Revisiting the Informal Sector

Sarbajit Chaudhuri . Ujjaini Mukhopadhyay

Revisiting the Informal Sector

A General Equilibrium Approach

Springer

Sarbajit Chaudhuri
Department of Economics
University of Calcutta
56A B.T. Road
Kolkata-700050
India
sarbajitch@yahoo.com

Ujjaini Mukhopadhyay
Department of Economics
Behala College
Kolkata-700060
India
mukherjee_uj@yahoo.co.in

ISBN 978-1-4419-1193-3 e-ISBN 978-1-4419-1194-0
DOI 10.1007/978-1-4419-1194-0
Springer New York Dordrecht Heidelberg London

Library of Congress Control Number: 2009935568

Printed on acid-free paper

Springer is part of Springer Science+Business Media (www.springer.com)

To Bela Chaudhuri and Professor Sambhunath Chaudhuri and Sibani Mukhopadhyay and Anil Mukhopadhyay

Foreword

Informal sector has emerged as a critical element in the development process of the entire developing world. It is now well recognised that such a sector provides employment to the majority of the workforce in the poor countries. Sometimes the share of employment in these activities goes way beyond 50% of total employment. Informal usually refers to extra-legal and non-recorded economic activities and can capture a whole array of diverse occupations, products and services. Development Economics as a discipline has not treated such topics with adequate reverence. Text books dealing with economic development do not have exclusive sections devoted to the discussion of growth, dynamics and sustenance of informal activities. In particular how informal transactions influence employment, output, productivity, wages and environment is seldom discussed formally in terms of analytical models. Informal sector does not operate in a vacuum. Thus the general equilibrium linkages involving the informal and formal activities also need to be explored in detail if development policies are to be properly evaluated. This volume successfully addresses both these issues and does it with competence and rigour.

Authors of this volume have been working on the frontiers of development policy research in the context of open developing economies, focusing mainly on general equilibrium implications of such policies. In fact one of the authors has written at length on informal credit market. Sustained research programme on such a topic of great significance lends credibility to this volume. It is also high time that several international publications of the authors in related areas are put together in a comprehensive monograph. I am definite such a volume will be very helpful to students, researchers, policy makers and anyone seriously interested in development economics.

Centre for Studies in Social Sciences, Calcutta, India Sugata Marjit

Preface

In the last few decades informal sector has drawn serious cognizance among economists in view of its role in developing economies. The earlier contention that the informal sector epitomises the 'residual' sector or a sector of last resort has been belied by a plethora of evidences indicating its dynamic character and its instrumental role in ameliorating unemployment and in propelling the developing economies towards growth and prosperity. This conceptual metamorphosis regarding the informal sector has stimulated revived interest in the phenomenon among development economists. There exist many books that deal with the sector analytically or empirically.

However, the theoretical analysis of the different aspects of the sector is equally important, especially for formulation of appropriate policy prescriptions. Comparative static results, in many cases, diverge from the conventional results. We noticed that although various authors have published theoretical papers in different journals, there are very few books that try to understand the informal sector in a theoretical framework. This lacuna inculcated in us an interest to write this book. The aim of the book is to comprehend better the diverse aspects of this sector and its role in the context of unemployment, child labour, globalisation, environment, etc. We have explored the workings of the informal sector in a general equilibrium framework. We have mainly used (with a few modifications) the tools developed by R.W. Jones (1965, pp. 557–572; 1971, pp. 3–21). Given the heterogeneous nature and ambiguity in the origin and development of the sector, this book cannot be claimed to be comprehensive enough to have dealt with all the issues that may emerge in connection with the informal sector.

The book is targeted towards postgraduate students of development economics with interest in the informal sector and researchers who are pursuing theoretical research on informal sector.

Some of the chapters are based on our articles published in different international journals. We would like to thank Professor Sugata Marjit, Director, Centre for Studies in Social Sciences (Kolkata), for letting us know his invaluable comments on the book and writing the foreword. The incorporation of his comments has made the book much richer. We also express our gratitude to our spouses

Pampa Chaudhuri and Dr. Ratnakar Pani for their support and encouragement and our daughters Salonkara and Mayurakshi for their extreme co-operation with us during the project.

Kolkata, India
14, June 2009

Sarbajit Chaudhuri
Ujjaini Mukhopadhyay

Contents

Chapter 1
Introduction

1.1 Genesis of Informal Sector: A Historical Perspective

In the aftermath of World War II, the global economy underwent significant structural changes, particularly the developing economies, which had by the time started being liberated from decades of colonial despotism. Under the dwindling influence of colonialisation and in a zest to catch on with the developed world, they, in conformity with the Prebisch doctrine of post-Keynesian developments, emphasised on appropriate macroeconomic policies and institutions for promotion of growth in leading sectors that would entail an overall growth of the economy. The trajectory of development was essentially through the growth of organised economic activities by rapid industrialisation that was expected to foster capital formation and expand domestic and export demand.

At this postcolonial juncture the developing countries were characterised by dualistic economic structures – with the existence of both a developed urban market economy and a backward agriculture-oriented subsistence economy. Expansion of industries and the resulting economic opportunities in urban areas triggered rural–urban migration and massive urbanisation. However, industrial development failed to generate adequate employment and income opportunities in the urban sector, so that the surplus urban labour force was compelled to generate its own means of employment and survival in the informal sector. In China, for example, the large number of rural–urban migrants (some 60 million) has been an important reason for creation of jobs in the informal economy[1]; in Colombia, migration condition[2] has a large impact on the probability of being employed in the informal sector (Florez, 2003). A brief summary of the urbanisation process and emergence of the informal sector has been provided by Sethuraman (1981).

[1] It should be noted that although informal sector is predominant in developing countries, it is not exclusive to them. The evidence from developed countries shows that cross-border migrants, especially those who have recently arrived in the country and do not speak the language, or women who are dependants of the primary migrant, tend to concentrate in the informal economy since they have few other jobs open to them. (ILO, 2002a).

[2] However, Mazumdar (1976) shows that the informal sector is *not* the major point of entry for fresh migrants from rural areas.

S. Chaudhuri, U. Mukhopadhyay, *Revisiting the Informal Sector*,
DOI 10.1007/978-1-4419-1194-0_1, © Springer Science+Business Media, LLC 2010

In the 1950s and the 1960s empirical investigations widely observed a dichotomy in the urban economies as well – where besides the organised industrial sector, there exists an unorganised, unprotected, traditional sector. It was Hart (1971) who first identified the latter as 'informal sector', introduced it as part of the urban labour force that takes place outside the formal labour market and considered it as almost synonymous with the category of the small self-employed. Despite the limitation of Hart's notion of the informal sector to the self-employed, the introduction of the concept enabled incorporation of activities that were previously ignored in theoretical models of development and in national economic accounts (Swaminathan, 1991).

However, the pioneering research on the informal sector is widely considered to be the report of the International Labour Office on employment in Kenya (ILO, 1972), which was part of a series of large multi-disciplinary 'employment missions' to explore the persistent widespread unemployment in various developing countries. The Kenya employment mission recognised that the traditional sector had not just persisted but expanded to include profitable and efficient enterprises as well as marginal activities. Initially, ILO considered the main aim of the informal sector to be the provision of subsistence to families but later subsequent research studies recognised another aspect of the informal sector, that is, dynamism and potential for economic growth and employment.

1.2 Towards Defining the Informal Sector

Although the term 'informal sector' has gained wide currency in recent years, even after over 30 years of research on informal activities, there is still no consensus on its definition.[3] As pointed out by Sethuraman (1981), the main problems confronted are the choice of an appropriate economic unit and the determination of the boundary separating the two sub-systems, formal and informal. The formal–informal sector dichotomy was first used by Hart (1971) in a study of urban Ghana. Weeks (1975) provided the distinction between formal and informal sectors on the basis of 'the organisational characteristics of exchange relationships and the position of economic activities vis-à-vis the State'. It was also suggested that the activities could be sorted out on the basis of mode of production, organisation, scale of operation, technology, productivity and labour markets (Papola, 1981).

The ILO/UNDP employment mission report on Kenya (1972) suggested the following characteristics of the informal sector: (i) easy entry for the new enterprises; (ii) reliance on indigenous resources; (iii) family ownership of enterprises; (iv) small

[3] The literature on informal sector is characterised by terminological confusion (Harding and Jenkins, 1989). Other synonymous terms found in the literature are 'urban traditional' (Todaro, 1969), 'lower circuit' (Santos, 1979), 'protoproletariat' (McGee, 1971), 'firm-centered economy' (Geertz, 1963), 'underground economy' (Feige, 1989), 'urban subsistence sector' (Cole and Sanders, 1985), etc. However, there are important differences so that characteristics included in one definition are often ignored in others and none is sufficiently comprehensive.

scale of operations and low productivity; (v) labour-intensive and adapted technology; (vi) reliance of workers on informal sources of education and skills; (vii) unregulated and competitive markets; and (viii) lack of governmental support.

As already mentioned, there is a wide heterogeneity in the definitions and characteristics of the informal sector forwarded by different authors and the ILO itself.[4] In January 1993, the *Fifteenth International Conference of Labour Statisticians (15th ICLS)* adopted an international statistical definition of the informal sector and characterised enterprises as informal on the basis of the following criteria:

- The enterprises are private unincorporated, i.e. owned by individuals or households and are not constituted as separate legal entities, and for which no complete accounts are available that would permit a financial separation of the production activities of the enterprise from the other activities of its owner(s).
- All or at least some of the goods or services produced are meant for sale or barter, with the possible inclusion of households that produce domestic or personal services in employing paid domestic employees.
- Their size in terms of employment is below a certain threshold to be determined according to national circumstances and/or they are not registered under specific forms of national legislation.
- They are engaged in non-agricultural activities, including secondary non-agricultural activities of enterprises in the agricultural sector.

However, it was later recognised that with the process of globalisation, enterprises are increasingly responding to the impending competitive pressure by resorting to mixed-mode labour arrangements in which labour regulations coexist with non-standard, irregular types of labour and various forms of subcontracting. To accommodate the new forms of employment, an alternative conceptual framework for defining informal employment was proposed in the ILO report on 'Decent Work and the Informal Economy' and the 17th ICLS adopted the guideline endorsing it as an international statistical standard (ILO, 2003). The guideline complements the 15th ICLS Resolution concerning statistics of employment in the informal sector. It defined informal employment to include the following types of jobs:

- own-account workers employed in their own informal sector enterprises;
- employers employed in their own informal sector enterprises;
- contributing family workers, irrespective of whether they work in formal or informal sector enterprises;
- members of informal producers' cooperatives;
- employees holding informal jobs whether employed by formal sector enterprises, informal sector enterprises or as domestic workers employed by households; and
- own-account workers engaged in the production of goods exclusively for own final use by their household.

---

[4] For alternative definitions, see Jhabvala et al. (2003).

According to the World Bank definition,[5] the informal sector 'covers a wide range of labour market activities that combine two groups of different nature. On one hand, the informal sector is formed by the coping behaviour of individuals and families in economic environment where earning opportunities are scarce. On the other hand, the informal sector is a product of rational behaviour of entrepreneurs that desire to escape state regulations'. The coping behaviour or survival activities consist of casual jobs, temporary jobs, unpaid jobs, subsistence agriculture and multiple job holding, while the entrepreneurial strategies include unofficial activities to evade taxes and avoid governmental regulations and illegal underground activities.[6]

1.3 Theoretical Approaches to Informal Sector

The theoretical literature on informal sector is generally presumed to subscribe to any of the three broad approaches. These approaches are briefly discussed below:

(i) *Dualistic labour market approach*
The essence of the dualistic view is that less-developed countries are characterised by two different sectors, a modern and dynamic sector typified by capitalist mode of production; and a marginal or 'subsistence' sector dominated by agriculture, characterised by pre-capitalist modes of production. It hypothesises that the wage determination process is different in the two sectors. It was Lewis (1954) who first developed a theoretical model of development in a dualistic economy. Although his model is based on classical school foundations containing two sectors, agriculture and non-agriculture, with asymmetric behaviour postulated for each, he rejected the neoclassical assumptions of full employment, market clearance and perfect competition. He analysed how surplus labour from the traditional agricultural sector could be withdrawn and productively used in the modern industrial sector to initiate the process of development. His main focus was in transition growth from a dualistic to a one-sector economy, i.e. from organisational dualism to organisational homogeneity. Fei and Ranis (1964) extended the Lewis model by superimposing product dualism on his organisational dualism. Other important extensions of the basic Lewis model can be found in Harris and Todaro (1970) and Fields

---

5 Concept of Informal Sector – The World Bank Group. < http://lnweb18.worldbank.org .

6 There is a debate with regard to the inclusion of illegal activities in the periphery of informal sector. The 15th ICLS in 1993 asserted, 'Activities performed by production units of the informal sector are not necessarily performed with the deliberate intention of evading the payment of taxes or social security contributions, or infringing labour or other legislations or administrative provisions. Accordingly, the concept of informal sector activities should be distinguished from the concept of activities of the hidden or underground economy.' The majority in the informal economy, although they are not registered or regulated, produces goods and services that are legal (ILO, 2002a).

(1975). Harris and Todaro (1970) explained the process of migration in a dualistic framework and introduced the notion that intersectoral labour reallocation is affected not only by the intersectoral wage gap but also by the probability of obtaining a formal sector job. In their model a migrant either gets formal employment or remains unemployed. Fields (1975) pointed out that there were three choices for migrants: a formal sector job, open urban unemployment and, a third possibility, a job in the urban informal sector. The Harris–Todaro (1970) model proposes that all migrants are intent upon eventual urban modern sector employment but does not explain the movement of those targeting the urban subsistence sector employment. But Cole and Sanders (1985) point out that when population pressure on fixed agricultural land reduces the rural subsistence wage significantly below that of the urban subsistence sector, or when growth of demand for urban subsistence sector pushes the wage in that sector significantly above that of the rural subsistence sector, the focus for migrants with low endowments is not on the modern sector but rather on the subsistence sector with its relative ease of entry. Banerjee (1983) corroborates this view in his empirical study of Delhi, which shows that the segmentation model is only partially valid and a substantial proportion of informal sector entrants were attracted to Delhi by opportunities in the informal sector.[7]

(ii) *Neo-liberal approach*

In this approach legal instruments are the main influence on the emergence and survival of informal sector (De Soto, 1989). Lengthy registration procedures, complex administrative steps and the costs involved in legalising an enterprise deter entrepreneurs from operating legally and induce them towards informal activities. Informal sector is viewed as the optimal and coherent response of economic units to government-induced distortions such as minimum wages and excessive taxation policies. Rauch (1991) describes in a neoclassical model the emergence of the informal sector as a voluntary phenomenon of firms to enjoy legal exemption from a mandated minimum wage policy that distorts resources away from first best allocations. Jones (1997), Suryahadi et al. (2003), Gindling and Terrell (2005) and Fortin et al. (1997) have empirically studied the effects of minimum wages on informal sector. The importance of tax policy on the size of the informal sectors has been considered in a number of papers like Sarte (2000), Boeri and Garibaldi (2002), Choi and Thum (2005), Dessy and Pallage (2003), Ihrig and Moe (2004), among others. The empirical findings by Loayza (1996), Johnson et al. (1997) and Botero et al. (2003) substantiate these theoretical formulations.

(iii) *Structural articulation approach*

This approach counters the neo-liberal school by emphasising the lack of association between the extent of constraint imposed by the institutional and legal framework, costs incurred by the entrepreneurs and the size of the informal

[7] It has also been pointed out by ILO (1972), 'it is not only the high-wage formal sector job that attracts the potential migrant, but also the income opportunity in the informal sector'.

sector.[8] In this approach,[9] the basic distinction between formal and informal activities is supposed to rely on the character of production and distribution processes. The different modes and forms of production are seen not only to coexist but also to be inextricably connected and interdependent. The traditional sectors are marginalised and impoverished in the process of expansion of the modern sectors (see, for example, McGee, 1973; Quijano, 1974; Mingione, 1984). There is heterogeneity within the informal sector with at least two sub-sectors: informal activities with direct subsistence goals and dynamic activities with decreasing labour costs and capital accumulation goals. The former is a disadvantaged sector with a counter-cyclical behaviour and the latter is integrated to the formal sector showing procyclical behaviour (Flórez, 2002). Ranis and Stewart (1999) differentiate among two urban informal sub-sectors, a V-goods sub-sector, which is dynamic and tied by subcontract to the urban formal sector, and an informal sponge sub-sector. Studies indicate that some of the dynamic growth-oriented segments in the informal economy require considerable knowledge and skills, for example, information and communications technology (ICT) sector in India (see Kumar, 2001). The dependent structural linkages between the informal and formal sectors are shaped by the wage and labour strategies of capitalist enterprises, which seek to lower costs by maintaining a reserve army of surplus labour.

1.4 Informal Sector Employment: Voluntary or Involuntary?

The contention of the dualistic models that the informal sector is the disadvantaged end of a segmented labour market and a temporary waiting ground for those awaiting entry into formal sector has been empirically refuted in a number of studies. In fact, informal employment has been found in many cases to be voluntary.[10] Fields (1990), recognising the existence of prosperous, voluntary group within the sector, argued that this constituted a second tier of the sector that made it more heterogeneous than the original Todaro dualistic formulation. Being in the informal sector is often the optimal decision of the workers, given their preferences, the constraints they face in terms of their level of human capital and the level of formal sector labour productivity in the country. Fields (1990) labelled the two segments as 'upper-tier'

---

[8] This relates to the fact that the informal sector is proportionally the largest in Bolivia and Guatemala, which have completely different legal and administrative framework (Maldonado, 1995).

[9] See Beneria (1989), Castells and Portes (1989), Portes and Schauffler (1993), Roberts (1989) and Moser (1978).

[10] In Mexico, wage rigidity, the main source of labour market segmentation, seems to be absent; minimum wages have not been binding for the last decade and wages have shown extraordinary downward flexibility during crises. The persistence of a very large informal sector despite relatively undistorted and flexible labour market provides a paradox and undermines the role of wage distortions in the emergence of informal sector (Capalleja, 1994).

informal activities and 'easy entry' ones.[11] Unemployed persons in transition countries and even in developed countries are often not able to get by on unemployment benefits, if they are available, and people have to supplement this income from a variety of informal activities or barter, taking care to avoid formal recognition that might lead to a loss of entitlements (Leonard, 2001).

There is a plethora of empirical evidences of the voluntary nature of informal sector. In Brazil and Mexico, over 60% of those in the informal self-employed sector left their previous job and entered the sector voluntarily with greater independence or higher pay as the principal motives (Maloney, 2004). In the Brazilian Annual National Domestic Survey, over 62% of self-employed men stated that they did not want a formal sector job, primarily because they were content with their current job (Cunningham and Maloney, 2001). In a survey of Argentina it was revealed that 80% of the self-employed had no desire to change jobs.[12] In Greater Buenos Aires, another survey found that while 36% would have preferred to work more hours, only 26% were looking for other work (SIEMPRO, 1998). In Paraguay, only 28% of those in the informal sector (both self-employed and salaried) stated a desire to change occupations.[13] Arias and Sosa (2004), in a study of Bolivia, find a premium to being informally self-employed.

The growth of labour force in relation to the economic growth pertinently influences the voluntary or involuntary nature of the informal sector. The remarkable economic growth of China, coupled with the one-child norm, entails rural–urban migration to sustain the increasing labour demand. But the political economy ensures protection of the urban residents from rural migrants by way of institutions such as residence registration, restricting the rights of migrants in the cities and collectivist mentality of many formal sector enterprises. The migrants failing to reside permanently in cities are left with the option to enter the informal sector. In contrast, in South Africa between 1995 and 2003 the labour force increased by a remarkable 4.2% per annum, while wage employment grew relatively slowly over that period, by 1.8% per annum. Those who could not obtain wage jobs were forced to enter self-employment or open unemployment (see Kingdon and Knight, 2007; Knight and Song, 2005; Knight, 2007).

1.5 Growth of the Informal Sector

The segmented labour market models postulated the informal sector as a temporary phenomenon, motivated by the objective of employment generation rather than profit maximisation and viewed it as a holding ground for workers awaiting entry into the modern sector. It was therefore assumed that the informal sector comprising

---

[11] See also House (1984), Tokman (1987), Marcouiller et al. (1997) and Ranis and Stewart (1999).

[12] Consultoria Nordeste (1998) (as cited in Maloney, 2004).

[13] Direccion General de Estadistica, Encuestas y Censos, Republica de Paraguay, 'Sector Informal,' based on the Encuesta Integrada de Hogares 1997/1998.

of petty traders, small producers and a range of casual workers would eventually be absorbed into the formal economy and disappear (Chen et al., 2002). But the evidence of increasing proportions of informal activities in developing countries coupled with economic progress has led economists to emphasise informal sector as the focal point of development.

In the 1980s, the economic crisis in Latin America served to highlight that employment in the informal sector tends to grow during periods of economic crisis (Tokman, 1992). In the Asian economic crisis about a decade later, millions of people who lost formal jobs in the former East Asian Tiger countries tried to find jobs or create work in the informal economy (Lee, 1988). Meanwhile, structural adjustment in Africa and economic transition in the former Soviet Union and in Central and Eastern Europe was also associated with an expansion of employment in the informal economy. It was realised that the phenomenon of informal sector, although pervasive in the developing countries, also exists in developed countries in transition. The size of the informal labour market varies from the estimated 4–6% in the high-income countries to over 50% in the low-income countries. Agenor (1996) and Schneider and Enste (2000) list a range of existing estimates of the size of the informal sector for a large cross-section of countries.

The ILO (2002a) noted that out of the 42 countries studied, 17 had more than half of their total employment in the informal sector and only 4 countries had less than 10% of total employment in the informal sector. Among the regions covered, sub-Saharan African countries have the highest proportion of informal to total employment. The South Asian countries such as India, Pakistan, Bangladesh and Nepal (with the exception of Sri Lanka) have more than 90% of the workers in the informal economy. In other Asian countries, the number of informal workers ranges from 45 to 85% of non-agricultural employment and 40–60% of urban employment. In parts of East Asia, namely Japan, the Republic of Korea, Singapore, Hong Kong and China, the informal economy declined as manufacturing and industry expanded and created jobs in the formal economy. According to Charmes (2000), informal work in Africa accounted for almost 80% of non-agricultural employment, over 60% of urban employment and over 90% of new jobs over the past decade or so. Table 1.1 shows the informal sector employment as a percentage of non-agricultural employment in non-OECD countries.

Table 1.1 Informal sector work in non-OECD countries, 1999–2005

HDI rank	Country	Survey year	Employment in non-agricultural informal sector, both sexes (% of non-agricultural employment)
38	Argentina	2003	40[a]
40	Chile	1996	36[a]
46	Uruguay	2000	30
48	Costa Rica	2000	20
52	Mexico	2005	33
62	Panama	2004	33
65	Mauritius	2004	8

Table 1.1 (continued)

HDI rank	Country	Survey year	Employment in non-agricultural informal sector, both sexes (% of non-agricultural employment)
67	Russian Federation	2004	12
70	Brazil	2003	37
74	Venezuela	2004	46
75	Colombia	2004	58[a]
76	Ukraine	2004	4
78	Thailand	2002	72
79	Dominican Republic	1997	48[a]
84	Turkey	2004	35
87	Peru	2004	56[a]
89	Ecuador	2004	40[a]
90	Philippines	1995	72[a]
91	Tunisia	1994–1995	50[a]
95	Paraguay	1995	66[a]
103	El Salvador	1997	57[a]
104	Algeria	1997	43[a]
107	Indonesia	1998	78[a]
108	Syrian Arab Republic	2003	22
110	Nicaragua	2000	55[a]
111	Moldova	2004	8
112	Egypt	2003	45[a]
115	Honduras	1997	58[a]
116	Kyrgyzstan	2003	43
117	Bolivia	1997	64[a]
121	South Africa	2004	16
126	Morocco	1995	45[a]
128	India	2000	56[a]
136	Pakistan	2003–2004	70
148	Kenya	1999	72[a]
159	Tanzania (United Republic of)	2001	43
160	Guinea	1991	72[a]
163	Benin	1992	93[a]
169	Ethiopia	2004	41
170	Chad	1993	74[a]
171	Central African Republic	2003	21[a]
172	Mozambique	1999	74[a]
173	Mali	2004	71
176	Burkina Faso	2000	77[a]

[a]Source: *ILO Bureau of Statistics, 2007* (Compiled from Human Development Report, 2007–2008).

1.6 Globalisation and the Informal Sector

Globalisation and its major driving force, liberalised trade paradigm, have often been cited in the literature as major reasons for the proliferation of the informal economy. Globalisation broadly refers to reductions in trade barriers, liberalised external capital flows, diffusion of technology and international migration of labour. Empirical studies reveal increasing 'informalisation' of the workforce, mainly attributable to the liberalised regime. The popular argument is that a growingly competitive and uncertain environment due to trade liberalisation leads entrepreneurs to embrace higher capital-intensive productions that affect the growth of informal sector in two ways: first, for mostly labour-abundant developing countries, moving away from labour-intensive production is a harbinger of unemployment, which people can ill-afford and subsequently seek employment in the informal sector, and second, in a bid to reduce costs to sustain competitive pressure entrepreneurs are keen to subcontract few or all the stages of their production process to informal units, whereby they can curtail their costs of training and maintenance of the labour force and vary their production with demand fluctuations. There are also cases where the hitherto protected industries, which get exposed to foreign competition, fail to sustain themselves and are compelled to lay off workers or, in extreme cases, pull down their shutters. These retrenched workers largely prefer informal sector employment to remaining unemployed.

Since the major impact of trade liberalisation is typically on the manufacturing and other organised sectors of the economy, while the urban informal sector and subsistence agriculture are largely the producers of non-tradables, the informal labour market and employment are affected indirectly by trade liberalisation through changes in relative prices and in the probability of obtaining employment in the organised sector. Moreover, there exists substantial heterogeneity in the employment profiles of individuals and households within these sectors that vary largely in terms of their skills and endowments of assets. This implies that the impact of trade liberalisation on employment also varies significantly according to these differences in initial conditions.

Goldberg and Pavcnik (2003) have examined the response of the informal sector to liberalisation in Brazil and Colombia, both of which experienced large trade barrier reductions in the 1980s and the 1990s. While in Brazil, no link between trade policy and informality has been found, there did exist such relationship in Colombia, but only for the period preceding a major labour market reform that increased the flexibility of the Colombian labour market. These results suggest that labour market institutions play an important role in determining the extent of reductions in formal employment due to trade reforms.[14] Deregulation of labour market is an important instrument of structural adjustment policies that generally accompany liberalised policies. Labour market reforms bring in more flexibility in labour markets

[14] See also Aghion et al. (2003) for a study of India.

by lowering the firms' hiring and firing costs and are likely to affect their incentives to employ informal workers. In a series of papers, Kugler (1999) showed that the labour market deregulation in Colombia led to an increase in formal employment. On the other hand, doing away with minimum wages, contractual agreements ensuring term of service and social security and benefits implies lower adjustment costs associated with employment of workers. The firms respond by engaging a large pool of workers who are casual and temporary in nature. Despite being employed in the formal sector they fall within the domain of informal workers. A study by Currie and Harrison (1997) on Morocco finds that firms started hiring more temporary workers after the completion of a comprehensive trade liberalisation programme.

An important policy within structural adjustment programmes aimed at consolidating the economy to deal with international debts more effectively consists of devaluation of the currency to raise exports. But the constant devaluation results in large-scale inflation, pushing the lower income groups to seek additional employment from informal sector. More and more children and women from the marginalised section are drawn in this sector (Hasan, 2002).

The international trade theory endorses trade liberalisation on the basis of the understandings of the Stolper–Samuelson (SS) theory. Freer trade is unambiguously beneficial for a developing country since it not only promotes efficiency and growth but also has gainful effects on the abundant factor in the economy, unskilled labour. However, the beneficial growth, employment and distributional implications of trade liberalisation hinge on the assumptions of existence of perfectly competitive markets and constant returns to scale. However, this is somewhat distant from reality, particularly in developing countries, where market imperfection is pervasive, industrial production is characterised by economies of scale and market failures are common. It has also been assumed in the standard trade theory that resources are fully employed and trade is always balanced. But in these countries, characterised by high unemployment levels, trade liberalisation can impinge heavy adjustment costs in the form of reduction in output and aggravating trade deficits and unemployment.

In these countries, trade liberalisation predominantly fosters import liberalisation that mainly involves lowering tariffs in unskilled labour-intensive protected sectors. In accordance with the SS theory this has the immediate effect of decline in factor reward to unskilled labour, widening the wage gap between skilled and unskilled labour and also loss of jobs for many unskilled workers. For example, in Argentina, economic reforms were targeted at reducing import tariffs in labour-intensive manufacturing industries like textiles, with the short-run effect of an increase in unemployment. Beker (2000) finds that while 'the average job destruction rate in the US is 10.3% ... for Argentina it is higher than 20% after 1990. About one in five manufacturing jobs disappeared every year. Only a little more than half of them were replaced.'

Apart from trade liberalisation, there are other dimensions of globalisation, like foreign direct investment (FDI) flows and immigration of labour, that have received somewhat limited cognizance in the literature, towards analysing the correlation between globalisation and informal sector employment and welfare. Evidently, if FDI concentrates on the capital-intensive sector there is a greater possibility of employment reductions, stimulating informal employment, while the flow of foreign capital in the labour-intensive sectors is likely to generate employment potentials and wage hikes. However, even in the latter case, in the presence of a wage gap between skilled and unskilled labour, if foreign firms tend to locate in skill-intensive sectors there is a relative expansion of skill-intensive sectors, improving the relative position of skilled workers and accentuating the wage differentials (Feenstra and Hanson, 1997). This makes the unskilled workers still worse off and they are embraced in the informal sector requiring limited skills. Empirical evidences depict different relations between FDI and wage inequality. While Feenstra and Hanson (1997) find a rise in demand for skilled labour in Mexican manufacturing due to FDI, Te Velde and Morrissey (2002) did not find strong evidence that FDI reduced wage inequality in five East Asian countries (Korea, Singapore, Hong Kong, Thailand and Philippines). Although FDI had raised wage inequality in Thailand, in others wage inequality has shown a decreasing trend, with hike in both skilled and unskilled workers.

1.7 Child Labour and Informal Sector

Child labour, the worst forms of violation of human rights, is found predominantly in the developing countries and is ubiquitous primarily in the informal segment of the labour market. Formal enterprises, which are generally subject to government regulation and union scrutiny, rarely employ children under the legal minimum age. Of the children working in the informal sector, 70% are in agriculture, commercial hunting and fishing or forestry, 8% in manufacturing, 8% in wholesale and retail trade, restaurants and hotels and 7% in community, social and personal service, such as domestic work (ILO, 2005). The informal manufacturing units in which the children are mostly engaged are shoe, garment, embroidery, furniture and handicrafts industries, home-based production and small-scale mining.

According to the estimates of the ILO (2002b), '246 million child workers aged between 5 and 17 were involved in child labour, of which 170 million were involved in work that by its nature is hazardous to their safety, physical or mental health, and moral development.' Of the total number of child labourers, 61% are in Asia, 32% in Africa and 7% in Latin America. Overall, 41% of all African children between the ages of 5 and 14 are involved in some form of economic activity, compared with 21% in Asia and 17% in Latin America. The proportion of child labourers varies a lot among countries and even regions inside those countries (see *Child Labour: Targeting the Intolerable*, Geneva, 1998, p. 7).

The ILO (2002b) lists many causes of child labour, such as poverty, economic instability, political turmoil, discrimination, migration, traditional cultural practices, inadequate social protection, absence of schools, low adult productivity, greed of employees and inadequacy of the enforcement machinery. Other empirical studies have identified poverty,[15] lack of education facilities with higher costs of schooling[16] and credit market imperfection[17] as some of the key perpetrators of child labour. Poverty is the foremost compelling force that makes parents send their children to work instead of receiving education. The rate of return to primary education is also very low in most of the developing countries due to the poor quality of schooling. Moreover, the decision of parents regarding sending their child to work or school is an intertemporal one, where they make a trade-off between the two choices and opt for child education only if the return to education is high enough to compensate for the foregone income from child labour. In this situation, prevalence of credit market imperfection intensifies the plight of poor families where lack of access to credit under reasonable terms dissuades them from sacrificing their income from child labour to meet present consumption needs.

In recent years, the revolutionary changes in the integrated world economic scenario ushering into the neo-liberal paradigm have diverse connotations for the incidence of child labour. The profit-motivated employers under increased competitive pressure due to globalisation prefer children to adults because child labour is cheaper and is amenable to control and exploitation. The informal sector, largely outside the purview of labour laws, serves as an ideal zone for the persistence of child labour. Such a market-based development strategy promoted by globalisation encourages child labour.

In a free market, high supply coupled with low demand for labour (especially unskilled)[18] leads to plunge in wages. The low adult wages entail entry of children into the labour market, which, in turn, depresses wages paid to adult workers perpetuating the vicious circles of poverty and child labour. On the other hand, segmented labour market exists for children, that is, the market has a 'pull' factor that draws children towards work. Thus, low adult wages create and sustain a segmented market for child labour (see *India Social Development Report, Council for Social Development*, 2006).

Kruger (2007), in a study of Nicaragua, finds that labour demand can influence how children work. Demand for low-skill products from rich countries can enhance the economic opportunities available in poor countries, increasing the child's potential economic contribution to the family. However, even if the children are getting increased prospects of being employed in the export sectors, it can hardly be claimed that the export opportunity causes them to work. The 'push' factors are equally important – even if the children would not have involved in the export sector, they

---

[15] A Child Labour Survey in Zimbabwe, conducted by the ILO in 1999, found that about 88% of economically active children aged 5–17 came from households with incomes below Z$2,000 (US$36) per month. As family incomes rose above Z$3,000 the participation rate dropped to less than 1%. See also Hamid (1994), Grootaert and Kanbur (1995), Bhalotra (1999) and Ray (1999).

[16] See Ray (2000, 2002) and Grote et al. (1998).

[17] See Jaffrey and Lahiri (2002) and Ranjan (2001).

[18] Owing to liberalised investment, entailing increased inflow of foreign capital that is usually accompanied by skill-biased technology, demand for unskilled labour falls with a corresponding surge in demand for their skilled counterparts.

cannot be expected to withdraw from work and grow up as educated persons. On the other hand, it is equally true that the structural adjustment programmes that accompany globalisation package in developing countries have resulted in loss of jobs of adult labour with deleterious effects on the prevalence of child labour. The prime force behind availability of children for work is abject poverty, compelling them to forego schooling and supplement their parents' meager incomes. Most of the parents of the working children are either engaged in informal sector or unemployed.

Edmonds et al. (2007), in a recent study on the impact of India's tariff reforms on children in rural India, find that despite the growth of the Indian economy, rural areas with concentrations of employment in industries that lost protection experienced smaller declines in poverty than the rest of the country. Children living in these areas did not experience as large an increase in school attendance or decline in work without school as children residing in areas with lower pre-reform employment in heavily protected industries. The lower magnitude of child labour declines in these rural areas seems attributable to smaller reductions in poverty in these areas than elsewhere in India. They find little evidence of other potential causes of these relative declines in schooling and increases in work such as declining returns to education or rising unskilled wages.

The fact that reduction in poverty can effectively mitigate the incidence of child labour is also evident from the findings from a recent study of Vietnam by Edmonds and Pavcnik (2005). As a result of doing away with export quota and liberalisation of rice trade in Vietnam, allowing rice farmers to take advantage of higher international prices, the living standards of rice-producing households improved, with much lesser children in these households going to work, despite increasing employment opportunities.

1.8 Informal Sector: Effects on Environment

The environment is significantly affected by manufacturing activities by way of emissions and wastes. Consequent to the recent boost in environmental awareness, large-scale industries are becoming increasingly concerned about achieving and demonstrating sound environmental conservation performance due to compulsions from stringent environmental legislation. Also there is now an increased use of innovative and flexible incentives to induce them to clean up their act. These are the voluntary initiatives such as cleaner production, environment management systems, etc.

However, the informal units that largely use unsophisticated, indigenous technology are major sources of air and water pollution. They are also generators of hazardous wastes like heavy metal sludges, solvents, waste oils, acidic and alkaline wastes, photo wastes, etc. They use unsafe methods of disposing wastes like dumping solvents or heavy metal-laden waste water into drains or in a common place, which are difficult to monitor. Some of the polluting informal activities are tanneries, plastic, metal, chemical units, etc. Current efforts for global environmental protection are concentrated primarily around large- and small-scale industries within the organised sector. But the large number of informal units is left unnoticed despite their high resource intensity, inefficiency and high level of pollution per unit of production. Although more polluting, they cannot be circumscribed by any environmental regulation since they are largely unregistered and difficult to identify. However, the environmental implications of these informal units cannot be overlooked and policies and steps are immediately required to curb their perilous effects on environment. Nonetheless there exists scanty literature on the environmental impacts of informal sector.

The informal sector also has beneficiary effects on the environment by virtue of its overwhelming participation in waste management in developing countries. Developing country cities often collect only between 50 and 80% of waste generated, with open dumping being the only disposal method available (Medina and Dows, 2000). Insufficient collection and improper disposal in open dumps allow refuse to be readily available for informal waste recycling through scavenging or waste picking. A large number of waste pickers contribute in collecting wastes and a comprehensive informal recycling network is involved in processing and recycling of wastes. At least four categories of waste collection may be identified: itinerant waste buyers who are the door-to-door waste collectors who collect sorted recyclable materials from householders, which they buy or barter and then transport to a recycling shop; street waste picking in which recyclable wastes are recovered from mixed waste thrown on the streets or from communal bins before collection; and municipal waste collection crew in which secondary raw materials are recovered from vehicles transporting municipal solid waste to disposal sites and waste picking from dumps where scavengers sort through wastes prior to being recovered (Wilson et al. 2006).

The recycling network takes the form of a hierarchy in which a chain of intermediate dealers often exists between the scavengers and end-users. Recycling can effectively reduce pollution, lower green house gas emissions, provide environmentally preferable sources of raw materials and save energy. Informal recycling provides employment to a large pool of low-skilled labour and maintains a steady flow of secondary materials for local manufacturing units and reduces the costs associated with formal waste management systems. The informal waste management is both economically and environmentally beneficial in developing countries.

Chapter 2
Theoretical Foundations: A General Equilibrium Approach

The discussions in the subsequent chapters of the book are based mainly on the general equilibrium framework as developed by R.W. Jones in his 1965 and 1971 papers. Graduates and doctoral students are likely to be familiar with the simple general equilibrium theory. However, to have a deeper understanding, they should acquaint themselves with the 'hat calculus' developed by Jones. While Jones (1965) deals with the 2×2 Heckscher–Ohlin–Samuelson (HOS) model, Jones (1971) is based on the 2×3 specific-factor full-employment model. In the next section we intend to present the essence of these two papers in the simplest possible manner. Later we shall discuss the technique of measuring social welfare in a small open economy and its changes resulting from changes in policy parameters.

2.1 The 2 × 2 Heckscher–Ohlin–Samuelson Model

The 2×2 Heckscher–Ohlin–Samuelson (HOS) model of production assumes that two commodities, X_1 and X_2, are produced using two factors, labour (L) and capital (K). The production function exhibits constant returns to scale with positive but diminishing marginal returns to each factor. The factors are fully employed and are mobile between the two sectors. Commodities can be classified in terms of relative factor intensities, and factor intensities are irreversible. The wage rate and the return to capital are denoted by W and r, respectively. It is assumed that perfect competition prevails everywhere so that commodity prices P_1 and P_2 reflect unit costs of production. Commodity prices and factor endowments are given exogenously.

The production functions are given by the following two equations:

$$X_i = F_i(L_i, K_i) \text{ for } i = 1,2 \tag{2.1 \& 2.2}$$

where L_i and K_i denote employment of labour and use of capital in the ith sector, respectively. Since the production functions exhibit CRS, the equations of unit isoquants are obtained as follows:

$$1 = f_i(a_{Li}, a_{Ki}) \tag{2.3}$$

S. Chaudhuri, U. Mukhopadhyay, *Revisiting the Informal Sector*,
DOI 10.1007/978-1-4419-1194-0_2, © Springer Science+Business Media, LLC 2010

where a_{Li} and a_{Ki} denote, respectively, the labour and capital requirement per unit of X_i.

Now given the output level, profit maximisation means minimisation of costs. In other words, the producers minimise cost along the unit isoquant. At the point of cost minimisation, the iso-cost line, with slope (–W/r), is tangent to the unit isoquant with slope ($\mathrm{d}a_{Ki}/\mathrm{d}a_{Li}$). Thus cost minimisation with respect to both the commodities implies

$$W\mathrm{d}a_{L1} + r\mathrm{d}a_{K1} = 0 \tag{2.4}$$

$$W\mathrm{d}a_{L2} + r\mathrm{d}a_{K2} = 0 \tag{2.5}$$

The above two equations are called the 'envelope conditions'.

Rewriting Equations (2.4) and (2.5) in accordance with the '^' notation implying proportional change, we get

$$\theta_{L1}\hat{a}_{L1} + \theta_{K1}\hat{a}_{K1} = 0 \tag{2.4.1}$$

$$\theta_{L2}\hat{a}_{L2} + \theta_{K2}\hat{a}_{K2} = 0 \tag{2.5.1}$$

where θ_{ji} is the relative share of the jth input in the total value of production of the ith commodity, $i = 1, 2$ and $j = L, K$, for example $\theta_{L1} = (Wa_{L1}/P_1)$.

These are the alternative expressions of the 'envelope conditions'.

The competitive profit conditions (equality between price and unit cost) in each sector are represented as

$$a_{L1}W + a_{K1}r = P_1 \tag{2.6}$$

$$a_{L2}W + a_{K2}r = P_2 \tag{2.7}$$

Now, the full-employment conditions of labour and capital are given as

$$a_{L1}X_1 + a_{L2}X_2 = L \tag{2.8}$$

$$a_{K1}X_1 + a_{K2}X_2 = K \tag{2.9}$$

The model consists of four independent Equations (2.6), (2.7), (2.8) and (2.9). There are four variables, W, r, X_1 and X_2, and four parameters, P_1, P_2, L and K. Thus the system is determinate and each variable can be uniquely determined provided the factor intensities between the two sectors differ. Given the commodity prices, the factor prices can be determined from the price system alone consisting of Equations (2.6) and (2.7). Thus, any changes in factor endowments cannot affect factor prices. This kind of a system where factor prices are independent of factor endowments is called a decomposable system.

Equations of Change

To examine the comparative static properties of the model, that is, to determine the effects of a change in the parameters on the variables of the model, let us transform the equations of the system into equations of change. It is convenient to express these changes in terms of the rate of change, denoted by '^', for example $\hat{L} = (dL/L)$.

Totally differentiating Equations (2.6) and (2.7) in the price system and using the '^' notation, we obtain

$$\theta_{L1}\hat{W} + \theta_{K1}\hat{r} = \hat{P}_1 - [\theta_{L1}\hat{a}_{L1} + \theta_{K1}\hat{a}_{K1}] \tag{2.10}$$

$$\theta_{L2}\hat{W} + \theta_{K2}\hat{r} = \hat{P}_2 - [\theta_{L2}\hat{a}_{L2} + \theta_{K2}\hat{a}_{K2}] \tag{2.11}$$

Using the above 'envelope conditions' as given by Equations (2.4.1) and (2.5.1), Equations (2.10) and (2.11) can be reduced to

$$\theta_{L1}\hat{W} + \theta_{K1}\hat{r} = \hat{P}_1 \tag{2.10.1}$$

$$\theta_{L2}\hat{W} + \theta_{K2}\hat{r} = \hat{P}_2 \tag{2.11.1}$$

Equations (2.10.1) and (2.11.1) imply that for each commodity, the distributive-share weighted average of proportional factor-price changes equals the proportional commodity price change. The above two equations are written in the matrix form as follows:

$$\begin{bmatrix} \theta_{L1} & \theta_{K1} \\ \theta_{L2} & \theta_{K2} \end{bmatrix} \begin{bmatrix} \hat{W} \\ \hat{r} \end{bmatrix} = \begin{bmatrix} \hat{P}_1 \\ \hat{P}_2 \end{bmatrix} \tag{2.12}$$

The Stolper–Samuelson Theorem

The changes in factor prices can be determined uniquely by solving Equation (2.12) using Cramer's rule. Thus,

$$\hat{W} = (1/\,|\theta|\,)[\theta_{K2}\hat{P}_1 - \theta_{K1}\hat{P}_2] \tag{2.13}$$

and

$$\hat{r} = (1/\,|\theta|\,)[\theta_{L1}\hat{P}_2 - \theta_{L2}\hat{P}_1] \tag{2.14}$$

where $|\theta|$ is the determinant of coefficient matrix in Equation (2.12) and is given by

$$|\theta| = \begin{vmatrix} \theta_{L1} & \theta_{K1} \\ \theta_{L2} & \theta_{K2} \end{vmatrix} = (\theta_{L1}\theta_{K2} - \theta_{K1}\theta_{L2}) \tag{2.15}$$

By the very definition, $(\theta_{L1} + \theta_{K1}) = 1$ and $(\theta_{L2} + \theta_{K2}) = 1$, that is, each row in $|\theta|$ adds up to unity. Therefore, $|\theta|$ can also be expressed as

$$|\theta| = \theta_{L1} - \theta_{L2} = \theta_{K2} - \theta_{K1} \tag{2.16}$$

Now, subtracting Equation (2.14) from Equation (2.13) yields

$$(\hat{W} - \hat{r}) = (1/\,|\theta|\,)(\hat{P}_1 - \hat{P}_2)$$

or

$$|\theta|\,(\hat{W} - \hat{r}) = (\hat{P}_1 - \hat{P}_2) \tag{2.17}$$

It is evident that $\hat{W}$ and $\hat{r}$ can be determined if both the commodities are produced and $|\theta| \neq 0$.

Substituting the definition of each distributive share (for example $\theta_{L1} = (Wa_{L1}/P_1)$) from Equation (2.15) we obtain

$$|\theta| = \frac{Wr}{P_1P_2}(a_{L1}a_{K2} - a_{K1}a_{L2})$$

Therefore, $|\theta| \neq 0$ implies that for uniquely determining the factor prices, the factor intensities for production of the commodities must differ. Hence, $|\theta| > 0$, if the production of X_1 is labour-intensive, i.e. $(a_{L1}/a_{K1}) > (a_{L2}/a_{K2})$. This also implies from Equation (2.16) that $\theta_{L1} > \theta_{K1}$ and $\theta_{K2} > \theta_{K1}$ if X_1 is more labour-intensive vis-à-vis X_2.

From Equation (2.17), it follows that an increase in the price of labour-intensive X_1 raises the wage–rental ratio in a magnified amount. If $\hat{P}_1$ exceeds $\hat{P}_2$ and X_1 is labour-intensive, then

$$\hat{W} > \hat{P}_1 > \hat{P}_2 > \hat{r}$$

Analogously if X_1 is capital-intensive, $|\theta| < 0$. In this case, an increase in P_1 reduces the wage rate and raises the return to its intensive factor, capital.

These results are summarised in the Stolper–Samuelson theorem,[1] which states that a rise in the price of a commodity raises the real reward of its intensive factor and lowers the real reward of its unintensive factor.

The Rybczynski Theorem

Now let us consider the output system comprising of Equations (2.8) and (2.9). Totally differentiating the equations and using the '^' notation, we obtain

$$\lambda_{L1}\hat{X}_1 + \lambda_{L2}\hat{X}_2 = \hat{L} - (\lambda_{L1}\hat{a}_{L1} + \lambda_{L2}\hat{a}_{L2}) \tag{2.8.1}$$

$$\lambda_{K1}\hat{X}_1 + \lambda_{K2}\hat{X}_2 = \hat{K} - (\lambda_{K1}\hat{a}_{K1} + \lambda_{K2}\hat{a}_{K2}) \tag{2.9.1}$$

[1] See Stolper and Samuelson (1941).

where λ_{ji} denotes the proportion of the jth input used in the production of the ith commodity, $j = L, K$ and $i = 1, 2$, for example $\lambda_{L1} = (a_{L1}X_1/L)$. Equations (2.8.1) and (2.9.1) describe the relationship between the outputs and the endowments of the factors as well as the factor intensities.

Now let us consider the terms in parenthesis in Equations (2.8.1) and (2.9.1). One relationship between $\hat{a}_{L1}$ and $\hat{a}_{L2}$ follows from the concept of elasticity of substitution between labour and capital in the production of X_1.

By definition, the elasticity of substitution in sector 1 is given by

$$\sigma_1 = \frac{\hat{a}_{K1} - \hat{a}_{L1}}{\hat{W} - \hat{r}}$$

By using Equation (2.4.1) the above expression may be written as

$$\left.\begin{aligned} \hat{a}_{K1} &= \sigma_1\theta_{L1}(\hat{W} - \hat{r}) \\ \hat{a}_{L1} &= -\sigma_1\theta_{K1}(\hat{W} - \hat{r}) \end{aligned}\right\} \tag{2.18}$$

Similarly, for sector 2, we get

$$\left.\begin{aligned} \hat{a}_{K2} &= \sigma_2\theta_{L2}(\hat{W} - \hat{r}) \\ \hat{a}_{L2} &= -\sigma_2\theta_{K2}(\hat{W} - \hat{r}) \end{aligned}\right\} \tag{2.19}$$

Using Equations (2.18) and (2.19), Equations (2.8.1) and (2.9.1) can be rewritten as

$$\lambda_{L1}\hat{X}_1 + \lambda_{L2}\hat{X}_2 = \hat{L} + \delta_L(\hat{W} - \hat{r}) \tag{2.8.2}$$

$$\lambda_{K1}\hat{X}_1 + \lambda_{K2}\hat{X}_2 = \hat{K} - \delta_K(\hat{W} - \hat{r}) \tag{2.9.2}$$

where

$$\delta_L = \lambda_{L1}\theta_{K1}\sigma_1 + \lambda_{L2}\theta_{K2}\sigma_2$$

$$\delta_K = \lambda_{K1}\theta_{L1}\sigma_1 + \lambda_{K2}\theta_{L2}\sigma_2$$

The changes in output levels can be determined by solving Equations (2.8.2) and (2.9.2), which may be expressed in matrix notation as

$$\begin{bmatrix} \lambda_{L1} & \lambda_{L2} \\ \lambda_{K1} & \lambda_{K2} \end{bmatrix} \begin{bmatrix} \hat{X}_1 \\ \hat{X}_2 \end{bmatrix} = \begin{bmatrix} \hat{L} + \delta_L(\hat{W} - \hat{r}) \\ \hat{K} - \delta_K(\hat{W} - \hat{r}) \end{bmatrix} \tag{2.20}$$

Solving Equation (2.20) by Cramer's rule one gets

$$\hat{X}_1 = (1/\,|\lambda|\,)[\lambda_{K2}\{\hat{L} + \delta_L(\hat{W} - \hat{r})\} - \lambda_{L2}\{\hat{K} - \delta_K(\hat{W} - \hat{r})\}] \tag{2.21}$$

$$\hat{X}_2 = (1/|\lambda|)[\lambda_{L1}\{\hat{K} - \delta_K(\hat{W} - \hat{r})\} - \lambda_{K1}\{\hat{L} + \delta_L(\hat{W} - \hat{r})\}] \tag{2.22}$$

where $|\lambda|$ is the determinant of the coefficient matrix and is given by

$$|\lambda| = \begin{vmatrix} \lambda_{L1} & \lambda_{L2} \\ \lambda_{K1} & \lambda_{K2} \end{vmatrix}$$

Thus,

$$|\lambda| = (\lambda_{L1}\lambda_{K2} - \lambda_{L2}\lambda_{K1}) \tag{2.23}$$

By definition $(\lambda_{L1} + \lambda_{L2}) = 1$ and $(\lambda_{K1} + \lambda_{K2}) = 1$. In this case also each row in $|\lambda|$ adds up to unity. Therefore, $|\lambda|$ can also be expressed as

$$|\lambda| = \lambda_{L1} - \lambda_{K1} = \lambda_{K2} - \lambda_{L2} \tag{2.24}$$

Subtracting Equation (2.22) from Equation (2.21) yields

$$(\hat{X}_1 - \hat{X}_2) = \frac{(\hat{L} - \hat{K})}{|\lambda|} + \frac{(\delta_L + \delta_K)}{|\lambda|}(\hat{W} - \hat{r}) \tag{2.25}$$

By definition $|\lambda| = \lambda_{L1}\lambda_{K2} - \lambda_{L2}\lambda_{K1}$. Substituting the definition of input–output ratios for each commodity (for instance, $\lambda_{L1} = (a_{L1}X_1/L)$) yields

$$|\lambda| = \frac{X_1X_2}{LK}(a_{L1}a_{K2} - a_{K1}a_{L2}) \tag{2.26}$$

Now, $|\lambda| \neq 0$ only if the factor intensities in the two sectors differ. If X_1 is labour-intensive, i.e. $\frac{a_{L1}}{a_{K1}} > \frac{a_{L2}}{a_{K2}}$, $|\lambda| > 0$. Alternatively, this implies from Equation (2.24) that $\lambda_{L1} > \lambda_{K1}$ and $\lambda_{K2} > \lambda_{L2}$.

From Equation (2.25), it follows that if X_1 is labour-intensive, an increase in the labour endowment raises X_1 by a magnified amount and lowers X_2. If $\hat{L}$ exceeds $\hat{K}$ then

$$\hat{X}_1 > \hat{L} > \hat{K} > \hat{X}_2$$

But if X_1 is capital-intensive, $|\lambda| < 0$. In this case, an increase in L leads to higher production of X_2 and a decline in that of X_1.

This result entails the Rybczynski theorem,[2] which states that a rise in the endowment of a factor at constant commodity prices leads to the expansion of the commodity that uses the factor intensively and contraction of the other commodity.

[2] See Rybczynski (1955).

Responses of Outputs to Changes in the Commodity Prices

Equation (2.25) shows the relationship of changes in outputs with changes in factor endowments and factor prices. The output response to changes in factor endowment is captured by the Rybczynski theorem. To examine the effects of changes in commodity prices on the outputs, let us substitute the link between factor prices and commodity prices depicted in Equation (2.17) to obtain

$$(\hat{X}_1 - \hat{X}_2) = \frac{(\hat{L} - \hat{K})}{|\lambda|} + \frac{(\delta_L + \delta_K)}{|\lambda|\,|\theta|}(\hat{P}_1 - \hat{P}_2) \tag{2.25.1}$$

As already stated, δ_L and δ_K are both positive. Now, $|\lambda|$ and $|\theta|$ must have the same sign. If X_1 is labour-intensive, both $|\lambda|$ and $|\theta|$ are positive, whereas if X_1 is assumed to be capital-intensive, both $|\lambda|$ and $|\theta|$ are negative, so that the product $|\lambda||\theta|$ is always positive.

Thus, if $\hat{P}_1 > \hat{P}_2$ then $\hat{X}_1 > \hat{X}_2$. In particular, from Equations (2.21) and (2.22) it follows that $\hat{X}_1 > 0$ and $\hat{X}_2 < 0$. If $\hat{P}_1 = \hat{P}_2 > 0$, then $\hat{W} = \hat{P}_1 = \hat{P}_2 = \hat{r} > 0$ so that $(\hat{W} - \hat{r}) = 0$ and $\hat{X}_1 = \hat{X}_2 = 0$.

Therefore an increase in the price of a commodity leads to rise in production of that commodity and fall in that of the other commodity. If both the commodity prices change at the same rate, the production of both commodities remains unchanged.

If technologies of production are of fixed-coefficient type, i.e. $\sigma_1=\sigma_2=0$ then δ_L and δ_K are equal to 0. Then from Equations (2.21) and (2.22) it follows that $\hat{X}_1 = \hat{X}_2 = 0$.

So any changes in commodity prices have no effect on the composition of outputs.

2.1.1 An Alternative Presentation

The discussion in the preceding section regarding the effects of changes in factor endowments and commodity prices on the outputs can also be expressed in a slightly different fashion. We use a few different notations only to obtain the same results as described above.[3]

Given that $a_{L1} = a_{L1}\ (W, r)$ and $a_{K1} = a_{K1}\ (W, r)$, total differentiation and the use of '^' notation yield, respectively, the following:

$$\left.\begin{aligned} \hat{a}_{L1} &= S^1_{LL}\hat{W} + S^1_{LK}\hat{r} \\ \hat{a}_{K1} &= S^1_{KL}\hat{W} + S^1_{KK}\hat{r} \end{aligned}\right\} \tag{2.18.1}$$

[3] Both types of notations have been used in the subsequent chapters of the book. This alternative version is particularly useful when three factors are used to produce a commodity so that equations of changes involve partial elasticities as well, making the analysis complicated if the earlier version is used.

Similarly, from $a_{L2} = a_{L2}(W, r)$ and $a_{K2} = a_{K2}(W, r)$, we get

$$\left.\begin{aligned}\hat{a}_{L2} &= S^2_{LL}\hat{W} + S^2_{LK}\hat{r}\\ \hat{a}_{K2} &= S^2_{KL}\hat{W} + S^2_{KK}\hat{r}\end{aligned}\right\} \quad (2.19.1)$$

Using Equations (2.18.1) and (2.19.1), Equation (2.8.1) can be written as

$$\lambda_{L1}\hat{X}_1 + \lambda_{L1}(S^1_{LL}\hat{W} + S^1_{LK}\hat{r}) + \lambda_{L2}\hat{X}_2 + \lambda_{L2}(S^2_{LL}\hat{W} + S^2_{LK}\hat{r}) = \hat{L}$$

$$or,\ \lambda_{L1}\hat{X}_1 + \lambda_{L2}\hat{X}_2 = \hat{L} - (\lambda_{L1}S^1_{LL} + \lambda_{L2}S^2_{LL})\hat{W} - (\lambda_{L1}S^1_{LK} + \lambda_{L2}S^2_{LK})\hat{r} \quad (2.8.3)$$

Similarly, Equation (2.9.1) can be expressed as

$$\lambda_{K1}\hat{X}_1 + \lambda_{K2}\hat{X}_2 = \hat{K} - (\lambda_{K1}S^1_{KL} + \lambda_{K2}S^2_{KL})\hat{W} - (\lambda_{K1}S^1_{KK} + \lambda_{K2}S^2_{KK})\hat{r} \quad (2.9.3)$$

Here, S^i_{jk} is the degree of substitution between factors j and k in the ith sector, $j, k = L, K$ and $i = 1, 2$, for example in sector 1, $S^1_{LL} = (\partial_{L1}/\partial W)(W/a_{L1})$, $S^1_{LK} = (\partial a_{L1}/\partial r)(r/a_{L1})$. $S^i_{jk}>0$ for $j \neq k$ and $S^i_{jj}<0$. It should be noted that as the production functions are homogeneous of degree one, the factor coefficients, a_{ji}s, are homogeneous of degree zero in the factor prices. Hence the sum of elasticities for any factor of production in any sector with respect to factor prices must be zero. For example, in sector 1, with respect to labour, we have $(S^1_{LL} + S^1_{LK}) = 0$, while with respect to capital, $(S^1_{KL} + S^1_{KK}) = 0$. Similarly, in sector 2, $(S^2_{LL} + S^2_{LK}) = 0$ and $(S^2_{KL} + S^2_{KK}) = 0$.

Equations (2.8.3) and (2.9.3) can be expressed in the form of a matrix

$$\begin{bmatrix}\lambda_{L1} & \lambda_{L2}\\ \lambda_{K1} & \lambda_{K2}\end{bmatrix}\begin{bmatrix}\hat{X}_1\\ \hat{X}_2\end{bmatrix} = \begin{bmatrix}(\hat{L} - A_1\hat{W} - A_2\hat{r})\\ (\hat{K} - A_3\hat{W} - A_4\hat{r})\end{bmatrix}$$

where $A_1 = (\lambda_{L1}S^1_{LL} + \lambda_{L2}S^2_{LL}) < 0$

$$A_2 = (\lambda_{L1}S^1_{LK} + \lambda_{L2}S^2_{LK}) > 0$$

$$A_3 = (\lambda_{K1}S^1_{KL} + \lambda_{K2}S^2_{KL}) > 0$$

$$A_4 = (\lambda_{K1}S^1_{KK} + \lambda_{K2}S^2_{KK}) < 0$$

Solving by Cramer's rule, substituting the expressions for A_1–A_4 and simplifying, one gets

$$\hat{X}_1 = (1/|\lambda|)[(\lambda_{K2}\hat{L} - \lambda_{L2}\hat{K}) + \{\lambda_{L2}\lambda_{K1}S^1_{KL} + \lambda_{L1}\lambda_{K2}S^1_{LK} + \lambda_{L2}\lambda_{K2}(S^2_{KL} + S^2_{LK})\}(\hat{W} - \hat{r})] \tag{2.21.1}$$

and

$$\hat{X}_2 = (1/|\lambda|)[(\lambda_{L1}\hat{K} - \lambda_{K1}\hat{L}) - \{\lambda_{L2}\lambda_{K1}S^2_{LK} + \lambda_{L1}\lambda_{K2}S^2_{KL} + \lambda_{L1}\lambda_{K1}(S^1_{LK} + S^1_{KL})\}(\hat{W} - \hat{r})] \tag{2.22.1}$$

Subtracting Equation (2.22.1) from Equation (2.21.1) and using Equation (2.17) one gets

$$(\hat{X}_1 - \hat{X}_2) = \frac{(\hat{L} - \hat{K})}{|\lambda|} + \frac{(\eta_L + \eta_K)}{|\lambda|\,|\theta|}(\hat{P}_1 - \hat{P}_2) \tag{2.25.2}$$

where

$$\eta_L = \lambda_{L2}\lambda_{K1}S^1_{KL} + \lambda_{L1}\lambda_{K2}S^1_{LK} + \lambda_{L2}\lambda_{K2}(S^2_{KL} + S^2_{LK}) > 0$$

$$\eta_K = \lambda_{L2}\lambda_{K1}S^2_{LK} + \lambda_{L1}\lambda_{K2}S^2_{KL} + \lambda_{L1}\lambda_{K1}(S^1_{LK} + S^1_{KL}) > 0$$

Equation (2.25.2) is analogous to Equation (2.25.1). Hence the results pertaining to the Rybczynski theorem and output responses to changes in commodity prices obtained in the preceding section follow.

2.2 The 2×3 Full-Employment Model

Let us now consider a two-sector, specific-factor model of production where two commodities, X_1 and X_2, are produced. Labour and capital of type 1 (i.e. K_1) are used to produce X_1, while labour and capital of type 2 (i.e. K_2) are combined to produce X_2. Each type of capital is used specifically in one sector, while labour is mobile between both the sectors. The three inputs are fully employed. The wage rate is denoted by W, while the returns to capitals of type 1 and type 2 are represented by r_1 and r_2, respectively. All the other assumptions of the HOS model are retained.

Under competitive conditions, the zero-profit conditions in the two sectors are given by

$$a_{L1}W + a_{K1}r_1 = P_1 \tag{2.27}$$

$$a_{L2}W + a_{K2}r_2 = P_2 \tag{2.28}$$

The full-employment conditions of labour and both types of capital are given by

$$a_{L1}X_1 + a_{L2}X_2 = L \tag{2.8}$$

$$a_{K1}X_1 = K_1 \tag{2.29}$$

$$a_{K2}X_2 = K_2 \tag{2.30}$$

Use of Equations (2.29) and (2.30) and substitution in Equation (2.8) yields

$$(a_{L1}/a_{K1})K_1 + (a_{L2}/a_{K2})K_2 = L \tag{2.31}$$

This model consists of five independent Equations (2.27)–(2.31) and five endogenous variables, W, r_1, r_2, X_1 and X_2. The parameters of the system are P_1, P_2, L, K_1 and K_2. However, this model is indecomposable. The factor prices cannot be solved from the price system alone. The values of W, r_1 and r_2 are obtained by solving Equations (2.27), (2.28) and (2.31) simultaneously. Therefore, any changes in the factor endowments affect factor prices, which, in turn, affect the per unit input requirements, a_{ji}s, in each sector.[4]

Now, total differentiation of Equations (2.27) and (2.28) and the use of 'envelope conditions' in sectors 1 and 2 entail

$$\theta_{L1}\hat{W} + \theta_{K1}\hat{r}_1 = \hat{P}_1 \tag{2.32}$$

$$\theta_{L2}\hat{W} + \theta_{K2}\hat{r}_2 = \hat{P}_2 \tag{2.33}$$

Totally differentiating Equation (2.31) gives

$$\lambda_{L1}(\hat{a}_{L1} - \hat{a}_{K1}) + \lambda_{L1}\hat{K}_1 + \lambda_{L2}(\hat{a}_{L2} - \hat{a}_{K2}) + \lambda_{L2}\hat{K}_2 = \hat{L} \tag{2.31.1}$$

Now, the relationship between a_{ji}s and the factor prices as given by Equations (2.18) and (2.19) is modified to give the following expressions:

$$\left.\begin{aligned} \hat{a}_{Ki} &= \sigma_i\theta_{Li}(\hat{W} - \hat{r}_i) \\ \hat{a}_{Li} &= -\sigma_i\theta_{Ki}(\hat{W} - \hat{r}_i) \end{aligned}\right\} \tag{2.34}$$

Use of Equation (2.34) in Equation (2.31.1) yields

$$-(\lambda_{L1}\sigma_1 + \lambda_{L2}\sigma_2)\hat{W} + \lambda_{L1}\sigma_1\hat{r}_1 + \lambda_{L2}\sigma_2\hat{r}_2 = \hat{L} - \lambda_{L1}\hat{K}_1 - \lambda_{L2}\hat{K}_2 \tag{2.31.2}$$

Solving (2.32), (2.33) and (2.31.2) yields

$$\begin{aligned} \hat{W} =& (1/\Delta)[-\theta_{K2}\lambda_{L1}\sigma_1\hat{P}_1 - \theta_{K1}\lambda_{L2}\sigma_2\hat{P}_2 \\ &+ \theta_{K1}\theta_{K2}\hat{L} - \theta_{K1}\theta_{K2}\lambda_{L1}\hat{K}_1 - \theta_{K1}\theta_{K2}\lambda_{L2}\hat{K}_2] \end{aligned} \tag{2.35}$$

$$\begin{aligned} \hat{r}_1 =& (1/\Delta)[-\{\theta_{L2}\lambda_{L2}\sigma_2 + \theta_{K2}(\lambda_{L1}\sigma_1 + \lambda_{L2}\sigma_2)\}\hat{P}_1 + \theta_{L1}\lambda_{L2}\sigma_2\hat{P}_2 \\ &- \theta_{L1}\theta_{K2}\hat{L} + \theta_{L1}\theta_{K2}\lambda_{L1}\hat{K}_1 + \theta_{L1}\theta_{K2}\lambda_{L2}\hat{K}_2] \end{aligned} \tag{2.36}$$

---

[4]It is to be noted that the model loses its consistency if technologies are of the fixed-coefficient type, as Equation (2.31) does not contain factor prices implicitly.

$$\hat{r}_2 = (1/\Delta)[\theta_{L2}\lambda_{L1}\sigma_1\hat{P}_1 - \{\theta_{L1}\lambda_{L1}\sigma_1 + \theta_{K1}(\lambda_{L1}\sigma_1 + \lambda_{L2}\sigma_2)\}\hat{P}_2 \\ -\theta_{K1}\theta_{L2}\hat{L} + \theta_{K1}\theta_{L2}\lambda_{L1}\hat{K}_1 + \theta_{K1}\theta_{L2}\lambda_{L2}\hat{K}_2] \tag{2.37}$$

where

$$\Delta = -\theta_{L1}\theta_{K2}\lambda_{L1}\sigma_1 - \theta_{K1}\{\theta_{L2}\lambda_{L2}\sigma_2 + \theta_{K2}(\lambda_{L1}\sigma_1 + \lambda_{L2}\sigma_2)\} < 0$$

From Equations (2.35), (2.36) and (2.37), the following results are obtained:

$$\left.\begin{array}{l}
\text{(i) When } \hat{P}_1 > 0,\ \hat{W} > 0;\ \hat{r}_1 > 0 \text{ and } \hat{r}_2 < 0. \\
\text{(ii) When } \hat{P}_2 > 0,\ \hat{W} > 0;\ \hat{r}_1 < 0 \text{ and } \hat{r}_2 > 0. \\
\text{(iii) When } \hat{L} > 0,\ \hat{W} < 0;\ \hat{r}_1 > 0 \text{ and } \hat{r}_2 > 0. \\
\text{(iv) When } \hat{K}_1 > 0,\ \hat{W} > 0;\ \hat{r}_1 < 0 \text{ and } \hat{r}_2 < 0. \\
\text{(v) When } \hat{K}_2 > 0,\ \hat{W} > 0;\ \hat{r}_1 < 0 \text{ and } \hat{r}_2 < 0.
\end{array}\right\} \tag{2.38}$$

At constant overall factor endowments, the relation between the changes in commodity prices and factor prices can be established by subtracting Equation (2.33) from Equation (2.32), which gives

$$\theta_{K2}(\hat{W} - \hat{r}_2) - \theta_{K1}(\hat{W} - \hat{r}_1) = (\hat{P}_1 - \hat{P}_2)$$

The above expression entails that if $\hat{P}_1 > \hat{P}_2$ then $\hat{r}_1 > \hat{P}_1 > \hat{W} > \hat{P}_2 > \hat{r}_2$. Any change in commodity price drastically affects the returns to specific factors. The return to the mobile factor (labour) rises in terms of one factor and falls in terms of the other.

A crucial difference between the HOS model and the specific factor model is that in the former, factor prices remain unaffected by changes in factor endowments, while in the latter, changes in factor endowments produce significant changes in factor prices.

From the relationships depicted in Equation (2.38 – (iii), (iv) and (v)), it is evident that a rise in the endowment of the mobile factor brings about a fall in its return and augments the returns to both the specific factors, while an increase in the stock in one of the specific factors lowers the returns to both the specific factors and raises the return to the mobile factor.

Now, let us turn to examine the responses of output due to the changes in commodity prices and factor endowments. Total differentiation of Equations (2.29) and (2.30), the use of Equations (2.35), (2.36) and (2.37) and simplification yield, respectively, the following:

$$\hat{X}_1 = (1/\Delta)[-\theta_{L1}\sigma_1\lambda_{L2}\sigma_2\hat{P}_1 + \theta_{L1}\sigma_1\lambda_{L2}\sigma_2\hat{P}_2 - \theta_{L1}\sigma_1\theta_{K2}\hat{L} \\ -(\theta_{K1}\lambda_{L2}\sigma_2 + \theta_{K1}\theta_{K2}\lambda_{L1}\sigma_1)\hat{K}_1 + \theta_{L1}\sigma_1\lambda_{L2}\theta_{K2}\hat{K}_2 \tag{2.39}$$

$$\begin{aligned}\hat{X}_2 =&(1/\Delta)[\theta_{L2}\sigma_2\lambda_{L1}\sigma_1\hat{P}_1 - \theta_{L2}\sigma_2\lambda_{L1}\sigma_1\hat{P}_2 \\ &-\theta_{L2}\sigma_2\theta_{K1}\hat{L} + \theta_{L2}\sigma_2\lambda_{L1}\theta_{K1}\hat{K}_1 \\ &-(\theta_{K2}\lambda_{L1}\sigma_1 + \theta_{K1}\theta_{K2}\lambda_{L2}\sigma_2)\hat{K}_2\end{aligned} \tag{2.40}$$

From Equations (2.39) and (2.40), the following results follow:

$$\left.\begin{array}{l}\text{(i) When } \hat{P}_1 > 0, \hat{X}_1 > 0 \text{ and } \hat{X}_2 < 0. \\ \text{(ii) When } \hat{P}_2 > 0, \hat{X}_1 < 0 \text{ and } \hat{X}_2 > 0. \\ \text{(iii) When } \hat{L} > 0, \hat{X}_1 > 0 \text{ and } \hat{X}_2 > 0. \\ \text{(iv) When } \hat{K}_1 > 0, \hat{X}_1 > 0 \text{ and } \hat{X}_2 < 0. \\ \text{(v) When } \hat{K}_2 > 0, \hat{X}_1 < 0 \text{ and } \hat{X}_2 > 0.\end{array}\right\} \quad (2.41).$$

Thus, an increase in the price of a commodity expands the production of that commodity and reduces that of the other. If the endowment of the mobile factor increases, the outputs of both the commodities rise. An expansion in the stock of the specific factor raises the production of the commodity that uses the factor and reduces production of the other.

2.2.1 The Alternative Version

We now present the above analysis regarding the 2×3 full-employment model using the alternative set of notations as discussed in Section 2.1.1. In this model, $a_{Li} = a_{Li}\,(W, r_i)$ and $a_{Ki} = a_{Ki}\,(W, r_i)$; hence, $\hat{a}_{Li}$ and $\hat{a}_{Ki}$ can now be expressed as

$$\left.\begin{array}{l}\hat{a}_{Li} = S^i_{LL}\hat{W} + S^i_{LK}\hat{r}_i \\ \hat{a}_{Ki} = S^i_{KL}\hat{W} + S^i_{KK}\hat{r}_i\end{array}\right\} \tag{2.18.2}$$

Using Equation (2.18.2) and simplifying from Equation (2.31.1), we can derive

$$A\hat{W} + B\hat{r}_1 + C\hat{r}_2 = -\lambda_{L1}\hat{K}_1 - \lambda_{L2}\hat{K}_2 + \hat{L} \tag{2.31.2}$$

where

$$\begin{aligned}A &= [\lambda_{L1}(S^1_{LL} - S^1_{KL}) + \lambda_{L2}(S^2_{LL} - S^2_{KL})] < 0 \\ B &= \lambda_{L1}(S^1_{LK} - S^1_{KK}) > 0 \\ C &= \lambda_{L2}(S^2_{LK} - S^2_{KK}) > 0\end{aligned}$$

Solving Equations (2.32), (2.33) and (2.31.2) yields

$$\hat{W} = (1/\Delta)[\,-B\theta_{K2}\hat{P}_1 - C\theta_{K1}\hat{P}_2 + \theta_{K1}\theta_{K2}(\hat{L} - \lambda_{L1}\hat{K}_1 - \lambda_{L2}\hat{K}_2)] \tag{2.35.1}$$

$$\hat{r}_1 = (1/\Delta)[C\theta_{L1}\hat{P}_2 - \theta_{L1}\theta_{K2}(\hat{L} - \lambda_{L1}\hat{K}_1 - \lambda_{L2}\hat{K}_2) - (C\theta_{L2} - A\theta_{K2})\hat{P}_1] \tag{2.36.1}$$

$$\hat{r}_2 = (1/\Delta)[(A\theta_{K1} - B\theta_{L1})\hat{P}_2 + B\theta_{L2}\hat{P}_1 + \theta_{K1}\theta_{L2}(\hat{L} - \lambda_{L1}\hat{K}_1 - \lambda_{L2}\hat{K}_2)] \quad (2.37.1)$$

From the above three equations, the results obtained in Equation (2.38) follow.

Total differentiation of Equations (2.29) and (2.30) and the use of Equations (2.35.1), (2.36.1) and (2.37.1) yield, respectively, the following:

$$\begin{aligned}\hat{X}_1 =& (\hat{P}_1/\Delta)[S^1_{KL}\{\lambda_{L2}(S^2_{LL} - S^2_{KL}) - C\theta_{L2}] - (\hat{P}_2/\Delta)CS^1_{KK} - (\hat{L}/\Delta)S^1_{KL}\theta_{K2} \\ &+ (\hat{K}_1/\Delta)[-\lambda_{L1}S^1_{LK}\theta_{L1}\theta_{K2} - C\theta_{K1}\theta_{L2} + \{\lambda_{L1}S^1_{LL} + \lambda_{L2}(S^2_{LL} - S^2_{KL})\theta_{K1}\theta_{K2}] \\ &- (\hat{K}_2/\Delta)S^1_{KK}\lambda_{L2}\theta_{K2}\end{aligned} \quad (2.39.1)$$

and

$$\begin{aligned}\hat{X}_2 =& -(\hat{P}_1/\Delta)BS^2_{KK} - (\hat{P}_2/\Delta)[S^2_{KK}\{\theta_{K1}\lambda_{L1}(S^1_{LL} - S^1_{KL}) - B\theta_{L1}\}] - (\hat{L}/\Delta)S^2_{KL}\theta_{K1} \\ &- (\hat{K}_1/\Delta)S^2_{KK}\theta_{K1}\lambda_{L1} + (\hat{K}_2/\Delta)[-B\theta_{L1}\theta_{K2} - \theta_{K1}\lambda_{L2}S^2_{LK} + A\theta_{K1}\theta_{K2}]\end{aligned} \quad (2.40.1)$$

From Equations (2.39.1) and (2.40.1), the results obtained in Equation (2.41) follow.

2.3 Measurement of Social Welfare

Let us consider a production structure where two goods, X_1 and X_2, are produced with the help of labour (L) and capital (K). There is international trade and X_1 is the export good while X_2 is the import-competing good. Commodity 1 is chosen as the numeraire. The world price of good 2, P_2, is determined in the international market. There is a tariff at the ad valorem rate, t, on the import-competing sector so that the domestic price of commodity 2 is $P_2(1+t)$. Both the factors are fully employed and are mobile between the sectors producing the two goods. The total capital stock in the economy consists of domestic capital (K_D) and foreign capital (K_F) and these are perfect substitutes. Foreign capital income, rK_F, is completely repatriated, where r is the return to capital. It is assumed that good 1 is more labour-intensive than good 2 so that $(a_{L1}/a_{K1}) > (a_{L2}/a_{K2})$.

The competitive profit conditions imply

$$a_{L1}W + a_{K1}r = 1 \quad (2.42)$$

$$a_{L2}W + a_{K2}r = P_2(1 + t) \quad (2.43)$$

The full-employment conditions of labour and capital are depicted by

$$a_{L1}X_1 + a_{L2}X_2 = L \quad (2.44)$$

$$a_{K1}X_1 + a_{K2}X_2 = K = K_D + K_F \quad (2.45)$$

Each individual in the society derives positive utility from consumption of the two goods produced in the economy. Assuming that the individuals are homogenous in their preferences the strictly quasi-concave social welfare function is given by

$$V = V(D_1,D_2) \tag{2.46}$$

where D_i denotes the demand for the ith commodity for $i = 1, 2$.

Given that international trade occurs, trade balance requires

$$\begin{aligned}&(X_1 - D_1) = P_2(D_2 - X_2) + rK_F \\ &\text{or}\ \ D_1 + P_2^*D_2 = X_1 + P_2^*X_2 + tP_2(D_2 - X_2) - rK_F\end{aligned} \tag{2.47}$$

where $(X_1–D_1)$ is the amount of X_1 exported and $(D_2–X_2)$ denotes the amount of X_2 that is imported.

Differentiating Equation (2.46) yields

$$(\mathrm{d}V/V_1) = \mathrm{d}D_1 + P_2{}^*\mathrm{d}D_2 \tag{2.48}$$

National income at domestic prices is given by

$$Y = X_1 + P_2{}^*X_2 + tP_2M - rK_F \tag{2.49}$$

where M denotes the volume of import and is given by

$$M = D_2(P_2{}^*,Y) - X_2 \tag{2.50}$$

Differentiating Equation (2.47) one gets

$$\mathrm{d}D_1 + P_2{}^*\mathrm{d}D_2 = \mathrm{d}X_1 + P_2^*\mathrm{d}X_2 + tP_2\mathrm{d}M - r\mathrm{d}K_F \tag{2.51}$$

Using Equations (2.48) and (2.51), we write

$$(\mathrm{d}V/V_1) = \mathrm{d}X_1 + P_2{}^*\mathrm{d}X_2 + tP_2\mathrm{d}M - r\mathrm{d}K_F \tag{2.48.1}$$

From differentiation of Equation (2.49) one gets

$$\mathrm{d}Y = [\mathrm{d}X_1 + P_2{}^*\mathrm{d}X_2 + X_2\mathrm{d}P_2^* + tP_2\mathrm{d}M + P_2M\mathrm{d}t - r\mathrm{d}K_F] \tag{2.49.1}$$

Differentiating Equation (2.50) and using Equation (2.49.1) yield

$$\begin{aligned}\mathrm{d}M =&(\partial D_2/\partial P_2{}^*)\mathrm{d}P_2^* + (\partial D_2/\partial Y)[\mathrm{d}X_1 + P_2^*\mathrm{d}X_2 + X_2\mathrm{d}P_2{}^* \\ &+tP_2\mathrm{d}M + P_2M\mathrm{d}t - r\mathrm{d}K_F] - \mathrm{d}X_2\end{aligned} \tag{2.50.1}$$

Here note that $X_1{=}F^1$ $(L_1,\ K_1)$ and $X_2{=}F^2$ $(L_2,\ K_2)$ are the two production functions, while the full-employment conditions for the two inputs are

$$L_1 + L_2 = L \text{ and } K_1 + K_2 = K_D + K_F = K$$

Therefore, Equation (2.49.1) may be expressed as

$$\begin{aligned} \mathrm{d}Y &= [F_L^1\mathrm{d}L_1 + F_K^1\mathrm{d}K_1 + P_2^*F_L^2\mathrm{d}L_2 + P_2^*F_K^2\mathrm{d}K_2 + P_2X_2\mathrm{d}t + tP_2\mathrm{d}M \\ &\quad + P_2M\mathrm{d}t - r\mathrm{d}K_F] \\ &= [W\mathrm{d}L_1 + r\mathrm{d}K_1 + W\mathrm{d}L_2 + r\mathrm{d}K_2 - r\mathrm{d}K_F + P_2D_2\mathrm{d}t + tP_2\mathrm{d}M] \\ &= [W(\mathrm{d}L_1 + \mathrm{d}L_2) + r(\mathrm{d}K_1 + \mathrm{d}K_2) - r\mathrm{d}K_F + P_2D_2\mathrm{d}t + tP_2\mathrm{d}M] \\ \text{or, } \mathrm{d}Y &= P_2(D_2\mathrm{d}t + t\mathrm{d}M) \end{aligned} \tag{2.52}$$

Using Equation (2.52), Equation (2.50.1) may be expressed as

$$\begin{aligned} &\mathrm{d}M = (\partial D_2/\partial P_2^*)\mathrm{d}P_2^* + (\partial D_2/\partial Y)P_2(D_2\mathrm{d}t + t\mathrm{d}M) - \mathrm{d}X_2 \\ &\text{or, } \mathrm{d}M[1 - tP_2(\partial D_2/\partial Y)] = P_2dt\{(\partial D_2/\partial P_2^*) + D_2(\partial D_2/\partial Y)\} - \mathrm{d}X_2 \\ &\text{or, } \mathrm{d}M = v[HP_2\mathrm{d}t - \mathrm{d}X_2] \end{aligned} \tag{2.53}$$

where $v = [(1+t)/\{1+t(1-m)\}] > 0; m = P_2^*(\partial D_2/\partial Y)$ is the marginal propensity to consume commodity 2 and, $H = [(\partial D_2/\partial P_2^*) + D_2(\partial D_2/\partial Y)] < 0$ is the Slutsky's pure substitution term.

Using Equations (2.48.1) and (2.53) one gets

$$(\mathrm{d}V/V_1) = tP_2v[HP_2\mathrm{d}t - \mathrm{d}X_2] \tag{2.54}$$

From Equation (2.54), we find that

$$(1/V_1)(\mathrm{d}V/\mathrm{d}K_F) = -tP_2v(\mathrm{d}X_2/\mathrm{d}K_F) < 0 \text{ since } (\mathrm{d}X_2/\mathrm{d}K_F) > 0 \tag{2.55}$$

$$(1/V_1)(\mathrm{d}V/\mathrm{d}t) = tP_2v\{HP_2 - (\mathrm{d}X_2/\mathrm{d}t)\} < 0 \tag{2.56}$$

Now let us assume an imperfection in the labour market. Let sector 2 producing X_2 be the formal sector with unionised wage, while sector 1 that produces X_1 be the informal sector offering the competitive wage.

Let the unionised wage function in the formal sector be as follows:

$$W^* = W^*(W,U); (\partial W^*/\partial W) > 0, (\partial W^*/\partial U) > 0$$

Here U denotes the bargaining strength of the trade unions.

$E_W = (\partial W^*/\partial W)\,(W/W^*)$ is the elasticity of W^* with respect to W and $1 \geq E_W \geq 0$.
$E_U = (\partial W^*/\partial U)\,(U/W^*)$ is the elasticity of W^* with respect to U and $E_U > 0$.

Now, in the presence of unionised wage in the formal sector, the expressions for change in welfare with respect to change in tariff rate and change in the bargaining power are given, respectively, as

$$(1/V_1)(\mathrm{d}V/\mathrm{d}t) = v\{(W^* - W)(\mathrm{d}L_2/\mathrm{d}t) + tP_2(HP_2 - (\mathrm{d}X_2/\mathrm{d}t)\} \quad (2.56.1)$$

$$(1/V_1)(\mathrm{d}V/\mathrm{d}U) = v\{(W^* - W)(\mathrm{d}L_2/\mathrm{d}U) - tP_2(\mathrm{d}X_2/\mathrm{d}U)\} \quad (2.57)$$

The signs of ($\mathrm{d}V/\mathrm{d}t$) and ($\mathrm{d}V/\mathrm{d}U$) are ambiguous. Hence in the presence of labour market distortion in a two-sector full-employment model, a policy of trade liberalisation and/or labour market reform may not be welfare improving.

Chapter 3
The Harris–Todaro Migration Model and Introduction of the Informal Sector

3.1 Labour Market Segmentation

An important aspect of urban unemployment in developing countries is that it is predominantly open. The massive influx of rural migrants in the cities has been instrumental in fostering an overwhelmingly faster population growth in urban areas than in the rural ones. Rural workers are lured to migrate by economic incentives as well as by other attractions of an urbane life. While some of the migrants do manage to secure jobs in industries, the less-fortunate ones get absorbed only in the urban informal sector and the rest wait for their chance to get employment and thus swell the number of open urban unemployment. A substantial portion of the urban population in a country like India is engaged in the informal sector.

The urban labour market in the developing economies typically shows evidences of labour market segmentation. The labour market can be partitioned into two distinct segments: formal and informal. In the formal sector of the market, workers are unionised and they can wrest a high unionised wage through collective bargaining. On the contrary, workers in the informal sector earn a lower and competitive wage than their counterparts in the formal sector. In the next section, we explain how the unionised wage is determined in the organised (formal) sector of the labour market.

3.2 Determination of Unionised Wage Through Collective Bargaining

The informal sector wage rate plays a crucial role in determination of the unionised wage in the organised labour market. It is like a benchmark (reservation) wage over which the wage mark-up is determined through collective bargaining between the labour union and the firm. To explain how the unionised wage is actually determined, we make the following assumptions.

We consider a competitive formal sector industry. Production requires two inputs: labour (L) and capital (K). The capital market is perfect while the labour market facing the industry is unionised. Each firm in the industry has a separate trade

S. Chaudhuri, U. Mukhopadhyay, *Revisiting the Informal Sector*,

DOI 10.1007/978-1-4419-1194-0_3,

union. While determining the unionised wage, labour is considered as the only variable input of production. The unionised wage is determined as a solution to the Nash bargaining game between the representative firm and the representative labour union.

The representative firm's profit function is given by

$$\Pi = P_2 Q(L,K) - W^* L \tag{3.1}$$

where P_2 is the exogenously given price of the formal sector's product.

The representative labour union maximises the aggregate wage income of its members net of their opportunity wage income, i.e.

$$\Omega = (W^* - W)L \tag{3.2}$$

The informal sector wage, W, is the opportunity wage to the workers in the industry. This is because any worker failing to get employment in the formal sector will surely be getting a job in the informal sector.

We consider a cooperative game between the firm and the labour union that leads to determination of the unionised wage, W^*, and the employment level, L. If the two parties fail to reach an agreement, the game will not be played. In that case, no production will take place and the workers have to accept jobs in the informal sector. So given the objective functions of the two parties, represented by Equations (3.1) and (3.2), the disagreement pay-off is [0, 0]

The Nash bargaining solution is obtained from the following optimisation exercise.

$$\underset{W^*, L}{Max}\ J = [P_2 Q(L,K) - W^* L]^{(1-U)} \times [(W^* - W)L]^U \tag{3.3}$$

where U is the bargaining strength of the labour unions.

The first-order conditions for maximisation are

$$(1 - U)[(W^* - W)L] = U[P_2 Q(.) - W^* L] \tag{3.4}$$

and

$$(1 - U)(P_2 Q_L - W^*)L = -U[P_2 Q(.) - W^* L] \tag{3.5}$$

Using Equations (3.4) and (3.5) one obtains

$$P_2 Q_L = W \tag{3.6}$$

Differentiations of Equation (3.6) lead to

$$\left(\frac{\partial L}{\partial W}\right) = \frac{1}{P_2 Q_{LL}} < 0; \left(\frac{\partial L}{\partial P_2}\right) = -\frac{Q_L}{P_2 Q_{LL}} > 0 \tag{3.7}$$

Simplification from Equation (3.4) yields

$$W^* = U\frac{P_2Q(L,K)}{L} + (1-U)\,W \tag{3.8}$$

Equation (3.7) is the unionised wage function. In general form it is written as

$$W^* = W^*(P_2,W,U) \tag{3.8.1}$$

Differentiating Equation (3.8) and using Equation (3.7) we find that

$$\left.\begin{aligned}
\left(\frac{\partial W^*}{\partial U}\right) &= \left(\tfrac{1}{L}\right)(P_2Q(.) - WL) > 0\\
\left(\frac{\partial W^*}{\partial W}\right) &= (1-U) + \frac{U(WL - P_2Q(.))}{L^2P_2Q_{LL}} > 0\\
\left(\frac{\partial W^*}{\partial P_2}\right) &= \left[\frac{UP_2Q(.)(Q_{LL}L + Q_L) - UWLQ_L}{P_2Q_{LL}L^2}\right]
\end{aligned}\right\} \tag{3.9}$$

From Equation (3.9) it can be checked that

$$\left(\frac{\partial W^*}{\partial P_2}\right) > 0 \text{ if } (Q_{LL}L + Q_L) \leq 0 \text{ i.e. } \xi_L \geq 1 \tag{3.10}$$

where $\xi_L = -\left(\frac{LQ_{LL}}{Q_L}\right)$ is the elasticity of marginal product curve of labour.[1]

This establishes the following proposition.

Proposition 3.1 *The unionised wage is a positive function of both the informal wage and the bargaining strength of the labour union. It is also a positive function of the commodity price if the marginal product curve of labour is not inelastic.*

3.3 Two-Sector Mobile Capital Version of the Harris–Todaro Model

Before introducing the informal sector (and hence a dualistic urban industrial sector) let us present the essence of the basic 2×2 mobile capital version of the Harris–Todaro (1970) (hereafter HT) model which is also known as the Corden and Findlay (1975) model. A small open economy with two sectors, rural (sector *X*) and urban (sector *Y*), is considered. Sector *X* produces an agricultural commodity using labour and capital while sector *Y* produces a manufacturing good using the same two inputs. Capital is perfectly mobile between the two sectors and its economy-wide return is *r*. On the contrary, labour is imperfectly mobile between the sectors. Workers in

---

[1] This is only a sufficient condition. There can be another sufficient condition as well for which $(\partial W^*/\partial P_2) > 0$

the urban sector are unionised and receive a higher wage, $\overline{W}_Y$, than their counterparts in the rural sector who receive a low competitive wage, W_X. So $\overline{W}_Y > W_X$ and this intersectoral wage differential leads to rural–urban migration of labour. Markets are perfectly competitive except in the urban labour market. It is assumed that neoclassical production functions exhibit constant returns to scale with positive but diminishing marginal productivity to each factor. Finally, commodity 1 is taken to be the numeraire.

The usual zero-profit conditions for the two sectors are as follows:

$$W_X a_{LX} + r a_{KX} = 1 \tag{3.11}$$

$$\overline{W}_Y a_{LY} + r a_{KY} = P_Y \tag{3.12}$$

where a_{ji} is the amount of the jth factor required to produce 1 unit of commodity i, where $j = L, K$ and $i = X, Y$.

Capital is fully utilised. The full-employment condition for capital is given by

$$a_{KX} X + a_{KY} Y = K \tag{3.13}$$

There is unemployment of labour in the urban sector, which is denoted by L_{U}. The labour endowment equation is as follows:

$$a_{LX} X + a_{LY} Y + L_{\mathrm{U}} = L \tag{3.14}$$

Finally, the Harris–Todaro migration equilibrium condition is given by

$$\left(\frac{\overline{W}_Y a_{LY} Y}{a_{LY} Y + L_{\mathrm{U}}} \right) = W_X \tag{3.15}$$

Equation (3.15) states that the expected urban wage must be equal to the rural sector wage rate in the migration equilibrium. Using Equation (3.14), Equation (3.15) may be rewritten as follows:

$$\left(\frac{\overline{W}_Y}{W_X} \right) a_{LY} Y + a_{LX} X = L \tag{3.15.1}$$

Sectors can be classified in terms of relative factor intensities. It is assumed that sector X (sector Y) is more labour (capital) intensive than the other sector in value sense, i.e. $\left(\frac{W a_{LX}}{a_{KX}} > \frac{\overline{W} a_{LY}}{a_{KY}} \right)$. This trivially implies that sector X is more labour-intensive vis-à-vis sector Y in physical sense.

The general equilibrium structure consists of Equations (3.11), (3.12), (3.13), (3.14) and (3.15.1) and five endogenous variables, namely W_x, r, X, Y and L_{U}. This is a decomposable production structure. So factor prices depend on commodity prices but not on factor endowments. Given $\overline{W}_Y$, r is obtained from Equation (3.12). Inserting the value of r into Equation (3.11), W_x is obtained. Once factor prices are known, factor coefficients, a_{ji}s, are also known. The equilibrium values of X and

Y are determined from Equations (3.13) and (3.15.1). Finally, L_U is obtained from Equation (3.14).

From Equation (3.15.1) one can write

$$\left(\frac{\overline{W}_Y a_{LY} Y + W a_{LX} X}{L}\right) = W_X \tag{3.15.2}$$

Equation (3.15.2) states that the average wage of all workers in an HT economy is always equal to the rural sector wage. This is known as the envelope property of the HT structure.

The Harris–Todaro equilibrium is Pareto-suboptimal for two reasons. First, the wages across sectors are not equalised so that urban–rural wage differential persists, and second, there exists unemployment in the migration equilibrium.

The basic Harris–Todaro (1970) model has been re-examined and extended by different authors in different directions. However, most of the authors have come to the same broad conclusion that in the presence of rural–urban wage differential, the urban development policies cannot mitigate the problem of rising unemployment in the urban sector and therefore indicate to a rural development programme as a possible solution to the problem. This can be easily seen using the general equilibrium set-up we have just outlined.

In order to analyse the effects of different development policies on the urban unemployment level, we rewrite the two zero-profit conditions and the migration equilibrium conditions as follows:

$$W_X a_{LX} + r a_{KX} = (1 + S_P) \tag{3.11.1}$$

$$(1 - S_W)\overline{W}_Y a_{LY} + r a_{KY} = P_Y \tag{3.12.1}$$

$$\left(\frac{\overline{W}_Y}{1 + \left(\frac{L_U}{a_{LY} Y}\right)}\right) = W_X \tag{3.15.3}$$

where S_p and S_w are the rates of ad valorem price and wage subsidies given to the rural sector and the urban sector, respectively.

First, if the government gives a wage subsidy to the urban employers in order to create more jobs in the urban sector, the effective wage paid by the firm, $(1-S_W)\overline{W}_Y$, decreases although workers are still receiving $\overline{W}_Y$. From Equation (3.12.1) it is clear that the return to capital, r, rises to satisfy the zero-profit condition for sector Y. Then from Equation (3.11.1) it follows that the rural sector wage, W_x, has to fall. The wage–rental ratios in the two sectors thus get reduced. So producers will be substituting capital by labour, thereby increasing the labour–output ratios, a_{LX} and a_{LY}, and lowering the capital–output ratios, a_{KX} and a_{KY}. There will be an excess supply of capital at the given product mix. This produces a Rybczynski-type effect resulting in an increase in Y and a decrease in X. Since the urban sector expands in terms of both output and employment, the expected urban wage for a prospective rural migrant rises. On the other hand, the rural sector wage rate drops, leading to a fresh migration from the rural to the urban sector. The number of new migrants exceeds the number of new jobs created in the urban sector. As a result, the urban unemployment situation worsens, which is clear from Equation (3.15.3).

On the other hand, an increase in the price subsidy to the rural sector cannot affect the return to capital, r, as it is determined from Equation (3.12.1). But the policy raises the rural sector wage, W_x. As the (W_x/r) ratio rises the rural sector producers substitute labour by capital. Consequently, a_{KX} rises and a_{LX} falls. At the given output composition, adoption of more capital-intensive technology in the rural sector implies a shortage of capital. This produces a Rybczynski-type effect resulting in a contraction of the capital-intensive urban sector and an expansion of the labour-intensive rural sector. As the urban sector contracts in terms of both output and employment[2] and the wage rate in the rural sector increases, the expected urban wage falls short of the rural sector wage, resulting in a reverse migration of labour from the urban to the rural sector. Accordingly, the urban unemployment level falls in the new migration equilibrium, which is also clear from Equation (3.15.3). So the following proposition is now imminent.

Proposition 3.2 *In the HT model any urban development policy aggravates the problem of urban unemployment while rural development programme effectively mitigates it.*

However, there are two disconcerting features of the Corden and Findlay (1975) model which are worth mentioning. An increase in the capital endowment causes sector Y to expand and sector X to contract following a Rybczynski effect. Factor prices do not change. As sector Y expands in terms of both output and employment, the expected urban wage for a prospective rural migrant increases, which causes a fresh migration of labour from the rural to the urban sector. The number of new migrants exceeds the number of new jobs created in the urban sector. Consequently, the level of urban unemployment rises. On the contrary, an increase in the labour endowment causes sector Y to contract and the urban unemployment to alleviate. This establishes the following proposition.

Proposition 3.3 *In the two-sector mobile capital Harris–Todaro model an increase in the labour endowment lowers the problem of urban unemployment while a growth in the capital stock accentuates the problem.*

These results are surprising because capital scarcity is held responsible for unemployment in the capital-scarce developing economies. But, an inflow of capital from outside or even domestic capital formation raises the level of unemployment. On the other hand, population growth lowers urban unemployment. These undesirable properties can, however, be avoided in the absence of capital mobility between the sectors, i.e. if each sector uses capital specific to that sector.

---

[2] As the production techniques in the urban sector do not change a fall in Y implies a fall in $a_{LY}Y$.

3.4 Three-Sector HT Model, Urban Employment and Trade Liberalisation

We consider a three-sector dual economy with two urban sectors and one rural sector.[3] Sector 1 is the rural sector that produces a final agricultural commodity using labour and a non-traded input. One of the two urban sectors (sector m) produces the non-traded input for the rural sector using labour and capital. The other urban sector (sector 2) produces a manufacturing commodity with the help of labour and capital. This is the import-competing sector of the economy and is protected by an import tariff. The price of the non-traded input, P_m, is endogenously determined. As the other two commodities are internationally traded their prices are internationally given. In the two urban sectors, the wage rate is institutionally given at W^* while in the rural sector the wage rate, W, is flexible with $W^*>W$. The two wage rates are related by the Harris–Todaro migration equilibrium condition that states that the expected urban wage for a prospective rural migrant is equal to the actual rural wage. Production functions are of fixed-coefficient type. Markets, except the urban sector labour market, are perfectly competitive. Commodity 1 is assumed to be the numeraire.

Given the competitive product markets, the usual zero-profit conditions for the three sectors are given by the following three equations.

$$Wa_{L1} + P_m a_{m1} = 1 \tag{3.16}$$

$$W^* a_{L2} + r a_{K2} = P_2(1+t) \tag{3.17}$$

$$W^* a_{Lm} + r a_{Km} = P_m \tag{3.18}$$

Capital and the non-traded input are completely utilised. Therefore we have the following two equations.

$$a_{K2}X_2 + a_{Km}X_m = K \tag{3.19}$$

$$a_{m1}X_1 = X_m \tag{3.20}$$

There is unemployment of labour in the urban sector, which is denoted by L_U. The labour endowment equation of the economy is given by

$$a_{L1}X_1 + a_{L2}X_2 + a_{Lm}X_m + L_U = L \tag{3.21}$$

Finally, the Harris–Todaro migration equilibrium condition is as follows:

$$\left(\frac{W^*(a_{L2}X_2 + a_{Lm}X_m)}{a_{L2}X_2 + a_{Lm}X_m + L_U}\right) = W \tag{3.22}$$

---

[3] This section is based on Marjit and Beladi (1996).

Using Equation (3.21), Equation (3.22) can be rewritten as follows:

$$(W^*/W)(a_{L2}X_2 + a_{Lm}X_m) + a_{L1}X_1 = L \tag{3.22.1}$$

This production structure satisfies the decomposition property as there are three unknown input prices, W, r and P_m, and the same number of equations, namely Equations (3.16), (3.17) and (3.18). r is determined from Equation (3.17), as W^*, P_2 and t are exogenously given. Plugging the value of r into Equation (3.18), P_m is obtained. Inserting P_m into Equation (3.16) one can solve for W. X_1, X_2 and X_m are simultaneously solved from Equations (3.19), (3.20) and (3.22.1). Finally, L_U is determined from Equation (3.21).

Now if the government resorts to trade liberalisation, the tariff rate on the import of commodity 2, i.e. t takes a lower value. This lowers the domestic price of commodity 2, i.e. P_2 (1 + t).

For finding out the consequence of trade liberalisation on urban unemployment differentiating Equation (3.17) one gets

$$\hat{r} = \left(\frac{T\hat{t}}{\theta_{K2}}\right) \tag{3.23}$$

where

$$T = \left(\frac{t}{1+t}\right) > 0$$

Differentiation of Equation (3.18) and use of Equation (3.23) yield

$$\hat{P}_m = \left(\frac{\theta_{Km}}{\theta_{K2}}\right) T\hat{t} \tag{3.24}$$

Using Equation (3.24) and differentiating Equation (3.16) we find

$$\hat{W} = -\left(\frac{\theta_{m1}\theta_{Km}}{\theta_{L1}\theta_{K2}}\right) T\hat{t} \tag{3.25}$$

Differentiating from Equations (3.19) and (3.20) one can derive, respectively,

$$\lambda_{K2}\hat{X}_2 + \lambda_{Km}\hat{X}_m = 0 \tag{3.26}$$

and

$$\hat{X}_1 = \hat{X}_m \tag{3.27}$$

Hence sector 1 and sector m change in the same direction and in the same proportion.

From Equation (3.22.1) one gets

$$W^*(\lambda_{L2}\hat{X}_2 + \lambda_{Lm}\hat{X}_m) + \lambda_{L1}\hat{X}_1 = \hat{W}(1 - \lambda_{L1}) \tag{3.28}$$

Using Equation (3.27), Equation (3.28) can be rewritten as follows:

$$\left(\frac{W^*\lambda_{L2}}{W}\right)\hat{X}_2 + \left(\frac{W^*\lambda_{Lm}}{W} + \lambda_{L1}\right)\hat{X}_m = \frac{W^*}{W}(\lambda_{L2} + \lambda_{Lm})\hat{W} \tag{3.29}$$

Writing Equations (3.26) and (3.29) in a matrix notation we get

$$\begin{bmatrix} \lambda_{K2} & \lambda_{Km} \\ \left(\frac{W^*\lambda_{L2}}{W}\right) & \left(\frac{W^*\lambda_{Lm}}{W} + \lambda_{L1}\right) \end{bmatrix} \begin{bmatrix} \hat{X}_2 \\ \hat{X}_m \end{bmatrix} = \begin{bmatrix} 0 \\ \frac{W^*}{W}(\lambda_{L2} + \lambda_{Lm})\hat{W} \end{bmatrix} \tag{3.30}$$

where

$$|\lambda| = \lambda_{K2}\left(\frac{W^*\lambda_{Lm}}{W} + \lambda_{L1}\right) - \left(\frac{W^*\lambda_{L2}\lambda_{Km}}{W}\right) = \left(\frac{W^*}{W}\right)(\lambda_{K2}\lambda_{Lm} - \lambda_{L2}\lambda_{Km}) + \lambda_{L1}\lambda_{K2} \tag{3.31}$$

Solving Equation (3.30) by Cramer's rule one finds

$$\hat{X}_2 = -\frac{\lambda_{Km}W^*}{|\lambda|\, W}(\lambda_{L2} + \lambda_{Lm})\hat{W} \tag{3.32}$$

$$\hat{X}_m = \frac{\lambda_{K2}W^*}{|\lambda|\, W}(\lambda_{L2} + \lambda_{Lm})\hat{W} \tag{3.33}$$

Differentiating Equation (3.21) one finds

$$\lambda_{L1}\hat{X}_1 + \lambda_{L2}\hat{X}_2 + \lambda_{\mathrm{Lm}}\hat{X}_m + \lambda_{\mathrm{LU}}\hat{L}_{\mathrm{U}} = 0 \tag{3.34}$$

Using Equations (3.27), (3.32) and (3.33) from (3.34) we can derive

$$\hat{L}_{\mathrm{U}} = -\frac{W^*(\lambda_{L2} + \lambda_{\mathrm{Lm}})}{W\lambda_{\mathrm{LU}}\,|\lambda|}[(\lambda_{L1} + \lambda_{\mathrm{Lm}})\lambda_{K2} - \lambda_{L2}\lambda_{\mathrm{Km}}]\hat{W}$$

With the help of Equation (3.25), the above expression may be rewritten as follows:

$$\hat{L}_U = \frac{W^*(\lambda_{L2} + \lambda_{Lm})}{W\lambda_{LU}\,|\lambda|}[(\lambda_{K2}\lambda_{Lm} - \lambda_{L2}\lambda_{Km}) + \lambda_{L1}\lambda_{K2}]\left(\frac{\theta_{m1}\theta_{Km}}{\theta_{L1}\theta_{K2}}\right)T\hat{t} \tag{3.35}$$

From Equations (3.31) and (3.35) the following results are obtained.

(1) $\hat{L}_{\mathrm{U}} < 0$ when $\hat{t} < 0$ if $\left(\frac{\lambda_{K2}}{\lambda_{L2}}\right) > \left(\frac{\lambda_{Km}}{\lambda_{Lm}}\right)$, i.e. the protected sector is capital-intensive.

(2) $\hat{L}_U > 0$ when $\hat{t} < 0$ only if $|\lambda| < 0$. This means that a reduction in import tariff may accentuate the problem of urban unemployment only if the protected sector is labour-intensive. These results may be stated in terms of the following proposition.

Proposition 3.4 *A policy of trade liberalisation lowers the urban unemployment of labour if the protected sector is capital-intensive. On the contrary, removal of the protectionist policy may accentuate the unemployment problem only if the protected sector is labour-intensive.*

Proposition 3.4 can be intuitively explained as follows. Trade liberalisation lowers the domestic price of commodity 2 that, in turn, reduces r (Equation 3.17). This leads to a decrease in P_m (Equation 3.18). Finally, from the zero-profit condition for sector 1 (Equation 3.16) it follows that W rises, which, in turn, leads to a reverse migration and draws more labour in the rural sector. Consequently, the rural sector expands and raises the demand for the non-traded input. Sector m expands. If the rural sector expands by 1 unit, employment and the demand for the non-traded input increase by a_{L1} and a_{m1} units, respectively. If sector m expands by a_{m1} units, employment rises by $a_{Lm}\ a_{m1}$ units and the demand for capital rises by $a_{Km}\ a_{m1}$ units. As it is a full-employment model, that extra capital must come from sector 2. Consequently, sector 2 contracts by $(a_{Km}\ a_{m1}/a_{K2})$ units and employment falls by $(a_{Km}\ a_{m1}\ a_{L2}/a_{K2})$ units. So we find that owing to trade liberalisation, sectors 1 and m expand while sector 2 contracts.

Employment in the urban sector rises if $a_{Lm}\ a_{m1} > (a_{Km}\ a_{m1}\ a_{L2}/a_{K2})$, i.e. if $(a_{K2}/a_{L2}) > (a_{Km}/a_{Lm})$. In other words, aggregate employment in the urban sector rises if and only if the protected sector is capital-intensive. As the rural sector employment also increases, aggregate employment in the economy rises. On the contrary, if the protected sector is labour-intensive, aggregate employment in the urban sector falls. But the aggregate employment in the economy may still go up if the increase in the rural sector employment outweighs the fall in the urban sector employment. Hence that the protected sector is labour-intensive is only a necessary condition for the unemployment in the economy to increase.

3.5 Introduction of the Informal Sector

The HT model presumes that in the urban sector workers either find employment in the formal sector at the high unionised wage or they remain unemployed. However, a worker can remain unemployed either if he has not completely cut off his attachment with the rural sector or if he has some of his family members employed in the formal sector who would help him financially for the time being and keep his hope alive to be able to secure a formal sector job in the next period. But the documentation in a series of empirical studies[4] in several developing economies suggests that people

[4] See, for example, Papola (1981), Romatet (1983), Bose (1978) and Joshi and Joshi (1976).

who are unable to find employment in the urban formal sector end up working in the urban informal sector at low wages.[5] In the conventional dual economy models with an urban informal sector, the latter is viewed as a residual sector offering a low competitive wage which is less than both the rural and the formal sector wage rates.[6] If a worker fails to find a job in the formal sector, he is automatically absorbed in the informal sector. The informal sector wage rate is assumed to be perfectly flexible so as to clear the labour market in the urban sector. Hence, there is no open unemployment in the urban sector in the migration equilibrium.[7]

The informal sector as a residual sector can easily be introduced in a 2×2 mobile capital HT model. Consider the following general equilibrium set-up:

$$W_X a_{LX} + r a_{KX} = 1 \tag{3.36}$$

$$W_m a_{Lm} + r a_{Km} = P_m \tag{3.37}$$

$$\overline{W}_Y a_{LY} + r a_{KY} = P_Y \tag{3.38}$$

$$a_{KX} X + a_{Km} M + a_{KY} Y = K \tag{3.39}$$

$$a_{LX} X + a_{Lm} M + a_{LY} Y = L \tag{3.40}$$

Finally, the HT migration equilibrium condition is given by

$$\left(\frac{\overline{W}_Y a_{LY} Y + W_m a_{Lm} M}{a_{LY} Y + a_{Lm} M} \right) = W_X \tag{3.41}$$

Here sector M is the urban informal sector that produces an internationally traded commodity. So P_m is given internationally. Equations (3.39), (3.40) and (3.41) are the modified capital and labour endowment equations and the Harris–Todaro migration equilibrium condition, respectively. The Harris–Todaro (1970) migration equilibrium is now attained when the actual rural wage equals the expected urban

---

[5] See Chapter 1, Section 1.5 and Agenor (1996) for the size and growth of the informal sector. The percentage of population engaged in the informal sector has increased in the post-reform period. See Marjit (2003) and Dev (2000) in this context. That the informal sector is growing in most developing countries has also been pointed out in Djankov (2003).

[6] The rural–urban migration of labour in the presence of informal sector ensures that the rural sector wage rate settles down somewhere between the urban formal sector and informal sector wage rates. This is true in the Harris–Todaro migration framework where migration depends on expected wages only. However, there are alternative migration theories, in particular that of Katz and Stark (1986), where an individual's decision to migrate is part of the household's portfolio choice among different income streams. Thus, even if expected income in the rural sector is less, some family members may stay there because this allows diversifying the income risks of the household.

[7] In reality, the informal sector and open unemployment of unskilled labour coexist. This happens if the informal sector unskilled wage is also rigid in the downward direction. See Chapter 4 for details.

wage, which consists of both urban formal and informal wages. This model does not have urban unemployment, so that it is assumed that those who do not find formal sector employment are absorbed in the informal sector.

However, if the informal sector (sector M) produces a non-traded input for the urban formal sector, the price of the informal sector's product, i.e. P_m, is domestically determined. There would be an additional equation in the form of the demand and supply equality condition for the informal sector's product which is as follows:

$$M = a_{mY}Y \tag{3.42}$$

The zero-profit condition for the formal sector (Equation 3.38) has now to be replaced by the following equation:

$$\overline{W}_Y a_{LY} + r a_{KY} + P_m a_{mY} = P_Y \tag{3.38.1}$$

The modified production structure is an indecomposable one. This is because the price system now consists of Equations (3.36), (3.37) and (3.38.1) with four unknowns, namely W_x, W_m, r and P_m. So factor prices cannot be determined from the price system alone. One has to take help of the output system to solve for all the endogenous variables including the input prices. Hence, apart from the commodity prices, factor prices now depend on factor endowments.

Again, if the urban informal sector uses a specific input, the production structure would be as follows. The price–unit cost equality conditions in perfectly competitive markets of the three sectors are given by

$$W_X a_{LX} + r_1 a_{KX} = P_X \tag{3.43}$$

$$W_Y a_{LY} + r_2 a_{KY} = P_Y \tag{3.44}$$

$$\overline{W}_Z a_{LZ} + r_1 a_{KZ} = P_Z \tag{3.45}$$

The urban formal and rural sectors use capital of type 1 with interest rate r_1 and the informal sector uses capital of type 2 with interest rate r_2. Capital of type 1 is completely mobile between the urban formal and rural sectors while capital of type 2 is specific to the urban informal sector. Labour is imperfectly mobile among the three sectors of the economy.

Full employment of labour and complete utilisation of capital of the two types imply that

$$a_{LX}X + a_{LY}Y + a_{LZ}Z = L \tag{3.46}$$

$$a_{KX}X + a_{KZ}Z = K_1 \tag{3.47}$$

$$a_{KY}Y = K_2 \tag{3.48}$$

The Harris–Todaro (1970) migration equilibrium condition is now given by

$$\frac{W_Y a_{LY} Y + \overline{W}_Z a_{LZ} Z}{a_{LY} Y + a_{LZ} Z} = W_X$$

Use of Equation (3.46) and simplification yield

$$W_X a_{LX} X + W_Y a_{LY} Y + \overline{W}_Z a_{LZ} Z = W_X L \tag{3.49}$$

There are seven endogenous variables W_x, W_Y, r_1, r_2, X, Y and Z that can be solved from the above seven independent equations, namely Equations (3.43), (3.44), (3.45), (3.46), (3.47), (3.48) and (3.49). This is an indecomposable system where changes in factor endowments affect some of the factor prices and hence also the factor intensities.

Equations (3.43) and (3.45) form a decomposable subsector since W_X and r_1 can be solved from them. Hence, any change in factor endowments does not affect the factor prices in rural and formal sectors.

3.6 Subcontracting

Most of the studies conducted on the informal sector (see for example, Papola, 1981; Romatet, 1983; Joshi and Joshi, 1976; Bose, 1978) have found that the urban informal sector consists of many subcontract firms, which produce various parts and semi-processed components for the parent formal sector firms. Such subcontract firms are observed around machine and automobiles makers, garments and shoe industries in developing countries. These activities are typically characterised by small scale and among others a low wage rate suppressed by the parent firms.

Subcontracting alludes to the practice of farming out a part or whole of the production of a commodity by a larger (formal sector) firm to a smaller (informal sector) firm on a contractual basis. The terms of the contract, i.e the interest rate on credit and the price at which the formal sector firm (F_2) purchases the output of the informal sector firm (F_1), are determined by the former. This is analogous to the concept of credit–product interlinkage as observed in backward agriculture.

Formal sector firms have an advantage over the informal sector firms in the capital (credit) market while the latter firms enjoy the advantage of cheaper labour supply.

If the different cost advantages of the two sectors are combined, the production cost can be minimised. Thus, a possibility of interlinkage between these two sectors arises. Subcontracting is such an interlinkage. This system is Pareto-optimal and a principal–agent framework is adopted to analyse this contract.

Let the equation of the final demand curve facing the formal sector firm for its product, X, be

$$P = P(X);\ P' < 0;\ P'' \leq 0 \tag{3.50}$$

The total cost function for producing X is as follows:

$$\mathrm{C} = \mathrm{C}(X);\ \mathrm{C}' > 0;\ \mathrm{C}'' > 0;\ \mathrm{C}(0) \cong 0. \tag{3.51}$$

3.6.1 Two Alternative Contracts

We consider a subcontracting system between the representative formal sector firm and the informal sector firm. Two alternative contracts are available to both of these firms.

Contract I: The informal sector firm (F_1) sells its product in a competitive market at the price P^0 per unit. The large firm (F_2) purchases the product from F_1 at P^0 and resells it in the final market. F_1 takes credit from an informal source at the parametric interest rate g per period.

The profit function of F_1 is given by

$$\prod\nolimits_1 = P^0 X - (1+g)C(X) \tag{3.52}$$

The first-order condition of profit maximisation is given by

$$P^0 = (1+g)\,C'(.) \tag{3.53}$$

Solving Equation (3.53), the optimum supply or production of X is obtained as

$$X^0 = X^0(\underset{(+)}{P},\underset{(-)}{g}) \tag{3.54}$$

The optimum income of F_1 is

$$\prod\nolimits_1^0 = P^0 X^0 - (1+g)\,C(X^0) \tag{3.55}$$

The profit function of firm F_2 is

$$\prod\nolimits_2 = [P(X^0) - P^0]X^0 \tag{3.56}$$

Profit is maximised through a choice of X^0 and the first-order condition is

$$[P(X^0) + P'(X^0)\,X^0] = P^0 = (1+g)C'(X^0) \tag{3.57}$$

$$i.e.\ \mathrm{MR}\,(X^0) = \mathrm{MC}\,(X^0)$$

Contract II: This is subcontracting. Here F_2 supplies credit to F_1 at the interest rate r and purchases the output of the latter at the price P^* per unit. It then sells the product in the final commodity market.

The profit function of F_1 under this contract is

$$\prod_1 = P^*X - (1+r)\,C(X) \tag{3.58}$$

and this is maximised with respect to X. The first-order condition is as follows:

$$P^* = (1+r)\,C'(X) \tag{3.59}$$

Equation (3.59) leads to the following supply function of X:

$$\begin{aligned} X^* = X^*(&P^*, r) \\ &(+)(-) \end{aligned} \tag{3.60}$$

The optimum profit of the informal sector firm (F_1) is given by

$$\prod_1^* = P^*X^* - (1+r)\,C(X^*) \tag{3.61}$$

The profit of the formal sector firm (F_2) under subcontracting system is represented by

$$\prod_2 = [P(X^*) - P^*]\,X^* + (r - i)\,C(X^*) \tag{3.62}$$

where i is the opportunity interest rate of F_2.

The problem of F_2 is to maximise

$$\underset{P^*,\, i}{\text{Max}} \prod_2 = [P(X^*) - P^*]X^* + (r - i)\,C(X^*)$$

subject to the reservation income constraint of the informal sector firm given by

$$\prod_1^* \geq \prod_1^0$$

The Lagrange expression is as follows:

$$L = [P(X^*) - P^*]X^* + (r - i)C(X^*) + \lambda\left(\prod_1^* - \prod_1^0\right) \tag{3.63}$$

Assuming interior solutions for P^* and i the first-order conditions and the Kuhn-Tucker conditions are given as follows:

$$(\partial L/\partial P^*) = (\partial X^*/\partial P^*)\,[\mathrm{MR}(X^*) - P^* + (r - i)C'(.)] - X^*(1 - \lambda) = 0 \quad (3.64)$$

$$(\partial L/\partial r) = (\partial X^*/\partial r)\,[\mathrm{MR}\,(X^*) - P^* + (r - i)C'(.)] - C(X^*)(\lambda - 1) = 0 \quad (3.65)$$

$$(\partial \mathrm{L}/\partial \lambda) = 0;\ \text{and,} \quad (3.66)$$

$$\lambda(\partial \mathrm{L}/\partial \lambda) = 0,\ \lambda \geq 0 \quad (3.67)$$

Multiplying both sides of Equations (3.64) and (3.65) by $C(X^*)$ and X^*, respectively, and adding, one gets

$$[\mathrm{MR}\,(X^*) - P^* + (r - i)C'(.)][C(X^*)(\partial X^*/\partial P^*) + X^*(\partial X^*/\partial r)] = 0 \quad (3.68)$$

From Equation (3.68) one can easily verify that

$$[\mathrm{MR}\,(X^*) - P^* + (r - i)C'(.)] = 0 \quad (3.69)$$

(This is because it is easily seen that $[C(X^*)(\partial X^*/\partial P^*) + X^*(\partial X^*/\partial r)] \neq 0$)
Using Equation (3.59) from (3.69) it follows that

$$\mathrm{MR}(X^*) = (1 + i)C'(.) = \mathrm{MC}(X^*) \quad (3.70)$$

Using Equation (3.70) from Equation (3.64) or (3.65) one finds

$$\lambda = 1 > 0 \quad (3.71)$$

Using Equation (3.71) from Equation (3.67) it follows that

$$\prod_1^* = \prod_1^0 \quad (3.72)$$

This leads to the following proposition.

Proposition 3.5 *The informal sector firm does not get more than its reservation income in the subcontracting system.*

Now using Fig. 3.1 it is easy to prove that the subcontracting system is optimal for the formal sector firm (F_2).

In Fig. 3.1, *aD* is the market demand curve for the final product (X). The corresponding marginal revenue curve is *ab*. MC^0 and MC^* are the marginal cost curves under the two contracts, respectively. The respective equilibrium points are *c* and *d*. X^0 and X^* are the corresponding output levels. The profit of the formal sector firm (F_2) under contract 1 is

$$\prod_2^0 = m(OacX^0) - m(\Delta OcX^0) = m(\Delta Oac)$$

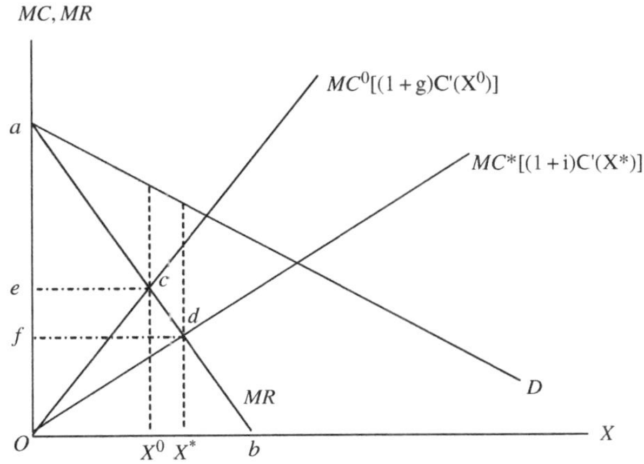

Fig. 3.1 The optimality of the subcontracting system

The profit of the formal sector firm (F_2) under subcontracting is

$$\prod\nolimits_2^* = m(OadX^*) - m(OdX^*) = m(\Delta Oad)$$

Hence, $(\prod_2^* - \prod_2^0) = m(\Delta Oad) - m(\Delta Oac) = m(\Delta Ocd) > 0$

Therefore, subcontracting is the optimal policy of the formal sector firm (F_2).

It is to be noted that the optimality of the system of subcontracting here has been proved in terms of credit market imperfection. In the absence of any credit market imperfections, $i = g$. In that case, $(\prod_2^* - \prod_2^0) = 0$. So there is no reason for subcontracting system to exist. So the following proposition readily follows.

Proposition 3.6 *The subcontracting system is the optimal policy to the formal sector firm provided there is imperfection in the credit market.*

Now if a credit subsidy is given to the informal sector firm (F_1), g falls and MC^0 curve moves to the right and $m(\Delta Ocd)$ decreases. Although the policy makes F_1 better off, the industrial productivity does not increase so long as F_1 is engaged in subcontracting. This leads to the following proposition.

Proposition 3.7 *A credit subsidy policy to the informal sector firm does not raise the industrial productivity so long as it is engaged in subcontracting arrangement with the formal sector firm.*

We have used the principal–agent framework to analyse the subcontracting system with formal sector firm (F_2) as the principal and informal sector firm (F_1) as the agent. The principal–agent framework is a special case of the Nash-bargaining game between the two players where the principal possesses all the bargaining capacity. On the contrary, the agent without having any bargaining power accepts the principal's offer of the interlinked contract and does not get more than its reservation income. So subcontracting is actually a system of creating economic surplus where the production is done by the agent and an instrument of extracting economic surplus on the part of the stronger party.

3.7 Does the Informal Sector Live or Die with the Formal Sector?

It has already been mentioned that the informal sector firms primarily produce intermediate inputs for the formal sector through an institutional arrangement, which is known as subcontracting. As the informal sector depends on the formal sector for marketing its output, a common contention is that the informal sector lives or dies with the formal sector. It is worthwhile to theoretically examine the validity of this conventional wisdom. In the following section, we do this exercise using a three-sector Harris–Todaro model with an urban informal sector.

We consider a model of rural–urban migration with three sectors: rural, urban informal and urban formal sectors. The rural sector produces an agricultural commodity, X, using labour and a sector-specific input land, the latter earning a return i. The urban informal sector produces an intermediate input, Y, for the formal sector with the help of labour and capital. In the rural and the urban informal sectors, labour markets are perfectly competitive and the wage rates are W_X and W_Y, respectively. The capital market facing the urban informal sector is imperfect. The interest rate on capital, R, is a positive function of the amount of capital borrowed and a decreasing function of the policy parameter, β. An increase in β implies a credit subsidy to the informal sector that lowers the interest rate. Therefore, we have

$$R = R(a_{KY}Y,\ \beta)\,\text{with}\,(\partial R/\partial a_{KY}Y) > 0\,;\text{and}\,(\partial R/\partial \beta) < 0. \tag{3.73}$$

Let us now explain in details the capital market dichotomy, which is a salient feature of the developing economies. The functional form of $R(.)$ suggests that capital cost in the informal sector increases with an increase in the amount of capital borrowed. In the absence of any significant provision for organised (formal) credit, the informal sector has to mainly rely on informal credit market for financing the costs of capital. The $R(.)$ function with $(\partial R/\partial a_{KY}Y) > 0$ and $(\partial R/\partial \beta) < 0$ is a possible way of formalising the informal sector's lack of access to the organised credit market. The idea is that the economy is endowed with a given amount of capital. Firms in sector Z have access to or connections with the owners of capital and they work out a rental rate, r, which is the competitive rate. The informal sector lacks this connection. Hence we can conceive of a set of middlemen who borrow capital from the capital owners at the competitive rate, r, and then lend them out to the workers in the informal sector at a higher rate given by $R(.)$, with $(\partial R/\partial a_{KY}Y) > 0$. This means sector Y can get an additional loan at the cost of a higher interest rate. This implies imperfection in the capital market. Similar treatment of credit market imperfection is available in Datta Chaudhuri (1989), Gupta (1993) and Chaudhuri (2000).

Lending of credit to the informal sector borrowers is always risky. There is a high probability of default of loans. The risk of default may arise due to many reasons.

First, there is the risk of involuntary default owing to unforeseen circumstances (unemployment, disease, death of the borrower, etc.). Hence, the borrower simply may not have sufficient money at the time of repayment of the loan. Second, there is possibility of voluntary default: the borrower may take the loan, not use the fund for production and refuse to repay. In developing countries where the legal machinery is not so strong and functions slowly, the risk of default is high. The larger the volume of loan, in order to cover risks, the higher the interest rate the informal sector lender would charge (see Bottomley (1975), Basu (1998) and Ray (1998) in this context). Nonetheless, in Appendix 3.1 we have shown mathematically why the informal interest rate, R, is an increasing function of the volume of loan and a decreasing function of the government's credit subsidy.

Finally, the urban formal sector faces a perfect capital market but a unionised labour market. The unionised wage in this sector, $\overline{W}$, is greater than both the rural and the informal sector wage rates. In particular, we have $\overline{W} > W_X > W_Y$. There are two production divisions in the formal sector. Division Z produces a final manufacturing commodity using labour, capital and the non-traded input, Y. Another division, M, produces at least a part of the requirement for the input in order to avoid complete dependence on the informal sector. The price of commodity Y is determined domestically while final commodity prices are given internationally. The technology for producing the intermediate good, Y, is identical in both sectors and coefficients of production in all the three sectors are fixed so that the a_{ji}s are technologically given. However, this is only a simplifying assumption. Finally, commodity X is chosen as the numeraire.

The usual zero-profit conditions are given by

$$W_X a_{LX} + i a_{NX} = 1 \tag{3.74}$$

$$W_Y a_{LY} + \underset{(+)(-)}{R(a_{KY}Y,\beta)} a_{KY} = P_Y \tag{3.75}$$

$$\overline{W} a_{LM} + r a_{KM} = P_Y \tag{3.76}$$

$$\overline{W} a_{LZ} + r a_{KZ} + P_Y a_{YZ} = \bar{P}_Z \tag{3.77}$$

All inputs are fully utilised. The full-employment conditions for land, capital, labour and the non-traded input are given by the following four equations, respectively.

$$a_{NX} X = N \tag{3.78}$$

$$a_{KY} Y + a_{KM} M + a_{KZ} Z = K \tag{3.79}$$

$$a_{LX} X + a_{LY} Y + a_{LM} M + a_{LZ} Z = L \tag{3.80}$$

$$Y + M = a_{YZ} Z \tag{3.81}$$

Finally, the Harris–Todaro migration equilibrium condition is given by

$$\left(\frac{W_Y a_{LY} Y + \overline{W} a_{LM} M + \overline{W} a_{LZ} Z}{a_{LY} Y + a_{LM} M + a_{LZ} Z}\right) = W_X \tag{3.82}$$

Here the endogenous variables are W_x, W_Y, i, P_Y, r, X, Y, M and Z. The policy parameter is β. An increase in β implies a credit subsidy policy to the urban informal sector.

$\overline{W}$ is the exogenously given wage rate in the urban formal sector. Given $\overline{W}$ and $\bar{P}_Z$, the equilibrium values of r and P_Y are determined from Equations (3.76) and (3.77). The values of W_X, i, X, Y, M and Z are determined by solving Equations (3.74), (3.78), (3.79), (3.80), (3.81) and (3.82) simultaneously. Once Y is known R is also known, and hence from Equation (3.74) W_Y is obtained. This is how the values of all endogenous variables are determined.

Now if a credit subsidy is given to the informal sector, β takes a higher value. Consequently, R decreases and W_Y increases as P_Y and r are determined from Equations (3.76) and (3.77). Sector Y also expands by the process. As the informal sector wage, W_Y, rises, the expected urban wage for a prospective rural migrant, given by the left-hand side of Equation (3.82), increases, leading to a migration of labour from the rural sector to the urban sector. There is no reason for sector Z to change. Thus, the demand for the intermediate input remains unchanged. The intermediate input-producing division of the formal sector must contract as the informal sector now produces more of input Y. Thus, as a whole the formal sector (final good plus intermediate input) contracts while the informal sector expands. So the following proposition can now be established.

Proposition 3.8 *A credit subsidy policy to the informal sector leads to an overall contraction of the formal sector while it expands the informal sector.*

Hence, there may be cases where the urban informal sector may expand even if the formal sector contracts and the former is dependent on the latter for marketing its output.

Appendix 3.1: Derivation of the *R* Function

Suppose an informal sector lender finds that on average, fraction q of his loans is not repaid. It is sensible to assume that q should be increasing in the volume of loan, K_Y, and decreasing in the government's credit subsidy, β. As the volume of credit increases the probability of default is expected to increase while a higher provision for subsidised formal credit would lower the average cost of borrowing funds for the informal sector borrowers and it would be easier for them to repay their loans. So we write

$$q = q(K_Y,\beta) \text{ with } (\partial q/\partial K_Y) > 0 \text{ and } (\partial q/\partial \beta) < 0 \tag{3.A.1}$$

The income of the informal sector lender, denoted as Q, is given by

$$Q = (1 - q)(1 + R)K_Y - K_Y \tag{3.A.2}$$

The effective informal interest rate net of the expected cost of default, denoted as d, is as follows:

$$d = \left(\frac{Y}{K_Y}\right) = (1 - q)(1 + R) - 1 \tag{3.A.3}$$

Competition between sectors will ensure that in equilibrium the effective informal interest is equal to the competitive interest rate in the organised credit market. So in equilibrium we have

$$(1 - q(.))(1 + R) - 1 = r$$

or

$$R = \left(\frac{r + q}{1 - q}\right) \tag{3.A.4}$$

It is easy to check that

$$(R - r) = \left(\frac{q(1 + r)}{1 - q}\right) > 0 \text{ if } q > 0. \tag{3.A.5}$$

So if the rate of default of loan, q, is positive, there exists positive interest rate differential between the informal and the formal credit markets.

From Equation (3.A.4) it is not difficult to check that

$$\left.\begin{aligned} &\left(\frac{\partial R}{\partial K_Y}\right) = \left[\frac{1+r}{(1-q)^2}\right]\left(\frac{\partial q}{\partial K_Y}\right) > 0; \text{ and,} \\ &\qquad\qquad\qquad\qquad (+) \\ &\left(\frac{\partial R}{\partial \beta}\right) = \left[\frac{1+r}{(1-q)^2}\right]\left(\frac{\partial q}{\partial \beta}\right) < 0. \\ &\qquad\qquad\qquad\qquad (-) \end{aligned}\right\} \tag{3.A.6}$$

Hence R is an increasing function of the volume of loan and a decreasing function of the credit subsidy.

Chapter 4
Informal Sector and Open Unemployment

4.1 Existing Literature and Empirical Evidences

In explaining urban unemployment in migration equilibrium, the Harris–Todaro (1970) model posits that due to the existence of minimum wages determined by institutional forces, a migrant entering the modern sector may not be absorbed at the prevailing urban real wage, that is, each migrant has only a 'probability' of obtaining modern sector job. There remains a time gap between the entry of a migrant in the urban labour force and his securing formal sector job. This implies that those not managing to secure modern sector employment are left to remain unemployed and search for employment. The job search strategy specified in the probabilistic models of Harberger (1971), Mincer (1976), Gramlich (1976) and Stiglitz (1982) allows for unemployment and full-time search.

The role of informal sector in the urban labour market is latent in the study of Todaro (1969), where he suggests that migrants find temporary employment in the urban 'traditional sector' before their eventual attainment of urban 'modern sector' job. Cole and Sanders (1983) introduce the informal sector in the Harris–Todaro (1970) model and emphasise that much of the migration takes place with the informal sector, not the modern sector as the intended destination. Those with adequate human capital migrate to the formal sector while others migrate to the informal sector. They argue that all informal sector migrants get employed. Therefore, the traditional view postulates that migrants not getting jobs in the formal sector are automatically employed in the informal sector, and in migration equilibrium, there does not exist any open unemployment in the urban sector.[1]

[1] See the models of Datta Chaudhuri (1989) and Grinols (1991). However, the Todaro (1969) model earlier had hinted that those who do not find employment in the formal sector accept temporary unemployment rather than menial jobs.

S. Chaudhuri, U. Mukhopadhyay, *Revisiting the Informal Sector*,
DOI 10.1007/978-1-4419-1194-0_4,

However, contrary to the traditional wisdom, empirical evidences[2] do indicate simultaneous existence of open unemployment and informal sector in developing countries. This calls for an explanation regarding the nature of unemployment and the factors responsible for the inability of the informal sector to sop up the residual labour force causing unemployment. Theoretical exposition on unemployment in the presence of informal sector depicts it as voluntary or involuntary. Voluntary unemployment is a supply side phenomenon where workers prefer remaining unemployed to being employed in the informal sector. Involuntary unemployment arises when workers are willing to accept informal jobs but are unable to find one. It is the latter type of unemployment that is more thought-provoking since it contradicts the conventional wisdom regarding the 'free-entry' nature of the informal sector that disallows open unemployment.

The earliest explanation for the existence of open unemployment in the presence of wage flexibility in the informal sector has been provided by Fields (1975). He posits a trade-off between informal sector employment and search for formal sector jobs. Those aspiring for formal sector employment have two options for job search: either they can get some informal employment with flexible work hours and tenure and search for formal sector job in the remaining hours of the day when they are not working or they can remain unemployed and devote their full time for seeking job in the formal sector. The greater effectiveness of search from being unemployed than informally employed and access to non-earned income may induce workers to choose to be unemployed. Unemployment in this case is essentially voluntary in nature.

However, there are several evidences that indicate that unemployment neither is always voluntary nor is the informal sector a free-entry zone as commonly perceived; rather conspicuous barriers to entry exist, which deter the unemployed from entering the sector (Banerjee, 1986; Gandhi-Kingdon and Knight, 2001). In a study of South Africa, Gandhi-Kingdon and Knight (2001) find that the unemployed are substantially worse-off than the informal sector workers in terms of income, living conditions and happiness. One may argue that the unemployed may be prepared to endure temporary penury and unhappiness to allow full-time search and thus optimise their 'inter-temporal search strategy'. This rationale is also consistent with voluntary unemployment. However, their study shows that only 9% of the unemployed searched full time (35 or more hours) for work in the reference week and 68% spent no more than 10 hours in job search. This rules out the possibility that

---

[2] In South Africa, the informal sector absorbs only 19% of the workforce, which is a very small proportion by developing country standards and open unemployment is more common. During the period 1995–2003, the labour force grew by over 5% per annum, wage employment rose by 1.8% per annum, self-employment grew by 5.1% per annum and unemployment grew by above 9% per annum (Kingdon and Knight, 2001, 2005). In Latin America, according to the ILO, the overall average unemployment rates have risen from 9.1% in 1995 to 11.1% in 1999, while several studies estimate the number of informal workers at between 20 and 35% of the urban economically active population (Portes and Schauffler, 1993). The 2000–2001 Labour Force Survey in Tanzania shows that the unemployment rate had increased by 1.5 points from 3.6% in 1990–1991 to 5.1 points in 2000–2001.

unemployment is a supply side phenomenon and suggests that limited scope for entering the informal sector may have pushed many workers into unemployment.

Nonetheless, minimal attention has been devoted in the literature to analyse and explain the phenomenon of involuntary unemployment and the deterrents for entry into informal sector in developing countries. Whatever studies do exist have mostly been carried out with respect to South Africa, typical with remarkably high open unemployment level despite the persistence of an informal sector. From those studies, three broad reasons that dissuade the unemployed from entering into the informal sector may be envisaged: first, lack of resources to enter the upper-tier informal sector; second, inhibitions and impediments to be engaged in self-employment; and third, wage rigidity in the informal wage employment.

In Zimbabwe, entry into the productive segment of the informal sector is restricted by lack of skills and capital. Voluntary entry is possible mostly for the erstwhile formal sector workers who had accumulated experience, knowledge and skills (Jenkins and Knight, 2002). Even for the educated young people it becomes difficult to be successful in self-employment, so that they prefer unemployment, in case they could not find formal sector jobs.

The hindrances to self-employment in South Africa may be classified as profit barriers where individuals do not view an informal activity as being able to generate profit, capital barriers that restrict an individual's access to funds, skill barriers in terms of technical or entrepreneurial skills, future-limiting barriers, which arise when informal work today limits an individual's opportunity to access formal employment in the future, lack of infrastructure, limited role of the government in assisting the unemployed and hidden cost barriers that include formal or informal restrictions and criminal activities (Skinner, 2005; Cichello, 2005; The Western Cape Provincial Economic Review & Outlook, 2007). Moreover, the subjugation of entrepreneurial activities under apartheid and the allied inhibition of entrepreneurial skills and social networks, and excessively restrictive bye-laws contribute to high entry barriers in South Africa (Chandra et al., 2002). Cichello et al. (2005) also identify the risk of impending business failure, high cost of transport and jealousy within the community as key deterrents in Khayelitsha, South Africa.

Wage rigidity in the informal sector can be explained in three ways. First, it is observed that in many developing countries the informal sector consists of several subcontract firms that produce various parts and semi-processed components for the parent formal sector firms. These activities are typically characterised by small scale and among others a low-wage rate suppressed by the parent firms. The informal sector workers do not get more than their reservation wages. Second, several authors (e.g. Banerjee, 1986; Gandhi-Kingdon and Knight, 2001) have noted that many activities in the so-called informal sector of developing countries are highly stratified, requiring skills, experience and contacts, with identifiable barriers to entry. For example, petty trading often has highly structured labour and product markets with considerable costs of entry. Even when skill and capital are not required, entry can be difficult because of the presence of cohesive networks, which exercise control over location and zone of operation. Finally, unemployment of unskilled labour may also arise if the workers are paid their nutritional efficiency wage that maximises the profits of their employers, even though the workers are willing to work at a lower wage which is equal to their reservation wage.

Apart from entry barriers and wage rigidity, the association between informal sector and unemployment has been analysed in terms of economic development with the help of the theoretical framework developed in the Lewis (1954) model. Following the model, two stages of the development process can be identified for an economy with labour mobility and market-clearing: first, the labour-surplus stage and, second, the labour-scarce stage; beyond the turning point, a shortage of labour begins to raise both urban real wages and rural real incomes more rapidly. In an economy where the turning point is being approached, the proportion of the labour force in free-entry informal activities declines while the more productive informal sector remains unchanged. On the other hand, where the turning point is receding, the free-entry informal sector and open unemployment together have to absorb the growing residual labour force. South Africa and Zimbabwe, characterised by fast labour force growth in relation to slow economic growth, appear to be moving further away from the turning point and therefore show evidences of simultaneous existence of informal sector and open unemployment (Ruffer and Knight, 2007; Knight, 2007).

A common conjecture is that growth can drastically curb unemployment. But globalisation-led growth leads to a complex problem. There is a soaring demand for skilled workers while a large pool of the unskilled labour remains 'unemployable'. The phenomenon of 'unsatisfied demand' coexists alongside 'an incredible surplus of labour power'. In many cases, like for example, Argentina, the revenues brought in through the privatisation process and the inflow of foreign investment did not go towards strengthening the country's productive base; instead, priority was put on the financial and speculative sectors. This led to a gradual contraction of industry and agriculture, aggravated by the opening of the economy to more competitive imports. Many people who had only informal sector jobs fell into perpetual unemployment.

Trade liberalisation, the most important ingredient of the globalisation process, exposes formal enterprises to increased foreign competition, which respond by reducing labour costs by cutting worker benefits, replacing permanent workers with part-time labour or subcontracting with establishments in the informal sector, including self-employed micro-entrepreneurs. Alternatively, they may also dismiss workers who subsequently seek employment in the informal sector. In many cases, an exceptionally large number of retrenched workers create considerable pressure on the already existing informal labour market, with the outcome of a pool of unemployed workers.

In the theoretical literature, Gupta (1993) first formalised the simultaneous existence of the informal sector and open unemployment in urban areas. Later, Chaudhuri (2000) and Chaudhuri et al. (2006) have also explained open unemployment in the urban sector despite the presence of the urban informal sector. It becomes imperative to examine the consequences of alternative development policies, particularly on the open unemployment in the urban sector within the backdrop of the simultaneous existence of the informal sector and open unemployment in the urban sector. In the subsequent sections we first present the Gupta (1993) and Chaudhuri (2000) models separately and then make a comparative analysis of different development policies on open unemployment in the urban area as found in these two models.

4.2 Gupta Model

The novelty of this model lies in the theoretical formulation of the functioning of informal sector in a Harris–Todaro (1970) type of dual economy. It extends the HT framework to explain the simultaneous existence of informal sector and open unemployment in migration equilibrium.[3]

4.2.1 The Model

A closed dual economy is considered to consist of an urban sector and a rural sector. The urban sector has two sub-sectors – a formal sector and an informal sector.

4.2.1.1 The Formal Sector

The urban formal sector (sector 1) produces a manufactured good using labour, capital and an intermediate input produced by the informal sector. Capital is assumed to be owned by the sector itself. So the cost of capital is not treated as variable cost in the process of profit maximisation. The production function of this sector is given by

$$Y_1 = F_1(L_1,R,K_1) \tag{4.1}$$

where Y_1 is the output level, L_1 and K_1 are the levels of labour and capital, respectively, and R is the amount of intermediate input used. The production function exhibits the following properties: (i) diminishing returns to scale technology; (ii) positive and diminishing productivity of each input; and (iii) separability in terms of its arguments.

Assuming the price of the formal sector output as the numeraire, the first-order conditions for profit maximisation are given by

$$(\partial Y_1/\partial L_1) = W_1^* - S_1 \tag{4.2}$$

$$(\partial Y_1/\partial R) = P_2 \tag{4.3}$$

[3] Here we present the Gupta (1993) model in the simplest possible manner. However, some of the results get affected due to this simplification.

where W^*_1 is the institutionally determined fixed wage rate in the urban formal sector, S_1 is a policy parameter denoting wage subsidy to sector 1 and P_2 is the price of the intermediate input produced in the informal sector.

Solving Equations (4.2) and (4.3) the input demand functions of sector 1 are obtained as follows:

$$L_1 = L_1(S_1); L_1'(S_1) > 0 \tag{4.4}$$

$$R = R(P_2); R'(P_2) < 0 \tag{4.5}$$

Equations (4.4) and (4.5) represent the employment function in the formal sector and the demand function for intermediate input, respectively.

4.2.1.2 The Informal Sector

The urban informal sector (sector 2) produces an intermediate input for the formal sector with the help of capital and labour, the latter being mainly the rural migrants unable to find formal sector jobs. There is perfect wage flexibility in the labour market, while the sector is characterised by capital market imperfection. This implies that capital is borrowed from the unorganised capital market at exceptionally high rates of interest. The informal sector interest rate r is given by

$$r = r_1 + r_2(K_2); r_2'(K_2) > 0 \tag{4.6}$$

where r_1 is a policy parameter. It implies that a credit subsidy policy to the informal sector lowers the value of r_1. K_2 is the amount of capital used in the informal sector. The assumption that $r_2'(K_2) > 0$ indicates that due to capital market imperfection, a higher amount of capital can be borrowed only at a higher interest rate.

The production function in sector 2 is given by

$$Y_2 = F_2(L_2, K_2) \tag{4.7}$$

where Y_2 and L_2 denote levels of output and employment, respectively. It satisfies all the properties satisfied by $F_1(.)$.

The first-order conditions for profit maximisation in sector 2 are given by

$$(P_2 + S_2)(\partial Y_2/\partial L_2) = W_2 \tag{4.8}$$

$$(P_2 + S_2)(\partial Y_2/\partial K_2) = r_1 + r_2(K_2) + r_2'(K_2)K_2 \tag{4.9}$$

Solving Equations (4.8) and (4.9) the demand functions for labour and capital can be obtained as

$$L_2 = L_2(P_2 + S_2, W_2); L_2^1 > 0, L_2^2 < 0 \tag{4.10}$$

$$K_2 = K_2(P_2 + S_2, r_1); K_2^1 > 0, K_2^2 < 0 \tag{4.11}$$

where W_2 is the informal sector wage rate and S_2 is the price subsidy to the informal sector.

Since the intermediate input produced in the informal sector is entirely used up by the formal sector, in equilibrium, the supply of Y_2 must equal its demand R in the formal sector. Thus, using Equations (4.7), (4.10) and (4.11) we get

$$\underset{(-)}{R(P_2)} = F_2(L_2(\underset{(+)}{P_2 + S_2}, \underset{(-)}{W_2}), K_2(\underset{(+)}{P_2 + S_2}, \underset{(-)}{r_1})) \tag{4.12}$$

For given values of S_2 and r_1, Equation (4.12) gives the alternative combinations of W_2 and P_2, at which the demand–supply equality of the informal sector output is maintained. On plotting the equation graphically on the W_2–P_2 plane, it generates the 'supply–demand equality' (SDE) curve. Since $\partial Y_2/\partial L_2 > 0$ and $L_2'(W_2) < 0$, an increase in W_2 brings about a fall in Y_2 so that to maintain the equilibrium, P_2 must rise. Therefore, the SDE curve is positively sloped.

4.2.1.3 The Rural Sector

The rural sector produces food using only labour. The production function is given by

$$Y_3 = F_3(L_3) \tag{4.13}$$

Assuming that the wage rate is determined in accordance with the marginal productivity principle, rural sector wage W_3 is given by

$$W_3 = P_3F_3' + S_3 \tag{4.14}$$

where P_3 is the procurement price of the crop and S_3 denotes the wage subsidy given to rural workers.

4.2.1.4 Marketable Surplus

The government procures food from the rural sector and provides subsidised supply of food to the urban population. The urban population consists of ($L_1 + L_2 + L_U$), where L_U represents the urban unemployed workers. The volume of procurement X is positively related to the size of urban population. Thus,

$$X = X(L_1 + L_2 + L_U); X' > 0 \tag{4.15}$$

The marketable surplus in the rural sector Z is assumed to positively depend on the price of food and its production level. Thus, the supply function of marketable surplus is given by

$$Z = Z(P_3, Y_3); Z^1, Z^2 > 0 \tag{4.16}$$

The endowment of labour in the economy is assumed to be equal to unity. Therefore,

$$L_1 + L_2 + L_3 + L_U = 1 \tag{4.17}$$

In equilibrium,

$$X = Z.$$

Using Equations (4.13), (4.15), (4.16) and (4.17), the above equilibrium condition can be rewritten as

$$X(1 - L_3) = Z(P_3, F_3(L_3)) \tag{4.18}$$

An increased subsidisation to food grains implies that although the buying price of food for the urban population remains the same, the rural producers are able to receive higher selling price. Therefore, P_3 is a policy parameter and depends on the food grain subsidisation policy of the government. L_3 remains the only variable which adjusts itself to maintain the $X = Z$ condition. The relationship between rural employment level and procurement price can be obtained from Equation (4.18) as

$$L_3 = L_3(P_3); L_3' < 0 \tag{4.19}$$

4.2.1.5 Rural–Urban Migration

The rural–urban migration considered here is of the Harris–Todaro (1970) type. The influx of rural migrants into the urban sector continues as long as the expected urban wage exceeds that of the actual rural wage. In migration equilibrium, the expected urban wage equals the actual rural wage. In the Harris–Todaro (1970) model, the urban sector employment consists of only formal sector (although implicitly, since it considers the sector with institutionally determined wages, which is analogous to the formal sector in this model). This model introduces the urban informal sector in the migration equilibrium to explain the phenomenon of unemployment. With $[L_1/(L_1 + L_2 + L_U)]$ and $[L_2/(L_1 + L_2 + L_U)]$ being the probabilities of obtaining formal and informal sector jobs, respectively, the migration equilibrium condition now becomes

$$\frac{W_1^* L_1 + W_2 L_2}{L_1 + L_2 + L_U} = W_3$$

Using Equations (4.4), (4.10), (4.17) and (4.19), the above migration equilibrium condition can be written as

$$\frac{W_1^* L_1(S_1) + W_2 L_2(P_2 + S_2, W_2)}{1 - L_3} = P_3 F_3'(L_3) + S_3 \tag{4.20}$$

With given values of the policy parameters S_1, S_3 and P_3, the employment levels in formal and rural sectors, L_1 and L_3, also remain unchanged. An increase in P_2 raises L_2 and augments the expected urban wage. The migration equilibrium is disturbed and to restore it back W_2 must change. Now, let $\Theta = -(\partial L_2/\partial W_2)(W_2/L_2)$ denote the wage elasticity of employment in the informal sector. It is assumed that $\Theta < 1$. This implies that a fall in W_2 leads to a decline in W_2L_2 and vice versa. So, in this case, equilibrium is restored by a fall in W_2 that lowers W_2L_2. On plotting Equation (4.20) on W_2–P_2 plane, the 'migration equilibrium' (ME) curve is obtained. It shows the alternative combinations of W_2 and P_2 at which migration equilibrium is maintained. It is negatively sloped if $\Theta < 1$ (Fig. 4.1).

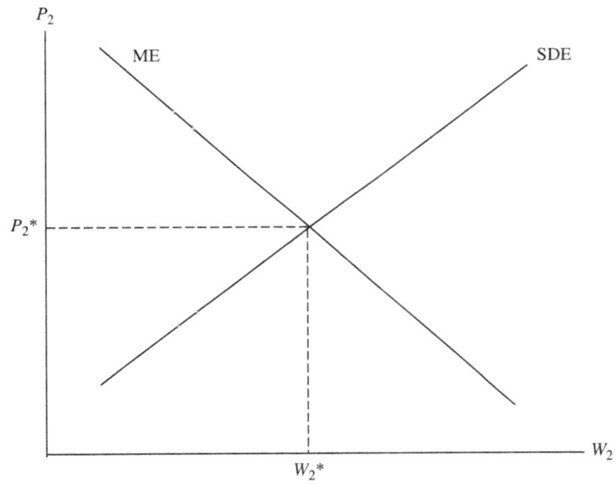

Fig. 4.1 Determination of equilibrium P_2 and W_2 in the Gupta (1993) model

The two basic endogenous variables in the model are P_2 and W_2 while the policy parameters are S_1, S_2, S_3, r_1 and P_3.

The two basic equations of the model may be rewritten as

$$\text{SDE: } R(P_2) = F_2(L_2(P_2 + S_2, W_2), K_2(P_2 + S_2, r_1)) \tag{4.12}$$

$$\text{ME: } W_1^* L_1(S_1) + W_2 L_2(P_2 + S_2, W_2) = W_3(1 - L_3) \tag{4.21}$$

P_2 and W_2 are obtained by solving Equations (4.12) and (4.21) simultaneously.

4.2.2 Effects of Policy Changes on Unemployment

In this section the effects on unemployment of wage subsidy, price subsidy and capital subsidy to the different sectors are analysed.

4.2.2.1 The Effect of Wage Subsidy Policy to the Formal Sector

First, let us consider what happens if there is a hike in S_1. If S_1 rises L_1 also goes up, leading to a surge in the expected formal sector wage. The migration equilibrium is disturbed, but can be restored by a fall in expected informal sector wage. Given W_2, P_2 has to fall so that L_2 shrinks, releasing labour and lowering W_2. Thus the ME curve shifts downwards and at the new equilibrium, both P_2 and W_2 decline. On the other hand, from the SDE equation it follows that the fall in P_2 raises the demand for R, which can be satisfied by rising L_2. However, L_3 remains unaffected since P_3 is unchanged. The boost in informal sector employment unambiguously lowers unemployment, L_U.

4.2.2.2 The Effect of Capital Subsidy Policy to the Informal Sector

An increase in capital subsidy to the informal sector r_1, *ceteris paribus*, raises capital employment in the sector, K_2. The informal sector output $F_2(.)$ also rises. To satisfy the SDE condition, given W_2, P_2 must fall. This results in a rightward shift of the SDE. The fall in P_2 leads to a contraction of L_2 in ME equation, so that W_2 must rise. Thus in the new equilibrium P_2 falls and W_2 rises. As a result, L_2 unequivocally falls. Since L_1 and L_3 remain unaltered, L_U aggravates.

4.2.2.3 The Effect of Price Subsidy Policy to the Informal Sector

As S_2 rises L_2, K_2 and hence F_2 increase. In order to satisfy the SDE condition, given P_2, W_2 has to rise. The SDE curve shifts outwards. The increase in W_2 augments L_2 in the ME condition so that P_2 must fall. As a consequence L_2 falls, and since L_1 and L_3 are unchanged, L_U rises in the new equilibrium.

4.2.2.4 The Effect of Wage Subsidy Policy to the Rural Sector

If S_3 rises there is a hike in W_3, leading to the rural wage exceeding the expected urban wage. To satisfy the ME condition, P_2 must rise, given W_2. The ME equation shifts out. Due to the rise in P_2, R falls whereas L_2, K_2 and hence F_2 increase. The right-hand side of the SDE equation increases. To maintain equality, W_2 must also rise. Thus in the new equilibrium, both P_2 and W_2 take higher values. L_1 and L_3 do not change and therefore L_U falls since L_2 rises.

4.2.2.5 The Effect of Price Subsidy Policy to the Rural Sector

A hike in the procurement price P_3 lowers L_3, leading to increases in both W_3 and W_3 $(1–L_3)$. Given W_2, P_2 must increase so as to satisfy the ME equation. As a result, the ME curve shifts out. The rise in P_2 lowers $R(P_2)$ but enhances F_2 such that there is excess supply in the SDE equation. F_2 can fall only if L_2 falls sufficiently, which is possible if W_2 increases. In the new equilibrium, both P_2 and W_2 assume higher values. The decrease in both L_2 and L_3 exacerbates unemployment.

The findings of the analysis can be summarised in terms of the following proposition.

Proposition 4.1 *A wage subsidy policy to the urban formal sector or rural sector lowers the urban unemployment of labour. On the contrary, a capital or price subsidy to the informal sector and/or a price subsidy policy to the rural sector accentuate the problem of unemployment in the urban area.*

So a wage subsidy policy to the urban sector or rural sector can be instrumental in alleviating unemployment whereas a policy of price subsidy pertaining to the rural sector actually perpetuates unemployment. The two of these results contradict the standard Harris–Todaro (1970) result.[4]

4.3 Chaudhuri (2000) Model

The model developed by Chaudhuri (2000) also shows the simultaneous existence of open urban unemployment and urban informal sector in migration equilibrium. However, the policy conclusions of this model are different from those found in Gupta (1993). This is due to the fact[5] that in Gupta (1993), the role of aggregate demand in determining the level of production and employment has been totally ignored. However, there is good evidence in the context of the developing countries that at least the manufacturing output is demand determined. This aspect has been taken care of in this model. The aggregate demand plays an important role in determining output and employment in all the three sectors of the economy. A price and/or a wage subsidy policy to the rural sector raises the aggregate income of the workers, which in turn raises the aggregate demand and, therefore, the level of employment in all the three sectors of the economy directly or indirectly. A demand management policy such as an export promotional scheme in the manufacturing sector also raises the aggregate demand in the two urban sectors, thereby causing their employment levels to increase. Consequently, the urban unemployment level falls. So the Chaudhuri (2000) model directs to a rural development programme or a demand management policy as a possible solution to the urban unemployment problem and the policy prescriptions are akin[6] to those generated by the standard Harris–Todaro (1970) model.

4.3.1 The Model

We consider a small open dual economy with three sectors, formal, informal and rural, represented by subscripts 1, 2 and 3, respectively. The urban sector consists

---

[4] The results of a price subsidy policy to the informal sector and a wage subsidy policy to the rural sector on the unemployment in the urban sector are different in the Gupta (1993) model.

[5] This aspect has been more elaborately discussed later.

[6] However, in the standard Harris–Todaro (1970) model, the role of a demand management policy, such as an export promotion scheme in the manufacturing sector, has not yet been studied.

of two segments: formal and informal. The urban sectors are completely dependent on the migrant labour force from the rural sector. We also assume that the economy is endowed with a given amount of capital stock, K_{D}, and that the domestic capital stock is owned by all the workers.[7] While the informal sector faces an imperfect capital market, the urban formal sector faces a perfect market. However, there is no capital constraint in the economy. There is free inflow (outflow) of capital into (from) the urban formal sector from (into) the foreign countries at the internationally given interest rate, r_1.

4.3.1.1 Urban Formal Sector

The urban formal sector (sector 1) produces a manufactured good X_1 using labour, an intermediate good and capital as inputs. The production function of this sector is of the fixed-coefficient type.[8] a_{K1} units of capital, a_{X2} units of the intermediate good and a_{L1} units of labour together produce one unit of X_1. The formal sector faces a unionised labour market. A given fraction z of the total amount of production of the manufactured good X_1 is exported to foreign countries and the remaining amount is sold at the domestic market at price P_1, given internationally. The exported amount of the manufacture represents the foreign import demand and is a component of aggregate demand of that commodity. An export promotional scheme is administered through a wage subsidy policy to the urban formal sector. The wage subsidy per unit of employment in this sector, S_1, is a positive function of the fraction of the manufactured good exported, z. If the formal sector improves its export performance, it receives more assistance from the government in the form of a wage subsidy. Given fixed coefficients of production, the price–unit cost equality condition for the formal sector is

$$P_1 = r_1 a_{K1} + P_2 a_{X2} + [W_1 - S_1(z)]a_{L1} \tag{4.22}$$

where W_1 is the wage rate in the formal sector. P_2 is the price of the intermediate input,[9] which is endogenously determined.

The relationship for the unionised wage rate is specified as

$$W_1 = \underset{}{f}\ (\underset{(+)}{W_2},\ \underset{(+)}{P_1},\ \underset{(+)}{P_f}) \tag{4.23}$$

where W_2 is the wage rate in the informal sector and P_{f} is the issue price[10] of food to the consumers. Equation (4.23) states that with an increase in the non-unionised

[7] This assumption has been borrowed from the literature on rural–urban migration. See Gupta (1995). This makes the rest of the analysis easier.

[8] This assumption has been made for the sake of analytical simplicity.

[9] Most of the theoretical papers in the existing literature on informal sector have made this assumption and it has also empirical base. See Section 3.6 of Chapter 3 for details.

[10] See footnote 13 in this context.

wage rate, the unionised wage goes up. Also with an increase in the cost of living, the unions bargain for a higher wage.

The level of employment in the formal sector L_1 is given by

$$L_1 = a_{L1}X_1 \quad (4.24)$$

where X_1 is the level of production of sector 1.

Now the demand for the intermediate input (produced in the informal sector) is given by

$$X_2^D = a_{X_2}X_1 \quad (4.25)$$

4.3.1.2 Informal Sector

The urban informal sector produces the intermediate input X_2, for the formal sector, by means of labour and capital. The production function of the informal sector is given by

$$X_2 = F_2(K_2, L_2) \quad (4.26)$$

where K_2 and L_2 denote the level of capital used and the level of employment in the informal sector, respectively. The production function satisfies all the standard properties including a special one that it is separable in terms of its arguments.[11]

The informal sector faces a perfect labour market and an imperfect capital market. The interest rate at which it can borrow capital is

$$r_2 = r_2(K_2);\ r'_2, r''_2 > 0 \quad (4.27)$$

The effective interest rate on capital that the informal sector faces is (r_2–S_2), where S_2 is the rate of capital subsidy given to this sector.

The profit function of the representative informal sector firm is

$$Y_1 = P_2F_2(K_2, L_2) - (r_2(K_2) - S_2)K_2 - W_2L_2$$

Profit is maximised with respect to K_2 and L_2 and the first-order conditions of maximisation are as follows:

$$P_2(\partial F_2/\partial K_2) = r_2(K_2) - S_2 + r'_2(K_2)K_2 \quad (4.28)$$

and

$$P_2(\partial F_2/\partial L_2) = W_2 \quad (4.29)$$

---

[11] This means that $(\partial^2 X_2/\partial L_2 \partial K_2) = 0$. This assumption has been made for the sake of analytical simplicity.

Solving Equations (4.28) and (4.29) we can obtain the demand function for capital

$$K_2 = \underset{(+)(+)}{K_2(P_2,\ S_2)} \tag{4.28.1}$$

and the demand function for labour

$$L_2 = \underset{(+)(-)}{L_2(P_2,\ W_2)} \tag{4.29.1}$$

In equilibrium, output of the informal sector must equal the demand for its product. So,

$$X_2 = X_2^D \tag{4.30}$$

Using Equations (4.25), (4.26), (4.28.1), (4.29.1) and (4.30) we have

$$F_2(K_2(P_2{,}S_2){,}L_2(P_2{,}W_2)) = a_{X2}X_1 \tag{4.31}$$

4.3.1.3 Rural Sector

The rural sector produces food using labour only. The production function[12] of this sector is

$$X_3 = F_3(L_3)\,\text{with}\,F_3' > 0\ \text{and}\ F''_3 < 0 \tag{4.32}$$

where X_3 and L_3 denote the levels of output and employment in the rural sector, respectively.

Assuming marginal productivity pricing of labour in the rural sector, we have

$$W_3 = P_3F'_3(L_3) + S_3 \tag{4.33}$$

where W_3 is the rural wage rate, P_3 is the procurement price of food[13] and S_3 is the wage subsidy per unit of employment in the rural sector.

[12] Land, as a sector specific input, may be included in the production function of the rural sector without affecting the qualitative results of the model.

[13] We assume that the government conducts the procurement of the crop – a practice followed, for example, in India in the case of food grains and some commercial crops. Government agencies like the Food Corporation of India procure food grains from the producers and use it for selling to the consumers through the public distribution system at a subsidised price, called the issue price. A price subsidy to the rural sector implies an increase in the procurement price of food, P_3. On the other hand, a reduction in the issue price of food, P_f, implies a subsidy on the consumption of food.

4.3.2 Equilibrium Conditions for Production of Food and Manufactures

All members (workers) of the economy are assumed to have identical preferences[14] defined over two goods: food and manufactures. We also assume that the aggregate demand functions for both food and manufactures exist, that a fraction b of the aggregate income, I, of the workers is spent on food and that

$$b = \underset{(+)(+)(-)}{b(P_{\text{f}}, P_1, I)} \tag{4.34}$$

Equation (4.34) states that the proportion of aggregate income of the workers spent on food, b, is an increasing function of the food price and the price of manufactures and a decreasing function of the aggregate income[15] of the labourers. Now (1–b) fraction of their aggregate income is spent on manufactures.

The aggregate income of the workers (wage income plus rental income) with complete repatriation of income on foreign capital is

$$I = (W_1L_1 + W_2L_2 + W_3L_3) + (r_1K_D + (r_2 - r_1)K_2) \tag{4.35}$$

In equilibrium, the output in each sector must be equal to the demand for its product. So we have the following two equilibrium conditions[16] in the production of food and manufactures, respectively:

$$b(.)[(W_1L_1 + W_2L_2 + W_3L_3) + (r_1K_D + (r_2 - r_1)K_2)] = P_{\text{f}}F(L_3) \tag{4.36}$$

$$(1 - b(.))[(W_1L_1 + W_2L_2 + W_3L_3) + (r_1K_D + (r_2 - r_1)K_2)] = P_1(1 - z)X_1 \tag{4.37}$$

where z is the fraction of the amount of production of the manufactured good which is exported. So the amount of production of the manufactured good must equal its aggregate demand, which is the sum of domestic demand and foreign import demand.

4.3.3 Other Equations of the Model

$$L_1 + L_2 + L_3 + L_u = 1 \tag{4.38}$$

[14] Labourers, although engaged in different sectors of the economy and earning different levels of wage income, may have identical preferences over two goods – food and manufactures since the rural sector is the origin of all the labourers in the economy.

[15] This means that the income elasticity of demand for food for all workers is less than unity. This is a direct consequence of Engel's law.

[16] Here it is assumed that the entire interest income earned from domestic capital is spent on two goods – food and manufactures. However, the qualitative results of the model remain unaffected if one alternatively assumes that only a fraction of the interest income is spent on the two goods.

where L_U is the number of unemployed workers in the urban sector. The total number of labourers is constant and is normalised to unity.

The rural–urban migration equilibrium condition is given by

$$[(W_1L_1 + W_2L_2)/(L_1 + L_2 + L_u)] = W_3 \tag{4.39}$$

The left-hand side of Equation (4.39) is the expected urban wage rate of a prospective rural migrant and is equal to the actual rural wage rate, W_3, in migration equilibrium.

4.3.4 General Equilibrium

By using Equation (4.38), Equation (4.39) can be expressed as

$$W_1L_1 + W_2L_2 + W_3L_3 = W_3 \tag{4.39.1}$$

With the help of Equations (4.34), (4.35) and (4.39.1), Equations (4.36) and (4.37) are rewritten as

$$b(P_f, P_1, W_3 + r_1K_D + (r_2 - r_1)K_2)[W_3 + r_1K_D + (r_2 - r_1)K_2] = P_fF(L_3) \tag{4.36.1}$$

$$(1 - b(.))[W_3 + r_1K_D + (r_2 - r_1)K_2] = P_1(1 - z)X_1 \tag{4.37.1}$$

In this model, there are 13 endogenous variables, namely X_1, X_2, X_3, L_1, L_2, L_U, W_1, W_2, W_3, I, P_2 and K_2. The policy variables of the government are S_2, S_3, P_3, P_f and z. P_1 and r_1 are internationally given. If the government adopts an export promotional scheme, z takes a higher value. There are 13 independent equations (4.22), (4.23), (4.24), (4.26), (4.28.1), (4.29.1), (4.31), (4.32), (4.33), (4.35), (4.36.1), (4.37.1) and (4.38) to solve for the 13 endogenous variables. From Equations (4.33) and (4.36.1) one can solve

$$L_3 = L_3(P_2, P_3, P_f, S_2, S_3) \tag{4.40}$$

Assuming that food is a non-inferior good, from Equations (4.33) and (4.36.1) one can easily show[17] that $(\partial L_3/\partial P_f)<0$ and $(\partial L_3/\partial P_2)$, $(\partial L_3/\partial P_3)$, $(\partial L_3/\partial S_2)$ and $(\partial L_3/\partial S_3)>0$. From Equations (4.33) and (4.40) we can obtain

$$\underset{}{W_3} = \underset{(-)(+)(+)(-)(+)}{W_3(P_2, P_3, P_f, S_2, S_3)} \tag{4.41}$$

Given W_3, the equilibrium value of X_1 is found from Equation (4.37.1) as

[17] These results have been proved in Appendix 4.1.

$$\underset{(+)(+)(+)(+)(+)(+)}{X_1 = X_1(P_2, P_3, P_f, S_2, S_3, z)} \tag{4.42}$$

By Equations (4.31) and (4.42) we can write

$$F_2(\underset{(+)(+)}{K_2(P_2, S_2)}, \underset{(+)(-)}{L_2(P_2, W_2)}) = a_{X1}\underset{(+)(+)(+)(+)(+)(+)}{X_1(P_2, P_3, P_f, S_2, S_3, z)} \tag{4.31.1}$$

As both the left-hand and the right-hand sides of Equation (4.31.1) are increasing in P_2 and S_2, we assume that the responsiveness of the supply of good 2, $F_2(.)$, with respect to P_2 (or S_2) is greater than that of good 1, $X_1(.)$. So when P_2 (or S_2) rises, the increase in $F_2(.)$ is greater than that of $ax_2X_1(.)$.[18]

An increase in W_2 leads to a fall in L_2, which in turn lowers $F_2(.)$. In order to keep Equation (4.31.1) undisturbed, P_2 must rise. So the curve (say, *AA*) which represents Equation (4.31.1) slopes positively in the W_2–P_2 space (see Fig. 4.2).

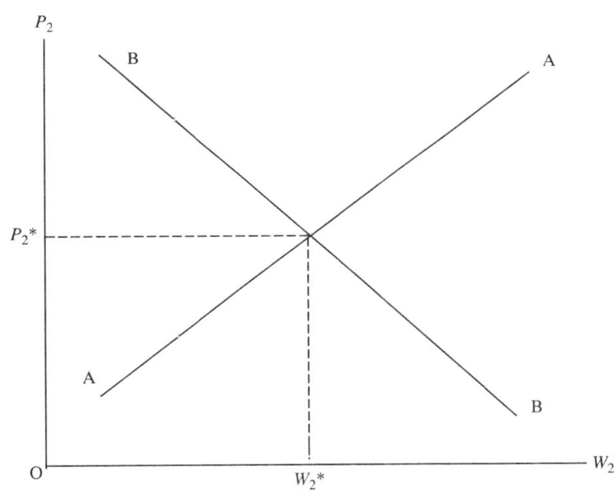

Fig. 4.2 Determination of equilibrium P_2 and W_2 in the Chaudhuri (2000) model

Now by Equations (4.22) and (4.23) we write

$$P_2 = [P_1 + S_1(z)a_{L1} - r_1a_{K1} - f(W_2, P_1, P_f)a_{L1}]/a_{x2} \tag{4.43}$$

Equation (4.43) is represented by the curve *BB* in the W_2–P_2 space (see Fig. 4.2). An increase in W_2 raises the unionised wage rate W_1. Consequently, P_2 falls when W_2 rises. This implies that the *BB* curve in Fig. 4.2 must slope negatively.

[18] This assumption causes the *AA* curve to be positively sloped, which makes the rest of the analysis much easier.

The equilibrium values of P_2 and W_2 are obtained by solving Equations (4.31.1) and (4.43) simultaneously. In terms of Fig. 4.2, the determination of the equilibrium values of P_2 and W_2 is shown by the point of intersection of the *AA* and *BB* curves.

Now given the equilibrium values of P_2 and W_2, the equilibrium values of W_1, K_2 and L_2 are determined from Equations (4.23), (4.28.1) and (4.29.1), respectively. We have already determined the equilibrium values of L_1, L_2 and L_3. The equilibrium level of urban unemployment, L_U, is then obtained from Equation (4.38).[19]

4.3.4.1 Effects of Policy Changes on Unemployment

As S_2 increases given P_2, the net effect will be a rise in $F_2(.)$. So W_2 has to go up to satisfy Equation (4.31.1). The *AA* curve in Fig. 4.2 shifts in the rightward direction. But the *BB* curve does not shift. So, in the new equilibrium, P_2 decreases and W_2 increases, resulting in a fall in L_2. Besides, L_1 rises as X_1 rises. L_3 also increases. But the net effect of an increase in S_2 on L_U is uncertain.

If P_f falls, L_3 rises but X_1 and L_1 fall. To satisfy Equation (4.31.1), given P_2, W_2 has to rise. This means that the *AA* curve shifts to the right. Also the *BB* curve which represents Equation (4.43) shifts in the upward direction when P_f decreases. As a result, W_2 rises but the effect on P_2 is uncertain. L_2 is likely to fall. However, the effect on L_U is again uncertain.

The above results can be summarised in the form of the following propositions.

Proposition 4.2 *The effect of a capital subsidy policy to the urban informal sector and/or a price subsidy policy to the consumers on the consumption of food on the open unemployment in the urban sector is ambiguous.*

On the other hand, when P_3 or S_3 goes up, X_1 and L_1 increase. L_3 also increases. To satisfy Equation (4.31.1), given P_2, W_2 has to fall. The *AA* curve shifts inwardly. But the *BB* curve does not shift. Consequently, P_2 increases and W_2 decreases, which in turn raises L_2.Therefore, L_U decreases. This leads to the following proposition.

Proposition 4.3 *If an additional wage or price subsidy is given to the rural sector, the employment levels in all the three sectors of the economy increase. The level of urban open unemployment falls as a consequence.*

Also, a rise in z raises X_1 and hence L_1. Given P_2, W_2 has to fall. So the *AA* curve, representing Equation (4.31.1), shifts in the inward direction. Now consider Equation (4.43). As z rises, S_1 also rises. This raises P_2 given W_2. So the *BB* curve in Fig. 4.2 shifts upwards. In the new equilibrium, P_2 increases but the effect on W_2 is uncertain. The latter depends on the relative magnitudes of shifts of the *AA* and *BB* curves. An increase in z directly raises X_1. Besides, it also raises P_2 resulting in increases in both X_1 and $F_2(.)$ indirectly. If the total expansionary effect on X_1 (direct plus induced) is greater than (equal to) the induced expansionary effect on

[19] Given the values of L_1, L_2 and L_3, Equation (4.38) may not always yield a strictly positive equilibrium level of urban unemployment. However, Propositions 4.2, 4.3 and 4.4 of Section 4.3 make sense only when there exists at least some urban unemployment.

$F_2(.)$, W_2 decreases (remains unchanged)[20] as a result. This is of course a reasonable assumption. So L_2 increases since P_2 increases due to an increase in z. In this case L_3 also rises since P_2 increases. The overall effect will be a fall in L_U. This establishes the following proposition.

Proposition 4.4 *If the government adopts an export promotional scheme in the manufacturing sector, the employment levels in all the three sectors of the economy expand and the urban unemployment level falls in the new equilibrium.*

So a capital subsidy policy to the urban sector may not be able to solve the urban unemployment problem. But a wage and/or a price subsidy policy to the rural sector and/or a demand management policy like an export promotional scheme in the manufacturing sector reduce the level of urban unemployment. These results are different from those found in the Gupta (1993) model.

Why the results of Chaudhuri (2000) are different from those of Gupta (1993) can be explicated as follows. In Gupta (1993), the role of the demand side in determination of the level of production has been completely ignored in both the manufacturing and rural sectors. The government procures food from the rural sector and distributes it among the urban consumers. So the government can effectively control the size of urban labour force by controlling the availability of food in that sector. Subsidy policies to the rural sector raise the availability of food in the urban sector resulting from an increase in total food production. This in turn causes the urban sector labour force to expand. On the other hand, a wage or a price policy in the urban sector increases the level of employment in the urban sector but does not disturb the rural sector in any way. Thus the urban unemployment level plummets. On the contrary, in Chaudhuri (2000), the demand side plays a very crucial role in determining the level of production in all the three sectors. A price or a wage subsidy policy to the rural sector raises the aggregate income of the workers in the economy, which in turn causes an increase in the level of demand in all the three sectors, directly or indirectly. As a result, the employment level in each of the three sectors increases, thereby causing a fall in the level of urban unemployment. Also a demand management policy, for example, an export promotional scheme in the manufacturing sector, raises the level of employment in each of the three sectors of the economy, directly or indirectly (through an increase in the informal sector's product price P_2). Thus urban unemployment level decreases due to an export promotional measure. An export promotional scheme is administered through a wage subsidy policy. If the urban formal sector improves its export performance, it receives more assistance from the government in the form of a wage subsidy. One may also consider other types of methods, for example, the imposition of a tax on the sales of the manufacturing output in the domestic market, through which an export promotional scheme can be implemented. On the other hand, a hike in the capital subsidy to the urban sector affects aggregate income of the workers and leads to an increase in the employment levels in both the rural sector and the urban formal sector. But this policy increases the informal sector wage rate and decreases the product price causing

[20] This is shown in Appendix 4.2.

the employment level in the sector to fall. Thus the net effect of this policy on the urban unemployment level is uncertain.

Appendix 4.1

Interest income of each worker in the economy, denoted by G, is

$$G = r_1 K_D + (r_2(K_2) - r_1)K_2 = G(P_2, S_2) \quad (4.A.1)$$

Since r_1 and K_D are constants, $r_2\prime(.) > 0$ and K_2 is a positive function of both P_2 and S_2, one can easily show that

$$(\partial G/\partial P_2) > 0 \text{ and } (\partial G/\partial S_2) > 0 \quad (4.A.2)$$

By Equations (4.33), (4.36.1) and (4.A.1) we can write

$$b(P_f, P_1, G + P_3F_3 + S_3)(G + P_3F_3 + S_3) = P_fF_3(L_3) \quad (4.A.3)$$

Totally differentiating Equation (4.A.3) we get

$$\begin{aligned} dL_3[I(\partial b/\partial I)P_3F''_3 + bP_3F''_3 - P_fF'_3] = {} & dP_f[F_3(L_3) - I(\partial b/\partial P_f)] \\ & -dP_2[b + I(\partial b/\partial I)](\partial G/\partial P_2) \\ & -dS_2[b + I(\partial b/\partial I)](\partial G/\partial S_2) \\ & -dS_3[b + I(\partial b/\partial I)] \\ & -dP_3[b + I(\partial b/\partial I)]F_3(L_3) \end{aligned} \quad (4.A.4)$$

Now

$$(b + (\partial b/\partial I)I) = b[1 + (I/b)(\partial b/\partial I)],$$

$$b = (P_fX_3)/I;\ (\partial b/\partial I) = [I(\partial X_3/\partial I) - X_3](P_f/I^2) = (P_fX_3/I^2)[(I/X_3)(\partial X_3/\partial I) - 1].$$

Again

$$[b + (\partial b/\partial I)I] = b[1 + (I/b)(P_fX_3/I^2)(E_{x3} - 1)] = b(.)E_{x3} > 0, \quad (4.A.5)$$

where E_{x3} is the income elasticity of demand for food and $E_{x3} > 0$ since food is a non-inferior good. So using Equation (4.A.5) we can write

$$\underset{(-)}{P_3F''_3}(b + (b/I)I) - \underset{(+)}{P_fF'_3} = D < 0 \quad (4.A.6)$$

Now from Equation (4.A.4) we get

$$\left.\begin{array}{l}(\partial L_3/\partial P_f) = [F_3(L_3) - I(\partial b/\partial P_f)]/D < 0 \\ \qquad\qquad\qquad (+) \qquad\quad (+)\ (-) \\ (\partial L_3/\partial P_2) = -[b + I(\partial b/\partial I)](\partial G/\partial P_2)/D > 0 \\ \qquad\qquad\qquad (+) \qquad\quad (+) \qquad (-) \\ (\partial L_3/\partial S_2) = -[b + I(b/I)](\partial G/\partial S_2)/D > 0 \\ \qquad\qquad\qquad (+) \qquad\quad (+) \qquad (-) \\ (\partial L_3/\partial S_3) = -[b + I(\partial b/\partial I)]/D > 0 \\ (\partial L_3/\partial P_3) = -[b + I(\partial b/\partial I)]F_3(L_3)/D > 0\end{array}\right\} \tag{4.A.7}$$

Totally differentiating Equation (4.33) we can derive the following results:

$$\begin{array}{l}(\partial W_3/\partial P_2) = P_3F''_3(\partial L_3/\partial P_2) < 0 \\ \qquad\qquad\qquad (-) \qquad (+) \\ (\partial W_3/\partial P_f) = P_3F''_3(\partial L_3/\partial P_f) > 0 \\ \qquad\qquad\qquad (-) \qquad (-) \\ (\partial W_3/\partial S_2) = P_3F''_3(\partial L_3/\partial S_2) < 0 \\ \qquad\qquad\qquad (-) \qquad (+) \\ (\partial W_3/\partial P_3) = P_3F''_3(\partial L_3/\partial P_3) + F'_3 > 0 \\ \qquad\qquad\qquad (-) \qquad (+)\ (+) \\ (\partial W_3/\partial S_3) = P_3F''_3(\partial L_3/\partial S_3) + 1 > 0\end{array}$$

When P_3 (or S_3) increases L_3 also increases. As a consequence, the right-hand side of Equation (4.36.1) also increases. $((\partial b/\partial W_3)W_3 + b) > 0$ since $(I(\partial b/\partial I) + b) > 0$ and G is independent of P_3 and S_3. So W_3 has to increase in order to satisfy Equation (4.36.1) as P_3 (or S_3) increases. So we have $(\partial W_3/\partial P_3)$, $(\partial W_3/\partial S_3) > 0$.

As P_2 (or P_3 or P_f or S_2 or S_3) increases W_3 and I also rise. As a consequence $b(.)$ falls. This means that the left-hand side of Equation (4.37.1) rises. An increase in z lowers the value of the right-hand side of Equation (4.37.1). In all these cases, X_1 has to increase in order to satisfy Equation (4.37.1). So we have $(\partial X_1/\partial P_2)$,$(\partial X_1/\partial P_3)$,$(\partial X_1/\partial P_f)$,$(\partial X_1/\partial S_2)$,$(\partial X_1/\partial S_3)$ and $(\partial X_1/\partial z) > 0$.

Appendix 4.2

For the sake of analytical simplicity we take $a_{L1} = a_{K1} = a_{x2} = 1$

Totally differentiating Equations (4.31.1) and (4.43) we, respectively, get

$$\begin{array}{l}dP_2[(\partial F_2/\partial L_2)(\partial L_2/\partial P_2) + (\partial F_2/\partial K_2)(\partial K_2/\partial P_2) - (\partial X_1/\partial P_2)] \\ = (\partial X_1/\partial z)dz - (\partial F_2/\partial L_2)(\partial L_2/\partial W_2)dW_2\end{array} \tag{4.A.8}$$

and

$$dP_2 = (\partial S_1/\partial z)dz - f_1(.)dW_2 \tag{4.A.9}$$

By Equations (4.A.8) and (4.A.9)

$$\begin{aligned}&T((\partial S_1/\partial z)\mathrm{d}z - Tf_1\mathrm{d}W_2 = (\partial X_1/\partial z)\mathrm{d}z - (\partial F_2/\partial L_2)(\partial L_2/\partial W_2)\mathrm{d}W_2\\ &\text{or, } (\mathrm{d}W_2/\mathrm{d}z) = [(\partial X_1/\partial z) - T(\partial S_1/\partial z)]/[(\partial F_2/\partial L_2)(\partial L_2/\partial W_2) - Tf_1]\end{aligned} \tag{4.A.10}$$

where

$$T = [(\partial F_2/\partial L_2)(\partial L_2/\partial P_2) + (\partial F_2/\partial K_2)(\partial K_2/\partial P_2) - (\partial X_1/\partial P_2)] > 0$$

By Equations (4.A.9) and (4.A.10) we can write

$$(\mathrm{d}P_2/\mathrm{d}z) = (\partial S_1/\partial z) - f_1[(\partial X_1/\partial z) - T(\partial S_1/\partial z)]/[(\partial F_2/\partial L_2)(\partial L_2/\partial W_2) - Tf_1]$$

After simplification this reduces to

$$\left(\frac{\mathrm{d}P_2}{\mathrm{d}z}\right) = \frac{[(\partial S_1/\partial z)(\partial F_2/\partial L_2)(\partial L_2/\partial W_2) - f_1(\partial X_1/\partial z)]}{[(\partial F_2/\partial L_2)(\partial L_2/\partial W_2) - Tf_1]} > 0 \tag{4.A.11}$$

From Equation (4.A.9) we have

$$(\mathrm{d}P_2/\mathrm{d}z) = (\partial S_1/\partial z) - f_1(\mathrm{d}W_2/\mathrm{d}z)$$

$$\text{or } (\partial \mathrm{S}_1/\partial z) = (\mathrm{dP}_2/\mathrm{d}z) + \mathrm{f}_1(\mathrm{dW}_2/\mathrm{d}z) \tag{4.A.9.1}$$

By Equations (4.A.10) and (4.A.9.1)

$$(dW_2/dz) = [(\partial X_1/\partial z) - T(dP_2/dz)]/[(\partial F_2/\partial L_2)(\partial L_2/\partial W_2)]$$

After inserting the value of T we get

$$\left(\frac{\mathrm{d}W_2}{\mathrm{d}z}\right) = \left[\frac{\begin{array}{l}[(\partial X_1/\partial z) + (\partial X_1/\partial P_2)(\mathrm{d}P_2/\mathrm{d}z)] - [(\partial F_2/\partial L_2)(\partial L_2/\partial P_2)\\ \quad + (\partial F_2/\partial K_2)(\partial K_2/\partial P_2)](\mathrm{d}P_2/\mathrm{d}z)\end{array}}{(\partial F_2/\partial L_2)(\partial L_2/\partial W_2)}\right]$$

$< (=) 0$ according to

$$\begin{aligned}&[(\partial X_1/\partial z) + (\partial X_1/\partial P_2)(\mathrm{d}P_2/\mathrm{d}z)] > (=)\\ &[(\partial F_2/\partial L_2)(\partial L_2/\partial P_2) + (\partial F_2/\partial K_2)(\partial K_2/\partial P_2)](\mathrm{d}P_2/\mathrm{d}z)\end{aligned}$$

i.e. according to the responsiveness of $X_1(.)$ (direct plus induced) with respect to $z >$ $(=)$ the responsiveness of $F_2(.)$ (induced) with respect to z.

Chapter 5
Foreign Capital Inflow, Informal Sector and Welfare

5.1 Introduction

In the first 30 years after World War II, the Development Consensus represented the fundamental approach in development strategies throughout the world. It emphasised on more stringent trade policies and inward-oriented strategies, making use of discriminating policies like tariffs, quotas and restricting inflow of foreign capital and imports. But the 'success story' of the East Asian Tigers brought about a change in the thinking about the appropriate road to development. A new approach known as the Washington Consensus started to be accepted widely as an alternative development strategy and it gained further momentum after the conclusion of the multilateral agreement and the formation of the World Trade Organization (WTO) in the Uruguay round of discussions. The perceptions about development have drastically changed from the Development Consensus, and the Washington Consensus has culminated into a paradigm shift in shaping the character of the world economy. The new prescription is for more openness and less intervention that is likely to entail efficiency and dynamism to the growth process. The bottomline is to head towards liberalised economies involving freer inflow of foreign capital, curbing down on the much conspicuous protectionist policies, structural reforms and integrating the domestic market with the world market.

The importance and desirability of inflow of foreign capital in the context of a developing economy have triggered much debate among trade and development economists. The optimism regarding foreign capital inflow tends to vary among different authors. Until the early 1980s entry of foreign capital was highly dejected in the developing countries as foreign capital was thought to be welfare-deteriorating. The much-needed theoretical foundation was provided by the well-known 'Brecher–Alejandro (1977) proposition'. The skepticism has undergone a diametrical change during the liberalised economic regime and many economists have successfully shown that foreign capital might be welfare-improving in several cases. In this chapter we discuss both the pessimistic and optimistic views on the role of foreign capital in a developing economy using the general equilibrium framework.

S. Chaudhuri, U. Mukhopadhyay, *Revisiting the Informal Sector*,
DOI 10.1007/978-1-4419-1194-0_5,

5.2 Pessimistic View

Let us begin our discussions on welfare consequence of foreign capital with the pessimistic view suggesting that growth with foreign capital in a small open economy is immiserising, i.e. welfare-worsening. In this section, we first elucidate the 'Brecher–Alejandro (1977) proposition' and then discuss a few extensions made by other economists where this result holds.

5.2.1 *Immiserising Growth: Brecher and Alejandro (1977) Proposition*

Brecher and Alejandro (1977) have considered the 2×2 Heckscher–Ohlin (H–O) framework to analyse the welfare consequence of an inflow of foreign capital in a small open economy. Two commodities, X and Y, are produced in the economy using two factors of production – labour and capital. Factors are fully employed and sector X is assumed to be more labour-intensive than sector Y. There is perfect competition in both product and factor markets and the production functions exhibit constant returns to scale with positive but diminishing marginal productivity to each factor. The economy exports good X and imports good Y and the import-competing sector is protected by a tariff. The aggregate capital stock of the economy consists of both domestic and foreign capital and these are assumed to be perfect substitutes. All foreign capital income is fully repatriated.

The competitive zero-profit conditions are given as

$$Wa_{LX} + ra_{KX} = P_X \tag{5.1}$$

$$Wa_{LY} + ra_{KY} = P_Y^* \tag{5.2}$$

where P_X and P_Y are the world prices of X and Y; $P_Y^* = (1+t)P_Y$; t is the ad valorem rate of tariff so that P_Y^* represents the domestic or tariff-inclusive price of Y; wage rate and interest rate on capital are denoted by W and r, respectively.

The full-employment condition of labour and capital are given, respectively, by

$$a_{LX}X + a_{LY}Y = L \tag{5.3}$$

$$a_{KX}X + a_{KY}Y = K_D + K_F = K \tag{5.4}$$

where K_D and K_F denote indigenous capital and foreign capital, respectively. L is the total labour endowment in the economy.

In this system there are four endogenous variables, W, r, X and Y, that can be solved from Equations (5.1) to (5.4). This is a decomposable system where the factor prices are independent of factor endowments. The factor prices W and r can be solved from the price Equations (5.1) and (5.2), while the levels of production of X and Y are then solved from the output Equations (5.3) and (5.4).

Here welfare is defined as a positive function of national income. The expression for national income at world prices, I, is given by

$$I = WL + rK_{\mathrm{D}} - tP_Y Y \tag{5.5}$$

WL is the aggregate wage income while rK_{D} is the income on domestic capital. Foreign capital income, rK_{F}, is completely repatriated. Finally, $tP_Y Y$ measures the distortionary cost of tariff of the production side.[1]

Now, with the endowment of labour remaining unchanged, an increase in the capital stock in the economy due to foreign capital inflow is considered.

Total differentiation of Equation (5.3) yields

$$\lambda_{LX}\hat{X} + \lambda_{LY}\hat{Y} = \hat{L} \tag{5.3.1}$$

Similarly, from Equation (5.4) one gets

$$\lambda_{KX}\hat{X} + \lambda_{KY}\hat{Y} = \hat{K} \tag{5.4.1}$$

Solving Equations (5.3.1) and (5.4.1) by Cramer's rule gives

$$\hat{X} = -(\lambda_{LY}/\Delta)\hat{K}$$

and

$$\hat{Y} = (\lambda_{LX}/\Delta)\hat{K}$$

where $\Delta = (\lambda_{LX}\lambda_{KY} - \lambda_{LY}\lambda_{KX}) > 0$ since it is assumed that sector X is more labour-intensive than sector Y. Hence, $\hat{X} < 0$ and $\hat{Y} > 0$, when $\hat{K} > 0$.

Therefore, in accordance with the Rybczynski theorem, with increased capital endowment, the production of the capital-intensive import substitution good Y expands. Since the increased production needs more labour as well, the output of X contracts so that the extra labour for production of Y is released in a full-employment situation.

Differentiating Equation (5.5) with respect to K gives[2]

$$(\mathrm{d}I/\mathrm{d}K) = -tP_Y(\mathrm{d}Y/\mathrm{d}K)$$

Now $(\mathrm{d}Y/\mathrm{d}K) = (\lambda_{LX}/\Delta)(Y/K) > 0$, which implies that $(\mathrm{d}I/\mathrm{d}K) < 0$.

---

[1] The presence of tariff artificially raises the domestic price of commodity Y and this leads to a misallocation of resources, as the producers will be producing more of Y and less of X than their free trade levels. Social welfare decreases owing to this commodity market distortion. Both producers' surplus and consumers' surplus will be lower than the optimum (free trade) levels.

[2] Since this is a decomposable system as already mentioned, $\hat{W} = \hat{r} = 0$ when $\hat{K} > 0$, so that $L(\mathrm{d}W/\mathrm{d}K) = 0$ and $K_{\mathrm{D}}(\mathrm{d}r/\mathrm{d}K) = 0$.

The important result that follows is that an inflow of foreign capital with full repatriation of its earnings is necessarily immiserising if the import-competing sector is capital-intensive and is protected by a tariff. This is called the Brecher–Alejandro proposition, also known as the immiserising effect of foreign capital. It is also evident that in the absence of tariff, foreign capital does not affect national income.

In the literature, the Brecher–Alejandro proposition has also been re-examined in terms of three-sector models. The third sector may be either a duty-free zone (DFZ) (sometimes called foreign enclave) as in Beladi and Marjit (1992a) or an urban informal sector as in Grinols (1991) and Chandra and Khan (1993). The Beladi and Marjit (1992a) model is a simple three-sector extension of the HOS framework, where the third sector, the DFZ, uses sector-specific capital that is foreign owned. They have shown that with full-repatriation of foreign capital income, an inflow of foreign capital may lead to immiserising growth in the presence of tariff- distortion even if the foreign capital is employed in the export sector. This generalises the main result in the existing literature, which primarily focuses on foreign capital inflow in the protected sector of the economy.

5.2.2 Introduction of Rural–Urban Migration

As the developing countries are plagued by labour market distortion, which tends to engender wage differentials between rural and urban sectors and consequently induce migration, some attempts have been made to analyse the welfare impact of foreign capital inflow using a Harris–Todaro (1970) framework. For example, Khan (1982) has considered a mobile capital generalised Harris–Todaro model with urban unemployment. A third sector, called an urban informal sector, has been introduced in the work of Chandra and Khan (1993). Khan (1982) has shown that the 'Brecher–Alejandro proposition' is valid even in a two-sector mobile capital Harris–Todaro model. The two-sector Heckscher–Ohlin model considered in the previous section is modified to capture the impact of rural–urban migration and the presence of urban unemployment. Total labour endowment L is used to produce X and Y and a part remains unemployed, i.e. $L = L_X + L_Y + L_U$. Here L_X and L_Y denote total employment in rural and urban sectors while L_U is urban unemployment. The model considers inter-sectoral wage differential. The rural wage W is perfectly flexible while there exists distortion in the urban labour market, which is institutionally fixed at $\overline{W}$ and $W < \overline{W}$. It is assumed that the urban sector is more capital-intensive vis-à-vis the rural sector in value terms.[3]

The price system depicted in the Brecher–Alejandro (1977) model is slightly modified to include the institutionalised wage in the urban sector (sector Y). The zero-profit condition for sector Y is modified as follows:

[3]This implies that $(\theta_{KY}/\theta_{LY}) > (\theta_{KX}/\theta_{LX})$, i.e. $(a_{KY}/\overline{W}a_{LY}) > (a_{KX}/Wa_{LX})$. It should be mentioned that if sector Y is capital-intensive in value sense, it implies that it is more capital-intensive than sector X in physical sense as well.

$$\overline{W}a_{LY} + ra_{KY} = P_Y^* \tag{5.2.1}$$

The labour endowment equation now includes urban unemployment and is given by

$$a_{LX}X + a_{LY}Y + L_U = L \tag{5.3.1}$$

The rural–urban wage differential induces rural workers to migrate to urban areas. The HT migration equilibrium condition is given by $\overline{W}\frac{L_Y}{L_Y+L_U} = W$. Using Equation (5.3.1) this can be rewritten as follows:

$$a_{LX}X + (\overline{W}/W)a_{LY}Y = L \tag{5.6}$$

The expression for the national income at world prices remains the same despite the introduction of labour market distortion and rural–urban migration. This is because of the 'envelope property' of the Harris–Todaro structure that states that the average wage of all workers in a Harris–Todaro economy is equal to the rural sector wage, W.

Now the output system consists of Equations (5.3.1), (5.4) and (5.6). This is again a decomposable system with an additional variable L_U and an additional Equation (5.6). Differentiating Equations (5.4) and (5.6) and considering $dL = 0$ one gets

$$\lambda_{KX}\hat{X} + \lambda_{KY}\hat{Y} = \hat{K} \tag{5.4.1}$$

$$\lambda_{LX}\hat{X} + (\overline{W}/W)\lambda_{LY}\hat{Y} = 0 \tag{5.6.1}$$

Solving Equations (5.4.1) and (5.6.1) by Cramer's rule the following expressions are obtained:

$$\hat{X} = \hat{K}[\{(\overline{W}/W)\lambda_{LY}\}/\Delta]$$

$$\hat{Y} = -\hat{K}[\lambda_{LX}/\Delta]$$

where $\Delta = \lambda_{KX}\lambda_{LY}\overline{W}_Y - W_X\lambda_{KY}\lambda_{LX} < 0$, since the urban sector is more capital-intensive than the rural sector in value terms.

Therefore, $\hat{X} < 0$ and $\hat{Y} > 0$, when $\hat{K} > 0$. As in the previous case, Rybczynski effect leads to expansion of sector Y and contraction of sector X.

As the expression for national income at world prices remains unchanged

$$(dI/dK) = -tP_Y(dY/dK)$$

Since $(dY/dK)>0$, $(dI/dK)<0$.

Therefore the immiserising effect of foreign capital continues to be valid even after the introduction of labour market imperfection, rural–urban migration and urban unemployment. The presence of labour market imperfection cannot affect the welfare consequence of foreign capital as the Harris–Todaro framework satisfies the 'envelope property', which suggests that the average wage of all workers in a Harris–Todaro economy is equal to the rural sector wage and an inflow of foreign capital cannot affect the factor prices including the rural wage.

5.2.3 Introduction of the Informal Sector: Chandra and Khan (1993) Model

Chandra and Khan (1993) have shown the validity of the immiserising effect even in the presence of an urban informal sector. They have used different concepts of informal sector and also distinguished between commodity and sector-specific capital–labour ratios, so that their actual work consists of several models dealing with different conceptualisations of the informal sector. However, we present here only the model that considers informal sector as producing an internationally traded final commodity and there is inter-sectoral capital mobility so that the rate of interest is the same for all three sectors. Chandra and Khan (1993) consider a dual economy with two sectors: urban and rural. The urban sector is further subdivided into informal and formal sectors so that in all there are three sectors. Let X, Y and Z denote the rural, urban informal and urban formal sectors, respectively. All the three sectors produce internationally traded commodities and their prices are given internationally due to the assumption of small open economy. Sector Z is the import-competing sector and is protected by an import tariff.

Given the perfectly competitive markets, the usual zero-profit conditions are given by

$$W_X a_{LX} + r a_{KX} = P_X \tag{5.7}$$

$$W_Y a_{LY} + r a_{KY} = P_Y \tag{5.8}$$

$$\overline{W}_Z a_{LZ} + r a_{KZ} = P_Z(1 + t) \tag{5.9}$$

where W_X, W_Y and $\overline{W}_Z$ denote the rural sector, urban informal sector and formal sector wage rates, respectively.

Full employment of labour is depicted by

$$a_{LX}X + a_{LY}Y + a_{LZ}Z = L \tag{5.10}$$

Complete utilisation of capital implies that

$$a_{KX}X + a_{KY}Y + a_{KZ}Z = K_D + K_F = K \tag{5.11}$$

The migration equilibrium condition is given by

$$\left(\frac{\overline{W}_Z a_{LZ} Z + W_Y a_{LY} Y}{a_{LZ} Z + a_{LY} Y}\right) = W_X$$

Using Equation (5.10) and simplifying, the above condition can be rewritten as follows:

$$a_{LX} X + (W_Y/W_X) a_{LY} Y + (\overline{W}_Z/W_X) a_{LZ} Z = L \tag{5.12}$$

The national income at world prices is now given by

$$I = W_X L + r K_{\mathrm{D}} - t P_Z Z \tag{5.13}$$

This is also a decomposable system where input prices are determined from the price system alone (Equations (5.7), (5.8) and (5.9)) without the use of the output system.

Subtraction of Equation (5.12) from Equation (5.10) yields

$$(W_X - W_Y)\lambda_{LY} + (W_X - \overline{W}_Z)\lambda_{LZ} = 0 \tag{5.14}$$

Now the effect of an increase in the inflow of foreign capital on welfare is considered. In the decomposable system, an increase in capital has no effect on factor prices, so that (W_i/r) also remains constant. Hence $a_{Li} = a_{Li}(W_i/r)$ and $a_{Ki} = a_{Ki}(W_i/r)$ remain constant as well. Therefore, differentiating Equation (5.14) one obtains

$$\hat{Y} = \hat{Z} \tag{5.15}$$

Differentiating Equations (5.11) and (5.12), using Equations (5.14) and (5.15) and considering $\mathrm{d}L = 0$, we get the following two expressions, respectively:

$$\lambda_{KX}\hat{X} + (\lambda_{KY} + \lambda_{KZ})\hat{Z} = \hat{K} \tag{5.16.1}$$

$$\lambda_{LX}\hat{X} + (\lambda_{LY} + \lambda_{LZ})\hat{Z} = 0 \tag{5.16.2}$$

Solving Equations (5.16.1) and (5.16.2) by Cramer's rule one finds

$$\hat{X} = (\lambda_{LY} + \lambda_{LZ})(\hat{K}/\Delta) \tag{5.17.1}$$

and

$$\hat{Z} = -(\lambda_{LX}\hat{K}/\Delta) \tag{5.17.2}$$

where

$$\Delta = [\lambda_{KX}(\lambda_{LY} + \lambda_{LZ}) - \lambda_{LX}(\lambda_{KY} + \lambda_{KZ})] \tag{5.17.3}$$

Now, according to the Chandra–Khan capital intensity condition (CKCIC) the urban sector as a whole (consisting of both formal and informal sectors) is capital-intensive if

$$[(\lambda_{KY} + \lambda_{KZ})/(\lambda_{LY} + \lambda_{LZ})] > (\lambda_{KX}/\lambda_{LX}) \qquad (5.17.4)$$

Hence, if CKCIC holds, it implies that $\Delta < 0$. This suggests that $\hat{X} < 0$ and $\hat{Z} < 0$, when $\hat{K} < 0$.[4]

It is evident that with increase in capital endowment, the overall urban sector expands and the rural sector contracts owing to Rybczynski effect if and only if CKCIC holds. The result holds even if the rural and/or informal sector does not use capital, that is, λ_{KX} and/or $\lambda_{KY} = 0$.

Now differentiating Equation (5.13) with respect to K we obtain

$$(\mathrm{d}I/\mathrm{d}K) = -tP_Z(\mathrm{d}Z/\mathrm{d}K) < 0 \text{ since } (\mathrm{d}Z/\mathrm{d}K) > 0 \qquad (5.18)$$

Hence an inflow of foreign capital is again immiserising if the CKCIC holds.

5.3 Gainful Effects of Foreign Capital

In spite of the standard welfare-deteriorating effects of foreign capital, evidence shows that the developing countries have been eager to attract a substantial amount of foreign capital in the last two decades by adopting liberalised investment and trade policies. As per the World Development Reports 1998–1999 and 2006, the amount of foreign direct investment (FDI) to the low-income countries has increased from 1,502 millions of dollars in 1980 to 13,283 millions of dollars in 2003. The corresponding figures for India are 162 and 4,289 millions of dollars, respectively. The magnitude of increase of FDI flow to China is worth mentioning. It increased from meager 3,487 millions of dollars in 1990 to 53,505 millions of dollars in 2003. Foreign capital accounts for 11% of fixed capital investment (10 times the share in 1980) and almost one-third of that in the manufacturing sector.[5] This paradox gives rise to a pertinent question that what drives the developing countries to yearn for foreign capital given the standard welfare-deteriorating effect of foreign capital. A few plausible explanations may be forwarded as follows. First, the immiserising result has been derived in the context of the standard HOS framework, where the decomposition property holds. So factor prices remain unchanged despite an inflow of foreign capital and welfare deteriorates as the tariff-protected import-competing sector expands. However, in an indecomposable production structure the result might be different.[6] Second, if foreign capital enters into the import-competing sector, the

---

[4] From Equations (5.15) and (5.17.2) it follows that $\hat{Y} = -(\lambda_{LX}\hat{K}/\Delta) > 0$

[5] See the Oxfam Report, 2002.

[6] See for example, Jones and Marjit (1992) and Grinols (1991). Grinols (1991) in terms of a three-sector-specific factor indecomposable system with an urban informal sector and Harris–Todaro

result should be immiserising. However, if foreign capital is allowed to enter only into an intermediate input (internationally traded or non-traded) producing sector, as Marjit and Beladi (1996) and Chaudhuri (2001) have shown, it might be welfare-improving. Besides, standard trade models do not adequately capture some of the essentials characteristics of a typical developing economy. Even in an HT structure, with agricultural dualism and non-traded commodities, it is possible to show that an inflow of foreign capital might be welfare improving (Chaudhuri, 2007). Finally, as we have seen in any decomposable two-sector or three-sector Harris–Todaro model, despite the presence of labour market distortion inflows of foreign capital worsen welfare. But, if a full-employment structure is followed, as Chaudhuri (2005) has shown, an inflow of foreign capital might be welfare-improving even in an otherwise 2 × 2 HOS model in the presence of tariff and labour market distortions. Let us explain the Chaudhuri (2005) model in details.

5.3.1 Chaudhuri (2005) Model: Role of Labour Market Distortion

The Chaudhuri (2005) model shows that even in a two commodity–two input full-employment structure with labour market distortion, an inflow of foreign capital without technology transfer may be welfare-improving. However, the existence of labour market distortion is a necessity to obtain this unconventional result. If an inflow of foreign capital takes place concurrently with labour market reform, the possibility of welfare gain due to foreign capital diminishes. On the contrary, if the inflow of foreign capital is accompanied by a transfer of labour-augmenting technology, welfare may improve even in the absence of labour market distortion.

Chaudhuri (2005) considers a small open economy, with two sectors where both the sectors operate at close vicinity. There are two inputs of production – labour and capital. Sector 1 is the informal sector producing a primary export commodity while the formal sector (sector 2) produces a manufacturing commodity. Now it is assumed that labour in sector 2 earns a unionised wage, W^*, while the wage rate in sector 1, W, is market determined. We shall assume that sector 2 is more capital-intensive relative to sector 1 in value sense. Besides, sector 2 is the tariff-protected import-competing sector of the economy. Two commodity prices are given internationally owing to our small open economy assumption. Production functions exhibit constant returns to scale with positive but diminishing marginal productivity to each factor. All markets except the labour market facing sector 2 are perfectly competitive. Factors of production are fully utilised.

The general equilibrium is represented by the set of following equations:

---

setting has argued that an inflow of foreign capital in the presence of a capital-intensive and tariff-protected import-competing sector is not necessarily immiserising. This is because of an increase in the return to the sector-specific input, which may outweigh the increased cost of tariff protection resulting from an expansion of the protected sector.

$$a_{L1}W + a_{K1}r = P_1 \tag{5.19}$$

$$a_{L2}W^* + a_{K2}r = P_2(1+t) \tag{5.20}$$

$$a_{L1}X_1 + a_{L2}X_2 = L \tag{5.21}$$

$$a_{K1}X_1 + a_{K2}X_2 = K \tag{5.22}$$

Equations (5.19) and (5.20) are the two zero-profit conditions, while Equations (5.21) and (5.22) are the two full-employment conditions for labour and capital, respectively. P_i and X_i denote internationally given price and the output level of the ith sector, respectively. L and K are the endowments of labour and capital. The capital stock of the economy consists of both domestic (K_D) and foreign capital (K_F) and these are perfect substitutes.

Sector 2 faces a unionised labour market. The relationship for the unionised wage rate is specified as[7]

$$W^* = f(W,U) \tag{5.23}$$

where U denotes the bargaining strength of the labour unions.

$f(.)$ satisfies the following properties: $W^* = W$ for $U = 0$, $W^* > W$ for $U > 0$; $f_1, f_2 > 0$.

Equation (5.23) states that $W^* > W$ when the trade unions exercise at least some power in the bargaining over wages. W^* is an increasing function of both W and U. The trade union power, denoted by U, is amenable to policy measures. If the government undertakes labour market reforms for curbing union power, e.g. partial or complete ban on resorting to strikes by the trade unions or reformation of employment security laws, U takes a lower value.

There are five endogenous variables in the system: W, W^*, r, X_1 and X_2. Using Equation (5.23), Equation (5.20) may be rewritten as follows:

$$a_{L2}f(W,U) + a_{K2}r = P_2(1+t) \tag{5.20.1}$$

W and r are determined from Equations (5.19) and (5.20.1). Then a_{ji}s are determined as functions of input price ratios. X_1 and X_2 are obtained from Equations (5.21) and (5.22). Finally, W^* is found from Equation (5.23).

We measure welfare of the economy by national income at world prices, I, which is given by

$$I = Wa_{L1}X_1 + W^*a_{L2}X_2 + rK_D - tP_2X_2 \tag{5.24}$$

It is assumed that the foreign capital income is fully repatriated. In Equation (5.24), $Wa_{L1}X_1$ and $W^*a_{L2}X_2$ give the total wage income of the workers employed in

[7] This function has already been derived in Chapter 3.

sectors 1 and 2 of the economy, respectively. rK_D is the rental income from domestic capital. Finally, tP_2X_2 measures the cost of tariff protection of the import-competing sector.

Differentiating Equations (5.21) and (5.22) and solving we can derive the following expressions:

$$\hat{X}_1 = -(1/|\lambda|)\lambda_{L2}\hat{K} \tag{5.25}$$

$$\hat{X}_2 = (1/|\lambda|)\lambda_{L1}\hat{K} \tag{5.26}$$

where $|\lambda| = (\lambda_{L1}\lambda_{K2} - \lambda_{L2}\lambda_{K1}) > 0$ as sector 2 is more capital-intensive vis-à-vis sector 1 both in physical and value terms.

Differentiating Equation (5.24) with respect to K and using Equations (5.25) and (5.26) we get the following expression:

$$(\mathrm{d}I/\mathrm{d}K) = (\lambda_{L1}a_{L2}X_2/|\lambda|K)(W^* - W) - (tP_2X_2\lambda_{L1}/|\lambda|K) \tag{5.27}$$

Now since $W^* > W$ and $|\lambda|>0$, from Equation (5.27) it follows that $(\mathrm{d}I/\mathrm{d}K) > 0$ iff $(a_{L2}\ (W^*-W)) > tP_2$. However, in the absence of any protectionist policy, i.e. when $t = 0$, $(\mathrm{d}I/\mathrm{d}K) > 0$, irrespective of any condition. This leads to the following proposition.

Proposition 5.1 *Welfare of the economy improves owing to an inflow of foreign capital in the presence of a tariff iff* $(a_{L2}\ (W^*-W)) > tP_2$. *In the absence of any tariff, foreign capital is unambiguously welfare-improving.*[8]

We explain Proposition 5.1 intuitively in the following fashion. An inflow of foreign capital leads to an expansion of the more capital-intensive sector 2 and a contraction of sector 1 following the Rybczynski effect. As sector 2 is the tariff-protected import-competing sector, its expansion lowers welfare by increasing the cost of tariff protection. This may be called the output effect (of sector 2). On the other hand, as the higher wage-paying sector 2 expands at the cost of lower wage-paying sector 1, the aggregate wage income rises. This we may call the labour reallocation effect, which produces a favourable effect on welfare. So two opposite forces on welfare are generated. If the latter effect, measured by $((\lambda_{L1}a_{L2}X_2/|\lambda|K)(W^* - W))$, dominates over the former (denoted by $(tP_2X_2\lambda_{L1}/|\lambda|K)$) in Equation (5.27), welfare of the economy improves.

It may be noted that the lesser the degree of labour market distortion, the lower will be the wage differential between the two sectors and hence the lower will be the magnitude of labour reallocation effect. If the government undertakes any policy of labour market reform, the bargaining power of the trade unions, denoted by U, falls.

---

[8] In the standard 2×2 Heckscher–Ohlin framework, welfare remains unaffected despite foreign capital inflow if there is no tariff protection. But in the present set-up one gets a different result because of the presence of labour market distortion. This result, however, cannot be obtained in a Harris–Todaro framework despite labour market distortion due to the envelope property implied by that structure.

As U falls, W^* decreases directly. Besides, r rises and W falls, which causes W^* to fall further. The inter-sectoral wage differential (W^*–W) goes down, as the decrease in W^* is greater than that of W. So a reduction in U lowers the magnitude of the labour reallocation effect and hence weakens the possibility of welfare gain due to foreign capital. So we can state the following proposition.

Proposition 5.2 *Any government policy aimed at reducing the labour market distortion weakens the possibility of improvement in welfare through foreign capital.*

The absence of any bargaining power of the trade unions implies that $W^* = W$. Then from Equation (5.27) it follows that

$$(\mathrm{d}I/\mathrm{d}K) = -(tP_2X_2\lambda_{L1}/|\lambda|K) < 0. \tag{5.27.1}$$

Thus, we find that as labour market distortion vanishes due to labour market reform, it boils down to the standard Brecher–Alejandro case and foreign capital inflow is welfare-deteriorating. It may be mentioned that in the presence of multiple distortions, welfare results related to a single distortion could easily change. However, the case cited in this chapter is an example, which illustrates the trade-off between labour market reform and location of foreign capital.

5.3.1.1 An Extension: Inclusion of Technology Transfer and Endogenous Determination of Foreign Capital Inflow

In the analysis of Section 5.3.1, the possibility of technology transfer from an inflow of foreign capital has not been taken into consideration. However, as a result of foreign direct investment, residents of the host country come into contact with foreign entrepreneurs who possess superior technical skills and knowhow. These new ideas lead to transfer of technology from the foreigners to the residents of the host country and it takes place through observation, discussion and training. This transmission can be considered as a spillover or external effect on the host country.[9] It can fairly be generalised that technology transfer in developing countries takes place mainly through foreign direct investment. Empirical investigations in this area by Mansfield (1961, 1968) also support the validity of this hypothesis.

Another shortcoming of the previous analysis is that the inflow of foreign capital has been assumed to be completely exogenous. There is no doubt that the major driving force behind FDI by the multinational enterprises (MNEs) in the developing countries is the higher rate of return on their capital in these countries relative to the international market.[10] Therefore, it would be more realistic to assume that the

---

[9] See Koizumi and Kopecky (1977). Findlay (1978) has also used this 'contagion hypothesis' in his theoretical analysis of technology transfer and relative backwardness.

[10] In many of the recent models of MNEs there is focus on Industrial Organization and oligopoly. See, for example, Markusen (1995, 2002), Norback and Persson (2002), Neary (2002, 2003), among others. In this literature, MNEs are seen as having firm-specific assets developed from R&D, or marketing, which enable these firms to penetrate foreign markets. When an MNE sets up

supply of foreign capital is a positive function of the rate of return to foreign capital in the host country.

The present section is designed to extend the earlier analysis in the two above-mentioned directions. It is now considered that the supply of foreign capital to our small open economy is a positive function of the net rate of return to capital. However, the assumption that foreign and domestic capital are perfect substitutes is retained.[11]

In addition to the symbols that we have used in Section 5.3.1 of the chapter, we shall here use the following symbols as well:

h = efficiency of each worker;
b = ad valorem tax rate on foreign capital income; and
K_F = supply of foreign capital.

The equational structure of the extended model is as follows:

The competitive equilibrium conditions for the two industries are again given by

$$Wa_{L1} + ra_{K1} = P_1 \tag{5.19}$$

$$f(W,U)a_{L2} + ra_{K2} = P_2(1+t) \tag{5.20.1}$$

There is a tax at the rate b on the foreign capital income. The supply function of foreign capital is given by

$$K_F = K_F(r(1-b)), K_F'(.) > 0 \tag{5.28}$$

a new production plant in a target country, it is in effect implementing an FDI. The MNEs may have a number of motives for its FDI decision. One such motive could be the cross-country return differential. There are different entry modes into a target production market, such as establishment of new plants, acquisitions of domestic firms or merger with domestic producers. It may be noted that the labour union activity could be a way to extract rents from the foreign MNEs. However, if union activity extracts too high wage premiums, the amount of FDI is likely to fall, especially when the motive behind an FDI is the cross-country reward differential. On the other hand, the host countries may be benefited from transfer of new and improved technologies of production by the MNEs.

[11] An alternative way to deal with the above issues is to introduce a third sector, called a 'foreign enclave', where foreign capital is a specific input. The assumptions of unionised labour market, supply of foreign capital positively related with net return to foreign capital and the efficiency-enhancing effect of foreign capital are retained. Instead of two, in this case there is only one – Rybczynski effect. An inflow of foreign capital into the foreign enclave, initiated by a reduction in tax on foreign capital income, raises the demand for labour in this sector. On the other hand, due to labour-augmenting technology transfer associated with foreign capital, the labour endowment of the economy measured in efficiency unit increases. Thus, there are two opposite forces working on the availability of labour to the two domestic sectors. This produces a Rybczynski effect. The import-competing sector contracts (expands) if the labour availability to the domestic sectors rises (falls). One may check that the qualitative results of this section may hold under different sufficient conditions.

where $r(1–b)$ is the net return to foreign capital.

The capital endowment equation of the economy is as follows:

$$a_{K1}X_1 + a_{K2}X_2 = K = K_D + K_F(r(1-b)) \quad (5.29)$$

The efficiency of each worker is considered to be a positive function of the amount of foreign capital[12] in the economy and is given by

$$h = h(K_F(r(1-b))), h' > 0 \quad (5.30)$$

After normalising the labour endowment in physical unit to unity, we write the labour endowment of the economy in efficiency unit as

$$a_{L1}X_1 + a_{L2}X_2 = h(K_F(r(1-b))) \quad (5.31)$$

Finally, national income at international prices is now given by

$$I = Wh(K_F(r(1-b))) + (W^* - W)a_{L2}X_2 + rK_D + brK_F(r(1-b)) - tP_2X_2 \quad (5.32)$$

where $brK_F(r(1-b))$ is the tax revenue from foreign capital income.

Now, totally differentiating Equations (5.29), (5.31) and (5.32) and simplifying we can derive the following expression:

$$\begin{aligned}(\mathrm{d}I/\mathrm{d}b) = &-r[(Wh' + br)K_F' - K_F] \\ &+(rK_F'X_2/|\lambda|)[(W^* - W)a_{L2} - tP_2][(h'K/h) - (\lambda_{L1}/\lambda_{K1})](\lambda_{K1}/K)\end{aligned} \quad (5.33)$$

From Equation (5.33) it is obvious that

$(\mathrm{d}I/\mathrm{d}b) < 0$ under the sufficient conditions: (i) $brK_F' \geq K_F$ and (ii) $[(W^*–W)a_{L2}–tP_2][(h'K/h)–(\lambda_{L1}/\lambda_{K1})] \leq 0$.

This leads to the following proposition.

Proposition 5.3 *An inflow of foreign capital induced by a reduction in the rate of tax on foreign capital income improves welfare in the host country if (i)* $brK_F' \geq K_F$ *and (ii)* $[(W^*–W)a_{L2}–tP_2][(h'K/h)–(\lambda_{L1}/\lambda_{K1})] \leq 0$.

We explain Proposition 5.3 in the following way. A decline in the tax rate on foreign capital income raises the net rate of return to foreign capital, which induces

[12] Here the efficiency-enhancing effect of an inflow of foreign capital has been modelled as a disembodied increase in labour endowment in efficiency unit. Labour efficiency units are freely mobile between the two sectors of the economy so that, in effect, the foreign capital brings to the economy additional labour supply. At least in the short run, it may be questionable whether labour would be more productive in all parts of the economy simply because foreign capital enters into one sector (the capital-intensive import-competing sector). It would have been more realistic if the labour efficiency gains were tied specifically to labour that works with the foreign capital and the same idea would go through. However, this way of treatment of technology transfer keeps the analysis simple. Besides, the efficiency-increasing effects of foreign capital are likely to spread over more and more workers of the economy with time.

a fresh inflow of foreign capital. Although the factor prices do not change, this may influence welfare of the economy in different ways. First, the aggregate capital stock of the economy swells up. This following a Rybczynski effect leads to an expansion (a contraction) of the import-competing (export) sector as sector 2 is more capital-intensive vis-à-vis sector 1. On the other hand, owing to the labour augmenting nature of technology transfer associated with foreign capital, the labour endowment of the economy in efficiency unit increases. This produces another Rybczynski effect, which produces an expansion of sector 1 and a contraction of sector 2. The net result of the two opposite Rybczynski effects would be an expansion (a contraction) of the import-competing sector if the former (latter) effect dominates over the latter (former). This happens iff $(h'K/h) < (>) (\lambda_{L1}/\lambda_{K1})$. As a consequence, the cost of tariff protection of the import-competing sector rises (falls). This, we call the net output effect (of the formal sector). This effect is zero if the magnitudes of the two opposite Rybczynski effects are equal, i.e. when $(h'K/h) = (\lambda_{L1}/\lambda_{K1})$. Second, any change in the composition of output affects the aggregate income of the workers (at the given labour endowment measured in efficiency unit) in the presence of wage differential between the two sectors. This is called the labour reallocation effect. If the formal sector expands (contracts) (does not change), the aggregate wage income rises (falls) (remains unaffected) due to a labour reallocation effect. The combined effect of the net[13] output (of the formal sector) effect and the labour reallocation effect is positive (zero) on welfare iff $[(W^*-W)\, a_{L2}-tP_2][(h'K/h)-(\lambda_{L1}/\lambda_{K1})]<(=)0$. Third, as the labour endowment in efficiency unit rises, this produces another positive effect on welfare. We call it the labour endowment effect. Finally, a decrease in the tax rate on the return to foreign capital affects the tax revenue of the government. The tax revenue rises (does not change) if $brK'_F > (=) K_F$. This is called the tax revenue effect. When $[(W^*-W)\, a_{L2}-tP_2][(h'K/h)-(\lambda_{L1}/\lambda_{K1})]=0$ and $brK'_F = K_F$, the aggregate wage income (at given labour endowment) and tax revenue from foreign capital income remain unchanged, but welfare may still improve due to the increase in the labour endowment (in efficiency unit).

In order to compare Proposition 5.1 with Proposition 5.3, it should be kept in mind that in the basic model the inflow of foreign capital was considered to be exogenous. But in the subsequent analysis, an inflow of foreign capital was initiated by a reduction in tax on foreign capital income, which might affect the welfare result by producing a tax revenue effect. To make the results comparable let us ignore this effect. In the basic model we have found that a labour market distortion

---

[13] In the analysis of Section 5.2.1, there was only one Rybczynski effect resulting from an inflow of foreign capital. The output of the import-competing sector expands and it produces a negative effect on welfare by increasing the cost of tariff protection. This was called the output effect (of sector 2). But here another Rybczynski effect takes place as the labour endowment of the economy measured in efficiency unit increases due to efficiency-enhancing effect of foreign capital. Therefore, there are now two Rybczynski effects on the output of sector 2 and hence on the cost of tariff-protection working in opposite directions to each other. The combined effect is called the net output (of the formal sector) effect.

is a necessity for foreign capital to be welfare-improving. An inflow of foreign capital leads to an expansion of the import-competing sector (formal sector) due to a Rybczynski effect. Thus, the output effect (of the formal sector) invariably produces a negative impact on welfare by increasing the cost of tariff protection. But in the extended model an inflow of foreign capital associated with labour-augmenting nature of technology transfer leads to an expansion of the effective labour endowment measured in efficiency unit. Thus, unlike the basic model, two Rybczynski effects are generated in the extended model, which work in the two opposite directions to each other. The net result, which we call the net output effect, may not be an expansion of the import-competing sector. If it contracts (or remains unaffected), the cost of tariff protection falls (or does not change). Even if this sector expands, its magnitude (and hence the negative impact on welfare) would be lower compared to the earlier case. On the contrary, the effect of labour reallocation effect on welfare may be negative (or zero) if the import-competing sector contracts (or remains unchanged). Even if it expands, the positive effect of the labour reallocation effect on welfare must be less than the original case. But it should be noted that for growth with foreign capital to be welfare improving, the existence of labour market distortion is no longer a necessary condition. There is now one additional effect (the labour endowment effect) that works favourably on welfare. Therefore, in the absence of wage differential between the two sectors, welfare may still improve even when the cost of tariff protection rises if the labour endowment effect is adequately strong.

It may be noted that in the extended model Proposition 5.2 may hold in a special case when $(h'K/h) < (\lambda_{L1}/\lambda_{K1})$, i.e. the tariff-protected import-competing sector expands due to net output effect. This may be explained as follows. Suppose that the tax revenue effect and the labour endowment effect on welfare are positive. But the protected sector expands due to net output effect. Also there are no labour market distortions so that the labour reallocation effect is zero. Then welfare may fall if the increase in the cost of tariff protection is sufficiently high. But the presence of labour market distortion and positive labour reallocation effect certainly weakens the possibility of welfare loss in this case. If the magnitude of wage differential is sufficiently high (which in turn implies an adequately strong labour reallocation effect), welfare may still improve. This establishes the following proposition.

Proposition 5.4 *In the extended model Proposition 5.2 may be valid when* $(h'K/h)$–$(\lambda_{L1}/\lambda_{K1})$.

Thus an inflow of foreign capital in a two-sector full-employment model with labour market distortion is welfare-improving if the consequent labour reallocation effect outweighs the output effect (of the import-competing sector). The existence of labour market distortion is a necessary condition for obtaining gainful effects of foreign capital and any attempt to lower the magnitude of labour market distortion lowers the possibility of welfare gain. However, if the inflow of foreign capital is accompanied by a transfer of technology that raises the technical efficiency of the workers, gainful effects of foreign can be achieved even without labour market imperfection.

5.3.2 *Gainful Effects of Foreign Capital in the Presence of an Urban Informal Sector and Open Unemployment of Labour*

In the previous chapter, we have stated that in reality the urban informal sector and open unemployment of labour coexist in the migration equilibrium. We have also theoretically explained their simultaneous existence. Now we proceed to show how inflows of foreign capital either into the export sector or into the tariff-protected import-competing sector might improve social welfare when the informal sector and open unemployment coexist in the urban sector.[14] This framework helps us to examine the consequences of liberalised investment policies on the open unemployment in the urban area.

Our small open dual economy is broadly divided into an urban sector and a rural sector. The urban sector is further subdivided into two sub-sectors so that there are three sectors in the economy. Sector 1 of the economy is the rural sector that is assumed to produce its product by means of labour and capital of type 1. The urban informal sector (sector 2) produces a non-traded input with the help of labour and capital of type 2. Finally, the urban formal sector (sector 3) requires labour, capital of type 2 and a non-traded input to produce a final manufacturing product. The per-unit requirement of the intermediate input is assumed to be technologically fixed in the formal sector.[15] Capital of type 2 is mobile between the two urban sub-sectors and labour is imperfectly mobile between the three sectors of the economy. But capital of type 1 is specific to sector 1. Let r and R denote the returns to capital of type 1 and type 2, respectively. There is Harris–Todaro type of unemployment denoted by L_U. The aggregate capital stock of the economy of either type consists of both domestic and foreign capital. Incomes earned from foreign capital are completely repatriated. Let us now assume that labourers in the urban formal and informal sectors earn exogenously given wages,[16] W_3^* and W_2^*, respectively, while the wage rate in the rural sector, W_1, is market determined. The three wage rates are related by the Harris–Todaro (1970) migration equilibrium condition where the expected urban wage rate equals the rural wage rate and $W_3^* > W_1 > W_2^*$.[17] Owing to the small

---

[14] This section is based on Chaudhuri et al. (2006).

[15] It rules out the possibility of substitution between the non-traded input and other factors of production in sector 3. Although this is a simplifying assumption, it is not totally unrealistic. This is partly justified by the fact that four tires are used to produce a car and one Brown tube is used for a TV set. In industries like shoe making and garments, large formal sector firms farm out their production to the small informal sector firms under the system of subcontracting. So the production is done in the informal sector firms while labelling, packaging and marketing are done by the formal sector firms. One pair of shoes produced in the informal sector does not change in quantity when it is marketed by the formal sector as a final commodity. Thus there remains a fixed proportion between the use of the intermediate input and the quantity of the final commodity produced and marketed by the formal sector. It may be noted that Gupta (1994) has used this assumption in the context of analyzing different expansionary policies of a duty-free zone in a developing economy. Chaudhuri (2003) has also made this assumption.

[16] The rigidity of the informal sector wage has been explained in Chapter 4.

[17] See Chapter 3 footnote 6.

open economy assumption, the prices of the two final commodities are given internationally. But the price of the non-traded input produced by the urban informal sector, P_2, is determined domestically by demand and supply forces. We assume that the urban formal sector is the import-competing sector of the economy and is protected by a tariff. Other standard assumptions made in the earlier sections are retained. Commodity 1 is chosen as the numeraire.

Some of the new notations used in this section are as follows:

$K_j =$ economy's aggregate capital stock of the jth type (domestic plus foreign), $(j = 1, 2)$;
$K_{Dj} =$ economy's domestic capital stock of the jth type, $j = 1, 2$;
$V =$ social utility;
$D_i =$ consumption demand for the ith final commodity, $i = 1, 3$;
$Y =$ national income at domestic prices; and
$M =$ import demand for commodity 3.

A general equilibrium of the system is represented by the following set of equations:

$$W_1 a_{L1} + r a_{K1} = 1 \tag{5.34}$$

$$W_2^* a_{L2} + R a_{K2} = P_2 \tag{5.35}$$

$$W_3^* a_{L3} + R a_{K3} + P_2 a_{23} = P_3(1+t). \tag{5.36}$$

Full-employment conditions for capital of types 1 and 2 are as follows:

$$a_{K1} X_1 = K_1 \tag{5.37}$$

$$a_{K2} X_2 + a_{K3} X_3 = K_2. \tag{5.38}$$

The demand–supply equality of X_2 implies that

$$a_{23} X_3 = X_2. \tag{5.39}$$

For the sake of analytical simplicity, the number of workers in the economy, L has been normalised to unity. The labour endowment equation is then given as follows:

$$a_{L1} X_1 + a_{L2} X_2 + a_{L3} X_3 + L_U = 1. \tag{5.40}$$

Introducing the informal sector to the Harris–Todaro framework would modify the labour allocation mechanism such that in the labour market equilibrium, the rural wage rate (W_1) equals the expected wage income in the urban area. Since the probability of finding a job in the manufacturing sector is $a_{L3}X_3/(a_{L2}X_2 + a_{L3}X_3 + L_U)$ in the present case, then the expected wage in the manufacturing sector is $W_3^* a_{L3} X_3/(a_{L2} X_2 + a_{L3} X_3 + L_u)$. Similarly, the expected wage in the informal sector is $W_2^* a_{L2} X_2/(a_{L2} X_2 + a_{L3} X_3 + L_U)$. Thus, the expected wage in the urban area (the manufacturing and informal sectors) is $(W_2^* a_{L2} X_2 + W_3^* a_{L3} X_3)/(a_{L2} X_2 + a_{L3} X_3 + L_u)$. Therefore, the labour allocation mechanism between rural and urban areas is expressed as

$$(W_2^* a_{L2} X_2 + W_3^* a_{L3} X_3)/(a_{L2} X_2 + a_{L3} X_3 + L_u) = W_1,$$

or equivalently

$$W_1 a_{L1} X_1 + W_2^* a_{L2} X_2 + W_3^* a_{L3} X_3 = W_1. \tag{5.41}$$

Following Beladi and Yabuuchi (2001) we assume that the wage in the informal sector is a constant fraction of the formal sector wage[18] and is given by

$$W_2^* = n W_3^* \tag{5.42}$$

where $0<n<1$ represents the distortionary wage differential between the two urban sectors. It is assumed that the urban informal sector consists of many subcontract firms, and as explained in Section 3.6, the workers employed do not get more than their reservation wages.

There are eight endogenous variables in the system: W_1, r, R, P_2, X_1, X_2, X_3 and L_U, and eight independent equations. The policy parameters are K_1 and K_2.[19] One can obtain R and P_2 by simultaneously solving Equations (5.35) and (5.36). Using Equations (5.37), (5.39) and (5.42), Equations (5.38) and (5.41) may be rewritten as the following, respectively:

$$(a_{K2} a_{23} + a_{K3}) X_3 = K_2 \tag{5.43}$$

and

$$(W_1 K_1 a_{L1}/a_{K1}) + (n W_3^* a_{L2} a_{23} + W_3^* a_{L3}) X_3 = W_1. \tag{5.44}$$

In the present set-up, W_1, R and X_3 are solved from Equations (5.34), (5.43) and (5.44). Once all the factor prices are known, the factor coefficients, a_{ji}s, are also known. Then X_1 and X_2 are found from Equations (5.37) and (5.39), respectively. Finally, L_U is obtained from Equation (5.40).

The demand side of the model is represented by a quasi-concave social utility function. Let V denote the social utility that depends on the consumption demand for the two final goods denoted by, D_1 and D_3. Thus, it is shown as

---

[18] This is not an essential assumption in this model. The constancy of the informal sector wage serves our purpose, which seems to be reasonable if the informal sector produces a non-traded input for the formal sector on a subcontracting basis.

[19] One can, of course, consider the tariff rate, t, as another policy parameter and carry out comparative statics with respect to that parameter.

$$V = V(D_1, D_3). \tag{5.45}$$

The balance of trade equilibrium requires that

$$D_1 + P_3 D_3 = X_1 + P_3 X_3 - r(K_1 - K_{D1}) - R(K_2 - K_{D2}), \tag{5.46}$$

or equivalently

$$\begin{aligned} Y &= D_1 + P_3^* D_3 \\ &= X_1 + P_3^* X_3 + tP_3 M - r(K_1 - K_{D1}) - R(K_2 - K_{D2}), \end{aligned} \tag{5.46.1}$$

where Y is national income at domestic prices and M $(= D_3\text{–}X_3)$ denotes import demand for good 3.

5.3.2.1 Effects of Foreign Capital Inflows on Welfare

We are now interested to analyse the consequences of liberalised investment policies on national welfare and open unemployment in the urban area. Liberalised investment policies imply increases in the stocks of the economy's two types of capital stock, K_1 and K_2, which arise due to inflows of foreign capital. According to the conventional wisdom an inflow of foreign capital in a developing economy is welfare-reducing. This is based on the argument that an inflow of foreign capital leads to an expansion of the protected import-competing sector, thereby lowering welfare by lowering the volumes of trade.

First, it is assumed that foreign capital of type 1 flows in, so that $\hat{K}_1 > 0$ with all other parameters remaining unchanged. We assume that the endowment of foreign capital is initially zero.

Differentiating Equations (5.45) and (5.46), we get (see Appendix 5.3)

$$dV/V_1 = dD_1 + P_3^* dD_3 = \nu[(1 - L_1)W_1\hat{W}_1 + tP_3(tP_3 H\hat{t} - X_3\hat{X}_3)], \tag{5.47}$$

where $V_1 = \partial V/\partial D_1, \nu = (1 + t)/\{1 + (1 - m)t\} > 0$,

$H = [(\partial D_3/\partial P_3^*) + (\partial D_3/\partial Y)D_3] < 0$ is Slutsky's pure substitution term and $m = P_3^*(\partial D_3/\partial Y)$ is the marginal propensity to consume good 3. Thus, welfare depends on the changes in the wage rate in sector 1 and the outputs in sector 3 since the rate of tariff does not change.

Comparative statics yield[20]

$$\hat{W}_1/\hat{K}_1 = -L_U \lambda_{L1}(\theta_{K3} + \theta_{K2}\theta_{23})/\Delta > 0, \tag{5.48}$$

and

$$\hat{X}_3/\hat{K}_1 = 0, \tag{5.49}$$

[20] See Appendix 5.2.

where Δ is the value of the determinant of the coefficient matrix of the system.[21] Note that $\lambda_{23} = a_{23}X_3/X_2 = 1$. Thus, the following proposition follows immediately.

Proposition 5.5 *Welfare improves unambiguously as a result of the inflow of foreign capital of type 1.*

Now it is assumed that $\hat{K}_2 > 0$, i.e. there is an inflow of foreign capital of type 2. Similar to the case of foreign capital of type 1, we have

$$\begin{aligned}\hat{W}_1/\hat{K}_2 &= -L_U\lambda_{K1}(\theta_{K3}+\theta_{K2}\theta_{23})(\tilde{\lambda}_{L3}+\tilde{\lambda}_{L2})/\Delta > 0,\\ &= -(\tilde{\lambda}_{L3}+\tilde{\lambda}_{L2})/(D+\lambda_{L1}S^1_{KK}/\theta_{K1}) > 0,\end{aligned} \tag{5.50}$$

and

$$\hat{X}_3/\hat{K}_2 = L_U\lambda_{L1}(\theta_{K3}+\theta_{K2}\theta_{23})(D+\lambda_{L1}S^1_{KK}/\theta_{K1})/\Delta = 1 > 0, \tag{5.51}$$

where $\tilde{\lambda}_{Li} = (W_i^*/W_1)\lambda_{Li}$ $(i = 2, 3)$ and $D = \lambda_{L1} - 1 + \lambda_{L1}S^1_{KK}/\theta_{K1} < 0$.

Substituting Equations (5.50) and (5.51) into Equation (5.47) with all other parameters remaining constant, we have

$$dV/V_1\hat{K}_2 = \nu[-(1-L_1)W_1(\tilde{\lambda}_{L3}+\tilde{\lambda}_{L2})/(D+\lambda_{L1}S^1_{KK}/\theta_{K1}) - tP_3X_3]. \tag{5.52}$$

So we can now establish the following proposition.

Proposition 5.6 *Foreign capital inflow of type 2 is welfare enhancing if and only if*

$$-(1-L_1)W_1(\tilde{\lambda}_{L3}+\tilde{\lambda}_{L2})/(D+\lambda_{L1}S^1_{KK}/\theta_{K1}) > tP_3X_3.$$

Propositions 5.5 and 5.6 can be intuitively explained as follows. An inflow of foreign capital of type 1 affects neither the rental to capital of type 2, R, nor the output of the formal sector, X_3, as it is specific to sector 1. So the cost of tariff protection tP_3X_3 does not change. But as the supply of this type of capital increases relative to its demand, the rental to capital of type 1, r, falls, which in turn raises the rural sector wage rate, W_1, to satisfy the zero profitability condition for sector 1 (see Equation 5.34). Thus, labour moves from urban to rural area. This contributes to increase total wage income and to reduce urban unemployment as shown below. Anyway, the hike in total wage income outweighs the drop in the rental income to capital of type 1. Hence welfare unambiguously improves.

On the other hand, an inflow of capital of type 2 does not affect its rental rate, R, as it is determined from the price system alone, independently of the output system. But since K_2 is used in sectors 2 and 3, there is a boost in X_2 and X_3. As the tariff-protected import-competing sector expands, the cost of tariff protection also rises. Now given W_2^* $(= nW_3^*)$, W_3^* and R, the factor coefficients a_{L2}, a_{L3}, a_{K2} and a_{K3} remain unchanged. But as X_2 and X_3 rise, the aggregate absorption of labour in the

[21] See footnote 20.

two urban sectors $(a_{L2}X_2 + a_{L3}X_3)$ increases. The necessary labour is supplied from the urban unemployment pool and the rural area. In this case, the change in unemployment is not unambiguous. It depends on the increase in labour demand in the urban sectors relative to the inflow of labour from the rural area. But the competitive rural wage rate rises unequivocally as the number of workers staying in the rural sector decreases.[22] So there would be three different effects on welfare. Welfare increases due to an increase in the total wage income through the reallocation of labour between the urban and rural areas. On the contrary, welfare deteriorates due to a decline in total rental income of type 1 capital and due to an increase in the cost of tariff protection of the import-competing sector. It can be easily checked that the net effect on welfare would be positive under the necessary and sufficient condition presented in the proposition.

5.3.2.2 Effects of Foreign Capital Inflow on Urban Unemployment

The growing incidence of urban unemployment has been a matter of deep concern to the developing economies. The ongoing process of economic liberalisation has probably aggravated this problem. We would now like to analyse the effects of liberalised investment policies on the level of urban unemployment.

The effect of an inflow of capital of type 1 on unemployment is derived as

$$\hat{L}_U/\hat{K}_1 = -\lambda_{L1}(\lambda_{L1} - 1)(\theta_{K3} + \theta_{K2}\theta_{23})/\Delta < 0. \tag{5.53}$$

This establishes the following proposition.

Proposition 5.7 *Foreign capital inflow of type 1 unambiguously lowers the urban unemployment level.*

Similarly, we get the effect of an inflow of capital of type 2 on unemployment as

$$\hat{L}_U/\hat{K}_2 = \lambda_{K1}(\theta_{K3} + \theta_{K2}\theta_{23})[(\lambda_{L3} + \lambda_{L2})(\tilde{\lambda}_{L3} + \tilde{\lambda}_{L2}) + \lambda_{L1}L_U S^1_{LL}/(\theta_{K1})^2]/\Delta. \tag{5.54}$$

This leads to the following proposition (see Appendix 5.4).

Proposition 5.8 *Foreign capital inflow of type 2 lowers the urban unemployment level if and only if* $\lambda_{L1}S^1_{LL}/(\theta_{K1})^2 > (\lambda_{L3} + \lambda_{L2})(\tilde{\lambda}_{L3} + \tilde{\lambda}_{L2})/(-L_U)$.

We explain Propositions 5.7 and 5.8 as follows. An inflow of foreign capital of type 1 leads to an increase in the rural sector wage rate, W_1, and an expansion of sector 1. As W_1 increases, there would be a reverse migration of labour from the urban sector to the rural sector. The consequence would be a fall in urban unemployment. On the other hand, if capital of type 2 flows into the economy, W_1 rises

[22] It is important to mention that owing to the 'envelope property' implied by the Harris–Todaro framework, the aggregate wage income of the workers in the economy increases as the rural sector wage, W_1, rises.

but both the urban sectors expand. Thus, two opposite effects on the urban unemployment level would be generated. If the expected urban wage rises relative to the rural sector wage rate, migration of labour from the rural to the urban sector rises. On the one hand, the level of urban unemployment falls as new jobs are created in the urban sector, and on the other, it rises if the size of the urban labour force swells up following a fresh migration from the rural sector. Our result shows that the unemployment level in the urban sector plummets if the expansion effect outweighs the migration effect, i.e. if the increase in the expected urban wage is greater than that in the rural wage rate. This happens subject to the precise condition provided in the proposition.

Contrary to the conventional immiserising result, the theoretical analysis of the previous section shows that an inflow of foreign capital in either of the two broad sectors of the economy may be welfare-improving mainly through the decrease in urban unemployment. Besides, an inflow of foreign capital into the urban sector leads to an expansion of the urban sector of the economy. This policy is to ameliorate the problem of urban unemployment.[23] These results are completely opposite to those generated by the standard Harris–Todaro model.

Appendix 5.1

Differentiating Equations (5.12) and (5.14) the following expressions are obtained:

$$\lambda_{L1}\hat{X}_1 + \lambda_{L2}\hat{X}_2 = -(h'K_F'br/h)\hat{b} \tag{5.A.1}$$

$$\lambda_{K1}\hat{X}_1 + \lambda_{K2}\hat{X}_2 = -(K_F'rb/K)\hat{b} \tag{5.A.2}$$

Solving Equations 5.A.1 and 5.A.2 by Cramer's rule one gets the following expression:

$$\hat{X}_2 = (brK_F'/|\lambda|)[(h'\lambda_{K1}/h) - (\lambda_{L1}/K)]\hat{b} \tag{5.A.3}$$

Now differentiating Equation (5.32) with respect to b we get

$$(\mathrm{d}Y/\mathrm{d}b) = -Wh'K_F'r + (W^* - W)a_{L2}(\mathrm{d}X_2/\mathrm{d}b) + rK_F(.) - br^2K_F' - tP_2(\mathrm{d}X_2/\mathrm{d}b)$$

Using Equation (5.A.3) and simplifying we get

$$\begin{aligned}(\mathrm{d}Y/\mathrm{d}b) = {} & -r[(Wh' + br)K_F' - K_F] \\ & +(rK_F'X_2/|\lambda|)[(W^* - W)a_{L2} - tP_2][(h'K/h) - (\lambda_{L1}/\lambda_{K1})](\lambda_{K1}/K)\end{aligned} \tag{5.A.4}$$

[23] It has also been noted that new employment opportunities have been created and labour force participation rates have increased in several large FDI recipient economies, especially in South, East and Southeast Asia (ILO 2002a).

From Equation (5.A.4) it is evident that

$$(dY/db) < 0\, if (i)\, brK'_F \geq K_F; and\, (ii)\, [(W^* - W)a_{L2} - tP_2][(h'K/h) - (\lambda_{L1}/\lambda_{K1})] \leq 0$$

Appendix 5.2

Differentiating Equations (5.34)–(5.41) and arranging terms, we obtain

$$\begin{bmatrix} 0 & 0 & 0 & 0 & 0 & \theta_{K3} + \theta_{K2}\theta_{23} \\ \lambda_{K1} & 0 & 0 & 0 & -\lambda_{K1}S^1_{KK}/\theta_{K1} & 0 \\ 0 & \lambda_{K2} & \lambda_{K3} & 0 & 0 & A \\ 0 & 1 & -1 & 0 & 0 & 0 \\ \lambda_{L1} & \lambda_{L2} & \lambda_{L3} & L_U & \lambda_{L1}S^1_{LL}/\theta_{K1} & C \\ \lambda_{L1} & \tilde{\lambda}_{L2} & \tilde{\lambda}_{L3} & 0 & D & C^* \end{bmatrix} \begin{bmatrix} \hat{X}_1 \\ \hat{X}_2 \\ \hat{X}_3 \\ \hat{L}_U \\ \hat{W} \\ \hat{R} \end{bmatrix} = \begin{bmatrix} 0 \\ \hat{K}_1 \\ \hat{K}_2 \\ 0 \\ 0 \\ 0 \end{bmatrix} \quad (5.A.5)$$

where $\tilde{\lambda}_{Li} = (W_i^*/W_1)\lambda_{Li}$ $(i = 2, 3)$, $T = t/(1 + t)$.

$$A = \lambda_{K2}S^2_{KK} + \lambda_{K3}S^3_{KK}\,, \quad C = \lambda_{L2}S^2_{LK} + \lambda_{L3}S^3_{LK},$$
$$C^* = \tilde{\lambda}_{L2}S^2_{LK} + \tilde{\lambda}_{L3}S^3_{LK} \text{ and } D = \lambda_{L1} - 1 + \lambda_{L1}S^1_{LL}/\theta_{K1} < 0,$$

Solving Equation (5.A.5) for $\hat{W}_1$ with respect to $\hat{K}_1$ and considering $\lambda_{K2} + \lambda_{K3} = 1$, we have Equation (5.48) in the main text.

$$\hat{W}_1/\hat{K}_1 = -L_U\lambda_{L1}(\theta_{K3} + \theta_{K2}\theta_{23})/\Delta > 0, \quad (5.48)$$

where Δ is the value of the determinant of the coefficient matrix of the system, and it is shown as

$$\Delta = L_U\lambda_{K1}(\theta_{K3} + \theta_{K2}\theta_{23})(D + \lambda_{L1}S^1_{KK}/\theta_{K1}) < 0.$$

Other comparative static results are obtained similarly.

Appendix 5.3

Differentiating Equations (5.45) and (5.46) with keeping initial holdings of foreign capital zero, we have

$$\begin{aligned} dV/V_1 &= dD_1 + P_3^* dD_3 \\ &= \mathrm{d}X_1 + P_3^*\mathrm{d}X_3 + tP_3\mathrm{d}M - r\mathrm{d}K_1 - R\mathrm{d}K_2, \end{aligned} \quad (5.A.6)$$

where $V_1 = \partial V/\partial D_1$ and $M = D_3(P_3^*, Y) - X_3$.

Differentiating M and arranging terms with keeping initial holdings of foreign capital zero, we obtain

$$\begin{aligned}\mathrm{d}M = (\partial D_3/\partial P_3^*)\mathrm{d}P_3^* + (\partial D_3/\partial Y)[\mathrm{d}X_1 + P_3^*\mathrm{d}X_3 + X_3\mathrm{d}P_3^* + tP_3\mathrm{d}M \\ + MP_3\mathrm{d}t - r\mathrm{d}K_1 - R\mathrm{d}K_2] - \mathrm{d}X_3,\end{aligned}$$

$$\mathrm{d}M = \nu[H\mathrm{d}P_3^* + (m/P_3^*)(\mathrm{d}X_1 + P_3^*\mathrm{d}X_3 - r\mathrm{d}K_1 - R\mathrm{d}K_2) - \mathrm{d}X_3] \qquad (5.A.7)$$

Differentiating production functions and considering Equations (4.38) and (4.41), we have

$$\begin{aligned}&\mathrm{d}X_1 + P_3^*\mathrm{d}X_3 - r\mathrm{d}K_1 - R\mathrm{d}K_2 \\ &= (F_L^1\mathrm{d}L_1 + F_K^1\mathrm{d}K_1) + P_3^*(F_L^3\mathrm{d}L_3 + F_K^3\mathrm{d}K_3 + F_2^3\mathrm{d}X_2) - r\mathrm{d}K_1 - R\mathrm{d}K_2 \\ &= (W_1\mathrm{d}L_1 + r\mathrm{d}K_1) + (W_3^*\mathrm{d}L_3 + R\mathrm{d}K_3) + (W_2^*\mathrm{d}L_2 + R\mathrm{d}K_2) - r\mathrm{d}K_1 - R\mathrm{d}K_2 \\ &= W_1\mathrm{d}L_1 + W_2^*\mathrm{d}L_2 + W_3^*\mathrm{d}L_3 \\ &= (1 - L_1)dW_1, \end{aligned} \qquad (5.A.8)$$

where F_j^k is the value of marginal product of the jth factor in the kth sector, which is equal to the factor price.

Substituting Equations (5.A.3) and (5.A.4) into Equation (5.A.2) yields

$$\mathrm{d}V/V_1 = \mathrm{d}D_1 + P_3^*\mathrm{d}D_3 = \nu[(1 - L_1)W_1\hat{W}_1 + tP_3(tP_3H\hat{t} - X_3\hat{X}_3)]. \qquad (5.47)$$

Appendix 5.4

Solving Equation (5.A.5) for $\hat{L}_U$ with respect to $\hat{K}_2$, and considering $S_{KK}^1 = \theta_{L1}S_{LL}^1/\theta_{K1}$,

$$(\lambda_{L1} - 1) = -(\tilde{\lambda}_{L3} + \tilde{\lambda}_{L2}),$$

and

$$L_U = (1 - \lambda_{L1}) - (\lambda_{L3} + \lambda_{L2}) = (\tilde{\lambda}_{L3} + \tilde{\lambda}_{L2}) - (\lambda_{L3} + \lambda_{L2}),$$

We have Equation 5.54 in the main text. Since $\Delta < 0$, therefore, $\hat{L}_U/\hat{K}_2 < 0$ from Equation 5.54 iff

$$[-(\lambda_{L3} + \lambda_{L2})(\tilde{\lambda}_{L3} + \tilde{\lambda}_{L2}) - \lambda_{L1}L_U S_{LL}^1/(\theta_{K1})^2] < 0. \qquad (5.A.9)$$

Thus, Equation (5.A.9) can be rewritten as

$$\lambda_{L1}S_{LL}^1/(\theta_{K1})^2 > (\lambda_{L3} + \lambda_{L2})(\tilde{\lambda}_{L3} + \tilde{\lambda}_{L2})/(-L_U).$$

This leads to the proposition.

Chapter 6
How and How Far to Liberalise a Developing Economy

6.1 Introduction

Many of the developing countries have chosen free trade as their development strategy and been vigorously implementing liberalised trade and investment policies for the last two decades or so. Liberalisation involves both inflow of foreign capital and reduction of protection of domestic industries, structural reforms like deregulating the labour market and integrating the domestic market with the world market.

The developing countries are plagued by many distortions. Commodity market distortion in the form of tariff protection in the import-competing sector and labour market distortion in the form of unionised formal sector labour market are the two most common types of distortion prevalent in these countries. Removal of distortions, according to the conventional wisdom, is likely to be welfare-improving, since this would lead to more efficient distribution of economics resources. The developing countries, therefore, have been advised by the WTO to include tariff and structural reform policies, like making the labour market more competitive by curbing the trade union power in determining the unionised wage in their globalisation programme packages.

However, it has been observed that some of the developing economies, notably the non-OECD countries, have not implemented tariff reforms to any significant extent, even after formally choosing free trade as their development strategy. The explanation to this seemingly puzzling situation has been provided by the existing tariff-jumping theory.[1] The tariff-jumping theory suggests a positive correlation between the amount of FDI in a country and tariff rates imposed by it. So, the countries in quest of foreign capital may be reluctant in implementing tariff reform seriously. But this theory fails to explain as to how many other countries have been

[1] The major driving force behind FDI by the MNEs in the developing countries is the higher rate of return on their capital in these countries vis-à-vis the international market. Countries with protected domestic markets are likely to attract foreign investment, but only for the purpose of jumping the tariff walls and reaping a good harvest by serving their markets directly. See, for example, Motta (1992) and Yanagawa (1990) for details.

S. Chaudhuri, U. Mukhopadhyay, *Revisiting the Informal Sector*,
DOI 10.1007/978-1-4419-1194-0_6,

able to attract a substantial amount of foreign investment even after lowering their tariff rates considerably.

As many of the developing economies have chosen free trade as their development strategy, thoughtfully or not, they are bound to open up their economies to the world and make domestic markets increasingly competitive. But how and how far to liberalise an economy are the vital questions of the hour. In other words, the crucial question is whether a developing economy should follow all the WTO-prescribed liberalising policies and to what extent. This is extremely important because available empirical evidences reveal that developing countries have been facing substantial adjustment costs in their endeavour in implementing different WTO-prescribed policies and opening up their economies to external competition at a brisk pace. Although many of the Sub-Saharan African countries have been subjected to IMF-imposed reforms for a decade or more, the overall performance of these economies yet remains remarkably poor, despite considerable progress on liberalisation and deregulation. The average annual growth of real GDP in these countries fell from 2.5% between 1985 and 1989 to 1.9% between 1990 and 1997.[2] During the 1990s, per capita income also declined in most of Africa's less developed countries (UNCTAD, 2000). In South Africa and in many of the Latin American countries, trade liberalisation during the 1990s was associated with falling employment and hence economic insecurity for the formal sector labour force. Most seriously, as noted by Kaplinsky (2001), trade reform measures have made the developing economies increasingly reliant on external economic events. In recent decades, this external environment has become increasingly volatile. The volatility of both capital flows and GDP growth was much greater in developing countries than in the industrial countries (Hausmann and Gavin, 1996). Besides, the costs of this volatility were greater for developing than for industrialised countries. More developing countries experienced currency crises than industrial ones, and with a greater negative impact on output (IMF, 1998). According to Stiglitz (2002), the results of IMF-sponsored economic reforms have been intensifying poverty for many people and instigating social and political chaos for many countries. Mistakes in sequencing and pacing of economic reforms have led to rising unemployment and increased poverty in many countries. Markets were opened up for competition too rapidly, which resulted in sharp increases in unemployment levels due to lack of strong financial institutions. After the 1997 Asian crisis, IMF policies exacerbated the crises in Indonesia and Thailand. Even those countries that have experienced some limited growth have seen the benefits accrue to the very well-off, leading to sharp increases in income inequalities.

In these circumstances, an effort has been made in this chapter to provide answers to the questions mentioned above in terms of a three-sector general equilibrium model with informal sectors, reasonable for a developing economy. Welfare effects of different trade and investment liberalisation policies have been first studied in a

---

[2] However, it has increased to 3.9% during 2000–2004 (World Development Report, 2006). The GDP per capita grew at 2.4% during 2003–2004.

full-employment set-up. The study has then been extended into an HT framework with an urban informal sector and capital market distortion.

6.2 The Analysis and Results

A small open economy with three sectors has been considered.[3] There are one formal and two informal sectors. One of the two informal sectors (sector 1) produces an agricultural commodity using capital and labour. The other informal sector (sector 2) produces a non-traded input[4] for the formal sector using capital and labour. The formal sector produces a manufacturing commodity with the help of capital, labour and the intermediate input produced in sector 2. The per-unit requirement of the intermediate input is assumed to be technologically fixed in sector 3.[5] Let us now assume that labour in the formal sector earns a contractual wage, W^*, while the wage rate in the two informal sectors, W, is market determined. Capital and labour[6] are perfectly mobile among all the three sectors of the economy. Owing to our small open economy assumption, we consider the prices of the commodities of sectors 1 and 3 to be given internationally. On the other hand, the price of the non-traded input produced in sector 2 is endogenously determined. We assume that the formal sector is the import-competing sector of the economy and is protected by a tariff. Production functions exhibit constant returns to scale with diminishing marginal productivity to each factor. All inputs are fully employed.[7] The endowment of labour is normalised to unity.

---

[3] This chapter draws upon Chaudhuri (2003).

[4] It may be pointed out that in the models of Grinols (1991) and Gupta (1997), it is assumed that the informal sector produces an internationally traded final commodity, which may seem hardly realistic, given the definition of informality. On the other hand, there is enough empirical evidence (see Section 3.6) in support of the fact that the informal sector units mostly produce non-traded intermediaries for the formal manufacturing industries.

[5] See footnote 15 in Chapter 5.

[6] Perfect labour mobility is compatible with the type of wage differential considered in this chapter. See Chapter 10 in Batra (1973) for an interesting exposition of this issue.

[7] The assumption of full-employment of labour in the context of a developing economy may seem to be awkward at the first sight. But in the presence of informal sectors where wages are completely flexible, this assumption may be justified. Datta Chaudhuri (1989), Grinols (1991), Chandra and Khan (1993) and Gupta (1997) consider that in the migration equilibrium in the presence of an informal sector, there does not remain any involuntary unemployment and the informal sector wage rate lies below that of the rural sector. There are also a few variants of the HOS framework with informal sector where full-employment is ensured relying on the complete flexibility of the informal sector wage rate. Marjit and Beladi (1996), Chaudhuri and Mukherjee (2002) and Chaudhuri and Mukhopadhyay (2002) are three of the few papers based on the HOS framework. The difference between the two types of frameworks is that in the models where an HT framework has been followed, wage rates differ between the rural and urban informal sectors, while in the HOS type of papers all the sectors operate at close vicinity and perfect labour mobility between the informal sectors ensures equalisation of the informal sector wage rates. However, in all these papers, there does not exist any involuntary unemployment of labour in equilibrium. Section 6.4 of this chapter has considered the HT case.

The general equilibrium is represented by the set of following equations:

$$a_{L1}W + a_{K1}r = P_1 \tag{6.1}$$

$$a_{L2}W + a_{K2}r = P_2 \tag{6.2}$$

$$a_{L2}W^* + a_{K3}r + a_{23}P_2 = P_3(1+t) \tag{6.3}$$

where r and P_2 denote the return to capital and the price of the non-traded input produced by sector 2, respectively. P_1, P_3 and t are the world prices of commodities 1 and 3 and the ad valorem rate of tariff on the import of commodity 3.

Equations (6.1), (6.2) and (6.3) are the three competitive industry equilibrium conditions in the two informal and the formal sectors, respectively.

Complete utilisation of capital (K) in the economy implies that

$$a_{K1}X_1 + a_{K2}X_2 + a_{K3}X_3 = K \tag{6.4}$$

Full employment of labour is implied by the following equation:

$$a_{L1}X_1 + a_{L2}X_2 + a_{L3}X_3 = 1 \tag{6.5}$$

The demand for the non-traded input must equal its supply. So we have

$$a_{23}X_3 = X_2 \tag{6.6}$$

The formal sector faces a unionised labour market. The relationship for the unionised wage rate is specified as[8]

$$W^* = W^*(W,U) \tag{6.7}$$

where U is the bargaining strength of the labour unions.

$W^*(.)$ satisfies the following properties[9]:

$$W^* = W \text{ for } U = 0,\ W^* > W \text{ for } U > 0;\ (\partial W^*/\partial W),\ (\partial W^*/\partial U) > 0$$

Using Equation (6.7), Equation (6.3) may be rewritten as follows:

$$a_{L3}W^*(W,U) + a_{K3}r + a_{23}P_2 = P_3(1+t) \tag{6.3.1}$$

---

[8] It may be noted that in a simple fixed wage differential model also, many of the qualitative results remain unaltered. Also one may include $P_3(1+t)$ in the $W^*(.)$ function. The welfare effects of trade liberalisation remain unaffected if the net effect on W^* of a decrease in t remains the same.

[9] See Section 5.3.1 for explanation.

There are seven endogenous variables in the system: W, W^*, r, P_2, X_1, X_2 and X_3. The parameters of the system are P_1, P_3, a_{23}, t, U, L and K, which are exogenously given. Equations (6.1), (6.2) and (6.3.1) form the price system of the model. We note that given the values of the parameters, the three unknown factor prices, W, P_2 and r, can be solved from the price system alone, independently of the factor endowments. Thus the production structure shows the decomposition property. Once the informal wage rate, W, is known, the unionised wage rate, W^*, is obtained from Equation (6.7). If factor prices are known, the factor coefficients, a_{ji}s, are also known. Equations (6.4), (6.5) and (6.6) then can be solved for X_1, X_2 and X_3.

The measure of welfare in this small open economy is national income measured at world prices, Y, which is expressed as follows:

$$Y = W(a_{L1}X_1 + a_{L2}X_2) + W^* a_{L3}X_3 + rK_D - tP_3X_3 \tag{6.8}$$

In Equation (6.8), $W(a_{L1}X_1 + a_{L2}X_2)$ and $W^* a_{L3}X_3$ give the total wage income of the workers employed in the two informal and the formal sectors of the economy, respectively. Rental income from domestic capital is rK_D, where K_D is the domestic capital stock. Finally, tP_3X_3 measures the cost of tariff protection[10] of the import-competing sector.

According to conventional wisdom, an inflow of foreign capital[11] in a developing economy leads to deterioration in its welfare while a reduction in tariff protection is welfare-improving. However, in this section we reanalyse the impact of foreign capital inflow and/or a reduction in import tariff on welfare of a small open economy. It is equally interesting in the present set-up to study the welfare consequences of any attempt of formal sector reforms, like deregulating the labour market. Although different liberalised policies in trade and investment are undertaken concurrently in a developing economy, to fix our ideas we may consider their effects one by one. We shall, however, discuss intuitively the net outcome of these policies on welfare, if carried out simultaneously.

Total differentials of Equations (6.1), (6.2) and (6.3.1) and use of envelope conditions yield

$$\theta_{L1}\hat{W} + \theta_{K1}\hat{r} = 0 \tag{6.1.1}$$

$$\theta_{L2}\hat{W} + \theta_{K2}\hat{r} - \hat{P}_2 = 0 \tag{6.2.1}$$

---

[10] The imposition of a tariff on the import-competing sector artificially raises the domestic price of the formal sector's product from its world price, which would lead to a misallocation of resources between the two traded sectors. Producers would produce more (less) of the importable (exportable) commodity vis-à-vis their free trade levels. tP_3X_3 measures the deadweight loss to the economy's welfare resulting from this inefficiency in production.

[11] Our assumption is that domestic capital and foreign capital are perfect substitutes. This simplified assumption has been made in Brecher and Alejandro (1977), Khan (1982), Grinols (1991), Chandra and Khan (1993), Gupta (1997), etc. However, in the papers of Beladi and Marjit (1992a, b) and Marjit and Beladi (1996), foreign capital has been treated differently from domestic capital and these two types of capital are not engaged in the same sector of the economy.

$$\theta_{L3}E_W\hat{W} + \theta_{K3}\hat{r} + \theta_{23}\hat{P}_2 = T\hat{t} - \theta_{L3}E_U\hat{U} \tag{6.3.1.1}$$

where $T = (t/1+t)>0$; $E_W = ((\partial W^*/\partial W)(W/W^*)) > 0$ and $E_U = ((\partial W^*/\partial U)(U/W^*)) > 0$. E_W and E_U are the elasticities of the unionised wage rate, W^*, with respect to the informal sector wage rate, W, and the trade union bargaining power, U, respectively.

Solving Equations (6.1.1), (6.2.1) and (6.3.1.1) by Cramer's rule one gets the following expressions:

$$\hat{W} = -(\theta_{K1}/|\theta|)(T\hat{t} - \theta_{L3}E_U\hat{U}) \tag{6.9.1}$$

$$\hat{r} = (\theta_{L1}/|\theta|)(T\hat{t} - \theta_{L3}E_U\hat{U}) \tag{6.9.2}$$

$$\hat{P}_2 = \{(\theta_{L1}\theta_{K2} - \theta_{K1}\theta_{L2})/|\theta|\}(T\hat{t} - \theta_{L3}E_U\hat{U}) \tag{6.9.3}$$

$$(\hat{W} - \hat{r}) = -\{(T\hat{t} - \theta_{L3}E_U\hat{U})/|\theta|\} \tag{6.9.4}$$

where $|\theta| = \theta_{L1}(\theta_{K2}\theta_{23} + \theta_{K3}) - \theta_{K1}(\theta_{L2}\theta_{23} + \theta_{L3}E_W) > 0$ as the vertically integrated formal sector is more capital-intensive vis-à-vis the agricultural informal sector and $0<E_W\leq 1$[12].

Also total differentiation of Equation (6.7) and use of Equations (6.9.1) and (6.9.2) yield

$$(\hat{W}^* - \hat{r}) = (\theta_{L1}E_U\hat{U}/|\theta|) - (T\hat{t}/|\theta|)(\theta_{L1} + E_W\theta_{K1}) \tag{6.9.5}$$

Now total differentiation of Equations (6.4) and (6.5) and use of Equation (6.6) yield, respectively,

$$\lambda_{K1}\hat{X}_1 + (\lambda_{K2} + \lambda_{K3})\hat{X}_3 = \hat{K} + A\hat{t} - B\hat{U} \tag{6.10.1}$$

$$\lambda_{L1}\hat{X}_1 + (\lambda_{L2} + \lambda_{L3})\hat{X}_3 = C\hat{U} - D\hat{t} \tag{6.10.2}$$

where

$A = [(T/|\theta|)\{\lambda_{K1}\theta_{K1}\sigma_1 + \lambda_{K2}\theta_{L2}\sigma_2 + \lambda_{K3}\theta_{L3}\sigma_3(\theta_{L1} + E_W\theta_{K1})\}] > 0$;
$B = (\theta_{L3}E_U/|\theta|)[\lambda_{K1}\theta_{L1}\sigma_1 + \lambda_{K2}\theta_{L2}\sigma_2 + \lambda_{K3}\sigma_3\{|\theta| + \theta_{L3}(\theta_{L1} + E_W\theta_{K1})\}] > 0$;
and
$C = (E_U/|\theta|)[(\lambda_{L1}\theta_{K1}\sigma_1 + \lambda_{L2}\theta_{K2}\sigma_2)\theta_{L3} + \lambda_{L3}\theta_{K3}\sigma_3\{|\theta| + \theta_{L3}(\theta_{L1} + E_W\theta_{K1})\}] > 0$;
and
$D = [(T/|\theta|)\{\lambda_{L1}\theta_{K1}\sigma_1 + \lambda_{L2}\theta_{K2}\sigma_2 + \lambda_{L3}\theta_{K3}\sigma_3(\theta_{L1} + E_W\theta_{K1})\}] > 0$

[12] This means that W^* and W move in the same direction. But the proportionate change in W^* is not greater than that in W. This is only a sufficient condition to make $|\theta|>0$, which means that the vertically integrated import-competing sector is more capital-intensive than the export sector in value terms.

and σ_i is the elasticity of substitution between labour and capital in the ith sector. Solving Equations (6.10.1) and (6.10.2) by Cramer's rule one obtains

$$\hat{X}_3 = (1/|\lambda|)[-\lambda_{L1}\hat{K} + \hat{U}(C\lambda_{K1} + \lambda_{L1}B)\} - \hat{t}(D\lambda_{K1} + A\lambda_{L1}) \tag{6.11}$$

where $|\lambda| = [\lambda_{K1}(\lambda_{L2} + \lambda_{L3}) - \lambda_{L1}(\lambda_{K2} + \lambda_{K3})] < 0$ as the vertically integrated import-competing sector is more capital-intensive than the export sector (sector 1).

Now using Equation (6.5) we rewrite the welfare function given by Equation (6.8) as

$$Y = W + (W^* - W)a_{L3}X_3 + rK_{\mathrm{D}} - tP_3X_3 \tag{6.8.1}$$

Totally differentiating Equation (6.8.1) the following expression can be obtained:[13]

$$\begin{aligned}
Y\hat{Y} = {} & -\hat{K}\underset{(-)}{(\lambda_{L1}/|\lambda|)}[(W^* - W)\lambda_{L3} - tP_3X_3] \\
& + \hat{U}\underset{(+)}{E_U}[\underset{(+)}{(r\theta_{L1}\theta_{L3}K_F/|\theta|)} - \{(W^* - W)\lambda_{L3}\theta_{K3}\sigma_3/\underset{(+)(+)}{|\theta|\}}\{|\theta| + \theta_{L3}\underset{(+)}{(\theta_{L1} + E_W\theta_{K1})\}} \\
& + \{\underset{(+)}{(C\lambda_{K1} + B\lambda_{L1})}/\underset{(+)(-)}{E_U\ \lambda|\}}\{(W^* - W)\lambda_{L3} - tP_3X_3\}] \\
& - \hat{t}T[\underset{(+)}{(\theta_{L1}rK_F/|\theta|)} - \{(W^* - W)\lambda_{L3}\theta_{K3}\underset{(+)}{\sigma_3}\underset{(+)}{(\theta_{L1} + E_W\theta_{K1})}/|\theta|\} \\
& + \{\underset{(+)}{(D\lambda_{K1} + A\lambda_{L1})}/\underset{(-)}{T\ \lambda|\}}\{(W^* - W)\lambda_{L3} - tP_3X_3\}]
\end{aligned} \tag{6.12}$$

From Equation (6.12) it follows that

$$(\mathrm{d}Y/\mathrm{d}K) = -\underset{(-)}{(\lambda_{L1}/K|\lambda|)}[(W^* - W)\lambda_{L3} - tP_3X_3] \tag{6.12.1}$$

From Equation (6.12.1) the following proposition can be established.

Proposition 6.1 *An inflow of foreign capital in the presence of tariff is welfare-improving iff* $(W^* - W)\lambda_{L3} > t_3P_3X_3$. *In the absence of any tariff protection, welfare unequivocally improves due to foreign capital inflow.*

Equation (6.12.1) can be interpreted in terms of the labour-reallocation effect and the output (of the formal sector) effect. Since the system possesses the decomposition property, factor prices and hence factor coefficients remain unaltered owing to foreign capital inflow, with only a change in the output composition of the economy. As the vertically integrated formal sector is more capital-intensive vis-à-vis the agricultural informal sector, the former (latter) sector expands (contracts) due to Rybczynski effect. The informal manufacturing sector that produces a non-traded input for the formal sector expands too. As the import-competing formal sector is

[13] See Appendix 6.1 for detailed derivation of this expression.

protected by a tariff, its expansion raises the distortionary cost of protection and hence lowers welfare. We call it the output (of the formal sector) effect. Owing to changes in the output composition, labour reallocation between the sectors of the economy takes place, thereby affecting the aggregate wage income of the workers. As the higher wage-paying formal sector expands at the cost of the lower wage-paying agricultural informal sector, the aggregate wage income increases, and as a consequence the welfare of the economy measured by the national income at world prices also goes up. This may be called the labour-reallocation effect. The necessary and sufficient condition under which $(\mathrm{d}Y/\mathrm{d}K)>0$ is that $(W^* - W)\lambda_{L3} > t_3 P_3 X_3$. This in turn implies that $[-(\lambda_{L1}/K|\lambda|)(W^* - W)\lambda_{L3} > tP_3 X_3(\lambda_{L1}/K|\lambda|)]$. The left-hand side of the inequality is the magnitude of labour-reallocation effect arising from an inflow of foreign capital, while the right-hand side measures the output effect (of the formal sector). Thus, under the necessary and sufficient condition that the labour-reallocation effect is stronger than the output effect of the formal sector, an inflow of foreign capital is welfare-improving.

It may be noted that in the absence of any labour market distortions, the labour reallocation effect will be completely absent. There would not exist any gainful effect on welfare due to labour reallocation between the three sectors resulting from foreign capital inflow. Aggregate income of the workers would remain unaffected even though the formal sector expands. From Equation (6.12.1) it then follows that

$$(\mathrm{d}Y/\mathrm{d}K) = -(\lambda_{L1}/|\lambda|K)tP_3X_3 < 0.$$

Thus when the labour markets are perfect, welfare unambiguously falls owing to an expansion of the tariff-protected formal sector in consequence of foreign capital inflow. The presence of any labour market imperfection is a necessary condition[14] for welfare improvement in the existing set-up.

We now analyse the welfare consequences of tariff reduction[15] and/or formal sector reforms. Owing to tariff reform, the domestic price of the formal sector's product falls, leading to a contraction of the tariff-protected formal sector. Welfare increases due to an increase in the efficiency of production. But a tariff reduction also affects domestic factor incomes, which may have a bearing on the economy's welfare in the opposite direction. On the contrary, if the government as a part of its structural adjustment programmes intervenes in the formal sector labour market by

---

[14] It should be mentioned that if there are more than one distortion (one of it being tariff protection), an inflow of foreign capital might alleviate some distortion at the expense of aggravating others. So the conditions derived in the chapter may be specific to this model and to distortions chosen. The results may change if another distortion is added or substituted for another one. If, for example, we relax the assumption of perfectly competitive product market for commodity 3 and consider increasing returns to scale, embedded in a monopolistically competitive market, an inflow of foreign capital in the formal sector may increase welfare even with a perfect labour market. A labour market distortion would no longer be necessary to derive the result.

[15] In order to analyse the welfare consequence of a tariff reform, one should ideally measure welfare in terms of a strictly quasi-concave social welfare function as apart from the usual income effect there is also a price effect resulting from the change in relative prices of commodities to the consumers. See Section 2.3 in this context.

weakening the unions' ability to mark-up wages, the unionised wage rate decreases. The tariff-protected formal sector expands, which will affect the economy's welfare negatively by reducing the efficiency in production. However, factor incomes will also be affected. These two forces may not work on welfare in the same direction. Thus no definite conclusion can be drawn regarding the welfare effects of tariff or formal sector labour market reforms.

However, from Equation (6.12) it follows that

$$\begin{aligned}(\mathrm{d}Y/\mathrm{d}t) = -\{1/(1+t)\}[&(\underset{(+)}{\theta_{L1} r K_F/|\theta|})\\ &-\underset{(+)}{(W^* - W)}\lambda_{L3}\{(\theta_{K3}\sigma_3\underset{(+)}{(\theta_{L1} + E_W\theta_{K1})/|\theta|})\\ &-(\underset{(-)}{(D\lambda_{K1} + A\lambda_{L1})/T|\lambda|})\}\\ &-tP_3X_3\{\underset{(+)}{(D\lambda_{K1}} + \underset{(-)}{A\lambda_{L1})/T|\lambda|}\}]\end{aligned} \tag{6.12.2}$$

A reduction in tariff affects welfare of the economy by affecting both the aggregate factor income and the cost of tariff protection of the import-competing sector. As t is lowered, the domestic price of the formal sector's product falls. The rate of return on capital, r, falls too, which in turn raises the informal sector wage rate, W. As W rises the unionised wage rate, W^*, also rises. The wage–rental ratios in all the three sectors of the economy rise, forcing the producers to adopt more capital-intensive techniques of production. Given the output composition, adoption of more capital-intensive techniques means a shortage of capital leading to a contraction of both sectors 2 and 3 and an expansion of sector 1, as the vertically integrated import-competing sector is more capital-intensive vis-à-vis sector 1 in value terms. This produces a favourable effect on welfare since the cost of tariff protection now falls. However, there are other effects on welfare too. As t decreases the rental income from capital unequivocally falls. On the contrary, the effect on the aggregate wage income is somewhat uncertain. The aggregate wage income of the workers is affected due to (i) direct positive effects on W and W^* following a reduction in t and due to (ii) labour reallocation effect as the higher (lower) wage-paying formal (informal agricultural) sector contracts (expands). To sum up, a tariff reduction produces three different effects on welfare (national income at world prices): (i) factor income effect at given X_is (i.e. changes in aggregate factor income excluding the labour reallocation effect), which is encapsulated by the term $\{1/(1+t)\}\{\theta_{L1} r K_F/|\theta|\}$, (ii) effect on wage income resulting from reallocation of labour, captured by the expression $-\{1/(1+t)\}(W^* - W)\lambda_{L3}\{(\theta_{K3}\sigma_3(\theta_{L1} + E_W\theta_{K1})/|\theta|) - ((D\lambda_{K1} + A\lambda_{L1})/T|\lambda|)\}$; and (iii) outcome on cost of tariff protection resulting from output effect of the formal sector, given by the term $-\{1/(1+t)\}tP_3X_3\{(D\lambda_{K1} + A\lambda_{L1})/T|\lambda|)\}$. When the stock of foreign capital, K_F, is 0 the aggregate factor income at given X_is would not change. Then, welfare decreases owing to tariff reform if and only if the labour reallocation effect on aggregate wage income is stronger than the output effect of the formal sector. On the contrary, if the size of foreign capital stock of the economy is positive, aggregate factor income at the given product mix would increase and welfare improves under the sufficient condition that the labour reallocation effect on wage income is not greater than the output effect of the formal sector. Even if the former effect outweighs the latter, welfare may still improve if the foreign capital stock is sufficiently large. This establishes the following proposition.

Proposition 6.2 *A tariff reform in the absence of any foreign capital in the economy is welfare-deteriorating if and only if* $[(W^* - W)\lambda_{L3}\{(\theta_{K3}\sigma_3(\theta_{L1} + E_W\theta_{K1})/|\theta|) - ((D\lambda_{K1} + A\lambda_{L1})/T|\lambda|)\}] > -[tP_3X_3\{(D\lambda_{K1} + A\lambda_{L1})/T|\lambda|\}]$. *However, in the presence of foreign capital, welfare improves due to tariff reform if* $(\theta_{L1}rK_F/|\theta|) \geq [(W^* - W)\lambda_{L3}\{(\theta_{K3}\sigma_3(\theta_{L1} + E_W\theta_{K1})/|\theta|) - ((D\lambda_{K1} + A\lambda_{L1})/T|\lambda|)\}]$.

Now to study the welfare impact of any labour market reform, from Equation (6.12) it is easy to derive the following expression:

$$
\begin{aligned}
(\mathrm{d}Y/\mathrm{d}U) = (E_U/U)[&(r\theta_{L1}\theta_{L3}K_F/|\theta|) \\
&\qquad\qquad\quad (+) \\
&-(W^* - W)\lambda_{L3}\{(\theta_{K3}\sigma_3/|\theta|)(|\theta| + \theta_{L3}(\theta_{L1} + E_W\theta_{K1}) \\
&\qquad (+) \qquad\qquad\quad (+)(+) \qquad\qquad\qquad (+) \\
&-((C\lambda_{K1} + B\lambda_{L1})/E_U|\lambda|)\} \\
&\qquad\quad (+) \qquad (-) \\
&-tP_3X_3\{(C\lambda_{K1} + B\lambda_{L1})/E_U|\lambda|\}] \\
&\qquad\qquad\qquad (+) \qquad (-)
\end{aligned}
\tag{6.12.3}
$$

Owing to government's measures to curb trade union power, the bargaining power of the trade unions, denoted by U, falls, which results in a lowering of W^*, the formal sector wage rate. To satisfy the zero-profit condition in sector 3, the rental on capital, r, must rise. This lowers the informal sector wage rate, W, too. Production techniques in all the three sectors become more labour-intensive as the wage–rental ratio in each sector falls. Given the product mix, this must imply an excess of capital, resulting in an expansion of the formal sector and a contraction of the informal agricultural sector as the vertically integrated formal sector is more capital-intensive than the agricultural sector. Unless U becomes 0, W^* exceeds W. Thus an expansion (a contraction) of the higher (lower) wage-paying sector implies an increase in the total labour income unless the wage rates fall. But as the wage rates have fallen, the net effect on the income of the workers is ambiguous. Aggregate rental income on capital unambiguously rises as rate of return on capital rises. On the contrary, as the formal sector expands, the cost of tariff protection rises and works unfavourably on welfare. Here the positive effect on welfare due to labour reallocation effect is given by $[(E_U/U)(W^* - W)\lambda_{L3}\{(\theta_{K3}\sigma_3/|\theta|)(|\theta| + \theta_{L3}(\theta_{L1} + E_W\theta_{K1})) - ((C\lambda_{K1} + B\lambda_{L1})/E_U|\lambda|)\}]$. On the other hand, the negative impact on welfare arising from output effect (of the formal sector) is expressed as $[(E_U/U)(tP_3X_3\{(C\lambda_{K1} + B\lambda_{L1})/E_U|\lambda|\}]$. Finally, the net effect on aggregate factor income, excluding the labour reallocation effect, i.e. at given X_is, is given by the term $[(E_U/U)(r\theta_{L1}\theta_{L3}K_F/|\theta|)]$. We now note that in the absence of any foreign capital, aggregate factor income at given X_is does not change. So, welfare improves if and only if the labour reallocation effect on wage income is stronger than the formal sector output effect on cost of tariff protection. But in the presence of foreign capital the outcome of labour market reform is likely to get reversed. This leads to the following proposition.

Proposition 6.3 *Labour market reform is welfare-improving in the absence of any foreign capital if and only if* $[(W^* - W)\lambda_{L3}\{(\theta_{K3}\sigma_3/|\theta|)(|\theta| + \theta_{L3}(\theta_{L1} + E_W\theta_{K1})) - ((C\lambda_{K1} + B\lambda_{L1})/E_U|\lambda|)\}] > -[tP_3X_3\{(C\lambda_{K1} + B\lambda_{L1})/E_U|\lambda|\}]$ *However, in the presence of foreign capital welfare deteriorates owing to any labour market reform if* $[(r\theta_{L1}\theta_{L3}K_F/|\theta|)] \geq [(W^* - W)\lambda_{L3}\{(\theta_{K3}\sigma_3/|\theta|)(|\theta| + \theta_{L3}(\theta_{L1} + E_W\theta_{K1})) - ((C\lambda_{K1} + B\lambda_{L1})/E_U|\lambda|)\}]$.

6.3 Implications of the Derived Results

From Propositions 6.2 and 6.3, we note that the presence and magnitude of foreign capital in the small open economy plays a very crucial role in determining the outcome of tariff and labour market reform policies. On the other hand, the relative magnitude of the labour reallocation effect and output effect of the formal sector also affects the welfare consequences of the policies. So, what liberalisation policies are to be undertaken and to what extent hinges on three factors: (i) extent of labour reallocation effect between different sectors; (ii) magnitude of the output effect of the tariff-protected formal sector; and (iii) the size of foreign capital stock of the economy.

Now depending on different relative magnitude of the labour reallocation and formal sector output effects, we may come across two alternative situations in the given set-up. First, one may think about the case where the labour reallocation effect is weaker than the formal sector output effect. Let us start from a situation where $K_F = 0$. Then allow an inflow of foreign capital. In this case (d*Y*/d*K*) will be clearly negative. So an inflow of foreign capital will be immiserising. Besides, in such a scenario, labour market reform will also be counterproductive while only a tariff reform does improve welfare. Now if all these three liberalisation policies are undertaken concurrently, the net outcome is likely to be a sharp decline in welfare as the investment and labour market reforms work unfavourably on welfare while only a tariff reduction produces a favourable effect. Thus, in this case the policy makers of the economy should think twice before going in for liberalisation programmes. Second, there may be another case where the labour reallocation effect is stronger than the output effect of the formal sector. We again start with a situation where $K_F = 0$. An inflow of foreign capital now works favourably on welfare. When K_F is low, (d*Y*/d*t*)>0 and (d*Y*/d*U*)<0. This implies that tariff reform lowers welfare but labour market reform is welfare-improving. However, as K_F rises with foreign capital inflow, the negative (positive) effect of tariff (labour market) reform measure on welfare decreases. Once K_F reaches a particular value, say K_F^*, (d*Y*/d*t*) becomes 0 and for any $K_F > K_F^*$,$(dY/dt) < 0$. This implies that for all $K_F > K_F^*$, tariff reform will be welfare-improving. On the other hand, at another specific value of K_F, say K_F^{**}, (d*Y*/d*U*) becomes 0 and any further inflow of foreign capital makes labour market reform counterproductive. So, the economy must stop undertaking labour market liberalisation policies at that point, i.e. when $K_F = K_F^{**}$. But the country can continue with tariff and investment liberalisation measures as both of these produce favourable effects on welfare. Thus, it follows that a country ought not carry on with labour market reform measures beyond a certain point. This is also necessary[16] in the present system because the gainful effects of foreign capital are obtained only in the presence of labour market distortion. In other words, in the absence of any labour market distortion, there would be no positive effect on welfare due to reallocation of labour between different sectors. Hence, the liberalising country in question must implement labour market reform very cautiously. It must be kept in mind that if labour market distortion is removed beyond a certain limit, gainful effects of investment and trade liberalisation policies may not be achieved and in the extreme these may even be counterproductive.

6.4 An Extension: A Harris–Todaro Framework with Imperfect Labour and Capital Markets

In this section of the chapter we study the welfare consequences of the different trade and investment liberalisation policies in HT framework with an urban informal sector and in the presence of capital market distortion. We consider an HT economy where there are two broad sectors: rural and urban. The urban sector is further divided into two sub-sectors: urban formal sector and informal sector. Each of the three sectors of the economy produces an internationally traded final commodity[17] using labour and capital. The urban formal sector faces a unionised labour market but a perfect capital market. On the other hand, the urban informal sector and the rural sector have competitive labour markets but imperfect capital market. The urban formal sector is the tariff-protected import-competing sector, while the other two sectors produce two exportable commodities.

In addition to the symbols that we have used in the full-employment version of the analysis, we shall here use the following symbols as well:

W_1 = rural sector wage rate;
W_2 = urban informal sector wage rate;
W_3^* = unionised wage rate in the urban formal sector;
R = rate of return on capital in the informal capital market;
r = rate of return on capital in the formal capital market;
β = parameter denoting the degree of imperfection in the informal capital market, and $\beta > 1$; and
K_I = supply of capital to the informal capital market.

[16] This aspect has been discussed in details in footnote 14.

[17] The assumption that the urban informal sector produces a traded final commodity is a simplifying one. Grinols (1991), Chandra and Khan (1993) and Gupta (1997) have used this assumption. This helps us to make the production structure a decomposable one.

The general equilibrium is represented by the following set of equations:

$$W_1 a_{L1} + R a_{K1} = P_1 \tag{6.13}$$

$$W_2 a_{L2} + R a_{K1} = P_2 \tag{6.14}$$

$$W_3^*(W_2, U) a_{L3} + r a_{K3} = P_3(1 + t) \tag{6.15}$$

Equations (6.13), (6.14) and (6.15) are the price–unit cost equality conditions for the rural, urban informal and formal sectors, respectively. The unionised wage rate of the formal sector, W_3^*, is a positive function of both the informal sector wage rate, W_2, and the bargaining power of the trade unions, U. We assume the following functional relationship between R and r, the informal and formal sector interest rates, respectively:

$$R = \beta r; \quad \beta > 1 \tag{6.16}$$

Here β denotes the degree of isolation of the informal credit market. $\beta>1$ implies that $R>r$. Thus the informal rate of interest, R, increases as the degree of capital market imperfection, β, and/or the formal sector interest rate, r, increases. The informal sector lenders generally borrow funds from the formal capital market for re-lending. Alternatively, r could simply be the opportunity cost of lending funds. Hence, the informal interest rate, R, depends positively on the formal sector interest rate, r. On the other hand, informal credit markets are modelled either as monopolies (see, e.g. Bhaduri, 1977; Rudra, 1982; Basu, 1984, 1998) or as fragmented oligopolies (Basu and Bell, 1991; Mishra, 1994). According to both lines of thinking, lenders in the informal credit markets have sufficient control over most of the borrowers, especially the smaller group of borrowers. A borrower cannot get credit from any lender according to his desire. The lower the number of alternative sources of credit to the borrowers, the greater is the degree of isolation that exists in the informal credit market and greater is the power of the informal sector lenders to mark up interest rate over that prevailing in the formal credit market.

We assume that the amount of capital supplied to the informal capital market, K_{I}, is a positive function of the interest rate differential between the two capital markets. So we have

$$K_{\text{I}} = K_{\text{I}}(R - r); \quad \text{and,} \quad K_{\text{I}} > (=)0 \quad \text{when } (R - r) > (=)0; \; K_{\text{I}}'(.) > 0 \tag{6.17}$$

We introduce a dichotomy between the two capital markets in this way[18]. Equation (6.17) implies that the informal capital market exists only in the presence of an interest rate differential between the two capital markets. However, it should be noted that so long as imperfection in the informal capital market exists, i.e. $\beta>1$, the interest rate differential exists and ensures the existence of the informal

[18] Another way of introducing capital market dichotomy has been discussed in Section 3.7.

capital market. This assumption is consistent with the lender's risk hypothesis, as explained by Bottomley (1975). According to this theory, an informal sector lender always suffers from the risk of default of loans advanced by him and the risk of default rises with loan volume. So it is rational for him to advance credit to informal sector borrowers only if the interest rate differential exists. The larger the interest rate differential between the two credit markets, the higher would be the amount of credit supplied to the informal capital market.

Informal credit is used by the rural and the urban informal sectors. So the complete utilisation of informal credit implies that

$$a_{K1}X_1 + a_{K2}X_2 = K_{\mathrm{I}} \tag{6.18}$$

The urban formal sector uses formal credit. Formal credit market equilibrium is given by

$$a_{K3}X_3 = K - K_{\mathrm{I}} \tag{6.19}$$

The labour endowment equation is as follows:

$$a_{L1}X_1 + a_{L2}X_2 + a_{L3}X_3 = 1 \tag{6.20}$$

Finally, the Harris–Todaro migration equilibrium condition is given by

$$(W_3^*/W_1)a_{L3}X_3 + (W_2/W_1)a_{L2}X_2 + a_{L1}X_1 = 1 \tag{6.21}$$

This extended model also possesses the decomposition property. So, factor prices are determined from the price system alone, namely from Equations (6.13), (6.14) and (6.15). Equation (6.18) is not an independent equation. Equation (6.16) determines R once r is known. K_{I} is found from Equation (6.17). Given K_{I}, X_3 is obtained from Equation (6.19). Once X_3 is known, X_1 and X_2 are found from Equations (6.20) and (6.21).

The expression for national income at world prices is given by

$$Y = W_1 + rK_D + (R - r)K_{\mathrm{I}} - tP_3X_3 \tag{6.22}$$

where W_1 is the aggregate wage income of the workers as the labour endowment has been normalised to unity. Besides, rK_{D} and $(R–r)K_{\mathrm{I}}$ denote rental incomes from domestic capital stock employed in the formal and informal capital markets, respectively. The deadweight loss to the society due to tariff is once again given by tP_3X_3.

To derive comparative static results, totally differentiating Equations (6.13)–(6.15) and using Equation (6.16) the following expressions are obtained:

$$\left.\begin{aligned}&\hat{r} = (1/\Delta)\theta_{L2}(T\hat{t} - E_U\theta_{L3}\hat{U}); \hat{W}_2 = -(\theta_{K2}/\Delta)(T\hat{t} - E_U\theta_{L3}\hat{U});\\&\hat{W}_3^* = (E_U\theta_{L2}\theta_{K3}/\Delta)\hat{U} - (E_W\theta_{K2}T/\Delta)\hat{t}; \hat{W}_1 = -(\theta_{K1}\theta_{L2}/\theta_{L1}\Delta)(T\hat{t} - E_U\theta_{L3}\hat{U})\end{aligned}\right\} \tag{6.23}$$

where $\Delta = \theta_{L2}\theta_{K3} - E_W\theta_{K2}\theta_{L3} > 0$ as the urban formal sector is more capital-intensive than the informal sector in value terms and $T = (t/(1+t)) > 0$.

Again totally differentiating Equation (6.19) and using Equations (6.16), (6.17) and (6.23), it is easy to derive the following:

$$\hat{X}_3 = (\hat{K}/\lambda_{K3}) + (T/\Delta)\hat{t}[\theta_{L3}\sigma_3(\theta_{L2} + E_W\theta_{K2}) - \{K_{\mathrm{I}}'(.)r(\beta - 1)\theta_{L2}/\lambda_{K3}K\}] \\ - (\theta_{L3}E_U/\Delta)\hat{U}[\theta_{L2}\sigma_3 - \{K_{\mathrm{I}}'(.)r(\beta - 1)\theta_{L2}/\lambda_{K3}K\}] \tag{6.24}$$

Differentiating Equation (6.22) with respect to K, t and U and using Equation (6.24), the following expressions are obtained, respectively:

$$\left.\begin{aligned}
(\mathrm{d}Y/\mathrm{d}K) &= -tP_3(X_3/K\lambda_{K3}) < 0;\\
(\mathrm{d}Y/\mathrm{d}t) &= (\theta_{L2}Tr/t\Delta)[\{(K_{\mathrm{D}} + (\beta - 1)K_{\mathrm{I}}(.) + r(\beta - 1)^2K_{\mathrm{I}}'(.))\} - (a_{K1}/a_{L1})]\\
&\quad -P_3X_3[1 + (T/\Delta)\{\theta_{L3}\sigma_3(\theta_{L2} + E_W\theta_{K2})\} - \{K_{\mathrm{I}}'(.)r(\beta - 1)\theta_{L2}/K\lambda_{K3}\}]\\
(\mathrm{d}Y/\mathrm{d}U) &= (\theta_{L2}E_U\theta_{L3}r/\Delta U)[(a_{K1}/a_{L1}) - \{(K_D + (\beta - 1)K_{\mathrm{I}}(.) + r(\beta - 1)^2K_{\mathrm{I}}'(.))\}]\\
&\quad + tP_3(X_3\theta_{L3}E_U\theta_{L2}/\Delta U)[\sigma_3 - \{K_{\mathrm{I}}'(.)r(\beta - 1)/K\lambda_{K3}\}]
\end{aligned}\right\} \tag{6.25}$$

In Equation (6.25) we find that the sign of the term, $[\{(K_{\mathrm{D}} + (\beta - 1)K_{\mathrm{I}}(.) + r(\beta - 1)^2K_{\mathrm{I}}'(.))\} - (a_{K1}/a_{L1})]$, is likely to be positive unless the stock of foreign capital in the initial aggregate capital endowment of the economy is sufficiently large. This is because of the following reasons. In an HT framework with informal sector, the rural sector is less (more) capital-intensive than the urban formal (informal) sector as $W_2 < W_1 < W_3^*$ and $R>r$. Therefore, it follows that $(a_{K3}/a_{L3}) > (a_{K1}/a_{L1}) > (a_{K2}/a_{L2})$. According to the capital-intensity condition of Chandra and Khan (1993), (a_{K1}/a_{L1}) is less than the aggregate capital–labour ratio of the urban sector (formal plus informal). Also, the capital intensity of the rural sector is less than, while that of the urban sector is greater than, the overall capital–labour ratio of the economy, (K).[19] But the overall capital–labour ratio is measured with respect to the aggregate capital stock of the economy that includes foreign capital apart from domestic capital, K_{D}. Hence, $\{(K_{\mathrm{D}} + (\beta - 1)K_{\mathrm{I}}(.) + r(\beta - 1)^2K_{\mathrm{I}}'(.))\} > (a_{K1}/a_{L1})$, unless the country has a sufficiently large amount of foreign capital at the initial equilibrium. If this is the case, from Equation (6.25) we find that $(\mathrm{d}Y/\mathrm{d}t)>0$ under the sufficient condition that $[1 + (T/\Delta)\{\theta_{L3}\sigma_3(\theta_{L2} + E_W\theta_{K2})\} - \{K_{\mathrm{I}}'(.)r(\beta - 1)\theta_{L2}/K\lambda_{K3}\}] \leq 0$. Besides, $(\mathrm{d}Y/\mathrm{d}U)<0$ if $[\sigma_3 \leq \{K_{\mathrm{I}}'(.)r(\beta - 1)K\lambda_{K3}\}]$. On the other hand, $(\mathrm{d}Y/\mathrm{d}K)<0$ irrespective of any condition. This establishes the following proposition.

Proposition 6.4 *An inflow of foreign with full repatriation of income on foreign capital is always immiserising in the existing set-up. Also a tariff reform lowers welfare of the economy if* $[1+(T/\Delta)\{\theta_{L3}\sigma_3(\theta_{L2}+E_W\theta_{K2})\}-\{K_{\mathrm{I}}'(.)r(\beta-1)\theta_{L2}/K\lambda_{K3}\}] \leq 0$. *On the contrary, a labour market reform is welfare-improving if* $[\sigma_3 \leq \{K_{\mathrm{I}}'(.)r(\beta - 1)K\lambda_{K3}\}]$.

19 Note that the labour endowment has been normalised to unity. So K gives the capital–labour ratio of the economy.

We explain Proposition 6.4 as follows. A major difference between the full-employment and the HT cases is that in the former case any policy change has a labour reallocation effect on welfare, while in the latter there is no such effect owing to the envelope property of the HT framework. An inflow of foreign capital cannot affect the factor prices but leads to an expansion of the tariff-protected urban formal sector. As the protected sector expands, the deadweight loss to the society due to a tariff protection rises and as a consequence welfare decreases. On the other hand, a reduction in tariff lowers the return to capital and raises the wage rates in the different sectors of the economy. Aggregate factor income of the economy falls unless the magnitude of foreign capital in the aggregate capital stock of the economy is sufficiently large at the initial equilibrium. Besides, producers in the different sectors of the economy adopt more capital-intensive techniques of production including the urban formal sector leading to increases in the a_{Ki}s. But as r falls $(R–r)$ falls too, resulting in a decrease (an increase) in the supply of capital to the informal (formal) capital market. So two opposite effects on X_3 are generated. An increase in a_{K3} lowers X_3 given the supply of capital to the formal capital market, $(K–K_I(.))$, while an increase in the latter raises X_3, given a_{K3}. If the sufficient condition $[1 + (T/\Delta)\{\theta_{L3}\sigma_3(\theta_{L2} + E_W\theta_{K2})\} - \{K_I'(.)r(\beta - 1)\theta_{L2}/K\lambda_{K3}\}] \leq 0$ is satisfied, X_3 and hence the cost of tariff protection do not fall. The consequence would be a deterioration in welfare of the economy. On the contrary, any labour market reform that lowers the bargaining strength of the trade unions lowers the wage rates and raises the return to capital. Aggregate factor income in this case rises if the magnitude of foreign capital in the economy is not sufficiently high. Also a_{Ki}s fall and the supply of capital to the informal (formal) capital market rises (falls). Again there would be two opposite effects on X_3. Both X_3 and the cost of tariff protection, tP_3X_3, do not rise under the sufficient condition that $[\sigma_3 \leq \{K_I'(.)r(\beta - 1)K\lambda_{K3}\}]$.

6.5 Policy Implications of Results of the Extended Model

We now try to explain the welfare consequences of different liberalisation policies, if undertaken concurrently. Let us start from a situation where the stock of foreign capital, denoted by K_F, is 0. Then we have $[\{(K_D + (\beta - 1)K_I(.) + r(\beta - 1)^2 K_I'(.))\} > (a_{K1}/a_{L1})]$. The magnitude of $K\lambda_{K3}$ would be relatively low and it is quite probable that the two sufficient conditions required to make $(dY/dt)>0$ and $(dY/dU)<0$ are satisfied. In such a case, any tariff reform is welfare-deteriorating while a labour market reform is welfare-improving. Now allow inflow of foreign capital. Welfare deteriorates due to growth with foreign capital. Also as the magnitude of foreign capital increases due to capital inflow, the possibility of the above capital intensity condition and the two sufficient conditions to hold diminishes. Along with this, the absolute magnitudes of (dY/dt) and (dY/dU) fall. There exist two critical levels of foreign capital for which (dY/dt) and (dY/dU) would be zero, respectively. If K_F exceeds those critical values a tariff reform would be welfare–improving, while a labour market deregulation policy would be counterproductive. So in the HT framework too, welfare outcomes of tariff and labour market reforms crucially depend on the presence and magnitude of the foreign capital in the liberalising country. But we should note that unlike the full-employment case, there is no labour reallocation effect in the HT case and that an inflow of foreign capital is always immiserising in the presence of a tariff.

Empirical evidence points out that trade and investment liberalisation has so far failed to provide any substantial welfare gains to the liberalising countries. Why liberalised trade and investment policies have not so far been successful in taking the developing countries into higher growth orbits is quite puzzling. One possible explanation may be that the liberalising countries have tried to free their economy in every possible way and at a very brisk pace, without pre-calculating their possible outcomes. Whether a country should follow every aspect of the WTO-prescribed policy package is an important question. We have found that an inflow of foreign capital is desirable only if there exists a certain degree of labour market distortion. So, the labour market reform, which aims at reduction of labour market distortion, a common characteristic of the developing countries, must be undertaken very cautiously. If labour market distortion is removed beyond a certain limit, gainful effects of investment liberalisation policy cannot be achieved and in the extreme cases this may even be counterproductive. On the other hand, a tariff reform measure has been found to be relatively safe in the existing set-up. In the Harris–Todaro setting, an inflow of foreign capital has been found to be immiserising. The welfare consequences of tariff and labour market reforms have been found to depend crucially on the presence and magnitude of foreign capital in the economy. If the magnitude of foreign capital is relatively small, deregulation of the labour market is likely to produce a favourable effect on national welfare while a tariff reform will be counterproductive. But these results are likely to get reversed in the presence of substantial amount of foreign capital in the economy. We, therefore, conclude that there may not be any need for a liberalising country to follow all the recommendations of the WTO, without taking into consideration the net outcome of these policies on national welfare. What policies to be followed and up to which limit will depend crucially on the institutional and technological characteristics and the trade pattern of the relevant country. Unless, a proper choice among different prescribed policies is made, implementation of reform measures may produce counterproductive result on welfare of a developing country.

Appendix 6.1: Derivation of Equation (6.12)

Totally differentiating Equation (6.8.1) the following expression can be obtained:

$$\mathrm{d}Y = \mathrm{d}W + (\mathrm{d}W^* - \mathrm{d}W)a_{L3}X_3 + (W^* - W)a_{L3}\mathrm{d}X_3 + (W^* - W)X_3\mathrm{d}a_{L3} + K_{\mathrm{D}}\mathrm{d}r - P_3X_3\mathrm{d}t - tP_3\mathrm{d}X_3$$

$$\text{or, } Y\hat{Y} = [W\hat{W} + (W^*\hat{W}^* - W\hat{W})\lambda_{L3}] + (W^* - W)\lambda_{L3}(\hat{a}_{L3} + \hat{X}_3) + rK_{\mathrm{D}}\hat{r} - tP_3X_3(\hat{t} + \hat{X}_3)$$

Using Equations (6.9.1), (6.9.2), (6.9.4), (6.9.5) and (6.11) the above expression becomes

$$\begin{aligned}
Y\hat{Y} = & -(\theta_{K1}/|\theta|)(T\hat{t} - \theta_{L3}E_U\hat{U})\{W(1-\lambda_{L3}) + \lambda_{L3}W^*E_W\} + \lambda_{L3}E_U W^*\hat{U} \\
& + (W^* - W)\lambda_{L3}[-\theta_{K3}\sigma_3\{E_U\hat{U}(1 + \theta_{L3}(\theta_{L1} + E_W\theta_{K1})/|\theta|) - (T/|\theta|)(\theta_{L1} \\
& + E_W\theta_{K1})\hat{t}\} \\
& + (1/|\lambda|)\{-\lambda_{L1}\hat{K} + \hat{U}(C\lambda_{K1} + B\lambda_{L1}) - \hat{t}(D\lambda_{K1} + A\lambda_{L1})\}] \\
& + (rK_D/|\theta|)T\hat{t} - \theta_{L3}E_U\hat{U})\theta_{L1} - tP_3X_3\hat{t} \\
& - (tP_3X_3/|\lambda|)\{-\lambda_{L1}\hat{K} + \hat{U}(C\lambda_{K1} + B\lambda_{L1}) - \hat{t}(D\lambda_{K1} + A\lambda_{L1})\} \\
= & -(\lambda_{L1}/|\lambda|)\hat{K}[(W^* - W)\lambda_{L3} - tP_3X_3] \\
& + E_U\hat{U}[(\theta_{K1}\theta_{L3}/|\theta|)\{W(1-\lambda_{L3}) + \lambda_{L3}W^*E_W\} + W^*\lambda_{L3} \\
& - (W^* - W)\lambda_{L3}\theta_{K3}\sigma_3\{1 + \theta_{L3}(\theta_{L1} + E_W\theta_{K1})/|\theta|\} + \{(W^* \\
& - W)\lambda_{L3}/E_U|\lambda|\}(C\lambda_{K1} + B\lambda_{L1}) \\
& - (rK_D\theta_{L3}\theta_{L1}/|\theta|) - (tP_3X_3/E_U|\lambda|)(C\lambda_{K1} + B\lambda_{L1})] \\
& - T\hat{t}[(\theta_{K1}/|\theta|)\{W(1-\lambda_{L3}) + \lambda_{L3}W^*E_W\} - \{(W^* - W)\lambda_{L3}\theta_{K3}\sigma_3(\theta_{L1} \\
& + E_W\theta_{K1})/|\theta|\} \\
& + \{(W^* - W)\lambda_{L3}/T|\lambda|\}(D\lambda_{K1} + A\lambda_{L1}) - (rK_D\theta_{L1}/|\theta|) + (tP_3X_3/T) \\
& - (tP_3X_3/T|\lambda|)(D\lambda_{K1} + A\lambda_{L1})]
\end{aligned} \tag{6.A.1}$$

Now $[(\theta_{K1}\theta_{L3}/|\theta|)\{W(1-\lambda_{L3}) + \lambda_{L3}W^*E_W\} + W^*\lambda_{L3} - (rK_D\theta_{L3}\theta_{L1}/|\theta|)]$

$$\begin{aligned}
= & (1/|\theta|)[\theta_{K1}\theta_{L3}W(1-\lambda_{L3}) + W^*\lambda_{L3}\{(\theta_{L1}\theta_{K2} - \theta_{K1}\theta_{L2})\theta_{23} + \theta_{L1}\theta_{K3}\} \\
& - rK_D\theta_{L3}\theta_{L1}] \\
= & (1/|\theta|)[\theta_{K1}\theta_{L3}W(1-\lambda_{L3}) + W^*\lambda_{L3}\{(\theta_{L1} - \theta_{L2})\theta_{23} + \theta_{L1}\theta_{K3}\} - rK_D\theta_{L3}\theta_{L1}] \\
= & (1/|\theta|)[(ra_{K1}/P_1)(W^*a_{L3}/P_3^*)W(a_{L1}X_1 + a_{L2}X_2) \\
& + W^*a_{L3}X_3\{(Wa_{L1}/P_1)(P_2a_{23}/P_3^*) \\
& - (Wa_{L2}/P_2)(P_2a_{23}/P_3^*) + (Wa_{L1}/P_1)(ra_{K3}/P_3^*)\} - rK_D(W^*a_{L3}/P_3^*)(Wa_{L1}/P_1)] \\
= & (WW^*a_{L3}/P_1P_3^*|\theta|)[ra_{K1}(a_{L1}X_1 + a_{L2}X_2) + X_3\{a_{L1}P_2(X_2/X_3) - a_{L2}(X_2/X_3)P_1 \\
& + ra_{L1}a_{K3}\} - rK_Da_{L1}] \\
= & (WW^*a_{L3}/P_1P_3^*|\theta|)[ra_{K1}(a_{L1}X_1 + a_{L2}X_2) + a_{L1}P_2X_2 - a_{L2}X_2P_1 + ra_{L1}a_{K3}X_3 \\
& - rK_Da_{L1}] \\
= & (WW^*a_{L3}/P_1P_3^*|\theta|)[a_{L2}X_2(ra_{K1} - P_1) + ra_{L1}(a_{K1}X_1 + a_{K3}X_3) + a_{L1}P_2X_2 \\
& - rK_Da_{L1}] \\
= & (WW^*a_{L3}/P_1P_3^*|\theta|)[a_{L1}X_2(P_2 - Wa_{L2}) + ra_{L1}(a_{K1}X_1 + a_{K3}X_3) - rK_Da_{L1}] \\
= & (WW^*ra_{L1}a_{L3}/P_1P_3^*|\theta|)[a_{K1}X_1 + a_{K2}X_2 + a_{K3}X_3) - K_D] \\
= & (\theta_{L3}\theta_{L1}r/|\theta|)K_F
\end{aligned} \tag{6.A.2}$$

Again,

$$
\begin{aligned}
&[(\theta_{K1}/|\theta|)\{W(1-\lambda_{L3})+\lambda_{L3}W^*E_W\}-(rK_D\theta_{L1}/|\theta|)+(tP_3X_3/T)]\\
&=[(\theta_{K1}/|\theta|)\{W(1-\lambda_{L3})+\lambda_{L3}W^*E_W\}+(1+t)P_3X_3-(rK_D\theta_{L1}/|\theta|)]\\
&=(1/|\theta|)[(\theta_{K1}\{W(1-\lambda_{L3})+\lambda_{L3}W^*E_W\}+P_3^*X_3\theta_{L1}(\theta_{K2}\theta_{23}+\theta_{K3})\\
&\quad -P_3^*X_3\theta_{K1}(\theta_{L2}\theta_{23}+\theta_{L3}E_W)-rK_D\theta_{L1}]\\
&=(1/|\theta|)[(ra_{K1}/P_1)\{W(1-\lambda_{L3})+\lambda_{L3}W^*E_W\}\\
&\quad +P_3^*X_3(Wa_{L1}/P_1)\{(ra_{K2}/P_2)(P_2a_{23}/P_3^*)\\
&\quad +(ra_{K3}/P_3^*)\}-P_3^*X_3(ra_{K1}/P_1)\{(Wa_{L2}/P_2)(P_2a_{23}/P_3^*)+(W^*a_{L3}E_W/P_3^*)\}\\
&\quad -rK_D(a_{L1}W/P_1)]\\
&=(r/P_1|\theta|)[a_{K1}\{W(a_{L1}X_1+a_{L2}X_2)+a_{L3}X_3W^*E_W\}+Wa_{L1}(a_{K2}X_2+a_{K3}X_3)\\
&\quad -a_{K1}(Wa_{L2}X_2+W^*a_{L3}X_3E_W)-a_{L1}WK_D]\\
&=(Wra_{L1}/P_1|\theta|)[a_{K1}X_1+a_{K2}X_2+a_{K3}X_3-K_D]\\
&=(\theta_{L1}rK_F/|\theta|)
\end{aligned}
\tag{6.A.3}
$$

Now by Equations (6.A.1), (6.A.2) and (6.A.3) we can write

$$
\begin{aligned}
Y\hat{Y}=&-(\lambda_{L1}/|\lambda|)[(W^*-W)\lambda_{L3}-tP_3X_3]\\
&+E_U\hat{U}[(\theta_{L3}\theta_{L1}r/|\theta|)K_F-\{(W^*-W)\lambda_{L3}\theta_{K3}\sigma_3/|\theta|\}\{|\theta|+\theta_{L3}(\theta_{L1}\\
&+E_W\theta_{K1})\}+\{(C\lambda_{K1}+B\lambda_{L1})/E_U|\lambda|\}\{(W^*-W)\lambda_{L3}-tP_3X_3\}]\\
&-T\hat{t}[(\theta_{L1}rK_F/|\theta|)-\{(W^*-W)\lambda_{L3}\theta_{K3}\sigma_3(\theta_{L1}+E_W\theta_{K1})/|\theta|\}\\
&+\{(D\lambda_{K1}+A\lambda_{L1})/T|\lambda|\}\{(W^*-W)\lambda_{L3}-tP_3X_3\}]
\end{aligned}
\tag{6.12}
$$

Chapter 7
Economic Liberalisation, Informal Wage and Skilled–Unskilled Wage Inequality

7.1 Introduction

Informal labour market characterised by competitive wage formation rather than unionised process of negotiations has emerged as an important institution in the entire developing world. The ongoing process of economic reforms has boosted significantly the role played by informal sectors in determining the pattern of employment in the developing countries. Many of the developing countries have been facing substantial adjustment costs in implementing economic liberalisation programmes, particularly in the employment front. Empirical evidence suggests that in South Africa and in many of the Latin American and other developing countries, trade liberalisation during the 1990s was associated with falling employment and hence economic insecurity for the formal sector labour force (ILO, 2006). Reformatory policies lead to contraction of the formal manufacturing sector and drive labour out into the informal segment of the labour market. Empirical studies[1] have reported that the size of the informal sector in the developing countries has increased considerably in the post-reform period. But the expanding informal sector has not been able to absorb the huge number of retrenched workers from the formal sector. The consequence has been a steep rise in the level of open unemployment in many of the developing economies.

When the size of the informal sector in the developing countries is increasing at a brisk pace, it is important to know how the liberalised economic policies have affected the working conditions and welfare of the informal sector workforce. As economic well-being of the workers and wage earnings are strongly correlated, the issue boils down to the study of the consequences of economic reforms on the informal sector wage. There are not enough direct empirical evidences as yet in understanding clearly the direction of movement of the informal sector wages in response to economic reforms. While Bhalotra (2002) reports that the real wage in the informal manufacturing sector has increased in the period of reforms, empirical studies of Khan (1998) and Tendulkar et al. (1996) have found that the incidence of

[1] See, for example, Bhalotra (2002), Dev (2000), ILO (2006) and Leite et al. (2006).

S. Chaudhuri, U. Mukhopadhyay, *Revisiting the Informal Sector*,
DOI 10.1007/978-1-4419-1194-0_7,

poverty has increased in India in the post-reform period. As informal sector workers belong to the poorer section of the population, an increase in poverty implies deterioration in their wage earnings. Besides, Leite et al. (2006) have reported a significant decrease in average real wage for informal workers in South Africa during 2000–2004.

The enormous theoretical literature on the informal sector[2] has not adequately addressed this aspect. An important exception in this context is Marjit (2003) who has examined the outcome of trade liberalisation on the informal wage using a three-sector general equilibrium model with two informal sectors. In his model one of the two informal sectors produces a non-traded input for the formal sector and capital is mobile only between the two informal sectors of the economy. Marjit (2003) has found that trade liberalisation may increase the informal sector wage under certain conditions. He argues that the positive effect on the informal wage would be strengthened if capital mobility between the informal and the formal sectors is allowed.

It should be pointed out that economic reforms involve not only removal of the protectionist policy but also liberalised investment policy resulting in inflows of foreign capital and structural reforms like deregulating the labour market. But liberalisation of labour laws is a politically sensitive issue. It is apprehended by the trade unions that any relaxation of labour laws will lead to general wage reductions[3] of the poorer group of the working population engaged in the informal sector of the economy[4]. Two other important aspects in this context are the empirical findings that the informal sector firms mainly produce intermediate inputs for the formal sector firms under the system of subcontracting and that capital is mobile between

---

[2]This includes works of Chandra and Khan (1993), Gupta (1993, 1997), Beladi and Yabuuchi (2001), Kar and Marjit (2001), Chaudhuri (2000, 2003), Chaudhuri and Mukherjee (2002), Chaudhuri et al. (2006), etc. But, none of these papers has exclusively examined the consequences of economic reforms on the wage rate and the well-being of the informal sector labour force and the role of the capital mobility between the formal and the informal sectors in this context.

[3]The firms in the urban (manufacturing) sector have well-organised trade unions. One of the most important roles of the labour unions is to bargain with the respective employers with respect to the betterment of the working conditions. Through offer of negotiation, threat of strike, actual strike, etc. they exert pressure on the employers (firms) in order to secure higher wages, reduced hours of work, share in profits and other benefits. Bhalotra (2002) has noted that in India before the initiation of economic reforms organised workers in large firms were able to reap wages higher than the supply price of labour due to the job security and minimum wage legislations. The higher the bargaining strength of the unions, the higher is expected to be the extent of benefits that can be wrested through collective bargaining. Now if the government undertakes measures, e.g. partial or complete ban on resorting to strikes by the trade unions, reformation of employment security laws to curb union power, the unions' power to mark up wages over the supply of labour decreases. The consequence would, therefore, be a fall in the unionised wage.

[4] Many of the developing countries, including India, are now seriously thinking in terms of implementing labour market reforms. But not much progress has been made so far towards implementation of such a highly politically sensitive measure and hence the outcome of this on the unionised wage cannot be statistically established a priori.

these two types of firms[5]. Three pertinent questions, therefore, are as follows: (i) Do different liberalised policies produce disparate effects on the informal wage? (ii) How far is the general apprehension that labour market reforms depress the informal wage valid? (iii) Do the consequences of economic reform really hinge on the nature of capital mobility between the formal and the informal sectors of the economy?

In the next section we attempt to provide answers to the above questions in terms of a three-sector general equilibrium model with two informal sectors.

7.2 Economic Liberalisation, Capital Mobility and Informal Wage

We consider a small open economy with three sectors: two traded sectors and one non-traded sector.[6] Sector 1 produces a primary agricultural commodity, X_1, using labour and land. Sector 2 produces a non-traded input for sector 3 using labour and one of the two inputs: land and capital. Finally, sector 3 (formal sector) may be either an agro-based industry or a manufacturing industry that uses labour, capital and the product of sector 2 to produce a final industrial commodity. So, we consider two cases depending on the nature of goods produced by sector 3. In the former case, sector 2 produces a commercial agricultural crop for the formal sector using only labour and land, while in the latter it produces a manufacturing intermediate input with the help of labour and capital. However, for constructing a general model from which the two cases arise as sub-cases, we assume that sector 2 uses both land and capital in its production. Sector 1 is the export sector while sector 3 is the import-competing sector protected by an import tariff.

The per-unit requirement of the intermediate input is assumed to be technologically fixed in sector 3.[7] Let us now assume that labour in the formal sector earns a contractual wage, W^*, while the wage rate in the two informal sectors, W, is market determined. So, labour is perfectly mobile between the two informal sectors but is imperfectly mobile between sector 3 and the rest of the economy. Land (capital) is perfectly mobile between sector 1 (sector 3) and sector 2 if sector 2 uses land (capital) while it is specific to sector 1 (sector 3) in the case where sector 2 produces a manufacturing (an agricultural) input for sector 3. The capital stock of the economy includes both domestic and foreign capital and these are perfect substitutes. Production functions exhibit constant returns to scale with diminishing marginal productivity to each factor. All inputs are fully employed. Owing to our small open economy assumption, we consider the prices of the commodities of sectors 1 and 3

[5] See Papola (1981), Romatet (1983), Sethuraman (1984), Sethuraman and Maldonado (1992), etc. in this context.

[6] This section is based on Chaudhuri and Banerjee (2007).

[7] It rules out the possibility of substitution between the non-traded input and other factors of production in sector 3. The rationale of this assumption has been discussed in earlier chapters.

to be given internationally while the price of the non-traded input produced in sector 2 is endogenously determined. Finally, commodity 1 is chosen as the numeraire.

Given the assumption of perfectly competitive markets, the usual price–unit cost equality conditions relating to the three sectors of the economy are given by the following three equations, respectively:

$$Wa_{L1} + Ra_{N1} = 1 \tag{7.1}$$

$$Wa_{L2} + Ra_{N2} + ra_{K2} = P_2 \tag{7.2}$$

$$W^*a_{L3} + ra_{K3} + P_2a_{23} = P_3(1+t) \tag{7.3}$$

where W, W^*, R, r and P_2 denote informal wage, unionised wage in the formal sector, return to land, return to capital and the price of the non-traded input produced by the informal sector, respectively.

Full utilisation of labour, land and capital imply the following three equations, respectively:

$$a_{L1}X_1 + a_{L2}X_2 + a_{L3}X_3 = L \tag{7.4}$$

$$a_{N1}X_1 + a_{N2}X_2 = N \tag{7.5}$$

$$a_{K2}X_2 + a_{k3}X_3 = K \tag{7.6}$$

where L, N and K are the endowments of labour, land and capital (domestic plus foreign), respectively, of the economy. X_i is the output of the ith sector and t is the ad valorem rate of tariff on the import of commodity 3.

The output of the informal sector, X_2, is used entirely for producing X_3, so that the supply of X_2 is circumscribed by its total demand by sector 3. The demand–supply equality condition is given by

$$X_2 = X_2^D = a_{23}X_3 \tag{7.7}$$

There are seven endogenous variables in the system: W, R, r, P_2, X_1, X_2 and X_3. The policy parameters are t, W^* and K. There are seven independent equations (7.1)–(7.7). The price system consists of Equations (7.1)–(7.3). The model does not satisfy the decomposition property. The working of the model is as follows. W, R and r are obtained from Equations (7.1) to (7.3) as functions of P_2 as W^*, P_3 and t are given exogenously. Once factor prices are determined, factor coefficients, a_{ji}s, are also determined as functions of P_2. Then from Equations (7.4) to (7.6), X_1, X_2 and X_3 are obtained. Finally, P_2 is found from Equation (7.7). Once P_2 is obtained the equilibrium values of all the endogenous variables are now found in terms of the parameters of the model.

Differentiating Equations (7.1)–(7.7), solving and using the stability condition in the market for the non-traded commodity, the final expression for $\hat{W}$ is derived.[8] Depending on the nature of the non-traded goods produced by sector 2 and the nature of capital mobility between the formal and the informal sectors, two cases are possible.

Sub-case I: Sector 2 produces an agricultural input for the formal sector and hence uses land and does not use capital. In this case there is complete mobility of land between the two informal sectors while capital is a specific input in sector 3. These imply that $a_{K2}, \lambda_{K2}, \theta_{K2} = 0$; $\lambda_{K3} = 1$; and $S^2{}_{KL}, S^2{}_{KN}, S^2{}_{LK}, S^2{}_{NK}, S^2{}_{KK} = 0$, where $S^i{}_{jk}$ is the partial elasticity of substitution between factors j and k in the ith sector. θ_{ji} and λ_{ji} have been defined in earlier chapters. It should be noted that sectors 1 and 2 together form a Hechscher–Ohlin subsystem (HCSS).

We assume that sector 2 is more labour-intensive than sector 1. The rationale behind this assumption becomes quite clear if one considers rice and cotton (or jute) as the two agricultural commodities. The production of rice involves less labour per unit of land vis-à-vis the processing of raw cotton/jute for delivery to the textile industry (formal sector). Even at the cultivation stage both products require the same labour/land ratio; cotton/jute must go through another process of conversion before it can be sent to the textile firms. This additional phase of production is likely to make the output of sector 2 labour-intensive.[9]

Using the above specifications the final expression for $\hat{W}$ is as follows:[10]

$$\left.\begin{aligned}
\hat{W} = &-\underset{(-)(+)}{\left(\frac{\theta_{N1}\hat{t}}{|\theta|\Delta}\right)}[-S^3_{KL}\underset{(-)}{(\lambda_{L1}\lambda_{N2} - \lambda_{L2}\lambda_{N1} - \lambda_{L3}\lambda_{N1})} + T\lambda_{L3}\lambda_{N1}S^3_{LK}]\\
&-\underset{(-)(+)}{\left(\frac{\theta_{N1}\hat{W}^*}{|\theta|\Delta}\right)}(\theta_{L3} + \theta_{K3})[S^3_{KL}\underset{(-)}{(\lambda_{L1}\lambda_{N2} - \lambda_{L2}\lambda_{N1})} - \lambda_{L3}\lambda_{N1}S^3_{LK}]\\
&+\underset{(-)(+)}{\left(\frac{\theta_{N1}\theta_{K3}\hat{K}}{|\theta|\Delta}\right)}\underset{(-)}{(\lambda_{L1}\lambda_{N2} - \lambda_{L2}\lambda_{N1} - \lambda_{L3}\lambda_{N1})}
\end{aligned}\right\} \qquad (7.8)$$

where

$$|\theta| = \theta_{K3}(\theta_{L1}\theta_{N2} - \theta_{N1}\theta_{L2}) < 0; \qquad (7.9)$$

$$|\lambda| = (\lambda_{L1}\lambda_{N2} - \lambda_{L2}\lambda_{N1}) < 0; \qquad (7.10)$$

and

$$T = \left(\frac{t}{1+t}\right) > 0 \qquad (7.11)$$

---

[8]See Appendices 7.1 and 7.2 for detailed derivation of this expression.

[9]See Marjit (1991) for details.

[10]This has been proved in Appendix 7.3.

$\Delta > 0$ in this case and its expression has been presented in Appendix 7.3. From Equation (7.8) one can easily establish the following proposition.[11]

Proposition 7.1 *When the informal sector produces an agricultural input for the formal manufacturing sector the informal wage (i) increases owing to an inflow of foreign capital; (ii) decreases due to removal of the protectionist policy; and (iii) rises following labour market reform.*

Proposition 7.1 can intuitively be explained as follows. We note that sectors 1 and 2 together form a HOSS. Now, an inflow of foreign capital lowers the rate of return to capital as the supply of capital rises given its demand. Sector 3 expands and demands more non-traded input, which in turn raises the price of the input, P_2. This produces a Stolper–Samuelson effect in the HOSS, leading to an increase in the competitive informal wage and a fall in the return to land as sector 2 is more labour-intensive relative to sector 1. On the other hand, a reduction in import tariff reduces the domestic price of commodity 3 and leads to a contraction of this sector. The demand for the non-traded input falls given its supply, resulting in a decrease in its price. The informal sector wage, W, now falls following a Stolper–Samuelson effect in the HOSS. Finally, a policy of labour market reform that takes the form of a reduction in the unionised wage, W^*, helps the formal manufacturing sector (sector 3) to save on labour input and enables it to expand, which in turn increases its demand for the non-traded input. This raises the price of the non-traded input, which in turn pulls up the informal wage once again following a Stolper–Samuelson effect in the HOSS.

We may consider a special case where sector 2 is land-intensive relative to sector 1 and the proportion of the workforce employed in the formal sector is significantly low. All these suggest that $|\theta|, |\lambda| > 0$; $\Delta < 0$; and $\lambda_{L3} \cong 0$. Using these specifications from the final expression for $\hat{W}$ (as presented in Appendix 7.1) the following proposition can be easily proved.[12]

Proposition 7.2 *In the case where the non-traded sector produces an agricultural input the informal wage (i) rises following a reduction in import tariff; (ii) falls due to labour market reform; and (iii) rises owing to an inflow of foreign capital if and only if* $|\theta|, |\lambda| > 0$; *and* $\lambda_{L3} \cong 0$.

Under the necessary and sufficient condition that $|\theta|, |\lambda| > 0$; and $\lambda_{L3} \cong 0$, the policy changes produce exactly the opposite effects on the informal wage to what we had derived in Proposition 1. Policy consequences on the price of the non-traded good remain unaltered. But the price change and the consequent Stolper–Samuelson effect would make the informal wage to move in the opposite direction, as the informal sector (sector 2) is now land-intensive. It is worthwhile to mention that Marjit (2003) has considered this case and obtained the counterintuitive effect of a reduction in import tariff on the informal sector wage.

Let us now turn to analyse the other sub-case.

Sub-case II: Sector 2 produces a non-traded manufacturing input for the formal sector. So it uses capital but not land. Land is now specific to sector 1 while capital

[11] Proofs of this are available in Appendix 7.3.

[12] This has been proved in Appendix 7.3.

is perfectly mobile between sectors 2 and 3. All these imply that $a_{N2}, \lambda_{N2}, \theta_{N2} = 0$; $\lambda_{NI} = 1$; and $S^2_{NL}, S^2_{NN}, S^2_{LN}, S^2_{NK}, S^2_{KN} = 0$. It is sensible to assume that the formal sector is more capital-intensive vis-à-vis the non-traded sector (sector 2) in both physical and value terms.

Using these stipulations from the final expression for $\hat{W}$ (as presented in Appendix 7.3) the following proposition can now be established.

Proposition 7.3 *In the case where the non-traded informal sector produces a manufacturing input for the formal sector the informal wage (i) decreases due to removal of the protectionist policy and (ii) increases owing to an inflow of foreign capital. On the other hand, a policy of labour market reform raises the competitive informal wage if* $(\lambda_{L2}\theta_{L2}\theta_{K3} \geq \theta_{K2}(\theta_{23} + \theta_{K3})\lambda_{L3})$.

We explain Proposition 7.3 in the following fashion. A policy of trade liberalisation lowers the domestic price of commodity 3 and leads to a contraction of this sector. Sector 3 now demands less capital, which in turn lowers the return to capital, r. The demand for the non-traded input also falls, which consequently lowers its price, P_2. Following the contraction of sector 3, sector 2 also reduces in size as its output is used in fixed proportion in the former. Now a fall in r implies that producers in both the manufacturing sectors use more (less) capital-intensive (labour-intensive) techniques of production than before. Labour is released by these two sectors, which now goes to sector 1, pressing down the competitive informal wage. On the other hand, an inflow of foreign capital leads to a fall in r and hence a hike in P_2 so as to satisfy the zero-profit condition for sector 3 (Equation 7.3). As the capital stock of the economy swells up, both the capital-using sectors expand. It raises the demand for labour in the two manufacturing sectors, making less labour available to sector 1 and hence exerts an upward pressure on the informal wage. Finally, a drop in the unionised wage makes it possible for the formal sector to save on labour input and raises the effective price of this commodity that the producers face. This leads to an expansion of this sector. An expansion of sector 3 raises the demand for the non-traded input. The price of the non-traded input, P_2, rises as a consequence. The demand for capital also goes up in this sector and so would be the return to capital. So capital moves out of sector 2 to sector 3. This raises the return to capital in sector 2. Given P_2, an increase in r implies a plunge in the informal wage, W (see Equation (7.2)). But, as P_2 has increased, it effectively produces a Stolper–Samuelson effect in the two manufacturing sectors and exerts an upward pressure on W (note that sector 2 is labour-intensive vis-à-vis sector 3 in value sense). Thus, there are two opposite effects on the informal wage, W. The positive effect on W is stronger than the negative effect under the sufficient condition as stated in the proposition.

7.3 Policy Implications of the Results

We have shown that trade liberalisation, except in a very special case, produces depressing effect on the informal wage while inflows of foreign capital and/or structural reforms like deregulating the labour market are likely to produce favourable effects on the wage earnings of the poor workers. The latter result is extremely crucial as it explains why labour market reform should form an integral constituent of the liberalised economic package in the liberalising countries. Furthermore, these results do not hinge on the nature of the capital mobility between the formal and informal sectors and, therefore, are robust. So, removal of the protectionist policy, which aims at reduction of commodity market distortion, a common characteristic of the developing countries, must be undertaken very cautiously as it is likely to hurt the interest of the poorer group of the workforce. On the other hand, investment and labour market reforms should be encouraged.[13] Therefore, the liberalising countries should not attempt in implementing all reforms at a very brisk pace, without pre-calculating their possible outcomes. A proper balance among various policies should be made considering the institutional, technological and trade-related characteristics in order to protect the interests of the poor informal sector workers. Making this balance is utterly essential for attaining the ILO's (2006) objective of promotion of decent work for all.

7.4 Economic Reforms and Skilled–Unskilled Wage Inequality

Liberalised economic policies, according to the celebrated Stolper–Samuelson theorem, were expected to lower the wage inequality between skilled and unskilled labour in the developing countries following increases in the prices of the export commodities as these are generally exporters of commodities that are intensive in the use of unskilled labour.[14] But empirical studies strongly suggest that the wage inequality has increased in many developing economies during the liberalised regime. From the empirical studies of Robbins (1994a,b, 1995a, b, 1996a, b) and Wood (1997), it has been found that while the inequality has narrowed in the East Asian countries, the Latin American countries like Mexico, Chile, Costa Rica and Columbia have experienced increasing skilled–unskilled wage gap following the liberalised trade and investment policies. On the other hand, there are some indirect studies that point out that economic reforms have led to a widening of the skilled–unskilled wage inequality also in the South Asian countries including India. For example, the findings by Khan (1998) and Tendulkar et al. (1996) that the incidence of poverty has increased in the post-reform period indicate that the relative wage inequality has aggravated, since unskilled workers constitute a significant proportion of the poor.

The empirical literature in this area has identified the following as the prime factors responsible for the growing incidence of wage inequality in the Latin American

---

[13] However, as shown in Chapters 5 and 6, labour market reform may have an adverse effect on the overall welfare of the economy. The result may vary depending on the presence and absence of foreign capital in the economy.

[14] This section draws upon revised version of excerpts of Chaudhuri and Yabuuchi (2007).

countries: (i) removal of tariff restrictions from the sectors that were relatively intensive in the use of unskilled labour; (ii) growth in foreign direct investment, which is positively correlated with the relative demand for skilled labour; and (iii) falling real minimum wages and decline of union strength of the unskilled workers. See, for example, Harrison and Hanson (1999), Hanson and Harrison (1999), Curie and Harrison (1997), Robbins (1994a, b), Feenstra and Hanson (1997) and Beyer et al. (1999).

The theoretical literature explaining the deteriorating wage inequality in the Southern countries includes works of Feenstra and Hanson (1996), Marjit et al. (2000), Marjit et al. (2004), Marjit and Acharyya (2003), Chaudhuri and Yabuuchi (2007) and Yabuuchi and Chaudhuri (2007). They have shown how trade liberalisation, inflows of foreign capital and international mobility of labour, both skilled and unskilled, might produce unfavourable effects on the wage inequality in the developing world given the specific structural characteristics of the less-developed countries, such as features of labour markets, structures of production, nature of capital mobility, etc. The paper by Feenstra and Hanson (1996) is based on the famous Dornbusch–Fischer–Samuelson continuum-of-goods framework. According to them, inflow of foreign capital has induced greater production of skilled-intensive commodities in Mexico, thereby leading to a relative decrease in the demand for unskilled labour. Besides, Marjit et al. (2000) have examined the impact of trade liberalisation on wage inequality in the presence of informal sectors. They have shown that the impact of trade on skilled–unskilled wage gap crucially hinges on the nature of capital mobility between the formal and informal sectors. An important piece of work in this area is that of Marjit et al. (2004), who have analysed how diverse trade patterns and market fragmentations in world trade can adversely affect the skilled–unskilled wage inequality in the developing countries. They have also studied the consequences of an improvement of terms of trade and inflows of foreign capital on wage inequality with or without trade fragmentation.

One of the salient features of the developing economies is the existence of distortion in the unskilled labour market. Unskilled workers are employed in different sectors of a developing economy. Workers employed in the organised (formal) sectors receive relatively high contractual (unionised) wage while their counterparts engaged in the informal sector earn a lower competitive wage.[15,16] The unionised wage is positively related to the competitive informal wage. As unskilled

---

15 The segmented nature of the labour market in the developing countries has been empirically verified and theoretically analysed by different authors. See Cole and Sanders (1985), Majumdar (1983, 1993), Fields (1990), Turnham (1993), Agenor and Montiel (1995), Agenor (1996) and Marjit and Acharyya (2003), among others.

16 On an average, more than 70% of the working population in the developing countries is employed in the informal sector (see Agenor, 1996). The corresponding figure in case of India is more than 90% including agriculture. The percentage of population engaged in the informal sector has increased in the post-reform period. See Marjit (2003) and Dev (2000) in this context. That the informal sector is growing in most developing countries has also been pointed out in Djankov (2003).

workers earn two different wages in the two different segments of the labour market, the average unskilled wage should be a weighted average of the two wages with weights being the proportions of unskilled labour employed in the two segments of the unskilled labour market. There are theoretical papers in the existing literature, e.g. Carruth and Oswald (1981), Agenor and Montiel (1995), Marjit and Beladi (2002) and Marjit (2003), which have dealt with labour market distortion for different purposes.

In this section of the chapter we are going to construct a general equilibrium model outside the H–O structure that emphasises the existence of distortion in the market for unskilled labour and may be useful in explaining as to how some of the factors identified in the empirical literature can lead to deteriorating skilled–unskilled wage inequality in the developing countries in the post-reform period. A three-sector general equilibrium model which is similar to a full-employment analogue of Jones and Marjit (2003) has been developed for the purpose of the analysis.[17] Two of the three sectors use unskilled labour while in the other skilled labour is a specific input. Two types of distortion, a labour market distortion in the form of unionised unskilled labour market in the low-skill manufacturing sector and a commodity market distortion in the form of tariff protection of the import-competing sector, which the developing countries are plagued with, have been considered. Two different trade patterns[18] have been taken into account.

We consider a small open developing economy with three sectors. Sector 1 is the informal sector that produces a primary agricultural commodity using unskilled labour and land. Sector 2 produces a high-skill manufacturing commodity with the help of skilled labour and capital. Sector 3 uses unskilled labour and capital to produce a low-skill manufacturing product. So land and skilled labour are specific factors in sectors 1 and 2, respectively. The capital stock of the economy consists of both domestic and foreign capital, which are perfect substitutes. Capital moves freely between sectors 2 and 3 while unskilled labour is imperfectly mobile between the informal sector and the formal sector. Production functions exhibit constant returns to scale with diminishing marginal productivity to each factor. Markets, except for the low-skill manufacturing sector labour market, are perfectly competitive. Unskilled workers employed in sector 3 earn a unionised wage, W^*, while their counterparts in the informal (agricultural) sector earn a competitive wage, W, with $W^* > W$. Due to our small open economy assumption, product prices are given internationally. The following two alternative trade patterns[19] will be considered: the country exports both the agricultural and the high-skill commodities and is a net importer of the low-skill manufacturing commodity; alternatively, it only exports the agricultural commodity and is a net importer of the other two commodities. In both

[17] The similarities and differences between Jones and Marjit (2003) and the present analysis have been discussed in details in Chaudhuri and Yabuuchi (2007).

[18] See footnote 20 in this context.

[19] The results of the model do not depend on the trade pattern of the economy.

the cases the low-skill manufacturing sector (sector 3) is protected by an import tariff. A developing country that fits the first type of comparative advantage is India.[20] On the contrary, an example of the second type of country is Mexico.[21] Commodity 1 has been assumed to be the numeraire.

As usual the price–unit cost equality conditions relating to the three sectors are as follows:

$$Wa_{L1} + Ra_{N1} = 1 \tag{7.12}$$

$$W_S a_{S2} + r a_{K2} = P_2 \tag{7.13}$$

$$W^* a_{L3} + r a_{K3} = P_3^* \tag{7.14}$$

where W, W^* and W_S denote the informal skilled wage, formal unskilled and skilled wages, respectively. R and r are the returns to land and capital, respectively. Commodity prices are given internationally and $P_3^* = P_3(1+t)$, where t is the ad valorem tariff on commodity 3.

All inputs are fully employed. The full-employment conditions for land (N), skilled labour (S), unskilled labour (L) and capital (K) are given by the following equations:

$$a_{N1}X_1 = N \tag{7.15}$$

$$a_{S2}X_2 = S \tag{7.16}$$

$$a_{L1}X_1 + a_{L3}X_3 = L \tag{7.17}$$

$$a_{K2}X_2 + a_{K3}X_3 = K \tag{7.18}$$

The formal sector faces a unionised labour market. The relationship for the unionised wage rate is specified as[22]

$$W^* = W^*(W,U) \tag{7.19}$$

---

[20] It may be mentioned that besides primary agricultural commodities, India is also a large exporter of high-skill products like computer software.

[21] Empirical evidences (e.g. Revenga, 1997; Hanson and Harrison, 1999) suggest that Mexico does not have a comparative advantage in high-skill manufacturing commodities and that its exports are negatively correlated to skill intensity.

[22] See Chapter 3 for detailed derivation.

with $(\partial W^*/\partial W),(\partial W^*/\partial U) > 0$ [23,24] where W is the informal wage and U denotes the bargaining strength of trade unions.

There are eight endogenous variables in the system: W, W^*, W_S, R, r, X_1, X_2 and X_3. The parameters of the system are P_2, P_3, t, U, N, K, L and S, which are exogenously given. There are eight independent equations, namely Equations (7.12)–(7.19). Equations (7.12)–(7.14) and (7.19) together form the price system of the model. It is easy to note that this production structure does not possess the decomposition property. So the input prices cannot be solved from the price system alone, independent of the output system. From Equations (7.15)–(7.18), it is easy to derive the following equation:

$$[\{(a_{L1}/a_{N1})N\} + (a_{L3}/a_{K3})\{K - (a_{K2}/a_{S2})S\}] = L \tag{7.20}$$

The working of the general equilibrium model is as follows. The five input prices, W, W_S, W^*, R and r, are determined by solving Equations (7.12)–(7.14), (7.19) and (7.20) simultaneously. Once the factor prices are known, the factor coefficients, a_{ji}s, are also known. X_1 and X_2 are obtained from Equations (7.15) and (7.16), respectively. Finally, X_3 is found from either Equation (7.17) or Equation (7.18).

Unskilled workers in this system earn two different wages – either the unionised wage, W^*, in sector 3 or a lower competitive wage, W, in sector 1. The average wage for unskilled labour is given by

$$W_A \equiv (W\lambda_{L1} + W^*\lambda_{L3}) \tag{7.21}$$

where λ_{L1} and λ_{L3} denote the proportion of unskilled labour employed in sectors 1 and 3, respectively. In this case, the skilled–unskilled wage gap improves (worsens) in absolute terms if the gap between W_S and W_A falls (rises). On the other hand,

---

[23] On the one hand, the trade union requires a higher wage rate than the competitive one as usual and, on the other, the competitive wage rate itself rises as the union wage rate increases if the collective bargaining institutions exist and have some effects on the unskilled labour market. See Carruth and Oswald (1981) in this context. Besides, as mentioned earlier that many activities in the so-called informal sector of the developing countries are highly stratified, requiring skills, experience and contacts, with identifiable barriers to entry. Thus, impediments to entry make the wage rate downwardly rigid in many cases. Also, in the case of agriculture there are cases of downward wage rigidity that can be explained by the 'collusive theory of unemployment' (Osmani, 1991). However, as a first step to address the role of trade unionism on wage inequality, we emphasise in this chapter the role of trade union in the formal sector only.

[24] It should be pointed out, in this context, that the channels through which unionisation of the unskilled labour market affects the skilled–unskilled wage dispersion are far more complex (covering wages and benefits, work rules limiting the intensity of work, stabilising hours, reducing arbitrariness in management actions, etc.) than has been worked out here. Although, the unionised wage function used in the present analysis is simple in form and does not consider some of the complex issues relating to collective bargaining, it has solid micro-foundation with Nash bargaining behind the scene. Besides, use of this function provides us a theory of wage differential between the sectors and helps to derive some interesting results that are new in the literature on trade and development.

the wage inequality improves (deteriorates) both in absolute and relative terms if $(\hat{W}_S - \hat{W}_A) < (>)0$.

Here a liberalised economic policy implies any subset of the following: (i) an increase in the relative price of the high-skill manufacturing product, P_2; (ii) a reduction in the ad valorem rate of tariff on the import of the low-skill manufacturing product, t (i.e. a reduction in P_3^*); (iii) an inflow of foreign capital; and (iv) a decline of the trade union strength of the unskilled workers implying a reduction in the contractual wage rate, W^*. Although trade and investment liberalisation actually imply a subset of the above policy measures, to establish ideas we consider the effects of each of these changes one at a time.

Totally differentiating Equations (7.12)–(7.14), (7.19) and (7.20) and using envelope conditions we get the following expressions in the matrix form:[25]

$$\begin{bmatrix} \theta_{L1} & 0 & 0 & 0 & \theta_{N1} \\ 0 & \theta_{S2} & 0 & \theta_{K2} & 0 \\ 0 & 0 & \theta_{L3} & \theta_{K3} & 0 \\ -E_W & 0 & 1 & 0 & 0 \\ A & B & C & D & E \end{bmatrix} \begin{bmatrix} \hat{W} \\ \hat{W}_S \\ \hat{W}^* \\ \hat{r} \\ \hat{R} \end{bmatrix} = \begin{bmatrix} 0 \\ \hat{P}_2 \\ \hat{P}_3^* \\ E_U\hat{U} \\ -F\hat{K} \end{bmatrix} \tag{7.22}$$

where

$$\begin{aligned} &A = \lambda_{L1}(S_{LL}^1 - S_{NL}^1) < 0, \\ &B = -(\lambda_{K2}\lambda_{L3}/\lambda_{K3})(S_{KS}^2 - S_{SS}^2) < 0, \\ &C = \lambda_{L3}(S_{LL}^3 - S_{KL}^3) < 0, \\ &D = \lambda_{L3}\left\{(S_{LK}^3 - S_{KK}^3) - (\lambda_{K2}/\lambda_{K3})(S_{KK}^2 - S_{SK}^2)\right\} > 0, \\ &E = \lambda_{L1}(S_{LN}^1 - S_{NN}^1) > 0, \text{ and} \\ &F = (\lambda_{L3}/\lambda_{K3}) > 0 \end{aligned}$$

On the other hand, totally differentiating Equation (7.21), we find that[26]

$$\hat{W}_A = \left\{\alpha + \gamma(S_{LL}^1 - S_{NL}^1)\right\}\hat{W} + (1-\alpha)\hat{W}^* + \gamma(S_{LN}^1 - S_{NN}^1)\hat{R}, \tag{7.23}$$

where $\alpha = (W\lambda_{L1}/W_A) > 0$ and $\gamma = ((W - W^*)\lambda_{L1}/W_A) < 0$ (as $W < W^*$).

Now, let us investigate the effect of the change in the skilled-intensive manufacturing product on the wage inequality. First, we can solve Equation (7.22) for $\hat{W}$, $\hat{W}_S$, $\hat{W}^*$ and $\hat{R}$ with respect to $\hat{P}_2$ by using Cramer' rule as

$$\hat{W}/\hat{P}_2 = -\theta_{N1}\theta_{K3}B/\Delta < 0, \tag{7.24}$$

$$\hat{W}_S/\hat{P}_2 = -\theta_{N1}E_W(\theta_{K3}C - \theta_{L3}D)/\Delta < 0, \tag{7.25}$$

[25] See Appendix 7.4 for detailed derivations.

[26] See Appendix 7.5.

$$\hat{W}^*/\hat{P}_2 = -\theta_{N1}\theta_{K3}E_W B/\Delta < 0, \tag{7.26}$$

$$\hat{R}/\hat{P}_2 = \theta_{L1}\theta_{K3}(B - \theta_{S2}E)/\Delta > 0, \tag{7.27}$$

where Δ is the determinant of the coefficient matrix of the derived equation system (7.22), and it is expressed as

$$\Delta = \theta_{S2}\theta_{K3}(\theta_{N1}A - \theta_{L1}E) + \theta_{N1}E_W(\theta_{K2}\theta_{L3}B + \theta_{S2}\theta_{K3}C - \theta_{S2}\theta_{L3}D) < 0. \tag{7.28}$$

Subtracting Equation (7.23) from Equation (7.25) we obtain

$$(\hat{W}_S - \hat{W}_A)/\hat{P}_2 = [\hat{W}_S - \left\{\alpha + \gamma(S^1_{LL} - S^1_{NL})\right\}\hat{W} - (1-\alpha)\hat{W}^* - \gamma(S^1_{LN} - S^1_{NN})\hat{R}]/\hat{P}_2 \tag{7.29}$$

It can be seen that $(\hat{W}_S - \hat{W}_A)/\hat{P}_2 > 0$ since, $\hat{W}_S/\hat{P}_2 < 0$, $\hat{W}/\hat{P}_2 < 0$, $\hat{W}_S/\hat{P}_2 < 0$, $\hat{R}/\hat{P}_2 > 0$, $\gamma < 0$, $S^k_{jj} < 0$ and $S^k_{ji} > 0$ $(i \neq j)$. Therefore, Equation (7.29) implies that if $\hat{P}_2 > 0$, then $(\hat{W}_S - \hat{W}_A) > 0$.

Similarly we can examine the effect of the change in the price of the low-skill manufacturing product on wage inequality. We obtain the result that if $\hat{P}^*_3 > 0$, then $(\hat{W}_S - \hat{W}_A) > 0$.

Now let us investigate the effect of the change in capital endowment due to, for example, an inflow of foreign capital on wage inequality. We can solve Equation (7.22) for $\hat{W}$, $\hat{W}_S$, $\hat{W}^*$ and $\hat{R}$ with respect to $\hat{K}$ by using Cramer' rule as

$$\hat{W}/\hat{K} = -\theta_{N1}\theta_{S2}\theta_{K3}F/\Delta > 0, \tag{7.30}$$

$$\hat{W}_S/\hat{K} = -\theta_{N1}\theta_{K2}\theta_{L3}E_W F/\Delta > 0, \tag{7.31}$$

$$\hat{W}^*/\hat{K} = -\theta_{N1}\theta_{S2}\theta_{K3}E_W F/\Delta > 0, \tag{7.32}$$

$$\hat{R}/\hat{K} = \theta_{N1}\theta_{S2}\theta_{L3}E_W F/\Delta < 0 \tag{7.33}$$

Using Equation (7.23) and Equations (7.30)–(7.33) and simplifying we obtain

$$\begin{aligned}(\hat{W}_S - \hat{W}_A)/\hat{K} = \theta_{N1}F[\{-\theta_{K2}\theta_{L3} + (1-\alpha)\theta_{S2}\theta_{K3}\}E_W \\ + \left\{\alpha + \gamma(S^1_{LL} - S^1_{NL})\right\}\theta_{S2}\theta_{K3} - \gamma(S^1_{LN} - S^1_{NN})\theta_{S2}\theta_{L3}]/\Delta\end{aligned} \tag{7.34}$$

We can show that $(\hat{W}_S - \hat{W}_A)/\hat{K} < 0$ if $\theta_{S2}\theta_{K3} \geq \theta_{K2}\theta_{L3}$ since,

$$\begin{aligned}&\{-\theta_{K2}\theta_{L3} + (1-\alpha)\theta_{S2}\theta_{K3}\}E_W + \alpha\theta_{S2}\theta_{K3} \\ &> \{-\theta_{K2}\theta_{L3} + (1-\alpha)\theta_{S2}\theta_{K3} + \alpha\theta_{S2}\theta_{K3}\}E_W = (-\theta_{K2}\theta_{L3} + \theta_{S2}\theta_{K3})E_W\end{aligned} \tag{7.35}$$

(Note that $E_W \leq 1$).

Thus, we obtain the result that if $\hat{K} > 0$, then $(\hat{W}_S - \hat{W}_A) < 0$ under the sufficient condition $\theta_{S2}\theta_{K3} \geq \theta_{K2}\theta_{L3}$[27], i.e. $\theta_{K3} \geq \theta_{K2}$.[28] These results are summarised in the form of the following proposition.

Proposition 7.4 *An increase in the relative price of the high-skill manufacturing product and/or a reduction of tariff restriction on the import of the low-skill manufacturing product unambiguously worsens the skilled–unskilled wage inequality. Besides, the wage inequality improves owing to an inflow of foreign capital if* $\theta_{K3} \geq \theta_{K2}$.

These results are more or less consistent with the empirical findings that have been mentioned at the very outset of the section. We explain the results presented in Proposition 7.4 as follows. As the system does not possess the decomposition property and the five unknown factor prices are obtained by solving five equations simultaneously, any parametric changes in the system can affect all factor prices and output levels.

An improvement in the relative price of the high-skill product leads to an expansion of sector 2. This raises the demand for skilled labour (a specific input) and capital. The skilled wage rate, W_S, and the return to capital, r, both increase as a consequence. Capital moves from sector 3 to sector 2 leading to a contraction of the former. This releases unskilled labour to the informal sector (sector 1). As the expanding sector 1 has now to absorb more unskilled labour than before, the informal unskilled wage rate, W, falls. This also lowers the unionised unskilled wage, W^*, in sector 3 given the bargaining strength of the trade unions, U. Thus we find that both W and W^* fall and the higher (lower) wage-paying sector 3 (sector 1) contracts (expands). The average unskilled wage rate, W_A, falls and the skilled–unskilled wage inequality deteriorates unambiguously.

On the other hand, a reduction of import tariff lowers the relative domestic price of the low-skill manufacturing commodity, P_3^*. This leads to a contraction of sector 3 and releases both capital and unskilled labour. The released capital goes to sector 2, which lowers the return to capital and leads to an expansion of sector 2. The demand for the sector-specific input, skilled labour, rises. The skilled wage, W_S, rises as a consequence. On the other hand, unskilled labour released from sector 3 moves to sector 1. The informal unskilled wage rate falls, which also lowers the unionised wage in sector 3. The two reasons that the unskilled wage rates have fallen and that the lower wage-paying sector has expanded at the cost of the higher wage-paying sector cause the average unskilled wage to fall. The skilled–unskilled wage inequality worsens unequivocally.

An inflow of foreign capital, ceteris paribus, leads to a decrease in the return to capital, r. Both sectors 2 and 3 expand as they use capital. The demand for

---

[27] While examining the consequence of emigration of skilled and unskilled labour on the wage inequality in an otherwise 2×3 specific factor model of Jones (1971), Marjit and Kar (2005) have shown that with international factor flows factor shares matter in determining the trend in wage distribution.

[28] Note that $(\theta_{S2} + \theta_{K2}) = 1 = (\theta_{L2} + \theta_{K2})$.

skilled labour rises in sector 2 and that of unskilled labour increases in sector 3. Consequently, W_S and W increase. A rise in W implies an increase in the unionised unskilled wage rate, W^*. The informal sector contracts and releases unskilled labour to the expanding sector 3. The proportion of unskilled labour employed in the higher (lower) wage-paying sector increases (decreases). Therefore, the average unskilled wage, W_A, rises as a consequence. What happens to the skilled–unskilled wage inequality crucially depends on the rates of increase in W_S and W_A. However, if sector 3 is capital-intensive in a sense that $\theta_{K3} \geq \theta_{K2}$,[29] the fall in the return to capital is larger than that in sector 2. Thus, this implies that the increase in W^* is larger than the increase in W_S from Equations (7.13) and (7.14). This improves the wage inequality.

Finally, we want to examine the consequence of labour market reform on both the informal wage rate and relative wage inequality. In this model, labour market reform implies a decline in the bargaining power of the trade unions, denoted by U. We can solve Equation (7.22) for $\hat{W}, \hat{W}_S, \hat{W}^*$ and $\hat{R}$ with respect to $\hat{U}$ using Cramer' rule as

$$\hat{W}/\hat{U} = -(E_U\theta_{N1}/\Delta)[B\theta_{L3} + C\theta_{S2}\theta_{K3} - D\theta_{S2}\theta_{L3}] > 0, \quad (7.36)$$

$$\hat{W}^*/\hat{U} = (E_U\theta_{S2}\theta_{K3}/\Delta)(\theta_{N1}A - \theta_{L1}E) < 0, \quad (7.37)$$

$$\hat{R}/\hat{U} = (\theta_{L1}E_U/\Delta)[\theta_{S2}(C\theta_{K3} - D\theta_{L3}) + B\theta_{K2}\theta_{L3}] < 0, \quad (7.38)$$

$$\hat{W}_S/\hat{U} = (\theta_{K2}\theta_{L3}E_U/\Delta)(\theta_{N1}A - \theta_{L1}E) < 0 \quad (7.39)$$

Now using Equations (7.23) and (7.36)–(7.39) it is easy to find that

$$\begin{aligned}(\hat{W}_S - \hat{W}_A) = [&(E_U\hat{U}/\Delta)(\theta_{N1}A - \theta_{L1}E)(\theta_{K2}\theta_{L3} - \theta_{S2}\theta_{K3}) + \alpha\hat{W}^* \\ &-\gamma(S^1_{LN} - S^1_{NN})\hat{R} - \{\alpha + \gamma(S^1_{LL} - S^1_{NL})\}\,\hat{W}]\end{aligned} \quad (7.40)$$

From Equation (7.40) it follows that if $\hat{U} < 0$, then $(\hat{W}_S - \hat{W}_A) < 0$ under the sufficient condition $\theta_{K2} \geq \theta_{K3}$. This establishes the following proposition.

Proposition 7.5 *A decline in the trade union strength of unskilled labour unambiguously raises the competitive unskilled wage and does not necessarily lead to deterioration in the skilled–unskilled wage inequality in the existing set-up. This policy actually improves the wage inequality if* $\theta_{K2} \geq \theta_{K3}$.

Proposition 7.5 can be intuitively explained as follows. A decline of the trade union strength of the unskilled workers, U, implies a reduction in the contractual

---

[29] Here sectors 2 and 3 use two different types of labour. However, there is one intersectorally mobile input, which is capital. So, these two industries cannot be classified in terms of factor intensities as is usually done in the HOS model. Despite this, a special type of factor intensity classification in terms of the relative distributive shares of the mobile factor, i.e. capital, may be used for analytical purposes. The industry in which this share is higher relative to the other may be considered as capital-intensive in a special sense. See Jones and Neary (1984) for details.

wage rate, W^*, given the informal wage, W. A reduction in the wage cost in sector 3 leads to an expansion of this sector, which in turn implies higher demand for both capital and unskilled labour. Capital is drained out of sector 2 to sector 3. The increased demand for unskilled labour is met by release of that input by the informal sector. Both sectors 1 and 2 contract. The demand for skilled labour in sector 2 falls. Both r and W increase while W_S falls. Two opposite forces work on W^*. While W^* falls directly due to a fall in U, it rises with an increase in W. However, the net result would be a fall in W^*. Thus, W rises but W^* falls. Besides, the proportion of unskilled labour employed in the higher wage-paying sector 3 (i.e. λ_{L3}) rises. But, what happens to W_A is somewhat uncertain. However, the wage inequality improves under the simple sufficient condition $\theta_{K2} \geq \theta_{K3}$.

7.5 Policy Implications of the Results

The model of this section, although stylised, does point to possible channels of influence that would explain as to why many of the developing countries have experienced deteriorating skilled–unskilled wage inequality in the regime of trade and investment liberalisation, belying the expectations of the proponents of these policies. The empirical literature in this area has identified a few factors responsible for the deteriorating wage inequality in the liberalised regime. This model has made an attempt to provide a theoretical foundation of those empirical findings in terms of a three-sector general equilibrium model reasonable for at least a few developing economies.

The analysis has found that the wage inequality rises unambiguously due to policies like an increase in the relative price of the high-skill commodity and a reduction of import tariff from the low-skill manufacturing sector. On the other hand, an increase in capital endowment due to, for example, an inflow of foreign capital improves the wage inequality if the skill-intensive sector is not more capital-intensive (in a special sense) vis-à-vis the low-skill manufacturing sector. Interestingly, contrary to the common wisdom a decline in the trade union power of the unskilled labour that results from a policy of labour market reform does not necessarily lead to deterioration in the skilled–unskilled wage inequity. In fact, such a policy may improve the wage inequality under reasonable condition. This result is important especially when many of the developing countries are hesitant to undertake labour market reforms seriously in the fear that such a move would be vehemently resisted by the political parties and trade unions on the plea that it would lead to general wage reductions of the poorer groups of the working population engaged in different sectors of the economy and accentuate the wage inequality. But this model has shown that there is very little substance in such a common and populist belief. The vast section of the poor working population engaged in the different unorganised sectors of the economy will ultimately be benefited from such a policy and the wage inequality is also much likely to improve.

Appendix 7.1

Totally differentiating Equations (7.1)–(7.3), using the envelope conditions and solving by Cramer's rule, the following expressions can be derived easily:

$$\hat{W} = -(\frac{\theta_{N1}}{|\theta|})[(\theta_{K3} + \theta_{23}\theta_{K2})\hat{P}_2 - \theta_{K2}T\hat{t} + \theta_{K2}\theta_{L3}\hat{W}^*] \tag{7.A.1}$$

$$\hat{R} = (\frac{\theta_{L1}}{|\theta|})[(\theta_{K3} + \theta_{23}\theta_{K2})\hat{P}_2 - \theta_{K2}T\hat{t} + \theta_{K2}\theta_{L3}\hat{W}^*] \tag{7.A.2}$$

$$\hat{r} = \frac{(\theta_{L1}\theta_{N2} - \theta_{N1}\theta_{L2})}{|\theta|}(T\hat{t} - \theta_{23}\hat{P}_2 - \theta_{L3}\hat{W}^*) \tag{7.A.3}$$

where

$$T = (\frac{t}{1+t}) > 0;$$

and,

$$|\theta| = \theta_{K3}(\theta_{L1}\theta_{N2} - \theta_{N1}\theta_{L2}) \tag{7.A.4}$$

Now differentiating Equations (7.4)–(7.6), using Equations (7.A.1)–(7.A.3) and solving, the following expressions can be obtained:

$$\begin{aligned}\hat{X}_2 = (\tfrac{1}{|\lambda|})[&(\lambda_{L1}\lambda_{K3}A_4 + \lambda_{N1}\lambda_{K3}A_1 + \lambda_{L3}\lambda_{N1}A_7)\hat{P}_2 \\ &-(\lambda_{L1}\lambda_{K3}A_5 + \lambda_{N1}\lambda_{K3}A_2 + \lambda_{L3}\lambda_{N1}A_8)\hat{t} \\ &+(\lambda_{L1}\lambda_{K3}A_6 + \lambda_{N1}\lambda_{K3}A_3 + \lambda_{L3}\lambda_{N1}A_9)\hat{W}^* + \lambda_{L3}\lambda_{N1}\hat{K}]\end{aligned} \tag{7.A.5}$$

and

$$\begin{aligned}\hat{X}_3 = (\tfrac{1}{|\lambda|})[&(\lambda_{L1}\lambda_{N2}A_7 - \lambda_{L1}\lambda_{K2}A_4 - \lambda_{L2}\lambda_{N1}A_7 - \lambda_{N1}\lambda_{K2}A_1)\hat{P}_2 \\ &-(\lambda_{L1}\lambda_{N2}A_8 - \lambda_{L1}\lambda_{K2}A_5 - \lambda_{L2}\lambda_{N1}A_8 - \lambda_{N1}\lambda_{K2}A_2)\hat{t} \\ &+(\lambda_{L1}\lambda_{N2}A_9 - \lambda_{L1}\lambda_{K2}A_6 - \lambda_{L2}\lambda_{N1}A_9 - \lambda_{N1}\lambda_{K2}A_3)\hat{W}^* + (\lambda_{L1}\lambda_{N2} - \lambda_{L2}\lambda_{N1})\hat{K}]\end{aligned} \tag{7.A.6}$$

where

$$|\lambda| = (\lambda_{L1}\lambda_{N2}\lambda_{K3} - \lambda_{L2}\lambda_{N1}\lambda_{K3} + \lambda_{L3}\lambda_{N1}\lambda_{K2}) \tag{7.A.7}$$

$$A_1 = (\tfrac{1}{|\theta|})[(\theta_{K3} + \theta_{23}\theta_{K2})\bar{\lambda}_{Li}\bar{S}^k_{Lj} - \theta_{23}(\theta_{L1}\theta_{N2} - \theta_{N1}\theta_{L2})(\lambda_{L2}S^2_{LK} + \lambda_{L3}S^3_{LK})];$$

$$A_2 = (\tfrac{T}{|\theta|})[\theta_{K2}\bar{\lambda}_{Li}\bar{S}^k_{Lj} - (\theta_{L1}\theta_{N2} - \theta_{N1}\theta_{L2})(\lambda_{L2}S^2_{LK} + \lambda_{L3}S^3_{LK})];$$

$$
\begin{aligned}
A_3 &= (\tfrac{1}{|\theta|})[\theta_{K2}\theta_{L3}\bar{\lambda}_{Li}\bar{S}^k_{Lj} - (\theta_{L1}\theta_{N2} - \theta_{N1}\theta_{L2}) \\
&\quad \left\{\theta_{L3}\lambda_{L2}S^2_{LK} + \lambda_{L3}S^3_{LK}(\theta_{L3} + \theta_{K3})\right\}]; \\
\bar{\lambda}_{Li}\bar{S}^k_{Lj} &= (\lambda_{L1}S^1_{LN} + \lambda_{L2}S^2_{LN} + \lambda_{L2}S^2_{LK}\theta_{N1}) > 0; \\
A_4 &= (\tfrac{1}{|\theta|})[(\theta_{K3} + \theta_{23}\theta_{K2})\bar{\lambda}_{Ni}\bar{S}^k_{Nj} + \theta_{23}(\theta_{L1}\theta_{N2} - \theta_{N1}\theta_{L2})\lambda_{N2}S^2_{NK}]; \\
A_5 &= (\tfrac{T}{|\theta|})[\theta_{K2}\bar{\lambda}_{Ni}\bar{S}^k_{Nj} + (\theta_{L1}\theta_{N2} - \theta_{N1}\theta_{L2})\lambda_{N2}S^2_{NK}]; \\
A_6 &= (\tfrac{\theta_{L3}}{|\theta|})[\theta_{K2}\bar{\lambda}_{Ni}\bar{S}^k_{Nj} + (\theta_{L1}\theta_{N2} - \theta_{N1}\theta_{L2})\lambda_{N2}S^2_{NK}]; \\
\bar{\lambda}_{Ni}\bar{S}^k_{Nj} &= (\lambda_{N1}S^1_{NL} + \lambda_{N2}S^2_{NL} + \lambda_{N2}S^2_{NK}\theta_{L1}) > 0; \\
A_7 &= (\tfrac{1}{|\theta|})[(\theta_{K3} + \theta_{23}\theta_{K2})(S^2_{KL}\theta_{N1} - S^2_{KN}\theta_{L1})\lambda_{K2} - \theta_{23}(\theta_{L1}\theta_{N2} \\
&\quad -\theta_{N1}\theta_{L2})\bar{\lambda}_{Ki}\bar{S}^k_{Kj}]; \\
A_8 &= (\tfrac{T}{|\theta|})[\theta_{K2}\lambda_{K2}(\theta_{N1}S^2_{KL} - \theta_{L1}S^2_{KN}) - (\theta_{L1}\theta_{N2} - \\
&\quad \theta_{N1}\theta_{L2})\bar{\lambda}_{Ki}\bar{S}^k_{Kj}]; \\
A_9 &= (\tfrac{1}{|\theta|})[\theta_{L3}\theta_{K2}\lambda_{K2}(\theta_{N1}S^2_{KL} - \theta_{L1}S^2_{KN}) - \\
&\quad (\theta_{L1}\theta_{N2} - \theta_{N1}\theta_{L2})\bar{\lambda}_{Ki}\bar{S}^k_{Kj}\bar{\theta}_{L3}]; \\
\bar{\lambda}_{Ki}\bar{S}^k_{Kj} &= [\lambda_{K2}(S^2_{KL} + S^2_{KN}) + \lambda_{K3}S^3_{KL}] > 0; \text{ and,} \\
\bar{\lambda}_{Ki}S^k_{Kj}\bar{\theta}_{L3} &= [\lambda_{K3}S^3_{KL}(\theta_{L3} + \theta_{K3}) + \theta_{L3}\lambda_{K2}(S^2_{KL} + S^2_{KN})] > 0 \qquad (7.A.8)
\end{aligned}
$$

Differentiating Equation (7.7) and using Equations (7.A.5) and (7.A.6) and simplifying we obtain

$$
\begin{aligned}
\hat{P}_2 = &(\tfrac{\hat{t}}{\Delta})[A_8(\lambda_{L1}\lambda_{N2} - \lambda_{L2}\lambda_{N1} - \lambda_{L3}\lambda_{N1}) - A_5\lambda_{L1} - A_2\lambda_{N1}] \\
&-(\tfrac{\hat{W}^*}{\Delta})[A_9(\lambda_{L1}\lambda_{N2} - \lambda_{L2}\lambda_{N1}) - A_6\lambda_{L1} - A_3\lambda_{N1}] \qquad (7.A.9) \\
&-(\tfrac{\hat{K}}{\Delta})(\lambda_{L1}\lambda_{N2} - \lambda_{L2}\lambda_{N1} - \lambda_{L3}\lambda_{N1})
\end{aligned}
$$

where

$$
\Delta = [A_7(\lambda_{L1}\lambda_{N2} - \lambda_{L2}\lambda_{N1} - \lambda_{L3}\lambda_{N1}) - \lambda_{L1}A_4 - \lambda_{N1}A_1] \qquad (7.A.10)
$$

Finally, using Equation (7.A.9) and collecting terms, Equation (7.A.1) can be rewritten as follows:

$$
\begin{aligned}
\hat{W} =&-(\tfrac{\theta_{N1}\hat{t}}{|\theta|})[\{A_8(\lambda_{L1}\lambda_{N2} - \lambda_{L2}\lambda_{N1} - \lambda_{L3}\lambda_{N1}) - A_5\lambda_{L1} - A_2\lambda_{N1}\}(\tfrac{\theta_{K3}+\theta_{23}\theta_{K2}}{\Delta}) \\
&+\theta_{K2}T] \\
&+(\tfrac{\theta_{N1}\hat{W}^*}{|\theta|})[\{A_9(\lambda_{L1}\lambda_{N2} - \lambda_{L2}\lambda_{N1}) - A_6\lambda_{L1} - A_3\lambda_{N1}\}(\tfrac{\theta_{K3}+\theta_{23}\theta_{K2}}{\Delta}) - \theta_{K2}\theta_{L3}] \\
&+(\tfrac{\theta_{N1}}{|\theta|})(\theta_{K3} + \theta_{23}\theta_{K2})(\tfrac{\hat{K}}{\Delta})(\lambda_{L1}\lambda_{N2} - \lambda_{L2}\lambda_{N1} - \lambda_{L3}\lambda_{N1})
\end{aligned}
$$

(7.A.11)

Appendix 7.2: Derivation of stability condition in the market for the non-traded input

As commodity 2, produced by sector 2, is internationally non-traded, its market must clear domestically through adjustments in its price, P_2. The stability condition in the market for commodity 2 requires that

$(d(X_2^D - X_2)/dP_2) < 0$. This implies around equilibrium, initially, $X_2^D = X_2$. Thus,

$$((\hat{X}_2^D/\hat{P}_2) - (\hat{X}_2/\hat{P}_2)) < 0. \qquad (7.A.12)$$

Now the demand for the non-traded input is given by

$X_2^D = a_{23}X_3$. Differentiating this equation we find
$\hat{X}_2^D = \hat{X}_3$. Using Equation (7.A.6) one can find

$$\left(\frac{\hat{X}_3}{\hat{P}_2}\right) = \left(\frac{1}{|\lambda|}\right)(\lambda_{L1}\lambda_{N2}A_7 - \lambda_{L1}\lambda_{K2}A_4 - \lambda_{L2}\lambda_{N1}A_7 - \lambda_{N1}\lambda_{K2}A_1) \qquad (7.A.13)$$

On the other hand, from Equation (7.A.5) it follows that

$$\left(\frac{\hat{X}_2}{\hat{P}_2}\right) = \left(\frac{1}{|\lambda|}\right)(\lambda_{L1}\lambda_{K3}A_4 - \lambda_{N1}\lambda_{K3}A_1 - \lambda_{L3}\lambda_{N1}A_7) \qquad (7.A.14)$$

Using Equations (7.A.12)–(7.A.14) we find the following stability condition for equilibrium in the market for commodity 2:

$$\left(\frac{1}{|\lambda|}\right)[A_7(\lambda_{L1}\lambda_{N2} - \lambda_{L2}\lambda_{N1} - \lambda_{L3}\lambda_{N1}) - \lambda_{L1}A_4 - \lambda_{N1}A_1] < 0;$$

i.e.

$$\left(\frac{\Delta}{|\lambda|}\right) < 0 \qquad (7.A.15)$$

Appendix 7.3: Two possible cases

Depending on the nature of the non-traded input produced by sector 2 and the nature of capital mobility between the formal and the informal sectors, the following two cases are possible.

Sub-case I: Sector 2 produces an agricultural input for the formal sector and hence uses land and does not use capital. These imply that

$$a_{K2},\lambda_{K2},\ \theta_{K2}=0;\ \lambda_{K3}=1;\quad \text{and,}\ S^2_{KL},S^2_{KN},S^2_{LK},S^2_{NK},S^2_{KK}=0. \qquad (7.A.16)$$

As per our assumption that sector 2 is more labour-intensive than sector 1 we have $|\theta|,|\lambda|<0$.

Using Equation (7.A.16), the expressions presented in Equations (7.A.7) and (7.A.8) can be reduced to

$$|\lambda|=(\lambda_{L1}\lambda_{N2}-\lambda_{L2}\lambda_{N1})<0; \qquad (7.A.17)$$

$$\begin{aligned}
A_1 &= (\tfrac{1}{|\theta|})[\theta_{K3}(\lambda_{L1}S^1_{LN}+\lambda_{L2}S^2_{LN})-\lambda_{L3}S^3_{LK}\{\theta_{23}(\theta_{L1}\theta_{N2}-\theta_{N1}\theta_{L2})\\
&\qquad -\theta_{N1}(\theta_{K3}+\theta_{L3})\}]<0\\
A_2 &= -[(T/\theta_{K3})\lambda_{L3}S^3_{LK})]<0;\ A_3=-[(\lambda_{L3}/\theta_{K3})S^3_{LK}(\theta_{L3}+\theta_{K3})]<0;\\
A_4 &= (\tfrac{1}{|\theta|})[\theta_{K3}(\lambda_{N1}S^1_{NL}+\lambda_{N2}S^2_{NL})]<0;\ A_5=A_6=0;\\
A_7 &= (\tfrac{S^3_{KL}}{|\theta|})[\theta_{N1}(\theta_{K3}+\theta_{23}\theta_{K2})-\{(\theta_{23}/\theta_{K3})\,|\theta|-\theta_{N1}\theta_{L2}\}]<0;\\
A_8 &= -(TS^3_{KL}/\theta_{K3})<0;\ A_9=-[(S^3_{KL}/\theta_{K3})(\theta_{K3}+\theta_{L3})]<0.
\end{aligned} \qquad (7.A.18)$$

Using Equations (7.A.16)–(7.A.18) and Equation (7.10) it is easy to check from Equation (7.A.15) that $\Delta>0$.

With the help (7.A.17) and (7.A.18) and simplifying from (7.A.9) one can write

$$\begin{aligned}
\hat{P}_2 &= \underset{(+)}{(\tfrac{\hat{t}}{\theta_{K3}\Delta})}[-S^3_{KL}\underset{(-)}{(\lambda_{L1}\lambda_{N2}-\lambda_{L2}\lambda_{N1}-\lambda_{L3}\lambda_{N1})}+T\lambda_{L3}\lambda_{N1}S^3_{LK}]\\
&\quad +\underset{(+)}{\left(\frac{\hat{W}^*}{\theta_{K3}\Delta}\right)}(\theta_{L3}+\theta_{K3})[S^3_{KL}(\lambda_{L1}\lambda_{N2}-\lambda_{L2}\lambda_{N1})-\lambda_{L3}\lambda_{N1}S^3_{LK}]\\
&\quad -\underset{(+)}{(\tfrac{\hat{K}}{\Delta})}\underset{(-)}{(\lambda_{L1}\lambda_{N2}-\lambda_{L2}\lambda_{N1}-\lambda_{L3}\lambda_{N1})}
\end{aligned} \qquad (7.A.19)$$

From Equation (7.A.19) we find the following:
(i) $\hat{P}_2<0$ when $\hat{t}<0$; (ii) $\hat{P}_2>0$ when $\hat{W}^*<0$; and (iii) $\hat{P}_2>0$ when $\hat{K}>0$.

Using Equations (7.A.17) and (7.A.18) the expression (7.A.11) can be rewritten as follows:

$$\begin{aligned}
\hat{W} &= -\underset{(-)(+)}{(\tfrac{\theta_{N1}\hat{t}}{|\theta|\Delta})}[-S^3_{KL}\underset{(-)}{(\lambda_{L1}\lambda_{N2}-\lambda_{L2}\lambda_{N1}-\lambda_{L3}\lambda_{N1})}+T\lambda_{L3}\lambda_{N1}S^3_{LK}]\\
&\quad -\underset{(-)(+)}{(\tfrac{\theta_{N1}\hat{W}^*}{|\theta|\Delta})}(\theta_{L3}+\theta_{K3})\underset{(-)}{[S^3_{KL}(\lambda_{L1}\lambda_{N2}-\lambda_{L2}\lambda_{N1})-\lambda_{L3}\lambda_{N1}S^3_{LK}]}\\
&\quad +\underset{(-)(+)}{(\tfrac{\theta_{N1}\theta_{K3}\hat{K}}{|\theta|\Delta})}\underset{(-)}{(\lambda_{L1}\lambda_{N2}-\lambda_{L2}\lambda_{N1}-\lambda_{L3}\lambda_{N1})}
\end{aligned} \qquad (7.8)$$

The following results are evident from Equation (7.8):

(i) $\hat{W} < 0$ when $\hat{t} < 0$; (ii) $\hat{W} > 0$ when $\hat{W}^* < 0$; and (iii) $\hat{W} > 0$ when $\hat{K} > 0$

A special case

We consider a special case where sector 2 is land-intensive relative to sector 1 and the proportion of the workforce employed in the formal sector is significantly low. These imply that

$$|\theta|, |\lambda| > 0; \text{ and } \lambda_{L3} \cong 0. \tag{7.A.20}$$

Using these specifications from Equation (7.A.10) one finds that

$$\Delta < 0 \tag{7.A.21}$$

Now using Equations (7.A.20) and (7.A.21) from Equation (7.8) the following results are obtained: $\hat{W} > 0$ when $\hat{t} < 0$; (ii) $\hat{W} < 0$ when $\hat{W}^* < 0$; and (iii) $\hat{W} < 0$ when $\hat{K} > 0$. We should note that these results hold under the necessary and sufficient conditions that $|\theta|, |\lambda| > 0; \Delta < 0$; and $\lambda_{L3} \cong 0$.

Sub-case II: Sector 2 produces a non-traded manufacturing input for the formal sector. So it uses capital and not land. All these suggest that

$$a_{N2}, \lambda_{N2}, \theta_{N2} = 0;\ \lambda_{N1} = 1; \text{ and, } S^2_{NL},\ S^2_{NN},\ S^2_{LN},\ S^2_{NK},\ S^2_{KN} = 0 \tag{7.A.22}$$

Sector 3 is capital-intensive relative to sector 2 in both physical and value terms. This implies that $(\lambda_{K3}\lambda_{L2} > \lambda_{K2}\lambda_{L3})$ and $(\theta_{K3}\theta_{L2} > \theta_{K2}\theta_{L3})$.

Using Equation (7.A.22) the expressions presented in Equations (7.A.4), (7.A.7) and (7.A.8) can be reduced to as follows:

$$|\theta| = \theta_{N1}(\theta_{K2}\theta_{L3} - \theta_{K3}\theta_{L2}) < 0; \tag{7.A.23}$$

$$|\lambda| = \lambda_{N1}(\lambda_{K2}\lambda_{L3} - \lambda_{L2}\lambda_{K3}) < 0 \tag{7.A.24}$$

$$\left.\begin{array}{l}
A_1 = (\frac{1}{|\theta|})[(\theta_{K3} + \theta_{23}\theta_{K2})\lambda_{L1}S^1_{LN} + \theta_{N1}(\lambda_{L2}S^2_{LK} + \lambda_{L3}S^3_{LK})] < 0 \\
A_2 = (\frac{T}{|\theta|})[\theta_{K2}\lambda_{L1}S^1_{LN} + \theta_{N1}(\lambda_{L2}S^2_{LK} + \lambda_{L3}S^3_{LK})] < 0; \\
A_3 = (\frac{1}{|\theta|})[\theta_{K2}\theta_{L3}\lambda_{L1}S^1_{LN} + \theta_{N1}\theta_{L3}\lambda_{L2}S^2_{LK} + (\theta_{N1}\theta_{L3} - |\theta|)\lambda_{L3}S^3_{LK}] < 0; \\
A_4 = (\frac{1}{|\theta|})[(\theta_{K3} + \theta_{23}\theta_{K2})S^1_{NL}] < 0;\ A_5 = (\frac{T\theta_{K2}S^1_{NL}}{|\theta|}) < 0; \\
A_6 = (\frac{\theta_{L3}\theta_{K2}S^1_{NL}}{|\theta|}) < 0;\ A_7 = [(\frac{\theta_{N1}}{|\theta|})(\lambda_{K2}S^2_{KL} + \lambda_{K3}S^3_{KL})] < 0; \\
A_8 = [(\frac{T}{|\theta|})\theta_{N1}(\lambda_{K2}S^2_{KL} + \lambda_{K3}S^3_{KL})] < 0; \\
A_9 = (\frac{1}{|\theta|})[\theta_{L3}\theta_{N1}\lambda_{K2}S^2_{KL} + \lambda_{K3}S^3_{KL}(\theta_{N1}\theta_{L3} - |\theta|)] < 0
\end{array}\right\} \tag{7.A.25}$$

Using Equations (7.A.23)–(7.A.25), from Equation (7.A.10) one finds that $\Delta > 0$.

Using Equations (7.A.23)–(7.A.25) and collecting terms from Equation (7.A.9) one can write

$$\begin{aligned}\hat{P}_2 = &-\left(\tfrac{T\hat{t}}{\Delta|\theta|}\right)[\lambda_{L1}\theta_{K2}(S^1_{LN} + S^1_{NL}) + \theta_{N1}(\lambda_{L2}S^2_{LK} + \lambda_{K2}S^2_{KL})\\ &\quad (+)(-) \qquad\qquad\qquad\qquad\qquad (+)\\ &+\{(\lambda_{L2} + \lambda_{L3})(\lambda_{K2}S^2_{KL} + \lambda_{K3}S^3_{KL})\}]\\ &\qquad\qquad\qquad (+)\\ &+\left(\tfrac{\hat{W}^*}{\Delta|\theta|}\right)[\lambda_{L1}\theta_{L3}\theta_{K2}(S^1_{LN} + S^1_{NL}) + \theta_{N1}\theta_{L3}\lambda_{L2}(\lambda_{K2}S^2_{KL} + \lambda_{L2}S^2_{LK})\\ &\quad (+)(-) \qquad\qquad\qquad\qquad\qquad (+)\\ &+(\theta_{N1}\theta_{L3} - |\theta|)(\lambda_{L3}S^3_{LK} + \lambda_{K3}\lambda_{L2}S^3_{KL})] + \left(\tfrac{\hat{K}}{\theta_{L2}\Delta}\right)(\lambda_{L2} + \lambda_{L3})\\ &\qquad (-) \qquad\qquad (+) \qquad\qquad\qquad (+)\end{aligned} \tag{7.A.26}$$

From Equation (7.A.26) it follows that
(i) $\hat{P}_2 < 0$ when $\hat{t} < 0$; (ii) $\hat{P}_2 > 0$ when $\hat{W}^* < 0$; and (iii) $\hat{P}_2 > 0$ when $\hat{K} > 0$.
Finally, using Equations (7.A.22) – (7.A.25) and simplifying, Equation (7.A.11) can be rewritten as follows:

$$\begin{aligned}\hat{W} = &-\left(\tfrac{T(\theta_{N1})^2\hat{t}}{\Delta(|\theta|)^2}\right)[(\lambda_{L2} + \lambda_{L3})(\lambda_{K2}S^2_{KL} + \lambda_{K3}S^3_{KL})\\ &\quad (+) \qquad\qquad\qquad (+)\\ &+(\theta_{K3}\theta_{L2} - \theta_{K2}\theta_{L3})(\lambda_{L2}S^2_{LK} + \lambda_{L3}S^3_{LK})]\\ &\qquad\qquad (+)\\ &-\left(\tfrac{\theta_{N1}\hat{K}}{\Delta|\theta|}\right)[(\theta_{K3} + \theta_{23}\theta_{K2})(\lambda_{L2} + \lambda_{L3})]\\ &\quad (+)(-) \qquad (+)\\ &+\left(\tfrac{\theta_{N1}\hat{W}^*}{\Delta(|\theta|)^2}\right)[\theta_{N1}\theta_{L3}(\lambda_{L2}S^2_{LK} + \lambda_{L3}S^3_{LK})(\theta_{K3}\theta_{L2} - \theta_{K2}\theta_{L3})\\ &\quad (+)(+) \quad + \theta_{N1}\theta_{L3}\{\theta_{K3}\theta_{L2}\lambda_{L2} - \theta_{K2}(\theta_{L3}\lambda_{L2} + \lambda_{L3})\}(\lambda_{K2}S^2_{KL} + \lambda_{K3}S^3_{KL})\\ &\qquad\qquad - |\theta|(\theta_{K3} + \theta_{23}\theta_{K2})(\lambda_{L3}S^3_{LK} + \lambda_{K3}S^3_{KL})]\\ &\qquad\qquad\qquad (-) \qquad\qquad\qquad (+)\end{aligned} \tag{7.A.27}$$

From Equation (7.A.27) the following results trivially follow:
(i) $\hat{W} < 0$ when $\hat{t} < 0$; (ii) $\hat{W} > 0$ when $\hat{K} > 0$; and (iii) $\hat{W} > 0$ when $\hat{W}^* < 0$ if $(\lambda_{L2}\theta_{L2}\theta_{K3} \geq \theta_{K2}(\lambda_{L2}\theta_{L3} + \lambda_{L3}))$

Appendix 7.4: Derivation of Equation (7.22)

Totally differentiating Equation (7.12), we have

$$a_{L1}\mathrm{d}W + a_{N1}\mathrm{d}R = 0, \tag{7.A.28}$$

since $Wda_{L1} + Rda_{N1} = 0$ by the envelope property of the unit cost function. Thus, from Equation (7.A.28), we obtain

$$\theta_{L1}\hat{W} + \theta_{N1}\hat{R} = 0. \tag{7.A.29}$$

Similarly we have the following equations corresponding to Equations (7.13) and (7.14), respectively

$$\theta_{S2}\hat{W}_S + \theta_{K2}\hat{r} = \hat{P}_2 \tag{7.A.30}$$

and

$$\theta_{L3}\hat{W}^* + \theta_{K3}\hat{r} = \hat{P}_3^*. \tag{7.A.31}$$

Now totally differentiating Equation (7.19), we obtain

$$\hat{W}^* = E_W\hat{W} + E_U\hat{U}. \tag{7.A.32}$$

where

$$E_W = (\partial W^*/\partial W)(W/W^*) \text{ and } E_U = (\partial W^*/\partial U)(U/W^*).$$

Finally, totally differentiating Equation (7.20), we have

$$\begin{aligned} &Nda_{L1}/a_{N1} - Na_{L1}da_{N1}/(a_{N1})^2 + X_3da_{L3} + a_{L3}\{dK - Sda_{K2}/a_{S2} \\ &+Sa_{K2}da_{S2}/(a_{S2})^2\}/a_{K3} - a_{L3}(K - a_{K2}/a_{S2})da_{K3}/(a_{K3})^2 = 0. \end{aligned} \tag{7.A.33}$$

Each coefficient is a function of the factor prices employed in the sector, for example, $a_{L1} = a_{L1}(W,R)$. Thus, the derivative is expressed as

$$da_{L1} = S_{LL}^1 dW + S_{LN}^1 dR, \tag{7.A.34}$$

where $S_{LL}^1 = (W/a_{L1})(\partial a_{L1}/\partial W)$ and $S_{LN}^1 = (R/a_{L1})(\partial a_{L1}/\partial R)$. Using the same calculation to other coefficients, and arranging terms, we obtain

$$A\hat{W} + B\hat{W}_S + C\hat{W}^* + D\hat{r} + E\hat{R} = -F\hat{K}, \tag{7.A.35}$$

where A to F are defined in the main text. Equations (7.A.29)–(7.A.32) and (7.A.35) are expressed as Equation (7.22) in the matrix form.

Appendix 7.5: Derivation of Equation (7.23)

Equation (7.21) can be rewritten as

$$W_A = \lambda_{L1}W + \lambda_{L3}W^* = \lambda_{L1}W + (1 - \lambda_{L1})W^*, \tag{7.A.36}$$

since $\lambda_{L1} + \lambda_{L3} = 1$ by definition. Totally differentiating (7.A.36), we have

$$dW_A = \lambda_{L1}dW + \lambda_{L3}dW^* + Wd\lambda_{L1} - W^*d\lambda_{L1}. \tag{7.A.37}$$

Since $\lambda_{L1} = a_{L1}X_1/L$, we obtain using (7.A.34)

$$\hat{\lambda}_{L1} = S_{LL}^1 \hat{W} + S_{LN}^1 \hat{R} + \hat{X}_1, \tag{7.A.38}$$

On the other hand, from Equation (7.15), we have

$$\hat{X}_1 = -\hat{a}_{N1} = -(S_{NL}^1 \hat{W} - S_{NN}^1 \hat{R}). \tag{7.A.39}$$

Thus, substituting (7.A.38) and (7.A.39) into (7.A.37), we obtain

$$\hat{W}_A = \left\{\alpha + \gamma(S_{LL}^1 - S_{NL}^1)\right\} \hat{W} + (1-\alpha)\hat{W}^* + \gamma(S_{LN}^1 - S_{NN}^1)\hat{R},$$

where $\alpha = W\lambda_{L1}/W_A$ and $\gamma = (W - W^*)/W_A < 0$ as $W < W^*$.

Chapter 8
Incidence of Child Labour, Informal Sector and Economic Liberalisation

8.1 Introduction

Child labour is presently a phenomenon pervasive mostly in the transitional societies of the developing economies where multi-class social structures exist and a complex of traditional and pre-capitalist production relations are operative in an articulated capitalist mode of production and exploitation. In particular, child labour is predominant in the informal segment of the labour markets in developing countries, which are generally outside the purview of governmental regulation. It is mainly the poor working families employed in the informal sector who are the largest potential suppliers of child labour. Economic liberalisation has led to a contraction of the formal segment of the labour market and a significant expansion of the informal sector. The consequences of liberalised policies on the incidence of child labour depend on how the poor working families get affected by these policies.

According to ILO (2002b) one in every six children aged between 5 and 17 or 246 million children are involved in child labour in the developing countries.[1] India is one among these countries where the concentration of child labour is the highest in the world. Out of 246 million about 170 million child workers were found in different hazardous works. Some 8.4 million children were caught in the worst forms of child labour including slavery, trafficking, debt bondage and other forms of forced labour, forced recruitment for armed conflict, prostitution, pornography and other illicit activities.

In the recent literature, the supply of child labour has been attributed to factors such as poverty,[2] lack of educational facilities and poor quality of schooling, capital market imperfection, parental attitudes[3] and their objectives to maximise present

[1]If the 'invisible' workers who perform unpaid and household jobs are included, it is likely that the estimate would shoot up significantly further.

[2]Perceived poverty instead of actual poverty and desire for consumer goods and better living standards may sometimes contribute to the incidence of child labour.

[3]Parental attitudes, reflecting cultural norms and social values, nevertheless play a major role in sending a child to work or to school. Parents' expectations that children will provide for them in their old age may lead to their having larger numbers of children and, where household incomes are limited, there may be a lower level of investment in each child, including in education. Parents

S. Chaudhuri, U. Mukhopadhyay, *Revisiting the Informal Sector*,
DOI 10.1007/978-1-4419-1194-0_8, © Springer Science+Business Media, LLC 2010

income, and a dualistic economy characteristic of developing countries with the coexistence of formal and informal sectors. However, it is generally contemplated that the root cause is abject poverty, which induces people to have large families and children to go out in the job market and supplement their low family income.

However, policy prescriptions directed towards poverty alleviation are difficult to be implemented properly due to various bottlenecks and vicious circles typical of developing economies; even if implemented, they take a long time to mitigate the problem, so that legal restrictions can be more instrumental to deal with child labour. Legislative fiats to combat child labour range from an outright ban on child labour to social labelling of products. A total ban, again, would be counterproductive in the sense that it may adversely affect the welfare of the poor households and force the children to take resort to more hazardous and illegal activities. Moreover, most of the children work in domestic service or informal sector, where labour law enforcement is virtually absent. Social labelling can be applied only to a few products (mostly exported ones), so that the potential effect is limited; it is also difficult to monitor the labelling operations and may have disastrous consequences on the developing economies as the Bangladeshi experience[4] has shown. It is largely believed that the betterment of educational opportunities and a policy of compulsory education designed for human capital formation can more effectively remove children from work[5].

In the recent theoretical literature on child labour the notable contributors are Eswaran (1996), Basu and Van (1998), Ranjan (1999, 2001), Baland and Robinson (2000), Jafarey and Lahiri (2002) and Dessy (2000). Eswaran (1996) has found an explanation in the need for old-age security of the parents behind the incidence of high fertility rate and lower investment on the education of their offspring (and hence the high incidence of child labour) in a backward society where the child mortality rate is quite high. Thus he has suggested improvement in healthcare services and legislation of compulsory education to eradicate child labour from the system. Basu and Van (1998) have shown that if child labour and adult labour are substitutes (Substitution Axiom) and if child leisure is a luxury commodity to the poor households (Luxury Axiom), unfavourable adult labour market, responsible for low adult wage rate, is the driving force behind the incidence of child labour. According to the Luxury Axiom,[6] there exists a critical level of adult wage rate, and any adult worker

---

may genuinely believe that they are doing the best for their children by allowing or encouraging them to work, not realising the hazards that the work might entail (ILO, 2002b).

[4]Owing to the possibility of introduction of the US Harkins Bill, which calls for complete ban on imports of any good that were manufactured wholly or partly by child workers, the employers in the booming garments industry in Bangladesh who had employed a large number of child labourers began removing the child workers drastically. The consequence was a chaotic process that left many children worse off than they had been before. See UNICEF (1997).

[5]To eradicate the incidence of child labour, *World Development Report 1995* called for a multifaceted approach with programmes that increase income security, reduce education costs and improve the quality of schooling.

[6]See footnote 8 for the Substitution Axiom.

earning below this wage rate considers himself poor and does not have the luxury to send his offspring to school. He is forced to send his children to the job market to complement low family income out of sheer poverty. What follows from the paper by Basu and Van (1998) is that labour market interventions that raise adults' wages are expected to mitigate the problem of child labour. There are some papers in the literature focusing on capital market failure. Ranjan (1999), Baland and Robinson (2000) and Jafarey and Lahiri (2002) emphasise the importance of capital-market imperfection as a contributing factor to child labour. The dynamic implications of capital market imperfection have been studied by Ranjan (2001), with similar conclusions reached by Basu (1999). On the other hand, Dessy (2000) has advocated in favour of imposition of compulsory education as a means to combat the incidence of child labour. Dessy (2000) has shown that in an economy where the benefits of having children are outweighed by rearing costs, a policy of free education with no compulsory education laws may lead the economy to an underdevelopment trap with high fertility rate and higher incidence of child labour. On the contrary, a compulsory education policy is expected to eradicate the existence of the evil from the system.

The ongoing process of globalisation was expected to produce considerable downward pressure on the problem of child labour in the developing countries by reducing the extent of poverty. It was believed that liberalised economic policies would take the developing countries into higher growth orbits, the benefits of which would eventually percolate down to the bottom of the society, thereby leading to reduction of poverty and poverty-driven child labour incidence. Despite most of the developing economies choosing free trade as their development strategies, empirical evidence suggests that in many of the transition economies the incidence of child labour has been on the rise. For example, a recent study of child labour by Swaminathan (1998) in a city in western India concluded, 'The prevalence and absolute expansion of child labour in a period and region of relatively high growth of aggregate output indicates that the nature of economic growth is flawed.' Why liberalised trade policies and free education policy have not so far been successful in eradicating the problem is quite puzzling.

Unfortunately, the existing theoretical literature on child does not deal adequately[7] with issues like the supply of child labour and its linkages with the adult labour markets in a multi-sector general equilibrium framework, which is especially crucial when child labour and adult labour are substitutes[8] in different informal

[7]The Basu and Van (1998) model, of course, can be easily embedded in a general equilibrium framework. Besides, Jafarey and Lahiri (2002) and Gupta (2002) have examined the efficacy of imposition of trade sanctions on export items of the developing countries produced by child labour as a policy in curbing the incidence of child labour in terms of general equilibrium models.

[8]In the developing economies child workers are mostly found in the production of carpets, glass, bangles, leather bags, shoes, garments, matchbox and fireworks and cattle feeding. It is sensible to assume that adults can perform all these tasks. First, all these industries exist in countries where there is no child labour. Second, not all the firms producing these goods in countries where child labour exists actually use child labour – after all, this is the justification for 'social labelling'. The 'nimble fingers' argument, which once has been put forward, especially to carpet weaving, is an

sectors of a developing economy. One cannot get the overall effect of a policy on the incidence of child labour in a partial equilibrium framework. This is because, as the Bangladeshi experience has shown, a policy designed to mitigate the problem of child labour in a targeted sector may drive the children into other sectors of the economy and undertake illegal and more hazardous activities. So, one cannot evaluate the success of a particular policy unless one takes into account its effect on the aggregate number of child workers, spread over different sectors of a developing economy. Neither do we find any work where the effect of an education subsidy policy on the supply of child labour has been studied although the traditional wisdom recommends a hike in educational opportunities to eradicate the problem. Also, economists have not so far paid adequate attention to analyse the implications of the liberalised economic policies on the problem of child labour.[9] This attempt should have been made earlier, especially when trade liberalisation was expected to exert downward pressures on the incidence of poverty-driven child labour.

This chapter aims at filling up this gap in the existing literature by constructing two general equilibrium models with child labour. First, a three-sector full-employment model with informal sector and child labour is considered and then a three-sector Harris–Todaro type general equilibrium model is used for examining the implications of a free education policy and liberalised economic policies on the incidence of poverty-induced child labour and adult labour market in a developing economy.

8.2 Effects of Education Subsidy and Economic Liberalisation on the Incidence of Child Labour

We begin our theoretical analysis with a three-sector full-employment model where there are two informal sectors and one formal sector. One of the two informal sectors produces an agricultural product, X, with the help of labour and capital. The informal manufacturing sector uses labour and capital to produce an internationally non-traded input, Y, for the formal manufacturing sector. In the two informal sectors both adult labour and child labour are used and these are perfect substitutes to each other.[10]

Following Basu and Van (1998), we make the assumption of 'substitution' in the informal sectors, which suggests that adult labour is a perfect substitute for child

excuse given by employers and fails to convince researchers (see Burra, 1995; Weiner, 1991). Even if present technologies required the use of child labour and not adult labour in certain production activities, major changes in economic conditions coupled with the mobility of capital across sectors would certainly result in the adoption of different technologies allowing the substitution of adult for child labour.

[9] Chaudhuri and Gupta (2004) and Chaudhuri and Dwibedi (2006, 2007) are among the few notable exceptions.

[10] In the second model we will consider the case where child labour may be an essential input in the urban informal sector.

labour, or more generally, adults can do what children do. It is assumed that an adult worker is equivalent to μ number of child labourers, where $\mu>1$. Thus, adult and child labour are perfect substitutes subject to a child-equivalent scale correction of μ. So when the adult wage rate is W the child wage rate, W_C, must be equal to (W/μ). Complete mobility of both types of labour between these two sectors ensures that the respective wage rates must be the same across both the informal sectors.

The formal sector is the tariff-protected import-competing sector producing a manufacturing good, Z. It uses adult labour, capital and the produced input from the informal sector. Owing to effective wage legislation and unionisation of labour, the adult wage rate in the formal sector, W^*, is greater than the competitive informal sector adult wage rate, W.[11]

Production functions in sectors X and Y satisfy constant returns to scale with positive but diminishing returns to each factor. But, fixed-coefficient technology is assumed for sector Z. Markets, except for the formal sector labour market, are perfectly competitive and all inputs are fully employed. Owing to the small open economy assumption, prices of the traded goods, X and Z, are given internationally. Since Y is non-traded its price is endogenously determined by the demand–supply mechanism. We assume that sectors Y and Z as a whole is more capital-intensive[12] than sector X.

8.2.1 Derivation of Supply Function of Child Labour

We assume that there are L numbers of working families in the economy, which are classified into two groups with respect to the earnings of their adult members. The adult workers who work in the higher paid formal manufacturing sector comprise the richer section of the working population. On the contrary, labourers who are engaged in the informal sectors constitute the poorer section. Following the 'Luxury Axiom'[13] of Basu and Van (1998), we assume that there exists a critical level of

[11]In a developing economy the supply of child labour comes largely from the poor working families employed in the informal sectors. Their incomes from non-child labour sources are quite low and uncertain. In the rural areas, workers get employment in the peak season. But in the lean season, employment is not guaranteed, as the demand for labour remains low. However, it has been observed that the market for child labour remains relatively stable throughout the year as child workers are mainly employed to look after the cattle (see Gupta, 2000). Therefore, the poor families often send out their children to work for the purpose of 'consumption smoothing'. In urban areas also there is very little employment security for the workers employed in the informal sectors. The present analysis, unfortunately, cannot take into consideration the aspect of income uncertainty on the part of informal sector workers. However, there is no reason to deny that the incidence of child labour is likely to fall significantly if the poor working families are protected by employment and social securities.

[12]Chandra and Khan (1993) and Gupta (1997) have also made this assumption. However, in these papers, the Harris–Todaro framework has been considered.

[13]An empirically testable hypothesis of Basu and Van's model is that child labour arises if adult household income falls below some benchmark level. This hypothesis has been tested by different

family (or adult labour) income, $\overline{W}$, from non-child labour sources, such that the parents will send their children out to work if and only if the actual adult wage rate is less than this critical level. We can fairly assume that each worker in the formal manufacturing sector earns a wage income, W^*, sufficiently higher than this critical level. So, the workers belonging to this group do not send their children to work. On the other hand, adult workers employed in the informal sectors earn W amount of wage income, which is less than $\overline{W}$ and, therefore, send many of their children to the job market to supplement low family income.

The supply function of child labour by each poor working family is determined from the utility maximising behaviour of the representative altruistic household. We assume that each working family consists of one adult member and 'n' number of children. The altruistic adult member of the family (guardian) decides the number of children to be sent to the workplace. The rest of the children are sent to schools. We also assume that there is only public educational system[14,15] available to the children in the economy and it is entirely financed by government subsidy on this account. The richer section of the workers does not send their children to the job market. In a society with high fertility rate, poor perception of the parents about future benefits of children's education, low quality of schooling and households' objectives to maximise present income, one of the main motives behind the decision of the poorer households in sending some of their offspring to public schools is to derive the immediate benefits of free education policy.[16] In the public education system in the developing economies there are provisions for the children from the poorer families to get stipend, free educational goods and free mid-day meals.[17] It

economists for different countries. Studies by Ray (1999) for India, Ray (2000) for Pakistan and Peru, Addison et al. (1997) for Ghana and Pakistan and Bhalotra (2000) for Pakistan have found the 'Luxury Axiom' of Basu and Van (1998) more or less to be statistically valid.

[14]Governments all over the world devote substantial resources to their education sector. This is especially true in developing countries. In 1995, public spending on education accounted for 15.7% of total government expenditure in developing countries (see Bedi and Garg, 2000). Furthermore, the majority of students in developing countries are educated in publicly funded and publicly managed educational institutions. According to Jimenez and Lockheed (1995), almost 90% of all primary and 70% of all secondary enrolments in developing countries are in public schools.

[15]Here we do not deal with an important aspect of child labour – its relation to education and human capital. However, Basu and Van (1998) also share the same limitation.

[16]In this context, mention should be made of the empirical paper by Ravallion and Wodon (1999) who have found that the school enrolment subsidy reduced the incidence of child labour in Bangladesh. However, they have admitted that the magnitude of decline in the incidence of child labour as a proportion of the total amount of enrolment subsidy is insignificant. This is because parents are clearly substituting other uses of their children's time, so as to secure the current income gain from access to the programme with modest impact on earnings from their children's work.

[17]The education subsidy policy is undertaken in different countries in a number of ways. Among the most popular incentive schemes are school meal programmes. In countries like Brazil, Egypt, South Africa and India mid-day meals are offered to poor children attending schools. However, as noted by Brown et al. (2001), school-lunch programmes themselves do not provide a sufficient incentive to draw children out of work and into school. As a result of the low financial value of the meal combined with the poor quality of schools, school-lunch programmes cannot generally

is sensible to assume that the higher the subsidy on education, E, the higher would be the free educational facilities and the related benefits, B, associated with child schooling. On the other hand, the larger the number of children sent to schools, the higher would be the aggregate benefits accruing to the poor families. We make the simplifying assumption that the money value of such benefits is strictly proportional to the number of children sent to schools. The utility function of the household is given by

$$U = U(C_X, C_Z(n - l_C))$$

The household derives utility from the consumption of the final goods, C_X and C_Z, and from the children's leisure measured by $(n–l_C)$, where l_C denotes the supply of child labour by each poor working family. However, children's leisure here does not imply that the children who are not sent out to work are kept at home. They are rather sent to schools.[18] The altruistic guardian of the family derives utility from this source because at least some of his children have been kept out from the work hazards. Besides, by sending some of the children to schools, the family secures current income gain from access to the different incentives that the free education scheme provides. For analytical simplicity let us consider the following Cobb–Douglas type of the utility function.

$$U = A(C_X)^{\alpha}(C_Z)^{\beta}(n - l_C)^{\gamma} \tag{8.1}$$

with $A>0$ and $1>\alpha, \beta, \gamma>0$ and $(\alpha+\beta+\gamma)=1$

It satisfies all the standard properties and is homogeneous of degree 1. The parameter γ denotes the degree of altruism of the guardian towards the well being of his children. The value of γ crucially depends on the social values and norms of the society towards child labour. In a relatively educationally advanced society the value of γ is likely to be comparatively high.[19]

Ruling out the possibility for any child worker attending school to undertake any part-time job, the budget constraint of the representative poor household is given by the following:

$$P_X C_X + P_Z(1 + t)C_z = (W_C l_C + W) + (n - l_C)B(E) \tag{8.2}$$

alter the poor parents' calculation of the value of school relative to work. Alternatively, in a few countries like Bangladesh and Mexico, governments have instituted cash stipends or in-kind gifts for children attending schools. Ravallion and Wodon (2000) have found the Food-for-Education (FFE) programme quite successful in keeping the children from poor families into schools in rural Bangladesh. However, the impact of this programme on the incidence on child labour was not satisfactory.

[18] This is a static model. So the aspects of education and human capital formation and its role on the incidence of child labour have not been dealt here.

[19] A comparative static result relating to a change in γ on the incidence of child labour in the economy has been discussed in details in footnote 25.

where W is the income of the adult worker, $W_C l_C$ measures the income from child labour and $(n–l_C)B(E)$ is the money value of the benefits derived by the household from sending $(n–l_C)$ number of children to schools. Note that $B'(\cdot)$ is positive. Here the effective child wage rate is $(W_C–B(E))$.[20]

Maximisation of the utility function subject to the above budget constraint gives us the following first-order conditions:

$$((\alpha U)/(P_X C_X)) = ((\beta U)/(P_Z(1+t)C_Z)) = ((\gamma U)/(n-l_C)(W_C - B(E))) \quad (8.3)$$

From Equation (8.3) we get the following expressions:

$$C_X = \{\alpha(n - l_C)(W_C - B(E))/(\gamma P_X)\} \quad (8.4)$$

$$C_Z = \{\beta(n - l_C)(W_C - B(E))/(\gamma P_Z(1+t))\} \quad (8.5)$$

Substitution of the values of C_X and C_Z into the budget constraint and simplification give us the following labour supply function:

$$l_C = \frac{[n\{(\alpha+\beta)W_C - B(E)\} - \gamma W]}{(W_C - B(E))} \quad (8.6)$$

This is the supply function of child labour by each poor family. We now analyse its properties. First, l_C varies negatively with the adult wage rate, W. A rise in W produces a positive income effect so that the adult worker sends a larger number of children to schools and therefore decides to send a lower number of children to the workplace. An increase in W_C (or an increase in $(W_C–B(E))$), on the other hand, produces a negative price effect, which increases the supply of child labour from the family.

As adult labour and child labour are perfect substitutes in this model subject to a child-equivalent scale correction of μ, the child wage rate, W_C, must be (W/μ) when the adult wage rate is W. Substituting (W/μ) in place of W_C in Equation (8.6) we get

$$l_C = \frac{[n\{(\alpha+\beta)(W/\mu) - B(E)\} - \gamma W]}{((W/\mu) - B(E))} \quad (8.6.1)$$

Differentiating Equation (8.6.1) with respect to W we get

$$(dl_C/dW) = \left[B(E)\gamma\left(1+\frac{n}{\mu}\right)\left(\frac{1}{(W/\mu) - B(E)}\right)^2\right] > 0.$$

In this case, the negative price effect of an increase in the adult wage rate, W, taking place through an increase in the effective child wage rate, $((W/\mu) - B(E))$,

[20] We assume that $W_C > B(E)$. Otherwise, no children are sent to the job market.

outweighs the positive income effect so that the net effect would be an increase in the supply of child labour. Thus, an increase in the adult wage, W, leads to an increase in the supply of child labour by each poor working family when the two types of labour are perfect substitutes.

There are $L_I(=L-a_{LZ}Z)$ number of adult workers engaged in the two informal sectors and each of them sends l_C number of children to the workplace. Thus, the aggregate supply function of child labour in the economy is given by

$$L_C = \left[\frac{[n\{(\alpha+\beta)(W/\mu) - B(E)\} - \gamma W]}{((W/\mu) - B(E))}\right](L - a_{LZ}Z) \tag{8.7}$$

Given the assumption of perfectly competitive markets the usual price–unit cost equality conditions relating to the three sectors of the economy are given by the following three equations:

$$a_{LX}W + a_{KX}R = P_X \tag{8.8}$$

$$a_{LY}W + a_{KY}R = P_Y \tag{8.9}$$

$$a_{LZ}W^* + a_{YZ}P_Y + a_{KZ}R = P_Z(1+t) \tag{8.10}$$

The formal sector faces a unionised labour market. The relationship for the unionized wage rate is specified as[21]

$$W^* = f(W,U) \tag{8.11}$$

$f(.)$ satisfies the following properties:

$W^*=W$ for $U=0$, $W^*>W$ for $U>0$; $f_1, f_2>0$. $W^*=W$ for $U=0$, $W^*>W$ for $U>0$; $f_1, f_2>0$.

Using Equation (8.11), Equation (8.10) may be rewritten as

$$a_{LZ}f(W,U) + a_{YZ}P_Y + a_{KZ}R = P_Z(1+t) \tag{8.10.1}$$

Since the intermediate input, Y, is used only in the production of Z, its full-employment condition is as follows:

$$a_{YZ}Z = Y \tag{8.12}$$

The capital endowment equation is given by

$a_{KX}X + a_{KY}Y + a_{KZ}Z = K$. Using Equation (8.12), this may be rewritten as follows:

$$a_{KX}X + (a_{KY}a_{YZ} + a_{KZ})Z = K. \tag{8.13}$$

[21] See Chapter 3 in this context.

As in the two informal sectors child labour and adult labour are perfect substitutes, the effective adult labour endowment equation of the economy is given by the following:

$$a_{LX}X + a_{LY}Y + a_{LZ}Z = (L + L_C/\mu)$$

Using Equations (8.7) and (8.12) and after simplification this may be rewritten as follows:

$$\begin{aligned} &a_{LX}X + \left[a_{LY}a_{YZ} + a_{LZ}\left\{1 + \frac{(n(\alpha+\beta)W - n\mu B(E) - \mu\gamma W}{(W - \mu B(E))}\right\}\right]Z \\ &\quad = L\left[1 + \frac{(n(\alpha+\beta)W - n\mu B(E) - \mu\gamma W)}{(W - \mu B(E))}\right] \end{aligned} \tag{8.14}$$

In this model there are eight endogenous variables W, W^*, R, P_Y, X, Y, Z and L_C and eight independent equations, (8.7), (8.8), (8.9), (8.10.1), (8.11), (8.12), (8.13) and (8.14). The parameters of the system are P_X, P_Z, K, L, E, t, U, α, β, γ, μ and n. Equations (8.8), (8.9) and (8.10.1) constitute the price system and the rest of the equations form the output system. The system possesses the decomposition property since the three unknown input prices, W, R and P_Y, can be determined from the price system alone, independent of the output system. Once the factor prices are known, the factor coefficients, a_{ji}s, are also determined. As W is already known, W^* is obtained from Equation (8.11). X and Z are simultaneously solved from Equations (8.13) and (8.14). Given Z the equilibrium value of Y is found from Equation (8.12). Finally, L_C is obtained from Equation (8.7).

In this section of the chapter, we examine the effectiveness of an improvement of the educational facilities and liberalised trade and investment policies to control the supply of child labour. Although these policies are undertaken simultaneously in a developing economy, we consider their effects one by one for better understanding of the ideas.

Totally differentiating Equations (8.8), (8.9) and (8.10.1) and solving by Cramer's rule the following expression can be obtained:[22]

$$\hat{W} = (1/|\theta|)[\hat{P}_X(\theta_{KY}\theta_{YZ} + \theta_{KZ}) - \theta_{KX}T\hat{t}] \tag{8.15}$$

and

$$\hat{R} = (1/|\theta|)[\theta_{LX}T\hat{t} - \hat{P}_X(\theta_{LY}\theta_{YZ} + \theta_{LZ}E_W)] \tag{8.16}$$

where $|\theta| = \{\theta_{LX}(\theta_{KY}\theta_{YZ} + \theta_{KZ}) - \theta_{KX}(\theta_{LY}\theta_{YZ} + \theta_{LZ}E_W)\} > 0$ as the industrial sector as a whole (sectors Y and Z taken together) is more capital-intensive than the agricultural sector (sector X), $T=(t/(1+t))>0$, $E_W=((\partial W^*/\partial W)(W/W^*))>0$. E_W is the

[22]See Appendix 8.1 in this context.

elasticity of the unionised wage rate, W^*, with respect to the informal sector wage rate, W.

So, a policy of trade liberalisation in agriculture or a reduction in import tariff unequivocally raises the informal sector wage rate.

Now totally differentiating Equations (8.14) and (8.13) one can derive[23] the following expressions, respectively:

$$\lambda_{LX}\hat{X} + \{\lambda_{LY} + \lambda_{LZ}(1 + l_C/\mu)\}\hat{Z} = A_1\hat{P}_X - A_2\hat{t} - A_3\hat{E} \tag{8.17}$$

where

$$A_1 = (1/|\theta|)\left[(\lambda_{LX}\theta_{KX}\sigma_X + \lambda_{LY}\theta_{KY}\sigma_Y)(1 - \theta_{LZ}(z - E_W)) + \frac{(L - a_{LZ}Z)W}{L^*(W - \mu B)}\{n(\alpha + \beta) - \mu\gamma - l_C\}(\theta_{KY}\theta_{YZ} + \theta_{KZ})\right] > 0;$$

$$A_2 = \left(\frac{T}{|\theta|}\right)\left[(\lambda_{LX}\theta_{KX}\sigma_X + \lambda_{LY}\theta_{KY}\sigma_Y) + \frac{\theta_{KX}(L - a_{LZ}Z)W\{n(\alpha + \beta) - \mu\gamma - l_C\}(\theta_{KY}\theta_{YZ} + \theta_{KZ})}{L^*(W - \mu B)}\right] > 0; \text{ and,}$$

$$A_3 = \left[\frac{\mu B' E(1 + n)(L - a_{LZ}Z)}{L^*(W - \mu B)}\right] > 0.$$

$$\lambda_{KX}\hat{X} + (\lambda_{KY} + \lambda_{KZ})\hat{Z} = \hat{K} - A_4\hat{P}_X + A_5\hat{t} \tag{8.18}$$

where

$$A_4 = [\{(\lambda_{KX}\theta_{LX}\sigma_X + \lambda_{KY}\theta_{LY}\sigma_Y)/|\theta|\}\{(1 - \theta_{LZ}(1 - E_W))\}] > 0; \text{ and,}$$

$$A_5 = [\{(\lambda_{KX}\theta_{LX}\sigma_X + \lambda_{KY}\theta_{LY}\sigma_Y)/|\theta|\}T] > 0.$$

Solving Equations (8.17) and (8.18) by Cramer's rule we get the following expression:

$$\hat{Z} = (1/|\lambda|)[\lambda_{KX}\hat{K} - (\lambda_{LX}A_4 + \lambda_{KX}A_1)\hat{P}_X + (\lambda_{LX}A_5 + \lambda_{KX}A_2)\hat{t} + \lambda_{KX}A_3\hat{E}] \tag{8.19}$$

where

$$|\lambda| = [\lambda_{LX}(\lambda_{KY} + \lambda_{KZ}) - \lambda_{KX}(\lambda_{LY} + \lambda_{LZ}(1 + l_C/\mu))] \tag{8.20}$$

So, $|\lambda| > (<)0$ iff $\{\lambda_{LX}(\lambda_{KY} + \lambda_{KZ}) - \lambda_{KX}(\lambda_{LY} + \lambda_{LZ})\} > (<) (\lambda_{KX}\lambda_{LZ}l_C/\mu)$. Alternatively, $|\lambda| > (<)0$ under the following necessary and sufficient condition:

[23]See Appendix 8.2 for detailed derivation.

$$\left[\frac{a_{LX}}{a_{KX}} - \frac{(a_{LY}Y + a_{LZ}Z)}{(a_{KY}Y + a_{KZ}Z)}\right] > (<) \left[\frac{(a_{LZ}l_C/\mu)}{a_{KY}Y + a_{KZ}Z}\right] \tag{8.21}$$

From Equation (8.19) one can now trivially establish the following proposition.

Proposition 8.1 *An inflow of foreign capital or a hike in subsidy on education leads to a contraction (an expansion) of the formal sector (sector Z) in terms of both employment and output if and only if* $|\lambda| < (>)0$. *On the other hand, sector Z contracts (expands) owing to an increase in the price of agricultural commodity or a reduction in the import tariff iff* $|\lambda| > (<)0$.

We shall now try to interpret the necessary and sufficient condition (given by Equation (8.21)) for $|\lambda|$ to be negative (positive). It should be remembered that each adult worker employed in the two informal sectors sends l_C number of his children to the job market and the rest are sent to schools. On the other hand, labourers engaged in the formal sector of the economy constitute the richer section of the working class and do not send their children to the job market. In the two informal sectors adult labour and child labour are perfect substitutes. So, the effective adult labour endowment of the economy including child labour is given by $L^*(= L + L_C/\mu)$. The labour–capital ratio in sector X is given by (a_{LX}/a_{KX}). Sector Z uses capital directly as well as indirectly through use of Y as production of one unit of Z requires a_{YZ} units of Y and sector Y also requires capital in its production. Thus, $(a_{KY}Y+a_{KZ}Z)$ gives the direct plus indirect requirement of capital in the production of Z. Sector Y requires labour in its production. So this should be included in the calculation of labour requirement for sector Z. The effective labour–capital ratio for sector Z is given by $\{(a_{LY}Y+a_{LZ}Z)/(a_{KY}Y+a_{KZ}Z)\}$. The left-hand side of Equation (8.21) gives the difference between the actual labour–capital ratio of sector X and the effective labour–capital ratio of sector Z. This difference is positive because it is sensible to assume that the agricultural sector (sector X) is more labour-intensive vis-à-vis the aggregate industrial sector (i.e. sectors Z and Y taken together). Now turning back to interpreting the right-hand side of Equation (8.21), we note that $a_{LZ}Z$ number of workers who are engaged in sector Z do not send their offspring to the job market. However, if they were employed in either of the two informal sectors each of them would have sent l_C number of children to work. As these $a_{LZ}Z$ numbers of workers are used in sector Z, the economy is deprived of having $a_{LZ}Zl_C$ number of potential child workers, which is equivalent to $(a_{LZ}Zl_C/\mu)$ units of adult labour. Thus, the right-hand side of Equation (8.21) gives the ratio between the forgone labour endowment and aggregate amount of capital used in the industrial sectors. Thus, $|\lambda|$ is negative (positive) under the necessary and sufficient condition that the latter ratio must be greater (less) than the difference between the labour–capital ratios of the agricultural and the industrial sectors. We should note that the a_{ji}s depend on the unknown factor prices, which in turn depend on the parameters in the price system like P_X, P_Z, t and U. The value of l_C, on the other hand, depends on the values of μ, α, β, γ, P_X, P_Z, t and U. So, depending on the parameter values $|\lambda|$ would be negative or positive.

Finally, totally differentiating Equation (8.7) using Equations (8.15), (8.19) and (8.20) and simplifying we can derive the following expression:[24, 25]

$$\begin{aligned}
\hat{L}_C = &-\left(\frac{l_C a_{LZ} Z \lambda_{KX}}{L_C|\lambda|}\right)\hat{K}\\
&+\hat{P}_X\left(\frac{1}{L_C|\lambda||\theta|}\right)\left[\frac{(L - a_{LZ}Z)W(\theta_{KY}\theta_{YZ} + \theta_{KZ})(n(\alpha+\beta) - \mu\gamma - l_C)}{(W - \mu B)}\right.\\
&\{\lambda_{LX}(\lambda_{KY} + \lambda_{KZ})\}\\
&-\{\lambda_{KX}(\lambda_{LY} + \lambda_{LZ})\} + l_C a_{LZ} Z(1 - \theta_{LZ}(1 - E_W))\\
&\{\lambda_{LX}(\lambda_{KX}\theta_{LX}\sigma_X + \lambda_{KY}\theta_{LY}\sigma_Y) + \lambda_{KX}(\lambda_{LX}\theta_{KX}\sigma_X + \lambda_{LY}\theta_{KY}\sigma_Y)\}]\\
&-\hat{t}\left(\frac{T}{|\lambda||\theta|L_C}\right)\left[\left\{\frac{\theta_{KX}W(L - a_{LZ}Z)(n(\alpha+\beta) - \mu\gamma - l_C)}{(W - \mu B)}\right\}\right.\\
&\{\lambda_{LX}(\lambda_{KY} + \lambda_{KZ}) - \lambda_{KX}(\lambda_{LY} + \lambda_{LZ})\}\\
&\left.+l_C a_{LZ} Z\{\lambda_{LX}(\lambda_{KX}\theta_{LX}\sigma_X + \lambda_{KY}\theta_{LY}\sigma_Y) + \lambda_{KX}(\lambda_{LX}\theta_{KX}\sigma_X + \lambda_{LY}\theta_{KY}\sigma_Y)\}\right]\\
&-\hat{E}\left[\frac{\mu B' E(L - a_{LZ}Z)}{L_C|\lambda|(W - \mu B)}\right][(n - l_C)\{\lambda_{LX}(\lambda_{KY} + \lambda_{KZ}) - \lambda_{KX}(\lambda_{LY} + \lambda_{LZ})\}\\
&+l_C\lambda_{LZ}\lambda_{KX}(1 + l_C)]
\end{aligned} \tag{8.22}$$

From Equation (8.22) we find that

(i) $\hat{L}_C > (<)0$ when $\hat{K} > 0$ iff $|\lambda| < (>)0$;
(ii) $\hat{L}_C > (<)0$ when $\hat{E} > 0$ iff $|\lambda| < (>)0$;

Let us now explain these results intuitively. We note that any policy change affects the supply of child labour in two ways: (i) through a change in the size of the

[24] See Appendix 8.3 for detailed derivations.

[25] It may be an interesting idea to carry out a comparative static exercise with respect to γ. The parameter denoting the degree of altruism on the part of the guardian of a poor working family depends crucially on the social values and tradition. Owing to mass literacy and adult education programmes and vigorous public campaign against child labour, social values and tradition may change over time and raise the value of γ. From Equation (8.6.1) it is easy to check that an increase in γ lowers the supply of child labour from each poor family, l_C. To find out the effect on the aggregate supply of child labour in the economy after differentiating Equation (8.7) with respect to γ and using Equations (8.15) and (8.19) we find that $(\mathrm{d}L_C/\mathrm{d}\gamma) = -(L_C/\gamma)\left[\frac{\mu\gamma W}{(W-\mu B)l_C|\lambda|}\right][\{\lambda_{LX}(\lambda_{KY} + \lambda_{KZ}) - \lambda_{KX}(\lambda_{LY} + \lambda_{LZ})\}$
$+l_C\lambda_{LZ}\lambda_{KX}(1 - 1/\mu)]$
From this expression it follows that $(\mathrm{d}L_C/\mathrm{d}\gamma) > (<)0$ if and only if $|\lambda| < (>)0$. So, the incidence of child labour declines iff $|\lambda|>0$. This result may be intuitively explained in terms of *direct effect* and *labour reallocation effect*.

informal sector labour force, ($L_I = (L - a_{LZ}Z)$), as these families are considered to be the suppliers of child labour (we call this the *labour reallocation effect*); and (ii) through a change in l_C (the number of child workers supplied by each poor family), which results either from a change in the adult wage rate, W, or from a change in the benefit derived from sending children to schools, $B(E)$ (this is called the *direct effect*).

An inflow of foreign capital cannot alter the factor prices including the informal sector adult wage rate, W, as the production system possesses the decomposition property. So the supply of child labour from each poor working family, l_C, does not change. However, it produces a Rybczynski effect leading to a contraction (expansion) of sector Z and an expansion (contraction) of sector X if and only if $|\lambda| < (>) 0$. As sector Z contracts (expands), more (less) adult workers would now be employed in the two informal sectors than before. Consequently, the number of poor families, from which the supply of child labour comes, increases (decreases). This is the labour reallocation effect. The supply of child labour in the economy increases (decreases) following an inflow of foreign capital if and only if $|\lambda| < (>) 0$.

On the other hand, an increase in the subsidy on education affects the incidence of child labour in two ways. First, it lowers the effective price of child labour, $((W/\mu) - B(E))$. This lowers the supply of child labour from each family, l_C. This is the direct effect of the policy, which exerts a downward pressure on the incidence of child labour. Second, an induced effect is generated as the direct effect lowers the number of available child labour and hence the effective adult labour endowment of the economy.[26] This causes sector Z to shrink (grow) and sector X to expand (contract) owing to Rybczynski effect if and only if $|\lambda| < (>) 0$.[27] If the formal sector contracts, the number of child labour supplying families employed in the informal sectors increases. This is the labour reallocation effect, which tends to push up the number of child labour in the society. The incidence of child labour gets a boost when the labour reallocation effect outweighs the contractionary direct effect. This happens under the necessary and sufficient condition that $|\lambda| < 0$. On the contrary, when $|\lambda| > 0$, a larger number of working families would now be engaged in the formal sector (sector Z) resulting in a decrease in the number of families supplying child labour. Hence, both the direct and induced effects of an education subsidy policy work together to lower the incidence of child labour in the society when $|\lambda| > 0$.

So the following proposition can now be established.

Proposition 8.2 *An increase in the subsidy on education and/or an inflow of foreign capital will raise (lower) the supply of child labour iff* $|\lambda| < (>) 0$.

We are now interested to study the consequences of the trade liberalisation policies. If trade in agriculture is liberalised in the developed nations, the prices of primary agricultural exports of the developing countries are expected to rise

---

[26] As child labour and adult labour are substitutes in X and Y sectors, the effective labour force must include child labour subject to a scale correction of μ. Thus, a reduction in the number of child labour lowers the effective adult labour endowment of the economy.

[27] The interpretation of this condition has already been provided.

possibly owing to the multilateral tariff reductions by the large trading countries and the consequent increase in their import demands. In the context of the present model, trade liberalisation in agriculture in the developed countries implies an increase in the price of the export commodity of the developing country, P_X. On the contrary, tariff reform in the case of manufacturing product means a reduction in the import tariff, t, on Z.

From Equation (8.22) it is easy to check that

(iii) $\hat{L}_C > (<)0$ when $\hat{t} < 0$ iff $|\lambda| > (<)0$; and
(iv) $\hat{L}_C > (<)0$ when $\hat{P}_X > 0$ iff $|\lambda| > (<)0$.

If the price of the agricultural commodity, P_X, soars or the import tariff on sector Z falls, the informal sector adult wage rate, W, rises following a Stolper–Samuelson effect as sector X is more intensive in the use of labour vis-à-vis the industrial sectors as a whole. The child wage rate, W/μ, also rises as a consequence. The supply of child labour from each poor family, l_C, swells (see Equation (6.1)). As a consequence, the incidence of child labour mounts up. This is the direct effect of the trade liberalisation policies, which exerts an upward pressure on the incidence of child labour. However, as the direct effect raises the number of available child labour and hence the effective adult labour endowment of the economy, sector Z expands (contracts) if and only if $|\lambda| < (>)0$. If the formal sector expands, some workers move out of the informal sectors to join the formal sector. Hence, the number of families, supplying child labour, shrinks. This is the labour reallocation effect, which produces a favourable effect on the incidence of child labour. The net result would be a decrease in the aggregate supply of child labour as the labour reallocation effect outweighs the direct effect. On the contrary, when $|\lambda| > 0$ sector Z contracts. More adult workers are now employed in the two informal sectors, thereby raising the total number of families supplying child labour. Thus, in this case both the direct effect and the labour reallocation effect work on the same direction and accentuate the incidence of child labour in the society. This leads to the following proposition.

Proposition 8.3 *Tariff reform in manufacturing import or a policy of trade liberalisation in agriculture lowers (raises) the incidence of child labour in the society if and only if* $|\lambda| < (>)0$.

A close look at Propositions 8.2 and 8.3 reveals that when $|\lambda| > 0$, an inflow of foreign capital or a hike in education subsidy lowers the incidence of child labour while a policy of tariff reform and/or trade liberalisation in agriculture accentuates the problem. On the contrary, the former policies raise the incidence of child labour while the latter produce the opposite effect when $|\lambda| < 0$. In a developing economy, a subsidy policy on education and trade and investment liberalisation policies are undertaken concurrently. In the given set-up, we find that if these policies are undertaken concurrently, some of these will work to reduce the incidence of child labour while the others will accentuate the problem, thereby counterbalancing each other's effects, partially, if not fully. Thus, the net effect may be ambiguous irrespective of the sign of $|\lambda|$. This establishes the final proposition of the model.

Proposition 8.4 *If a subsidy policy on education and different trade and investment liberalisation policies are adopted in a developing economy concomitantly, the net effect on the incidence of child labour may be uncertain.*

Thus our theoretical investigation has shown that if different trade and investment liberalisation programmes and a free education policy are undertaken simultaneously in a transition economy, their overall effect on the supply of child labour may not be quite satisfactory as different policies produce mutually opposite effects on the incidence of child labour, thereby nullifying each other's effects, at least partially. For example, when $\lambda>0$, an inflow of foreign capital or a hike in education subsidy exerts a downward pressure on the incidence of child labour while a policy of tariff reform or trade liberalisation in agriculture accentuates the problem. On the contrary, the former two policies raise the child labour incidence while the latter policies produce the opposite effect when $|\lambda| < 0$. The actual sign of $|\lambda|$ depends on the parameters of the system. So, taking into account all parameter values, the policymakers of the country should decide which policies ought to be given priority and carried out in order to mitigate the incidence of poverty-induced child labour in the system.

8.3 An Extension: Urban Unemployment of Adult Labour in a Harris–Todaro Framework

The analysis of the previous section has used a full-employment structure and hence ignored the problem of unemployment, which is one of the salient features of the developing countries. We are now going to build up a three-sector Harris–Todaro-type general equilibrium model to analyse the consequences of liberalised economic policies and an education subsidy policy on the child labour problem in the urban sector. We shall show that these policies may raise the level of urban unemployment of adult labour even when two types of labour are not substitutes to each other.

We consider a small open dual economy, which is broadly divided into an urban sector and a rural sector. The urban sector is subdivided into two sub-sectors – the urban informal sector and the urban formal sector, so that there are three sectors in the economy. The rural sector produces an agricultural product X, with the help of labour, both adult and child, and capital. Following Basu (1999), we assume that child labour and adult labour are substitutes in the rural sector. The rural sector is concerned mainly with activities relating to cultivation. For no such activities children are essential, so that adults can always replace them. Thus the substitution axiom is quite relevant in the rural sector. It is assumed that a child's labour is equivalent to β units of an adult's labour, where $0 <\beta < 1$. Thus, adult and child labour are perfect substitutes subject to an adult-equivalent scale correction of β. The adult labour earns an institutionally given rural wage[28] of $\overline{W}_X$, while a child

[28] An exogenously given rural wage for adult labour does not give rise to the possibility of rural unemployment of adult labour as we have considered a Harris–Todaro type economy. The levels of production and employment of labour in the rural sector (in other sectors of the economy as well)

labour earns $\beta\overline{W}_X$. The rigidity of rural wage can be justified[29] by the 'efficiency wage hypothesis' or the 'collusive theory of unemployment' (Osmani, 1991).

The informal sector uses adult labour, child labour and capital to produce an internationally non-traded input, Y, for the formal sector. Many of the large industries like the carpet weaving industries, the glass manufacturing industries, the bangles industries, leather bag and shoe manufacturing industries, garment industries, etc. have split up into tiny units and shifted the production process to urban slums, in order to utilise the services of children at lower wages. Some among these industries give subcontract to enterprises, which produce a component of the formal sector output, on an informal basis, hiring child labour. For many of these industries, child labour may be essential since their 'nimble fingers' are typically suited to perform activities like carpet weaving, stitching buttons, etc. Hence, we consider a separate child labour market in this sector, with perfectly flexible wage rate, W_C. The informal sector adult wage rate is W_Y and quite obviously, $W_C < W_Y$.

The formal sector is the tariff-protected capital-intensive import-competing sector producing manufactured goods, Z. It uses adult labour, capital and produced input from the informal sector. Owing to effective wage legislation and unionisation of labour, there is rigidity of wages, so that $\overline{W}_Z$ is given exogenously. Throughout we shall assume that the urban sector, as a whole, is more capital-intensive than the rural sector.

There is homogeneity of labour so that each adult worker has exactly α number of potential child worker at his disposal and without any loss of generality we can choose $\alpha=1$. So, each working family comprises one adult and one child worker each. Production functions are of fixed coefficient type; markets are competitive; capital is fully employed and is completely mobile among the three sectors. There is presence of Harris–Todaro type of adult unemployment, while child labour is

---

are determined by factor endowments, technological and other parameters of the system. Those adult workers who are unable to find employment in the rural sector migrate to the urban sector with their children as both adult and child wage rates in the urban informal sector are absolutely flexible. The complete flexibility of informal sector wage rates leads to the equality between the expected urban income for a prospective rural migrant family and their actual family income in the rural sector (given by Equation (8.29)). In a completely different context, Gupta (1994) has also made the same assumption and explained the simultaneous existence of informal sector and open unemployment in the urban area.

[29] According to the 'wage efficiency hypothesis' the nutritional efficiencies of the workers are positively related to their respective wage incomes (at least for some minimum levels). Thus the employers in the rural labour market would prefer to pay efficiency wages to their respective workers rather than lower wages even if there is excess supply in the labour market. In this situation, competition would fail to lower the wage rates and clear the labour market. For surveys of the nutritional evidence from the perspective of economics one can look at Dasgupta and Ray (1990) and Osmani (1990). On the other hand, Osmani (1991) has observed that in the casual labour market in the rural areas, workers generally refuse to undercut other workers, even if they are unemployed, for fear that this would lower wages for everybody at present and in the future. In other words, they may prefer to remain unemployed in the hope that in the next period they would find employment at the prevailing high wage rates. Thus, the wage rates would not fall even when there is open unemployment in the labour market.

assumed to be fully employed.[30] We assume that a child worker cannot migrate[31] to the urban sector unless his guardian migrates. In other words, migration of an adult worker is always accompanied by migration of the child worker in his family. The rural and urban adult and child wage rates are related by the migration equilibrium condition where the wage income of a rural working family is equal to the expected urban wage, consisting of expected urban adult wage and child labour wage rate. Owing to the small open economy assumption, prices of the traded goods, X and Z, are given internationally. Since Y is non-traded its price is endogenously determined by the demand–supply mechanism – the supply of Y is constrained by the demand for Y in the formal sector.

In addition to the symbols used so far we will use the following as well:

a_{CY}: child labour–output ratio in sector Y;
W_Y: adult wage rate in the informal sector;
$\overline{W}_i$: institutionally given wage rates in the i-th sectors, $i = X, Z$;
r: rate of return to capital;
L: total adult labour endowment;
L_U: level of unemployment of adult labour in the urban sector; and
L_C: supply of child labour in the urban sector.

A general equilibrium of the system is given by the following set of equations:

$$\overline{W}_X a_{LX} + r a_{KX} = P_X \tag{8.23}$$

$$W_C a_{CY} + W_Y a_{LY} + r a_{KY} = P_Y \tag{8.24}$$

$$P_Y a_{YZ} + \overline{W}_Z a_{LZ} + r a_{KZ} = P_Z(1+t) \tag{8.25}$$

$$\frac{a_{LX}X}{(1+\beta)} + a_{LY}Y + a_{LZ}Z + L_U = L, \tag{8.26}$$

$$a_{CY}Y = L_C, \tag{8.27}$$

$$a_{KX}X + a_{KY}Y + a_{KZ}Z = K \tag{8.28}$$

Equations (8.23), (8.24) and (8.25) are the usual price-unit cost equality conditions in the three sectors of the economy. Equations (8.27) and (8.28) are the full-employment conditions of child labour and capital, respectively. Equation

[30] Complete flexibility of the wage rate of child labour ensures full-employment of child labour in the urban sector.

[31] This is not true in general. In some cases the children who especially work in the informal service sector of the urban area migrate without the other members of their families. Besides, there may be many cases where adult members of rural families come to the urban areas for work without their offspring. However, there is some empirical evidence in support of our assumption (see Mohsin, 1996).

(8.26) is the endowment equation of adult labour. In Equation (8.26), $(a_{LX}X/(1+\beta))$ is the number of adult workers (or working families) employed in the rural sector. This is because one working family, consisting of one adult and one child worker each, is equivalent to $(1+\beta)$ units of adult labourers.

The Harris–Todaro migration equilibrium condition is given by

$$\frac{W_Y a_{LY} Y + \overline{W}_Z a_{LZ} Z}{a_{LY} Y + a_{LZ} Z + L_U} + W_C = \overline{W}_X (1 + \beta). \tag{8.29}$$

The right-hand side of Equation (8.29) is the total income of a working family in the rural sector, which must be equal to the expected total income of the family in the urban sector (the left-hand side) in migration equilibrium.[32]

The supply of child labour in the urban sector[33] is given by

$$L_C = a_{LY} Y + L_U - f(E) \tag{8.30}$$

where $f(E)$ is the number of school-going children from the poorer section of the urban sector, $f' > 0$. This relationship can be explained as follows. Abject poverty and lack of educational facilities are claimed to be the two most important factors responsible for the persistence of child labour. If one admits the luxury axiom of Basu and Van (1998) there is enough justification to assume that a household would not send its children out to work if their incomes from non-child labour sources are sufficiently high. In the urban sector of the economy in our model, each worker employed in the formal sector earns relatively high contractual wage, $\overline{W}_Z$, while the labourers in the urban informal sector earn low-wage incomes and the unemployed adult workers have no income at all. So it would be justified to assume that the last two categories of workers in the urban sector send their children out to work to supplement their low-income levels from non-child labour sources. Thus the higher the number of labourers in these two categories, the larger would be the potential supply of child labour. In accordance with our assumption that each adult worker has exactly one child in his family, the number of potential child workers in the urban area will be $(a_{LY}Y+L_U)$. To get the actual supply of child labour one has to deduct the number of school-going children from the potential supply of child labour. Now, the higher the subsidy on education, E, the higher would be the free educational facilities and the related incentives to attract children from the poorer urban households and the larger would be the number of school-going children, $f(E)$.

[32] The Harris–Todaro (1970) model with urban unemployment fails to provide a satisfactory answer to the question as to how the unemployed workers persevere having no income at all. It is supposed that they survive as social parasites on the earnings of their employed counterparts. Fortunately, the present analysis furnishes a more acceptable answer to the above question. It explains that the offspring who find no problem to be absorbed in the urban informal sector take up the responsibility to feed their unemployed guardians and this case is common in the developing countries.

[33] We here assume that no child in the rural sector goes to school. This is not totally unrealistic because in the rural sector of the developing countries the very availability of educational opportunities is extremely limited.

Thus an increase in E lowers the actual supply of child labour, L_C, and vice versa. We also assume that the school-going children cannot undertake any part-time job.

The demand–supply equality condition for the intermediate good, Y, is given by

$$a_{YZ}Z = Y. \tag{8.31}$$

There are nine endogenous variables in the system, $W_C, W_Y, r, P_Y, X, Y, Z, L_C$ and L_U, which are solved from Equations (8.23), (8.24), (8.25), (8.26), (8.27), (8.28), (8.29), (8.30) and (8.31). This is an indecomposable system. Given $\overline{W}_X$ and P_X, r can be determined from Equation (8.23). Substituting the value of r in Equation (8.25), P_Y is determined. W_Y and W_C can be obtained by solving Equations (8.24) and (8.29). Using Equation (8.31), X can be expressed as a function of Y. Inserting the expression for X into Equation (8.26), one can obtain an equation containing the two variables Y and L_U. Also, using Equations (8.27) and (8.30), another equation with Y and L_U is found. The equilibrium values of Y and L_U are obtained as functions of parameters of the system by solving these two equations simultaneously. Once Y is known, Z is found from Equation (8.31). From the expression for X, the equilibrium level of X is obtained. Finally, L_C is found from (8.27) as Y is known. It is easy to check that the level of urban unemployment for adult labour is positive in migration equilibrium under the simple sufficient condition $a_{LY} \leq a_{CY}$.

A pertinent question at this juncture is why urban unemployment of adult labour may exist particularly when the urban informal sector wage rate is flexible. Given the fixed coefficient nature of the production technologies in different sectors of the economy, the output composition does not depend on factor prices. It entirely depends on the factor endowments, technological and other parameters of the system. Sector Y produces a non-traded intermediate input, which is solely used by sector Z. So, the demand for the informal sector's product (and hence its level of production) completely depends on the output of sector Z and the technological parameter, a_{YZ}. This together with another technological parameter, a_{LY}, ultimately determines the level of employment in the urban informal sector. Hence, unemployment[34] for adult labour in this model arises due to the inadequacy of demand for the intermediate input used in sector Z. The simultaneous existence of the informal sector and open unemployment in the urban sector has been dealt in Chapter 4.

The effects of subsidy on education and foreign capital inflow on the supply of child labour in the urban sector

To analyse the impacts of any changes in the amounts of subsidy on education and inflow of foreign capital on the child labour market we proceed as follows.

Using Equations (8.27) and (8.30) we can write

$$a_{CY}Y = a_{LY}Y + L_U - f(E) \tag{8.30.1}$$

---

[34] In a very special case, however, full employment of adult labour may occur depending on the parameter values of the system.

Totally differentiating Equations (8.26), (8.30.1), (8.28) and (8.31) and solving by Cramer's rule, the following expressions can be derived:

$$\hat{X} = -(\lambda_{LU}/\Delta_1)[\{\lambda_{LY} + \lambda_{LZ} + \lambda_{LU} - (f(E)/L)\}\hat{K} + (\lambda_{KY} + \lambda_{KZ})f'(.)E\hat{E} \quad (8.32.1)$$

$$\hat{Y} = (\lambda_{LU}/\Delta_1)[\lambda_{LX}\hat{K} + \lambda_{KX}f(.)E\hat{E}] \quad (8.32.2)$$

and

$$\hat{L}_U = (\lambda_{LX}/\Delta_1)[f'(.)E(\lambda_{LY} + \lambda_{LZ})\{((\lambda_{KY} + \lambda_{KZ})/(\lambda_{LY} + \lambda_{LZ})) - (\lambda_{KX}/\lambda_{LX})\}\hat{E} + \{\lambda_{LU} - f(E)/L)\}\hat{K}] \quad (8.32.3)$$

where

$$\Delta_1 = \lambda_{LU}\lambda_{LX}\{\lambda_{LY} + \lambda_{LZ} + \lambda_{LU} - (f(E)/L)\}[\{(\lambda_{KY} + \lambda_{KZ})/(\lambda_{LY} + \lambda_{LZ} + \lambda_{LU} - (f(E)/L))\} - (\lambda_{KX}/\lambda_{LX})]$$

As the urban sector as a whole is more capital-intensive than the rural sector, we have $[\{(\lambda_{KY} + \lambda_{KZ})/(\lambda_{LY} + \lambda_{LZ} + \lambda_{LU} - (f(E)/L))\} > (\lambda_{KX}/\lambda_{LX})]$, which implies that $\Delta_1 > 0$.

Now from Equation (8.32.3) we find that $\hat{L}_U > 0$ when $\hat{E} > 0$ as $[\{(\lambda_{KY} + \lambda_{KZ})/(\lambda_{LY} + \lambda_{LZ} + \lambda_{LU})\} > (\lambda_{KX}/\lambda_{LX})]$ if the urban sector as a whole is more capital-intensive than the rural sector. Also $\hat{L}_U > 0$ when $\hat{K} > 0$ if and only if $\lambda_{LU} > (f(E)/L)$. So the following proposition is imminent.

Proposition 8.5 *A policy of free education to the children in the urban sector raises the level of urban unemployment of adult labour. Inflow of foreign capital also leads to an increase in adult unemployment iff* $\lambda_{LU} > (f(E)/L)$.

The urban families whose adult members either are employed in the informal sector or remain unemployed are termed as the poor urban families. The number of such families, denoted L_P, is given by

$$L_P = a_{LY}Y + L_U \quad (8.33)$$

Totally differentiating Equation (8.33) and using Equations (8.32.2) and (8.32.3), one can easily derive[35] the following expression:

$$(L_P/L)\hat{L}_P = \hat{K}\underset{(+)}{(\lambda_{LU}\lambda_{LX}L_C/L\Delta_1)} + \hat{E}[\underset{(+)(+)}{(E\lambda_{LU}f'(.)/\Delta_1)}[\lambda_{LY}\lambda_{KX} + \lambda_{LX}(\lambda_{LY} + \lambda_{LZ})\underset{(+)}{\{(\lambda_{KY} + \lambda_{KZ})/(\lambda_{LY} + \lambda_{LZ})\} - (\lambda_{KX}/\lambda_{LX})}] \quad (8.34)$$

---

[35] This has been derived in Appendix 8.4.

So, from Equation (8.34) it follows that $\hat{L}_P > 0$ if $\hat{K},\hat{E} > 0$. However, $\hat{L}_P = 0$ if t falls or P_X rises as t and P_X are not included in Equation (8.34). This establishes the following corollary.

Corollary 8.1 *An increase in education subsidy or inflow of foreign capital raises the number of poor urban families. On the other hand, any reduction in the import tariff or an increase in the primary agricultural commodity cannot change it.*

The intuition behind corollary 8.1 is fairly straightforward. Inflow of foreign capital and/or an increase in the education subsidy leads to an expansion of the urban sector as a whole (formal plus informal). The expected urban income for a rural migrant family rises, leading to more migration from the rural sector. However, the number of new jobs created in the urban formal sector always falls short of the number of newly migrated families to the urban sector. The consequence would be an increase in the number of poor families in this sector.

Now, differentiation of Equation (8.27) yields

$$\hat{L}_C = \hat{Y} \tag{8.27.1}$$

Thus, from Equations (8.32.2) and (8.27.1) it follows that

$$\hat{L}_C = (\lambda_{LU}/\Delta_1)[\lambda_{LX}\hat{K} + \lambda_{KX}f'(.)E\hat{E}] \tag{8.27.2}$$

So $\hat{L}_C > 0$ when $\hat{E}$ and/or $\hat{K} > 0$ (as $\Delta_1, f'(.)>0$)

This establishes the following proposition.

Proposition 8.6 *A policy of providing free education to children in the urban sector and /or inflow of foreign capital unambiguously accentuates the incidence of child labour in the urban area.*

Propositions 8.5 and 8.6 can be intuitively explained as follows. A policy of providing free education to the urban children raises the number of school-going children, which in turn temporarily lowers the supply of child labour in the urban sector. As a consequence, the urban informal sector that produces an intermediate input for the formal sector contracts releasing capital. Now if the urban sector, as a whole, is more capital-intensive than the rural sector, both the urban sectors would ultimately expand at the expense of the rural sector. But as child labour is an essential input in the urban informal sector, its expansion implies an ultimate increase in the supply of child labour. This may seem to be puzzling when the supply of child labour decreased initially following an increase in the number of school-attending children. We should note that as the formal manufacturing sector expands, the expected income of a rural migrant family in the urban sector rises, leading to more migration from the rural sector. This raises the level of adult unemployment in the urban sector as new migrants outnumber the new job opportunities. Children from these new migrant families add to the size of the child workforce in the urban sector, which outweighs the initial drop in their number resulting from an increase in the free educational opportunities. So the net effect would be an increase in the number of child workers in the urban sector.[36] However, this lowers the incidence of child labour in the rural sector as more and more adult workers along with their children are drawn from the rural sector to the urban sector and as the family size of each working family has been assumed to be the same and given exogenously across the families irrespective of the employment status of their adult members. On the other hand, inflow of foreign capital leads to an expansion of the two urban sectors and a contraction of the rural sector due to Rybczynski effect. Expansion of the informal manufacturing sector implies an increase in the supply of child labour that comes from the newly migrated working families into the urban sector. However, given the fixed-coefficient production technologies, as the capital endowment of the economy has risen in this case, the employment opportunities of the adult workers would increase relatively more compared to the education subsidy case. Thus the effect on the level of urban unemployment of adult labour is ambiguous. It increases if and only if $\lambda_{LU} > (f(E)/L)$.

The effects of education subsidy and trade liberalisation on the child wage rate and welfare of the poorer section of the urban working families

Now we are interested in studying the effects of free education policy and different liberalised trade policies on the child wage rate and also on the welfare of the poorer section of the working families in the urban sector. The working families, in which the adult members either are unemployed or find employment only in the low-wage-paying informal sector, constitute the poorer section of the urban families. The welfare of each family in this category of urban families, for the sake of analytical simplicity, is measured simply by the average income of these families although there are actually two sub-sections within the poorer section of families depending on the status of employment of their adult members.

To analyse the effects of the tariff reform and possible trade liberalisation in agriculture in developed nations, after differentiating Equations (8.23), (8.24), (8.25) and (8.29), using Equations (8.26), (8.32.1) and (8.32.2) and solving by Cramer's rule we get[37]

$$\hat{W}_C = (1/\Delta_2)[\underset{(+)}{W_Y}\underset{(+)}{\lambda_{LY}}(T\hat{t} - H\hat{P}_X) + \theta_{LY}(\underset{(+)}{A}\hat{K} + \underset{(-)}{B}\hat{E})] \tag{8.35}$$

and

$$\hat{W}_Y = (1/\Delta_2)[-\theta_{CY}(\underset{(+)}{A}\hat{K} + \underset{(-)}{B}\hat{E}) - W_C(1 - \lambda_{LX})(\underset{(+)}{T}\hat{t} - \underset{(+)}{H}\hat{P}_X)] \tag{8.36}$$

where

$$\Delta_2 = -(W_C\theta_{LY}/L)[a_{LZ}Z + f(E)] < 0$$

[36] See footnote 15 in this context.

[37] See Appendix 8.5 for detailed derivations of Equations (8.35) and (8.36).

From Equations (8.35), it is seen that $\hat{W}_C > 0$ if $\hat{t} < 0$ or $\hat{P}_X > 0$ or $\hat{E} > 0$. On the contrary, $\hat{W}_C < 0$ if $\hat{K} > 0$. This establishes the following proposition.

Proposition 8.7 *The wage rate of child labour in the urban sector rises if (i) the education subsidy increases; or if (ii) import tariff on the final manufacturing product falls; and if (iii) the price of the primary export commodity rises owing to worldwide liberalised trade policies in agriculture.*

The total number of the poor families in the urban sector is $(a_{LY}Y + L_U)$. Some of the adult members of these families find employment in the informal sector at the wage rate, W_Y, while the others remain unemployed and earn nothing. A few of the children from these families go to schools and the rest work in the informal sector at the child wage rate, W_C. So the average income of these working families, G, is given by the following:

$$G = [\{W_Y a_{LY} Y + W_C L_C\}/\{a_{LY}Y + L_U\}] = [\{Y(a_{LY}W_Y + a_{CY}W_C)\}/(a_{LY}Y + L_U)]. \tag{8.37}$$

We should note that the total income of the urban poor families entirely comes from the urban informal sector. In Equation (8.37), $(a_{LY}W_Y + a_{CY}W_C)$ is the share of adult and child labour in the value of production of the informal sector per unit.

As the price of the primary commodity, produced by the rural sector, P_X hikes, the rental on capital r also rises as the rural sector wage rate, $\overline{W}_X$, is given, which in turn lowers the price of the product produced by the informal sector, P_Y, to satisfy the zero profitability condition. Again, a reduction of the import tariff, t, on the formal sector's product lowers P_Y directly as r is determined from the price–unit cost equality condition (Equation (8.23)) of the rural sector. In both of these cases, $(a_{LY}W_Y + a_{CY}W_C)$ falls (see Equation (8.24)). Y also does not change (see Equation (8.32.2)). So, the aggregate income of the poor urban families falls. However, the number of urban poor families does not change (see corollary 8.1). The consequence would be a drop in the average income of the deprived families of the urban sector.

On the contrary, an increase in the amount of education subsidy and/or inflow of foreign capital leads to an expansion of both of the two urban sub-sectors, as the urban sector as a whole is more capital-intensive vis-à-vis the rural sector. The share of adult and child labour in the value of production of the informal sector per unit, $(a_{LY}W_Y + a_{CY}W_C)$, does not change. But the aggregate income of the urban sector poor families rises as Y rises. On the other hand, the total number of poor families also rises (see Corollary 8.1). The net effect on their average income must depend upon the relative increases of the two terms. It can be easily shown[38] that in the case of foreign capital inflow the proportionate increase in their aggregate income would be greater than the rate of increase in their family number. On the contrary, in the case of a hike in education subsidy the opposite will happen. Thus, the average income of the poor families in the urban sector rises due to foreign capital inflow

[38] This has been proved in Appendix 8.6.

but it falls owing to an education subsidy policy. So, we can now state the following proposition.

Proposition 8.8 *Trade reforms in the form of tariff reductions and/or increase in the price of the export commodity, and increases in subsidy on education lower the welfare of the urban poor families. On the contrary, the urban poor people experience an increase in their welfare owing to foreign capital inflows.*

Thus, our analysis[39] has shown that inflow of foreign capital in the economy and/or a free education policy may raise the supply of child labour in the urban sector by forcing rural workers to migrate to the urban sector with their children and accentuate the problem of urban unemployment of adult labour. Besides, trade reforms like tariff reductions on the urban final manufacturing product or rise in the price of the export commodity resulting from worldwide liberalised trade policies in agriculture and the education subsidy policy lower the welfare of the poor people of the urban sector while foreign capital inflow unambiguously improves their welfare.

Appendix 8.1:

Totally differentiating Equations (8.8), (8.9) and (8.10.1) we get the following expressions:

$$\theta_{LX}\hat{W} + \theta_{KX}\hat{R} = \hat{P}_X \tag{8.A.1}$$

$$\theta_{LY}\hat{W} + \theta_{KY}\hat{R} - \hat{P}_Y = 0 \tag{8.A.2}$$

$$\theta_{LZ}E_W\hat{W} + \theta_{KZ}\hat{R} + \theta_{YZ}\hat{P}_Y = T\hat{t} \tag{8.A.3}$$

where $T = (t/(1+t)) > 0$ and $E_W = ((\partial W^*/\partial W)(W/W^*))$. E_W is the elasticity of the unionised wage rate, W^*, with respect to the informal sector wage rate, W.

Solving Equations (8.A.1), (8.A.2) and (8.A.3) by Cramer's rule one gets expressions (8.15) and (8.16) presented in the text.

Appendix 8.2:

Totally differentiating Equation (8.14) one gets the following:

$$\begin{aligned}\lambda_{LX}\hat{X} + \{\lambda_{LY} + \lambda_{LZ}(1 + l_C/\mu)\}\hat{Z} &= \lambda_{LX}\theta_{KX}\sigma_X(\hat{W} - \hat{R}) + \lambda_{LY}\theta_{KY}\sigma_Y(\hat{W} - \hat{R})\\ &+ \frac{(L - a_{LZ}Z)}{L^*(W - \mu B)^2}[(W - \mu B)\{n(\alpha + \beta)W\hat{W} - \mu\gamma W\hat{W} - n\mu B'E\hat{E}\}]\\ &-\{n(\alpha + \beta)W - n\mu B - \mu\gamma W\}(W\hat{W} - \mu B'E\hat{E})\end{aligned}$$

[39] There are a large number of assumptions embodied in the model, some of which are restrictive. Fixed-coefficient technologies have been assumed in all the three sectors of the economy. Otherwise, it becomes very difficult to derive straightforward analytical results. Also, the assumption that a child worker cannot migrate to the urban sector unless his/her guardian migrates is restrictive. Although there is some empirical evidence in support of this assumption, it may not be the case in general.

where $L^* = (L + L_C/\mu)$ is the effective adult labour endowment of the economy. Thus, $\lambda_{Li} = (a_{Li}X_i/L^*)$ for $i = X, Y, Z$. Note that $\hat{a}_{Li} = -\theta_{Ki}\sigma_i(\hat{W} - \hat{R})$ where σ_i is the elasticity of substitution between labour and capital in the ith sector for $i = X, Y$. But $\sigma_Z = 0$, since we have assumed fixed-coefficient technology for sector Z. Simplification gives

$$\lambda_{LX}\hat{X} + \{\lambda_{LY} + \lambda_{LZ}(1 + l_C/\mu)\}\hat{Z} = (\lambda_{LX}\theta_{KX}\sigma_X + \lambda_{LY}\theta_{KY}\sigma_Y)(\hat{W} - \hat{R})$$
$$+\frac{(L - a_{LZ}Z)}{L^*(W - \mu B)}[W\hat{W}\{n(\alpha + \beta) - \mu\gamma\} - n\mu B'E\hat{E}$$
$$-l_C(W\hat{W} - \mu B'E\hat{E})]$$

Using Equations (8.15) and (8.16) we write

$$\lambda_{LX}\hat{X} + \{\lambda_{LY} + \lambda_{LZ}(1 + l_C/\mu)\}\hat{Z} = \frac{(\lambda_{LX}\theta_{KX}\sigma_X + \lambda_{LY}\theta_{KY}\sigma_Y)}{|\theta|}[\{1 - \theta_{LZ}(1 - E_W)\}$$
$$\hat{P}_X - Q_{KX}T\hat{t}] + \frac{(L - a_{LZ}Z)W}{L^*(W - \mu B)|\theta|}\{n(\alpha + \beta) - \mu\gamma - l_C\}[(\theta_{KY}\theta_{YZ} + \theta_{KZ})\hat{P}_X - \theta_{KX}T\hat{t}]$$
$$-\left[\frac{\mu B'E(1 + n)(L - a_{LZ}Z)}{L^*(W - \mu B)}\right]\hat{E}$$

or

$$\lambda_{LX}\hat{X} + \{\lambda_{LY} + \lambda_{LZ}(1 + l_C/\mu)\}\hat{Z} = A_1\hat{P}_X - A_2\hat{t} - A_3\hat{E} \tag{8.A.4}$$

where

$$A_1 = (1/|\theta|)[(\lambda_{LX}\theta_{KX}\sigma_X + \lambda_{LY}\theta_{KY}\sigma_Y)(1 - \theta_{LZ}(1 - E_W)$$
$$+\frac{(L - a_{LZ}Z)W}{L^*(W - \mu B)}\{n(\alpha + \beta) - \mu\gamma - l_C\}(\theta_{KY}\theta_{YZ} + \theta_{KZ})] > 0;$$

$$A_2 = \left(\frac{T}{|\theta|}\right)\Bigg[(\lambda_{LX}\theta_{KX}\sigma_X + \lambda_{LY}\theta_{KY}\sigma_Y)$$
$$+\frac{\theta_{KX}(L - a_{LZ}Z)W\{n(\alpha + \beta) - \mu\gamma - l_C\}(\theta_{KY}\theta_{YZ} + \theta_{KZ})}{L^*(W - \mu B)}\Bigg] > 0; \text{ and}$$

$$A_3 = \left[\frac{\mu B'E(1 + n)(L - a_{LZ}Z)}{L^*(W - \mu B)}\right] > 0.$$

Similarly totally differentiating Equation (8.13) we obtain

$$\lambda_{KX}\hat{X} + (\lambda_{KY} + \lambda_{KZ})\hat{Z} = \hat{K} + \left[\frac{(\lambda_{KX}\theta_{LX}\sigma_X + \lambda_{KY}\theta_{LY}\sigma_Y)\{T\hat{t} - \hat{P}_X(1 - \theta_{LZ}(1 - E_W))\}}{|\theta|} \right] = \hat{K} - A_4\hat{P}_X + A_5\hat{t} \quad (8.A.5)$$

where $A_4 = [\{(\lambda_{KX}\theta_{LX}\sigma_X + \lambda_{KY}\theta_{LY}\sigma_Y)/|\theta|\}\{(1 - \theta_{LZ}(1 - E_W)\}] > 0$; and $A_5 = [\{(\lambda_{KX}\theta_{LX}\sigma_X + \lambda_{KY}\theta_{LY}\sigma_Y)/|\theta|\}T] > 0$.

Solving Equations (8.A.4) and (8.A.5) by Cramer's rule we get the following expression:

$$\hat{Z} = (1/|\lambda|)[\lambda_{KX}\hat{K} - (\lambda_{LX}A_4 + \lambda_{KX}A_1)\hat{P}_X + (\lambda_{LX}A_5 + \lambda_{KX}A_2)\hat{t} + \lambda_{KX}A_3\hat{E} \quad (8.19)$$

Appendix 8.3:

Totally differentiating Equation (8.7) we write

$$L_C\hat{L}_C = \frac{(L - a_{LZ}Z)}{(W - \mu B)}[nW(\alpha + \beta)\hat{W} - n\mu B'E\hat{E} - \mu\gamma W\hat{W} - l_C(W\hat{W} - \mu B'E\hat{E})] - l_C a_{LZ}Z\hat{Z}$$

or

$$\hat{L}_C = \frac{(L - a_{LZ}Z)}{L_C(W - \mu B)}\{n(\alpha + \beta) - \mu\gamma - l_C\}W\hat{W} - \mu B'E(n - l_C)\frac{(L - a_{LZ}Z)}{L_C(W - \mu B)} - (l_C a_{LZ}Z/L_C)\hat{Z}$$

Using Equations (8.15) and (8.19), the above expression can be rewritten as follows:

$$\hat{L}_C = \left[\frac{(L - a_{LZ}Z)W}{L_C(W - \mu B)|\theta|}\{n(\alpha + \beta) - \mu\gamma - l_C)\}\right][(\theta_{KY}\theta_{YZ} + \theta_{KZ})\hat{P}_X - \theta_{KX}T\hat{t}] - \frac{\mu B'E(n - l_C)(L - a_{LZ}Z)}{L_C(W - \mu B)}\hat{E} - \left(\frac{l_C a_{LZ}Z}{L_C|\lambda|}\right)\left[\lambda_{KX}\hat{K} - (\lambda_{LX}A_4 + \lambda_{KX}A_1)\hat{P}_X + (\lambda_{LX}A_5 + \lambda_{KX}A_2)\hat{t} + \lambda_{KX}A_3\hat{E}\right]$$

Rearranging terms one finds

$$\hat{L}_C = -\left(\frac{l_C a_{LZ} Z \lambda_{KX}}{L_C|\lambda|}\right)\hat{K}$$

$$+\hat{P}_X\left[\frac{(L - a_{LZ}Z)W\{n(\alpha+\beta) - \mu\gamma - l_C\}(\theta_{KY}\theta_{YZ} + \theta_{KZ})}{L_C(W - \mu B)|\theta|}\right.$$

$$\left.+\frac{l_C a_{LZ} Z(\lambda_{LX}A_4 + \lambda_{KX}A_1)}{L_C|\lambda|}\right]$$

$$-\hat{t}\left[\frac{T\theta_{KX}W(L - a_{LZ}Z)\{n(\alpha+\beta) - \mu\gamma - l_C\}}{L_C(W - \mu B)|\theta|} + \frac{l_C a_{LZ} Z(\lambda_{LX}A_5 + \lambda_{KX}A_2)}{L_C|\theta|}\right]$$

$$-\hat{E}\left[\frac{\mu B' E(n - l_C)(L - a_{LZ}Z)}{L_C(W - \mu B)} + \frac{l_C a_{LZ} Z \lambda_{KX} A_3}{L_C|\lambda|}\right] \tag{8.A.6}$$

Now

$$\left[\frac{\mu B' E(n - l_C)(L - a_{LZ}Z)}{L_C(W - \mu B)} + \frac{l_C a_{LZ} Z \lambda_{KX} A_3}{L_C|\lambda|}\right]$$

$$= \left[\frac{\mu B' E(n - l_C)(L - a_{LZ}Z)}{L_C(W - \mu B)} + \frac{l_C a_{LZ} Z \lambda_{KX} \mu B'(1+n)(L - a_{LZ}Z)}{L_C|\lambda|L^*(W - \mu B)}\right]$$

$$= \left[\frac{\mu B' E(L - a_{LZ}Z)}{L_C|\lambda|(W - \mu B)}\right][(n - l_C)|\lambda| + \lambda_{LZ} l_C \lambda_{KX}(1+n)]$$

Inserting the value of $|\lambda|$ and after simplification the above expression becomes

$$\left[\frac{\mu B' E(n - l_C)(L - a_{LZ}Z)}{L_C(W - \mu B)} + \frac{l_C a_{LZ} Z \lambda_{KX} A_3}{L_C|\lambda|}\right]$$

$$= \left[\frac{\mu B' E(L - a_{LZ}Z)}{L_C|\lambda|(W - \mu B)}\right][(n - l_C)\{\lambda_{LX}(\lambda_{KY} + \lambda_{KZ}) - \lambda_{KX}(\lambda_{LY} + \lambda_{LZ})\}$$

$$+ l_C \lambda_{LZ} \lambda_{KX}\{(1+n) - (n - l_C)/\mu\}] \tag{8.A.7}$$

Again,

$$\left[\frac{T\theta_{KX}W(L-a_{LZ}Z)\{n(\alpha+\beta)-\mu\gamma-l_C\}}{L_C(W-\mu B)|\theta|}+\frac{l_C a_{LZ}Z(\lambda_{LX}A_5+\lambda_{KX}A_2)}{L_C|\theta|}\right]$$

$$=\left[\frac{T\theta_{KX}W(L-a_{LZ}Z)\{n(\alpha+\beta)-\mu\gamma-l_C\}}{L_C(W-\mu B)|\theta|}\right.$$

$$+\left(\frac{l_C a_{LZ}ZT}{|\lambda|L_C|\theta|}\right)\{\lambda_{LX}(\lambda_{KX}\theta_{LX}\sigma_X+\lambda_{KY}\theta_{LY}\sigma_Y)$$

$$\left.+\lambda_{KX}(\lambda_{LX}\theta_{KX}\sigma_X+\lambda_{LY}\theta_{KY}\sigma_Y)+\frac{\lambda_{KX}\theta_{KX}(L-a_{LZ}Z)W(n(\alpha+\beta)-\mu\gamma-l_C)}{L^*(W-\mu B)}\Big\}\right]$$

Inserting the value of $|\lambda|$ and after simplification the above expression becomes

$$\left[\frac{T\theta_{KX}W(L-a_{LZ}Z)\{n(\alpha+\beta)-\mu\gamma-l_C\}}{L_C(W-\mu B)|\theta|}+\frac{l_C a_{LZ}Z(\lambda_{LX}A_5+\lambda_{KX}A_2)}{L_C|\theta|}\right]$$

$$=\left(\frac{T}{|\lambda||\theta|L_C}\right)\left[\left\{\frac{\theta_{KX}W(L-a_{LZ}Z)(n(\alpha+\beta)-\mu\gamma-l_C)}{(W-\mu B)}\right\}\right.$$

$$\{\lambda_{LX}(\lambda_{KY}+\lambda_{KZ})-\lambda_{KX}(\lambda_{LY}+\lambda_{LZ})+\lambda_{KX}\lambda_{LZ}l_C(1-1/\mu)\}$$

$$\left.+l_C a_{LZ}Z\{\lambda_{LX}(\lambda_{KX}\theta_{LX}\sigma_X+\lambda_{KY}\theta_{LY}\sigma_Y)+\lambda_{KX}(\lambda_{LX}\theta_{KX}\sigma_X+\lambda_{LY}\theta_{KY}\sigma_Y)\}\right] \tag{8.A.8}$$

We also write

$$\left[\frac{(L-a_{LZ}Z)W\{n(\alpha+\beta)-\mu\gamma-l_C\}(\theta_{KY}\theta_{YZ}+\theta_{KZ})}{L_C(W-\mu B)|\theta|}+\frac{l_C a_{LZ}Z(\lambda_{LX}A_4+\lambda_{KX}A_1)}{L_C|\lambda|}\right]$$

$$=\left[\frac{(L-a_{LZ}Z)W\{n(\alpha+\beta)-\mu\gamma-l_C\}(\theta_{KY}\theta_{YZ}-\theta_{KZ})}{L_C(W-\mu B|\theta|)}\right.$$

$$+\frac{l_C a_{LZ}Z}{|\theta|L_C|\lambda|}\{\lambda_{LX}(1-\theta_{LZ}(1-E_W))(\lambda_{KX}\theta_{LX}\sigma_X+\lambda_{KY}\theta_{LY}\sigma_Y)$$

$$+\lambda_{KX}(\lambda_{LX}\theta_{KX}\sigma_X+\lambda_{LY}\theta_{KY}\sigma_Y)(1-\theta_{LZ}(1-E_W))$$

$$\left.+\lambda_{KX}\frac{(L-a_{LZ}Z)W(n(\alpha+\beta)-\mu\gamma-l_C)(\theta_{KY}\theta_{YZ}+\theta_{KZ})}{L^*(W-\mu B)}\Big\}\right]$$

Inserting the value of $|\lambda|$ and after simplification the above expression becomes

$$\left[\frac{(L - a_{LZ}Z)W\{n(\alpha + \beta) - \mu\gamma - l_C\}(\theta_{KY}\theta_{YZ} + \theta_{KZ})}{L_C(W - \mu B)|\theta|} + \frac{l_C a_{LZ} Z(\lambda_{LX}A_4 + \lambda_{KX}A_1)}{L_C|\lambda|}\right]$$

$$= \left(\frac{1}{L_C|\lambda||\theta|}\right)\left[\frac{(L - a_{LZ}Z)W(\theta_{KY}\theta_{YZ} + \theta_{KZ})(n(\alpha + \beta) - \mu\gamma - l_C)}{(W - \mu B)}\right.$$
$$\{\lambda_{LX}(\lambda_{KY} + \lambda_{KZ}) - \lambda_{KX}(\lambda_{LY} + \lambda_{LZ}) + \lambda_{KX}\lambda_{LZ}l_C(1 - 1/\mu)\}$$
$$+ l_C a_{LZ}Z(1 - \theta_{LZ}(1 - E_W))\{\lambda_{LX}(\lambda_{KX}\theta_{LX}\sigma_X + \lambda_{KY}\theta_{LY}\sigma_y)$$
$$\left. + \lambda_{KX}(\lambda_{LX}\theta_{KX}\sigma_X + \lambda_{LY}\theta_{KY}\sigma_Y)\}\right] \tag{8.A.9}$$

Using Equations (8.A.7), (8.A.8) and (8.A.9) from Equation (8.A.6) we finally get

$$\hat{L}_C = -\left(\frac{l_C a_{LZ} Z\lambda_{KX}}{L_C|\lambda|}\right)\hat{K}$$
$$+ \hat{P}_X\left(\frac{1}{L_C|\lambda||\theta|}\right)\left[\frac{(L - a_{LZ}Z)W(\theta_{YZ}\theta_{KZ} + \theta_{KZ})(n(\alpha + \beta) - \mu\gamma - l_C)}{(W - \mu B)}\right.$$
$$\{\lambda_{LX}(\lambda_{KY} + \lambda_{KZ}) - \{\lambda_{KX}(\lambda_{LY} + \lambda_{LZ})\} + l_C a_{LZ}Z(1 - \theta_{LZ}(1 - E_W))$$
$$\left.\{\lambda_{LX}(\lambda_{KX}\theta_{LX}\sigma_X + \lambda_{KY}\theta_{LY}\sigma_Y) + \lambda_{KX}(\lambda_{LX}\theta_{KX}\sigma_X + \lambda_{LY}\theta_{KY}\sigma_Y)\}\right]$$
$$- \hat{t}\left(\frac{T}{|\lambda||\theta|L_C}\right)\left[\left\{\frac{\theta_{KX}W(L - a_{LZ}Z)(n(\alpha + \beta) - \mu\gamma - l_C)}{(W - \mu B)}\right\}\right.$$
$$\{\lambda_{LX}(\lambda_{KY} + \lambda_{KZ}) - \lambda_{KX}(\lambda_{LY} + \lambda_{LZ})\}$$
$$\left. + l_C a_{LZ}Z\{\lambda_{LX}(\lambda_{KX}\theta_{LX}\sigma_X + \lambda_{KY}\theta_{LY}\sigma_Y) + \lambda_{KX}(\lambda_{LX}\theta_{KX}\sigma_X + \lambda_{LY}\theta_{KY}\sigma_Y)\}\right]$$
$$- \hat{E}\left[\frac{\mu B' E(L - a_{LZ}Z)}{L_C|\lambda|(W - \mu B)}\right][(n - l_C)\{\lambda_{LX}(\lambda_{KY} + \lambda_{KZ}) - \lambda_{KX}(\lambda_{LY} + \lambda_{LZ})\}$$
$$+ l_C\lambda_{LZ}\lambda_{KX}(1 + l_C)] \tag{8.22}$$

Appendix 8.4:

Totally differentiating Equation (8.33) one gets the following expression:

$$\mathrm{d}L_P = a_{LY}\mathrm{d}Y + \mathrm{d}L_U$$

or

$$(L_P/L)\hat{L}_P = \lambda_{LY}\hat{Y} + \lambda_{LU}\hat{L}_U$$

After inserting the expressions for $\hat{Y}$ and $\hat{L}_U$ from Equations (8.32.2) and (8.32.3), it becomes

$$\begin{aligned}(L_P/L)\hat{L}_P &= \lambda_{LY}(\lambda_{LU}/\Delta_1)[\lambda_{LX}\hat{K}\\ &\quad +\lambda_{KX}f'(.)E\hat{E}] + \lambda_{LU}(\lambda_{LX}/\Delta_1)[f'(.)E(\lambda_{LY}\\ &\quad +\lambda_{LY})\{((\lambda_{KY}+\lambda_{KZ})/(\lambda_{LY}+\lambda_{LZ}))\\ &\quad -(\lambda_{KX}/\lambda_{LX})\}\hat{E} + \{\lambda_{LU}-(f(E)/L)\}\hat{K}]\\ &= (\lambda_{LU}\lambda_{LX}/\Delta_1)[\lambda_{LY}+\lambda_{LU}-(f(E)/L)]\hat{K} + (\lambda_{LU}f'(.)E/\Delta_1)[\lambda_{LY}\lambda_{KX}\\ &\quad +\lambda_{LX}(\lambda_{LY}+\lambda_{LZ})\{((\lambda_{KY}+\lambda_{KZ})/(\lambda_{LY}+\lambda_{LZ}))-(\lambda_{KX}/\lambda_{LX})\}]\hat{E}\end{aligned}$$

With the help of Equation (8.30) it becomes

$$\begin{aligned}(L_P/L)\hat{L}_P = \hat{K}&\underset{(+)}{(\lambda_{LU}\lambda_{LX}L_C/L\Delta_1)} + \hat{E}[\underset{(+)(+)}{(E\lambda_{LU}f'(.)/\Delta_1)}[\lambda_{LY}\lambda_{KX}\\ &+\lambda_{LX}(\lambda_{LY}+\lambda_{LZ})\underset{(+)}{\{(\lambda_{KY}+\lambda_{KZ})/(\lambda_{LY}+\lambda_{LZ})\}-(\lambda_{KX}/\lambda_{LX})}]\end{aligned} \quad (8.34)$$

Appendix 8.5:

Total differentiation of Equations (8.23), (8.24) and (8.25) yields

$$\theta_{KX}\hat{r} = \hat{P}_X, \quad (8.A.10.1)$$

$$\theta_{CY}\hat{W}_C + \theta_{LY}\hat{W}_Y + \theta_{KY}\hat{r} = \hat{P}_Y \quad (8.A.10.2)$$

$$\theta_{YZ}\hat{P}_Y + \theta_{KZ}\hat{r} = \hat{t}(t/1+t) \quad (8.A.10.3)$$

From Equation (8.A.10.1) one can write

$$\hat{r} = \hat{P}_X(1/\theta_{KX}) \quad (8.A.10.4)$$

Substitution of $\hat{r}$ into Equation (8.A.10.3) yields

$$\hat{P}_Y = \hat{t}\{t/\theta_{YZ}(1+t)\} - \hat{P}_X(\theta_{KZ}/\theta_{YZ}\theta_{KX}) \quad (8.A.10.5)$$

After substituting $\hat{r}$ and $\hat{P}_Y$ into Equation (8.A.10.2), we get

$$\theta_{CY}\hat{W}_C + \theta_{LY}\hat{W}_Y + \hat{P}_X(\theta_{KY}/\theta_{KX}) = \hat{t}\{t/\theta_{YZ}(1+t)\} - \hat{P}_X(\theta_{KZ}/\theta_{YZ}\theta_{KX})$$

or

$$\begin{aligned}\theta_{CY}\hat{W}_C + \theta_{LY}\hat{W}_Y &= \hat{t}\{t/\theta_{YZ}(1+t)\} - \hat{P}_X[\{(\theta_{KZ}/\theta_{YZ}) + \theta_{KY}\}/\theta_{KX}]\\ &= T\hat{t} - H\hat{P}_X\end{aligned} \quad (8.A.11)$$

where $T = t/(1+t)\,\theta_{YZ} > 0$; $H = (1/\theta_{KX})[\theta_{KY} + (\theta_{KZ}/\theta_{YZ})] > 0$.

Using Equation (8.26), Equation (8.29) can be rewritten as

$$W_Y a_{LY} Y + \overline{W}_Z a_{LZ} Z = [\{\overline{W}_X(1+\beta) - W_C\}\{L - a_{LX}X/(1+\beta)\}] \qquad (8.A.12)$$

Totally differentiating Equation (8.A.12) we obtain

$$\begin{aligned} a_{LY}Y\mathrm{d}W_Y + a_{LY}W_Y\mathrm{d}Y + \overline{W}_z a_{LZ}\mathrm{d}Z = &-\{\overline{W}_X(1+\beta) - W_C\}\{a_{LX}/(1+\beta)\}\mathrm{d}X \\ &-\{L - a_{LX}X/(1+\beta)\}\mathrm{d}W_C \end{aligned}$$

or

$$\begin{aligned} W_C\{L - (a_{LX}X/(1+\beta))\}\hat{W}_C + a_{LY}YW_Y\hat{W}_Y &= -\{\overline{W}_X(1+\beta) - W_C\}(a_{LX}X/(1+\beta))\hat{X} \\ &\quad -[a_{LY}YW_Y + \overline{W}_Z a_{LZ}Z]\hat{Y} \text{ (since from (8.31.1), } \hat{Y} = \hat{Z}) \\ &= -\{\overline{W}_X(1+\beta) - W_C\}[\{a_{LX}X/(1+\beta)\}\hat{X} + \{L - (a_{LX}X/(1+\beta))\}\hat{Y}] \end{aligned}$$

(obtained using Equations (8.A.12) and (8.26))

Dividing both sides by L we get

$$W_C(1-\lambda_{LX})\hat{W}_C + \lambda_{LY}W_Y\hat{W}_Y = -\{\overline{W}_X(1+\beta) - W_C\}[\lambda_{LX}\hat{X} + (1-\lambda_{LX})\hat{Y}]$$

After inserting the values of $\hat{X}$ and $\hat{Y}$ from Equations (8.32.1) and (8.32.2) the above expression becomes

$$\begin{aligned} W_C(1-\lambda_{LX})\hat{W}_C + \lambda_{LY}W_Y\hat{W}_Y = &-\{\hat{W}_X(1+\beta) - W_C\}(\lambda_{LU}/\Delta_1)[(1-\lambda_{LX}) \\ &\{\lambda_{LX}\hat{K} + \lambda_{KX}f'E\hat{E}\} - \hat{K}\lambda_{LX}\{1 - \lambda_{LX}(f(E)/L)\} \\ &-\lambda_{LX}(1-\lambda_{KX})f'E\hat{E}] \end{aligned}$$

After a little manipulation this reduces to

$$W_C(1-\lambda_{LX})\hat{W}_C + \lambda_{LY}W_Y\hat{W}_Y = -A.\hat{K} - B.\hat{E} \qquad (8.A.13)$$

where

$$A = \{\underset{(+)}{\overline{W}_X(1+\beta) - W_C\}}\underset{(+)}{(\lambda_{LU}/\Delta_1)}\lambda_{LX}(f(E)/L)] > 0$$

and

$$B = \{\underset{(+)}{\overline{W}_X(1+\beta) - W_C\}}\underset{(+)(+)}{(\lambda_{LU}/\Delta_1)f'E}\underset{(-)}{(\lambda_{KX} - \lambda_{LX})} < 0$$

We should note that $\Delta_1 > 0$ and $\lambda_{KX} < \lambda_{LX}$ since it is assumed that the urban sector as a whole is more capital-intensive than the rural sector, in accordance with the Chandra–Khan capital-intensity condition with $L_U > 0$, i.e. $(a_{KX}(1+\beta)/a_{LX}) < \{(a_{KZ} + a_{YZ} \cdot a_{KY})/(a_{LZ} + a_{YZ} \cdot a_{LY} + L_U/L)\}$.

Solving Equations (8.A.11) and (8.A.13) by Cramer's rule, we get

$$\hat{W}_C = (1/\Delta_2)[W_Y\lambda_{LY}(\underset{(+)}{T}\underset{(+)}{\hat{t}} - H\hat{P}_X) + \theta_{LY}(\underset{(+)}{A}\hat{K} + \underset{(-)}{B}\hat{E})] \quad (8.35)$$

and

$$\hat{W}_Y = (1/\Delta_2)[-\theta_{CY}(\underset{(+)}{A}\hat{K} + \underset{(-)}{B}\hat{E}) - W_C(1-\lambda_{LX})(\underset{(+)}{T}\underset{(+)}{\hat{t}} - H\hat{P}_X)] \quad (8.36)$$

where

$$\begin{aligned}\Delta_2 &= W_Y\lambda_{LY}\theta_{CY} - W_C(1-\lambda_{LX})\theta_{LY}\\ &= (W_YW_Ca_{LY}/P_YL)[L_C - L + \{(a_{LX}X)/(1+\beta)\}]\\ &= (W_C\theta_{LY}/L)[a_{LY}Y + L_U - f(E) + \{a_{LX}X/(1+\beta)\} - L] \text{ (using (8.30))}\\ &= -(W_C\theta_{LY}/L)[a_{LZ}Z + f(E)] \quad \text{(obtained after using (8.26))}\\ &< 0\end{aligned}$$

Appendix 8.6:

With the help of Equations (8.24) and (8.27), the expression (8.37) may be rewritten as

$$G = [\{P_Y - ra_{KY}\}/\{a_{LY} + (L_U/Y)\}] = \{M/(a_{LY} + N)\} \quad (8.A.14)$$

where $M = \{P_Y - ra_{KY}\}$ and $N = (L_U/Y)$

Since the a_{ji}s are given owing to the assumption of fixed-coefficient technology, the effects of the policy changes on G must depend on the consequent changes on r, P_Y and (L_U/Y). Differentiating M and N and using Equations (A.10.4), (A.10.5), (32.2) and (8.32.3) we get the following expressions:

$$M\hat{M} = \{P_Yt/\theta_{YZ}(1+t)\}\hat{t} - \{(\theta_{KZ}/\theta_{YZ}) + \theta_{KY}\}(P_Y/\theta_{KX})\hat{P}_X \quad (8.A.15)$$

and

$$N\hat{N} = \{\underset{(+)}{f'(.)}\underset{(+)}{E}/\Delta_1\}[\underset{(+)}{\lambda_{LX}(\lambda_{KY} + \lambda_{KZ}) - \lambda_{KX}(\lambda_{LY} + \lambda_{LZ} + \lambda_{LU})}] - \underset{(+)}{\{\lambda_{LX}f(E)/L\Delta_1\}}\hat{K} \quad (8.A.16)$$

(Note that $\Delta_1>0$ and $\lambda_{LX}(\lambda_{KY} + \lambda_{KZ}) > \lambda_{KX}(\lambda_{LY} + \lambda_{LZ} + \lambda_{LU})$ as the urban sector as a whole is more capital-intensive than the rural sector.).

Now if $\hat{P}_X > 0$ or $\hat{t} < 0$ from Equation (8.A.15) it follows that $\hat{M} < 0$. From Equation (8.A.14) it now follows that G falls when P_X rises or t falls. Again, if $\hat{K} > 0$ from Equation (8.A.16) it follows that $\hat{N} < 0$. So G augments as K rises. On the contrary, $\hat{N} > 0$ when $\hat{E} > 0$. Thus, G falls if E goes up.

Chapter 9
Informal Sector, Pollution and Waste Management

9.1 Introduction

The Industrial Revolution in the nineteenth century has ushered into a new phase of industrialisation, propelling the world economy towards growth and prosperity. Improved economic performance due to industrial production has been accompanied by the inevitable consequence of discharges to the environment in the form of emissions, wastes and garbage causing pollution. Commensurate with growing consumption demand and population size over time, along with higher standards of living, industrial production has been impressively rising, inflicting further detriment to the environment. In the last few decades, environmental degradation due to rampant industrialisation has assumed such alarming proportions that pollution level has exceeded the carrying capacity of the earth, seriously jeopardising the environment and human life. The pursuit for economic growth and development is evidently consonant with environmental pollution and the menace of solid waste. Both environmental scientists and economists have been making ardent endeavours to identify the sources of this degradation and formulate policies to arrest it.

9.1.1 Informal Sector and Pollution

Most countries have taken significant strides to protect environment, and the developed ones have successfully been able to combat pollution to a large extent. But for the developing countries, a major problem in regulating environmental standards is the persistence of the informal sector. The informal sector plays a pivotal role in the context of environment pollution, referring primarily to emissions and discharges of hazardous effluents. Empirical evidences suggest that it is a major source of environmental pollution. For example, Biller and Quintero (1995) have examined leather tanneries in Bogota (Colombia) and also identified the metalworking, electroplating and textile industries, automobile repair shops and brick manufacturing as typical informal sector activities causing severe contamination. Blackman and Bannister (1996) have presented the results of an econometric analysis of the diffusion of propane among informal 'traditional' brick-makers in Cd. Juárez (Mexico).

S. Chaudhuri, U. Mukhopadhyay, *Revisiting the Informal Sector*,
DOI 10.1007/978-1-4419-1194-0_9,

In developed countries the major legislative instruments to combat pollution are command and control and economic incentives. In case of command and control, the regulator specifies the steps to control pollution after collecting the necessary information regarding the polluter. Economic incentives can take the form of pollution fees, marketable permits and liability.[1] However, these measures for environmental regulation become largely ineffective in developing countries due to the predominance of unregistered informal manufacturing units. They continue to operate with the help of indigenous, backward and obsolete technology, which are, in most cases, highly polluting. Yet they can be neither induced nor compelled to internalise the environmental costs inflicted on the society by their activities mainly due to two reasons. First, these units are unregistered, geographically dispersed and it is quite difficult to identify them. Hence they can hardly be brought under the surveillance of the regulating authority. Second, the informal sector units with a nominal capital base cannot afford to pay pollution fees or install pollution-abating equipments.

However, pollution control efforts have traditionally focused on large industrial sources, giving minimal cognizance whatsoever to the fact that a considerable magnitude of pollution emanates from the informal sector and its polluting effects may, in fact, have unfavourable impact on the efficacy of different pollution-regulating policies. It becomes imperative to explore and devise methods for bringing the informal sector into consideration while formulating environmental policies.

9.1.2 Informal Sector and Solid Waste Management

Along with pollution, solid waste constitutes a major problem in developing countries. Solid waste is defined to include refuse from households, non-hazardous solid (not sludge or semisolid) wastes from industrial and commercial establishments, refuse from institutions (including non-pathogenic waste from hospitals), market waste, yard waste and street sweepings (Cointreau-Levine, 1994). Solid waste is associated with both higher production and consumption. While in developed countries solid waste management is executed mainly by the formal sector with the involvement of the government, in developing countries, the formal or the municipal waste management network is crunched by budget crisis so that their contribution in collection and recycling of wastes is inadequate to tackle the huge magnitude of solid wastes.[2] The insufficient collection and inappropriate disposal of solid wastes represent, in turn, a source of water, land and air pollution, and pose risks to human health and the environment. The respite to this potential formidable situation is provided by the informal sector[3] comprising of street pickers, landfill scavengers and

---

[1] See Kolstad (2000) for more details.

[2] In India only about 50 % of the total refuse generated is collected, while the corresponding figures are 33 % in Karachi, 40 % in Yangoon, and 50 % in Cairo. Disposal receives even less attention: as much as 90 % of the munipal solid waste collected in Asian cities end up in open dumps.

[3] For Mexico, waste pickers are estimated to remove 10% of the municipal waste (Bartone et al., 1991). In Bangalore (India), the informal sector is claimed to prevent 15% of the municipal waste

itinerant buyers that are active in waste recovery or collection. They consider urban waste as economic resource and are self-motivated in waste management by income earning potentials.

The doctrine of 'waste management hierarchy' presents three ways to reduce the flow of waste. They are waste minimisation, reuse and recycling. Although waste minimisation is advocated to be the best solution, it hardly seems to be relevant and plausible for developing countries. Massive population growth and urbanisation foster increased production and consumption, both of which tend to generate large quantum of solid wastes. Unnecessary packaging materials and extravagant consumer behaviour are rare to be found in developing countries so that possibilities of prevention of consumption waste at source are remote. Waste generation is an unavoidable accomplice of development. Evidently, efforts to tackle the harmful effects of wastes on environment and human health by recycling are likely to be more appropriate. However, in these countries, a large quantity of waste is dumped in an uncontrolled manner or burned in open air. These have serious environmental and health hazards. The decomposition of organic materials produces methane, which can cause fire and explosions, and contributes to global warming. The biological and chemical processes that occur in open dumps produce strong leachates, which pollute surface and groundwater. It may be contemplated that recycling, although not the best, may be the only viable solution for managing solid wastes in these countries.

Recycling involves collecting end-of-life products, sorting and then transforming the scrap through a mechanical recycling process into either new secondary raw materials that can be fed back into the manufacturing process or reprocessed into another product. In developing countries, it is again the informal sector that plays a crucial role in recycling of wastes.[4] Recovery and pre-treatment of wastes constitutes a crucial stage in the recycling process. The collection and transformation are usually carried out in the informal sector. The secondary recycling industry using processed waste as raw material also largely operates in the informal sector. The comprehensive informal recycling network not only improves the environmental standard but also provides low-cost, labour-intensive solutions that reduce unemployment and poverty, particularly among the most underprivileged segments of the society.

Evidently, the informal sector has a dual impact on the environment in developing countries. On the one hand, absence of any governmental environmental regulations in the informal manufacturing sector engenders uncontrolled pollution, while, on the other, informal recycling of wastes produces significant benefits in terms of reduced

---

going to the dumpsite (Baud and Schenk, 1994). In Karachi, the informal sector reduces municipal waste collection by 10% (Ali et al., 1993). In Metro Manila, an estimated number of 17,000 people make their living as dumpsite scavengers (CAPS, 1992). The number of waste pickers in Bangalore is estimated to range from 20,000 to 30,000 (Baud et al., 1994), while over 20,000 women work as paper pickers in Ahmedabad (Bentley, 1988).

[4] In Cairo more than 400 small plastics reprocessing enterprises exist, which recycle approximately 70% of the waste plastics generated (EQI, 1991).

energy use and emissions, avoiding emissions from landfills and itinerators, conservation of raw materials and reduction in hazard due to improper disposal. It is essential to incorporate the informal sector in the understanding of environmental damages and formulation of policy prescriptions to regulate the environment.

9.2 Trade-Off Between Pollution and Welfare in the Presence of an Informal Sector

In developing countries, the existence of the informal sector is made use of by the formal sector to continue with their polluting production activities. Since the informal sector is outside the purview of governmental regulation, the formal sector often shifts its manufacturing processes to these informal units and manages to evade the abatement costs or penalty taxes for excessive pollution. Empirical evidences suggest that the urban informal sector units mostly produce intermediate inputs for the formal manufacturing sector on a subcontracting basis. Apart from facilitating elusion of environmental regulations, this is also economically cost-effective for the formal sector since due to the absence of labour legislation laws and consequent lower wages in the informal sector, labour can be fully exploited. Because of this outsourcing it is the informal units that become the major players in environmental pollution. For example, in the city of Kolkata in India leather-tanning process is carried on by the informal sector. In the garments industry the dyeing of garments are done by the informal sector participants on a subcontracting basis. Both tanning and dyeing pollute the environment considerably.

One of the possible solutions to tackle the pollution generated by the informal units may be to target the formal sector with the capability of bearing the external costs. If the formal sector is made to pay for its use of the output of the polluting informal sector, it may be effective as an indirect incentive to reduce informal sector production, generating less pollution. In this section, we develop a three-sector general equilibrium model with an informal sector, the output of which is used as an input in the formal sector. We assume that environmental pollution is generated through the production of goods in the informal sector. The formal sector firms are made to pay a pollution emission tax if the actual level of pollution exceeds a certain permissible limit, which is decided by the pollution regulatory authority. The tax revenue collected from this source is transferred to the workers, since they are victimised by environmental pollution. Labour endowment is measured in efficiency units where the efficiency of a representative worker is inversely related to the level of pollution. So, any change in the actual level of pollution affects the efficiency of the workers and hence affects the effective labour endowment. This again causes a change in the inter-sectoral output and the level of pollution. The higher the use of informal sector product, the higher the pollution created and the higher the discrepancy between actual and permissible levels of pollution, so that the emission taxes payable by the formal sector are also higher.

In this situation, we examine whether a reduction in the permissible pollution level by the regulating authority actually results in the desired outcome of diminishing pollution in the economy; the implications on welfare are also studied. Next, we analyse the effects of indirect policies like an inflow of foreign capital on the level of pollution and welfare of the economy. From the results we try to make a conjecture whether there exists a trade-off between economic welfare and pollution. This is extremely significant in today's perspective since we have to shift our approach from positive to normative and make a rational choice so that development goes hand in hand with environmental sustainability.

We consider a small open economy with three sectors operating at close vicinity. Sector 1 (rural sector) produces an agricultural (export) commodity using capital and labour. There are two manufacturing sectors: formal (sector 3) and informal (sector 2). The informal manufacturing sector produces a non-traded input for the formal sector using capital and labour. The formal sector is the tariff-protected import-competing sector producing a manufacturing commodity using capital, labour and the non-traded input produced by the informal sector. Capital is mobile among the three sectors. On the other hand, labour is perfectly mobile between the agricultural and informal manufacturing sectors. But the formal sector faces an imperfect labour market. It is assumed that labour in the formal sector earns a contractual wage, W^*, while the wage rate in the informal sector W is market determined and $W^* > W$. Owing to our small open economy assumption, we consider that the final commodity prices, P_1 and P_3, are given internationally. The price of the non-traded input, P_2, produced by sector 2 is determined endogenously. Production functions exhibit constant returns to scale[5] with diminishing marginal productivity to each factor. The three inputs, capital, labour and the non-traded input, are fully employed. The aggregate capital stock of the economy consists of both domestic and foreign capital and these are perfect substitutes. Income from foreign capital is completely repatriated. Finally, commodity 1 is chosen as the numeraire.

Given the assumption of perfectly competitive markets, the usual price–unit cost equality conditions of the three sectors of the economy are given by the following three equations, respectively:

$$Wa_{L1} + ra_{K1} = 1 \tag{9.1}$$

$$Wa_{L2} + ra_{K2} = P_2 \tag{9.2}$$

$$W^* a_{L3} + ra_{K3} + P_2 a_{23} = P_3(1+m) - \frac{T(Z(X_2) - \overline{Z})}{X_3} \tag{9.3}$$

[5]Production in the import-competing sector, apart from capital and labour inputs, requires a non-traded input, per-unit requirement of which is assumed to be technologically fixed. However, labour and capital are substitutes and the production function displays the property of constant returns to scale in these two inputs.

where $T(.)$, Z, $\overline{Z}$ and m denote aggregate pollution emission tax, permissible level of pollution, actual level of pollution in the economy and ad valorem rate of tariff on the import of commodity 3, respectively.

The rural sector does not generate any pollution[6] and without any loss of generality it is assumed that the informal sector is the only polluting sector[7] so that pollution level (industrial emission), Z, is a positive function of the production level of the informal sector, X_2, i.e.

$$Z = Z(X_2); Z' > 0.$$

For the sake of analytical simplicity, we assume that $Z(.)$ is strictly proportional to X_2. So, we write

$$Z = Z'X_2; Z' > 0, Z'' = 0 \tag{9.4}$$

In other words, Z' is a constant.

Even though the informal sector is the only polluting sector, it cannot be brought directly under government regulation simply because these are unregistered units. Hence it is only the formal sector that can be compelled to maintain the environmental standards by making them pay emission tax for the pollution created by them indirectly by the usage of the input produced by the polluting informal sector. $\overline{Z}$ is a policy parameter of the government. The greater the discrepancy between the permissible level, $\overline{Z}$, and the actual level of pollution, Z, the more the deterioration in environmental standards and hence the higher the aggregate pollution emission tax, T, to be borne by the formal sector.

We define the emission tax function as follows:

$$T = \begin{cases} 0 \text{ for } X_2 \leq \overline{X}_2; \text{ and,} \\ T(Z(X_2) - \overline{Z}); T' > 0 \text{ for } X_2 > \overline{X}_2 \end{cases} \tag{9.5}$$

We explain this emission tax function as follows. We have already stated that the informal sector is the only polluting sector, the level of pollution increases with an increase in the level of production of this sector and that there is a permissible level of pollution, denoted by $\overline{Z}$. Let $\overline{X}_2$ be the level of production at which $Z(.) = \overline{Z}$. So, for any $X_2 \leq \overline{X}_2$, the level of pollution in the economy does not exceed

[6] This is only a simplifying assumption. A typical rural sector is assumed to produce a primary exportable commodity. Production of primary exportable commodities also vitiates the environment through use of chemical fertilizers and pesticides. However, the amount of pollution generated by the rural sector is insignificant relative to that produced by the manufacturing sectors.

[7] Qualitative results of the model remain unchanged even if the formal sector is also assumed to produce pollution. As formal manufacturing sector uses an input produced by the informal sector at a fixed proportion, an expansion of the formal sector implies an expansion of the informal sector. Thus, the qualitative effect of any policy on the informal sector's output (and hence pollution) is equivalent to the case where both the sectors are assumed to generate pollution.

the permissible limit and the emission tax borne by the formal sector is zero. But, once X_2 surpasses $\overline{X}_2$, the pollution level goes above the permissible limit and the emission tax on the formal sector becomes positive. The amount of tax increases as the difference between X_2 and $\overline{X}_2$(and hence between $Z(.)$ and $\overline{Z}$) increases. As our policy analysis is meaningful only when $Z(.) > \overline{Z}$, we concentrate solely on the case where $X_2 > \overline{X}_2$.

The entire emission tax revenue is transferred to the workers in a lump-sum fashion. The right-hand side of Equation (9.3) denotes the unit domestic price of X_3 net of emission tax where $T(Z(X_2) - \overline{Z})/X_3$ is the effective emission tax per unit of output that the formal sector has to bear.

Complete utilisation of capital in the economy implies that

$$a_{K1}X_1 + a_{K2}X_2 + a_{K3}X_3 = K \tag{9.6}$$

The output of the informal sector, X_2, is used entirely for producing X_3, so that the supply of X_2 is circumscribed by its total demand by sector 3. The demand–supply equality condition is given by

$$X_2 = X_2^D = a_{23}X_3 \tag{9.7}$$

Here, a_{23} is assumed to be a constant. This means that to produce one unit of the formal sector's product a_{23} units of the non-traded input are required.[8]

It is assumed that the efficiency of a representative worker, h, is inversely related to the level of pollution, Z, in the economy. Environmental pollution leads to health hazards,[9] thus adversely affecting the worker's efficiency. Although in this model the informal sector only creates pollution, it is assumed that pollution affects the efficiency of the entire workforce, not only those who are engaged in the informal sector activities. This is because the three sectors operate at close vicinity so that environmental degradation affects all the members of the working class equally. Thus,

$$h = h(Z(X_2)); h' < 0. \tag{9.8}$$

After normalising the labour endowment in physical units to unity, the full employment of labour in efficiency units implies the following:

$$a_{L1}X_1 + a_{L2}X_2 + a_{L3}X_3 = h(Z(X_2)) \tag{9.9}$$

[8] See footnote 15 in Chapter 5.

[9] Air pollution can lead to irritation, breathing problems and lung diseases; water pollution causes contaminated drinking water; improper waste disposal management involves significant human pathogens; all these contribute directly to reduce human performance.

where $a_{Li} X_i$ is the employment of labour in the ith sector in efficiency units for $i = 1, 2$ and 3. As the labour endowment of the economy in physical units has been normalised to unity, the labour endowment in efficiency units is $h(Z(X_2))$.

Throughout the model, we assume that the agricultural sector is more labour-intensive than the formal manufacturing sector and that the industrial sector as a whole (formal plus informal) is more capital-intensive than the agricultural sector in value terms. The latter implies that the industrial sector is more capital-intensive vis-à-vis the agricultural sector in physical terms as well. In mathematical terms, we write the capital intensity conditions as follows:

$$\left.\begin{array}{l}(\lambda_{L1}\lambda_{K3} - \lambda_{L3}\lambda_{K1}) > 0;\\ \{\theta_{L1}(\theta_{K3} + \theta_{23}\theta_{K2}) - \theta_{K1}(\theta_{L3} + \theta_{23}\theta_{L2})\} > 0; \text{ and,}\\ \{\lambda_{L1}(\lambda_{K3} + \lambda_{23}\lambda_{K2}) - \lambda_{K1}(\lambda_{L3} + \lambda_{23}\lambda_{L2})\} > 0.\end{array}\right\} \quad (9.10)$$

From Equation (9.10) the following relationships trivially follow

$$\left.\begin{array}{l}\{\theta_{K3}\theta_{L1} + \theta_{23}(\theta_{L1} - \theta_{L2})\} > 0;\\ [\lambda_{K1}\{\lambda_{L2} + \lambda_{L3} - (h'(.)Z'X_2/h(.))\} - \lambda_{L1}(\lambda_{K2} + \lambda_{K3})\}] < 0\end{array}\right\} \quad (9.10.1)$$

However, the informal manufacturing sector can independently be either capital-intensive or labour-intensive relative to the agricultural sector. In this section, we concentrate on the case where the agricultural sector is more labour-intensive than the informal manufacturing sector.[10] In terms of algebra, this can be expressed as follows:

$$(\theta_{L1}\theta_{K2} > \theta_{L2}\theta_{K1}) \text{ i.e. } (\theta_{L1} > \theta_{L2}); \text{ and, } (\lambda_{L1}\lambda_{K2} > \lambda_{L2}\lambda_{K1}) \quad (9.11)$$

There are nine endogenous variables in the system: W, r, P_2, X_1, X_2, X_3, h, Z and T. This is an indecomposable production system where any changes in factor endowment affect factor prices and factor coefficients. By solving Equations (9.1) and (9.2), W and r can be obtained in terms of P_2. Substituting the values of W and r into Equation (9.3), solving simultaneously with Equations (9.6) and (9.9) and using Equation (9.7), the values of X_1, X_2 and P_2 can be obtained.[11] Having obtained X_2, one can find X_3 from Equation (9.7). Again, Z can be obtained from Equation (9.4)

[10] The case where the informal manufacturing sector is more labour-intensive vis-à-vis the agricultural sector has been taken up in Appendix 9.5. In that case, some of the results of the model hold under different sufficient conditions. Instead of dealing with both the cases, we consider only one case in details, since our main intention is to question the desirability of policies rendering a lower permissible level of pollution. If we can show this by considering just one case, our purpose is served.

[11] We should note that X_2 is nothing but the supply of commodity 2, i.e. X_2^S. Conversely, a_{23} X_3 in Equation (9.7) gives the demand for the non-traded input, i.e. X_2^D. Usually, X_2^D and X_2^S would not match if one starts from a random P_2. Therefore, we can define an excess demand function for commodity 2 as $E(P_2) = X_2^D(P_2) - X_2^S(P_2)$. Equation (9.7) is valid if and only if $E(P_2)=0$ say at $P_2 = P_2^e$. For making the entire system consistent, we assume that such a $P_2^e > 0$ exists and it is unique. See Marjit (2003) in this context.

and h from Equation (9.8) once X_2 is obtained. Having obtained Z, from Equation (9.5) T can be found.

The measure of welfare in this small open economy is national income at world prices, Y, which is expressed as follows[12]:

$$Y = W(a_{L1}X_1 + a_{L2}X_2) + W^* a_{L3}X_3 + rK_D + T(Z(X_2) - \overline{Z}) - mP_3X_3$$

Using Equation (9.9) the above expression becomes

$$Y = Wh(.) + (W^* - W)a_{L3}X_3 + rK_D + T(Z(X_2) - \overline{Z}) - mP_3X_3 \quad (9.12)$$

In Equation (9.12), $W(a_{L1}X_1 + a_{L2}X_2)$ is the total wage income of the workers engaged in the first two sectors of the economy. $W^* a_{L3} X_3$ is the amount of the wage income of the labourers employed in the formal sector. rK_D is the rental income from domestic capital.[13] $T(Z(X_2) - \overline{Z})$is the revenue from the emission tax, which the workers receive as transfer payments. Finally, $mP_3 X_3$ measures the cost of tariff protection of the import-competing sector.

According to the conventional wisdom, any policy that entails an improvement in environmental standards is welfare enhancing. Thus, a lowering of the permissible level of pollution by the pollution-controlling authority appears to be a highly desirable policy. But, in this section, we reanalyse the efficacy of such direct environmental policy in lowering pollution level and improving welfare in a developing country in the presence of an informal manufacturing sector generating considerable amount of pollution. We then examine the effects of an inflow of foreign capital on the level of environmental pollution as well as on welfare of the economy in the given set-up.

Total differentials of Equations (9.1) and (9.2) and use of envelope conditions yield

$$\theta_{L1}\hat{W} + \theta_{K1}\hat{r} = 0 \quad (9.13)$$

$$\theta_{L2}\hat{W} + \theta_{K2}\hat{r} = \hat{P}_2 \quad (9.14)$$

Solving Equations (9.13) and (9.14) by Cramer's rule, one gets the following expressions:

$$\hat{W} = -(\theta_{K1}\hat{P}_2)/|\theta| \quad (9.15)$$

---

[12] One may argue that the national welfare function does not explicitly contain any social cost due to pollution. However, the welfare function indirectly takes care of the cost due to pollution. This is because it contains the labour endowment in efficiency units, which is negatively related to the level of pollution. So as pollution level rises, the endowment of labour in efficiency unit falls, leading to a decrease in aggregate wage income. However, qualitative results of the paper hold under different sufficient conditions even if we consider welfare as $Y^* = Wh(.) + (W^* - W)a_{L3}X_3 + rK_D + T(Z(X_2) - \overline{Z}) - \beta Z(X_2)$, where β is the marginal social cost due to pollution.

[13] Income from foreign capital is fully repatriated. Hence, it is not included in Equation (9.12).

$$\hat{r} = \theta_{L1}\hat{P}_2/|\theta| \tag{9.16}$$

and

$$(\hat{W} - \hat{r}) = -(\hat{P}_2/|\theta|) \tag{9.17}$$

where

$$|\theta| = \theta_{L1}\theta_{K2} - \theta_{K1}\theta_{L2} = \theta_{L1} - \theta_{L2}$$

Now, differentiation of Equation (9.7) gives

$$\hat{X}_3 = \hat{X}_2 \tag{9.18}$$

Total differentiation of Equations (9.3), (9.9) and (9.6) and use of Equations (9.15), (9.16), (9.17) and (9.18) yield[14] the following expressions, respectively:

$$\begin{aligned}(\hat{P}_2/|\theta|)[\theta_{K3}\theta_{L1} + \theta_{23}(\theta_{L1} - \theta_{L2})] + (\theta_{23}/P_2X_2)\{T'(.)Z'X_2 - T(.)\}\hat{X}_2 \\ = (\theta_{23}/P_2X_2)(T'(.)\overline{Z}\hat{\overline{Z}})\end{aligned} \tag{9.19}$$

$$\begin{aligned}(\hat{P}_2/|\theta|)[\lambda_{L1}\theta_{K1}\sigma_1 + \lambda_{L2}\theta_{K2}\sigma_2 + (\lambda_{L3}\theta_{K3}\theta_{L1}\sigma_3/(1 - \theta_{23}))] + \{\lambda_{L2} + \lambda_{L3} \\ -(h'(.)Z'X_2/h(.))\}\hat{X}_2 + \lambda_{L1}\hat{X}_1 = 0\end{aligned} \tag{9.20}$$

and

$$\begin{aligned}(\hat{P}_2/|\theta|)[-\lambda_{K1}\theta_{L1}\sigma_1 - \lambda_{K2}\theta_{L2}\sigma_2 - (\lambda_{K3}\theta_{L3}\theta_{L1}\sigma_3/(1 - \theta_{23}))] + (\lambda_{K2} + \lambda_{K3})\hat{X}_2 \\ +\lambda_{K1}\hat{X}_1 = \hat{K}\end{aligned} \tag{9.21}$$

Solving Equations (9.19), (9.20) and (9.21) by Cramer's rule the following expressions can be obtained:

$$\begin{aligned}\hat{X}_2 = &-(1/\Delta|\theta|)[\theta_{K3}\theta_{L1} + \theta_{23}(\theta_{L1} - \theta_{L2})]\lambda_{L1}\hat{K} \\ &\qquad\qquad (+) \\ &-\hat{\overline{Z}}\{(\theta_{23}T'(.)\overline{Z})/(\Delta|\theta|P_2X_2)\}[\lambda_{K1}\lambda_{L1}\sigma_1 + \sigma_2(\lambda_{K1}\lambda_{L2}\theta_{K2} + \lambda_{L1}\lambda_{K2}\theta_{L2}) \\ &+(\theta_{L1}\sigma_3/(1 - \theta_{23}))(\lambda_{K1}\lambda_{L3}\theta_{K3} + \lambda_{L1}\lambda_{K3}\theta_{L3})] \\ &\qquad\qquad (+)\end{aligned} \tag{9.22}$$

and

$$\begin{aligned}\hat{P}_2 = &\hat{\overline{Z}}[\{(\theta_{23}T'(.)\overline{Z})/(\Delta P_2X_2)\}\{\lambda_{K1}(\lambda_{L2} + \lambda_{L3} - (h'(.)Z'X_2/h(.))) \\ &-\lambda_{L1}(\lambda_{K2} + \lambda_{K3})\}] \\ &(-) \\ &+\hat{K}[(\lambda_{L1}\theta_{23})\{T'(.)Z'X_2 - T(.)\}/(\Delta P_2X_2)]\end{aligned} \tag{9.23}$$

[14] See Appendix 9.1 for detailed derivation.

where

$$\begin{aligned}\Delta = &(1/|\theta|)[\{\theta_{K3}\theta_{L1} + \theta_{23}(\theta_{L1} - \theta_{L2})\} \\ &\qquad\qquad (+) \\ &\{\lambda_{K1}(\lambda_{L2} + \lambda_{L3} - h'(.)Z'X_2/h(.)) - \lambda_{L1}(\lambda_{K2} + \lambda_{K3})\}] \\ &\qquad\qquad (-) \\ &-[\theta_{23}\{T'(.)Z'X_2 - T(.)\}/(P_2X_2|\theta|)][\lambda_{K1}\lambda_{L1}\sigma_1 + \sigma_2(\lambda_{K1}\lambda_{L2}\theta_{K2} + \lambda_{L1}\lambda_{K2}\theta_{L2}) \\ &+(\theta_{L1}\sigma_3/(1-\theta_{23}))(\lambda_{K1}\lambda_{L3}\theta_{K3} + \lambda_{L1}\lambda_{K3}\theta_{L3})] \\ &\qquad\qquad (+)\end{aligned} \tag{9.24}$$

As commodity 2 is a non-traded input, its market must clear domestically and the comparative static exercises are meaningful only if the equilibrium in the market for commodity 2 is stable. It can be checked that the stability condition in the market for the non-traded input is as follows[15]:

$$(\Delta/\,|\lambda|\,) = (\Delta'/\,|\theta|\,|\lambda|\,) > 0. \tag{9.25}$$

where

$$\begin{aligned}|\theta| &= (\theta_{L1}\theta_{K2} - \theta_{K1}\theta_{L2}); \\ \Delta' &= [\{\theta_{K3}\theta_{L1} + \theta_{23}(\theta_{L1} - \theta_{L2})\}\{\lambda_{K1}(\lambda_{L2} + \lambda_{L3} - h'(.)Z'X_2/h(.)) \\ &\quad -\lambda_{L1}(\lambda_{K2} + \lambda_{K3})\}] \\ &\qquad (+) \qquad\qquad\qquad\qquad (-) \\ &\quad -[\theta_{23}\{T'(.)Z'X_2 - T(.)\}/(P_2X_2)][\lambda_{K1}\lambda_{L1}\sigma_1 + \sigma_2(\lambda_{K1}\lambda_{L2}\theta_{K2} + \lambda_{L1}\lambda_{K2}\theta_{L2}) \\ &\quad +(\theta_{L1}\sigma_3/(1-\theta_{23}))(\lambda_{K1}\lambda_{L3}\theta_{K3} + \lambda_{L1}\lambda_{K3}\theta_{L3})] \\ &\qquad\qquad (+)\end{aligned} \tag{9.26.1}$$

$$|\lambda| = [G(\lambda_{L1}\lambda_{K3} - \lambda_{L3}\lambda_{K1}) + H\{\lambda_{L1}\lambda_{K2} - \lambda_{K1}(\lambda_{L2} - h'(.)Z'X_2/h(.))\}]; \tag{9.26.2}$$

$$G = (T'(.)Z'X_2/P_3^*X_3) > 0; \tag{9.26.3}$$

and

$$H = (T(.)/P_3^*X_3) > 0. \tag{9.26.4}$$

In the present case where the agricultural sector is more labour-intensive vis-à-vis the informal manufacturing sector,[16] we have $|\theta| > 0$. Using Equations (9.26.3) and (9.26.4) from Equation (9.26.2) we obtain that $|\lambda| > 0$. Then using Equation (9.10.1), from Equations (9.25) and (9.26.1) we find that for the fulfilment of the stability condition in the market for the non-traded input one requires $\Delta > 0$ and $\Delta' > 0$. The necessary condition for $\Delta' > 0$ is $\{T'(.)Z'X_2 < T(.)\}$. This, in turn, implies that $(E_T < 1 - \overline{Z}/Z)$ where $E_T(= [\{dT(.)/d(Z - \overline{Z})\}\{(Z - \overline{Z})/T(.)\}])$ is the elasticity of the emission tax function.

---

[15]This has been derived in Appendix 9.2.

[16]See footnote 10 in this context.

9.2.1 Policy Effects on Environmental Pollution

In the stable equilibrium in the market for the non-traded input we have found that $\Delta > 0$. From Equation (9.22), it now follows that $\hat{X}_2 > 0$ when $\hat{\overline{Z}} < 0$ and $\hat{X}_2 < 0$ when $\hat{K} > 0$. Differentiating Equation (9.4) one gets

$$Z\hat{Z} = Z'X_2\hat{X}_2 \tag{9.27}$$

From Equation (9.27) it is easy to derive the following results:

$\hat{Z} > 0$ when $\hat{\overline{Z}} < 0$ and $\hat{Z} < 0$ when $\hat{K} > 0$. This leads to the following proposition.

Proposition 9.1 *A reduction in the permissible level of pollution in the presence of an informal sector leads to an increase in pollution while an inflow of foreign capital lowers the level of pollution in the economy.*

To explain these results in economic terms, let us first examine the effects of these policies on the effective pollution emission tax rate, say, F, where

$$F = \frac{T(Z(X_2) - \overline{Z})}{X_3}$$

Differentiating F, using Equation (9.22) and simplifying we get[17]

$$\begin{aligned} F\hat{F}X_3 = & -\hat{K}\{T'(.)Z'X_2 - T(.)\}[(1/\Delta\,|\theta|\,)\lambda_{L1}\underset{(+)}{\{\theta_{K3}\theta_{L1} + \theta_{23}(\theta_{L1} - \theta_{L2})\}}] \\ & -\hat{\overline{Z}}\{T'(.)\overline{Z}/(\Delta\,|\theta|\,)\}[\underset{(+)}{\{\theta_{K3}\theta_{L1} + \theta_{23}(\theta_{L1} - \theta_{L2})\}}\{\lambda_{K1}(\lambda_{L2} + \lambda_{L3} - h'(.)Z'X_2) \\ & \qquad \underset{(-)}{-\lambda_{L1}(\lambda_{K2} + \lambda_{K3})\}}] \end{aligned} \tag{9.28}$$

We have already mentioned that the comparative static exercises are meaningful only if equilibrium in the market for the non-traded input is stable. In the present case we have found that in the stable equilibrium $\Delta > 0$ and $\{T'(.)Z'X_2 < T(.)\}$. From Equation (9.28) it then follows that $\hat{F} > 0$ when $\hat{K} > 0$ and $\hat{F} < 0$ when $\hat{\overline{Z}} < 0$.

If in an attempt to check further deterioration in environmental quality, the pollution control authority fixes the permissible level of pollution at a lower level, $\overline{Z}$ takes a lower value. From Equation (9.28) it follows that the average pollution emission tax that the formal sector has to bear decreases. As a consequence, the effective price of the formal sector's product (net of average emission tax) rises leading to an expansion of the formal sector. As the formal sector uses the output of the informal sector at a fixed rate, the latter sector also expands, thereby raising the pollution level

[17] For detailed derivation see Appendix 9.3.

of the society. On the other hand, owing to an inflow of foreign capital the aggregate capital stock of the economy swells up. It produces a Rybczynski effect leading to an expansion of the formal sector (also informal manufacturing sector) and a contraction of the agricultural sector as the manufacturing sector as a whole (formal plus informal) is more capital-intensive than the agricultural sector. The average pollution emission tax, F, rises and the effective price of the formal sector's product decreases as $\Delta > 0$ (see Equation (9.28)). This produces a Stolper–Samuelson effect and exerts downward pressures on the output levels of the two manufacturing sectors. So two opposite effects on X_3 (and hence on X_2) are generated. Since the negative effect of an increase in F outweighs the positive Rybczynski effect, X_3 (and hence X_2) falls in the new equilibrium.

9.2.2 Policy Effects on Welfare

To analyse the welfare implications of the two policies, totally differentiating Equation (9.12) and using Equations (9.15), (9.16), (9.22) and (9.23) the following expression can be derived[18]:

$$\begin{aligned}
Y\hat{Y} = \hat{\overline{Z}}.\{(T'(.)\overline{Z})/(\Delta|\theta|P_2X_2)\}[A\theta_{23}\{\lambda_{K1}(\lambda_{L2} + \underset{(-)}{\lambda_{L3} - h'(.)Z'X_2/h(.))}\\
- \lambda_{L1}(\lambda_{K2} + \lambda_{K3})\}\\
\underset{(+)}{-B\theta_{23}C - (|\theta|\Delta P_2X_2)]}\\
+\hat{K}.(\lambda_{L1}/|\theta|\Delta)[(A\theta_{23}/P_2X_2)\{T'(.)Z'X_2 - T(.)\}\\
\underset{(+)}{-B\{\theta_{K3}\theta_{L1} + \theta_{23}(\theta_{L1} - \theta_{L2})\}]}
\end{aligned} \tag{9.29}$$

where

$$\begin{aligned}
A &= [\{(W^* - W)h(.)\lambda_{L3}\theta_{K3}\theta_{L1}\sigma_3/(1 - \theta_{23})\} - Wh(.)\theta_{K1}(1 - \lambda_{L3}) + rK_D\theta_{L1}],\\
B &= [(W^* - W)h(.)\lambda_{L3} + \{T'(.) + h'(.)W\}Z'X_2 - mP_3X_3], \text{ and}\\
C &= [\lambda_{K1}\lambda_{L1}\sigma_1 + \sigma_2(\lambda_{K1}\lambda_{L2}\theta_{K2} + \lambda_{L1}\lambda_{K2}\theta_{L2}) + (\theta_{L1}\sigma_3/(1 - \theta_{23}))(\lambda_{K1}\lambda_{L3}\theta_{K3}\\
&\quad + \lambda_{L1}\lambda_{K3}\theta_{L3})] > 0.
\end{aligned}$$

Using the stability condition from Equation (9.29) we find that $\hat{Y} < 0$ when $\hat{K} > 0$ and $\hat{Y} > 0$ when $\hat{\overline{Z}} < 0$ if (i) $A > 0$ and (ii) $B \geq 0$. This establishes the following proposition.

Proposition 9.2 *A reduction in the permissible level of pollution in the presence of an informal sector leads to an improvement in welfare if (i) $A > 0$ and (ii) $B \geq 0$. On*

[18] See Appendix 9.4 for detailed derivation.

the contrary, an inflow of foreign capital with full repatriation of income on foreign capital is welfare deteriorating under the same set of sufficient conditions.

Proposition 9.2 can be intuitively explained as follows. With the lowering of the permissible pollution level, $\overline{Z}$, the discrepancy between the actual and permissible pollution levels increases. However, from Equation (9.28) it follows that the average pollution emission tax that the formal sector has to bear decreases. The effective price of the formal sector's product (net of average emission tax) rises, leading to an expansion of the higher wage-paying formal sector. This we call the labour reallocation effect, which works favourably on welfare. The polluting sector (sector 2) also expands as its output is solely used in the formal sector in a fixed proportion. The labour endowment in efficiency units decreases as the level of pollution rises. Besides, a reduction in $\overline{Z}$ lowers P_2, which in turn raises r and reduces W following a Stolper–Samuelson effect. Thus, the aggregate wage income is affected due to three different effects: (i) direct negative effect on W following a reduction in $\overline{Z}$; (ii) the labour reallocation effect as the higher (lower) wage-paying formal (agricultural) sector expands (contracts); and (iii) changes in labour endowment of the economy in efficiency units. The net outcome on the aggregate wage income is ambiguous. There are other effects on welfare as well. Both the aggregate capital income and transfer payments to the workers (the pollution emission tax revenue collected from the formal sector) increase unambiguously. On the contrary, the cost of tariff protection rises as the formal sector expands. This lowers welfare. The net impact of all these effects would be an increase in welfare under the following sufficient conditions: (i) $A > 0$; and (ii) $B \geq 0$.

On the other hand, if foreign capital enters the economy with full repatriation of foreign capital income, the aggregate capital stock of the economy swells up. We have seen (proposition 9.1) that it leads to a contraction of the formal (and informal) sector. As the higher (lower) wage-paying formal (agricultural) sector contracts (expands), aggregate wage income falls due to the labour reallocation effect. However, there are two other effects on the aggregate wage income of the workers. As the polluting (informal manufacturing) sector contracts the labour endowment in efficiency units rises. Besides, an inflow of foreign capital lowers the price of the informal sector's price, P_2, which lowers W and raises r. There are again three different effects on the aggregate wage income. However, the aggregate capital income on domestic capital falls. Also, the transfer payments that the workers receive from the government also falls as the level of pollution (and hence the emission tax revenue) falls. On the contrary, the cost of tariff protection falls as the tariff-protected formal sector contracts, which works favourably on welfare. The net effect of all these effects on welfare is negative if: (i) $A > 0$; and (ii) $B \geq 0$. However, it is easy to check that welfare may fall due to an inflow of foreign capital even in the absence of any tariff protection.[19] Actually, in the absence of any tariff the possibility of welfare deteriorating effect of foreign capital is strengthened.

---

[19] This is an interesting result because it is different from the conventional Brecher–Alejandro proposition as discussed in Chapter 5.

Thus, we have shown that even if the permissible pollution level is reduced, the polluting sector may expand and lead to a deterioration in the environmental standard. Quite unexpectedly, this policy may improve welfare of the economy. This has a very important policy implication due to the counterintuitive results of direct environmental policies. On the contrary, an inflow of foreign capital may be effective in lowering the level of pollution although it may affect welfare of the economy adversely. Therefore, the above theoretical analysis finds that there might exist a trade-off between the economy's objectives of lowering the level of pollution and improving national welfare. These results are new in the literature on trade and environment, which would help the policy makers in the developing countries in designing appropriate policies because reduction of pollution level and improvement of national welfare are both desirable for a developing economy.

9.3 International Trade in Wastes and Recycling: Role of the Informal Sector

The informal waste management network usually operates in two stages – waste recovery and recycling.[20] Waste recovery involves the services of waste pickers or scavengers who sort out recyclable wastes from dumping grounds and sell it to itinerant waste buyers. The collected wastes are subsequently sold to waste dealers, wholesalers and finally to recycling units. The recycling units transform the recovered wastes either into new secondary raw materials for the formal sector manufacturing process or into final goods for consumption. The low production costs and consequently the low prices of the secondary intermediate products as well as final products create sufficient demand in the low-income countries (Beukering et al., 1997). Some of the most popular recycled items are metals, paper, plastics, textiles, glass and tyres.

The growing demands for both primary and secondary manufactured products encourage increased recycling activities. Waste recovery is an integral part in the expansion of the recycling industry. However, in developing countries, domestic waste recovery is inadequate due to budget constraints of the municipal authorities, lack of institutional infrastructure and political will, and fragmented divisions of labour and responsibility. There exist several bottlenecks of the informal recovery sector as well. As a result, recyclers often resort to the international market for waste trade.[21] The developing countries are primarily the importers of recyclable wastes.[22] Moreover, the recent sweep of liberalisation and free trade policies, which

[20] This section is based on Mukhopadhyay (2007).

[21] For details, refer Beukering et al. (1997), Beukering and Sharma (1996) and UNCTAD (1996).

[22] China is the world's largest importer of waste plastics (Beukering et al., 1997). Imports of waste paper currently constitute 60% of India's imports of pulp and waste paper (Beukering and Sharma, 1996). In 1992, the developing countries imported only 36% of globally traded primary plastics, while they accounted for 69% of the waste plastic trade (UNCTAD, 1996).

emphasise inflow of foreign capital and reduction in tariff protection, have been promoting the waste imports.

International trade in wastes is subject to controversies among economists and environmentalists. Critics of trade in wastes argue that imports are in reality a disguise for waste dumping by the exporting country. Besides, cheap imports of waste tend to crowd out the local recovery system, adding to domestic waste disposal problem (Duraiappah et al., 1999). A relaxation of restrictions in trade in wastes, arguably, is economically and environmentally not desirable since it results in the setback of the domestic recovery sector producing employment and disposal problems. However, proponents of waste trade are of the view that trade in recyclables offers economic and environmental benefits for importing developing countries (Ogilvie, 1996; Grace, 1978). They postulate that trade liberalisation is generally not the main source of environmental problems. It is market failure that causes environmental degradation, rendering policies directly addressing the failures to be the most functional. Trade liberalisation can affect the environment by increasing economic growth, which can, in the presence of environmental externalities, increase environmental problems. On the other hand, economic growth fosters increased expenses to be incurred on environmental upgradation. The net environmental effects of trade liberalisation[23] therefore depend on the relative strength of the two forces (Wilson, 1994).

It is relevant to note that the desirability of waste trade depends on its hazardous and non-hazardous nature.[24] Hazardous wastes, being environmentally perilous, are restricted for trans-boundary movements by international agreements like the Basel Convention on Trade in Hazardous Waste (1991), but there exists no explicit policy for trade in non-hazardous recyclable wastes. However, imports of recyclable wastes like paper, solid plastic, metal-bearing wastes and ceramic have been significantly growing in a large number of developing countries, especially those in South-East Asia. Thus, a pertinent question that arises is whether liberalisation in non-hazardous waste trade affects the economy and environment positively so that restrictions on waste trade should be increasingly relaxed or is it detrimental, requiring stringent regulations prohibiting waste trade.

On the other hand, the developing countries often have a fetish to attract foreign direct investment to strengthen their capital base, sometimes even by relaxing the environmental norms for industries where foreign capital flows in. However, due to financial crunch these countries are unable to provide proper disposal facilities for the wastes associated with higher industrial production. Therefore, the desirability

[23] In view of the fact that some western countries dumped refuse in China in the name of exporting recyclable materials, the Chinese government introduced a ban on imports of waste plastics. This policy received strong reactions because of its positive and negative effects. On the positive side, the policy aimed to protect the environment and safeguard national interests. On the negative side, many factories especially those engaged in plastic recycling with waste plastics as raw materials risked being forced out of the business.

[24] See UNEP/CHW.4/35, 18 March 1998 for classification.

of pursuance for foreign capital from the point of view of environmental issues is highly debatable.

In this section we examine the effects of liberalisation of waste trade and foreign capital inflow on waste management and pollution in a three-sector general equilibrium model. A small open economy is considered to consist of a formal manufacturing sector, an informal waste recovery sector and an informal waste-recycling sector that uses recovered wastes as intermediary good. It is to be noted that the existence of the informal sector has a two-fold benefit on environment. First, the recovery and processing sector contributes in solid waste management and makes the environment cleaner. Moreover, secondary production, using wastes as raw materials, has obvious advantages in terms of savings in energy and resources and the emission level is also lower than that of primary production, thus contributing significantly to environmental improvement (Beukering et al., 1997). In this situation, we analyse the effects of both reduction in tariff on wastes and foreign capital inflow on domestic waste recovery, recycling and pollution due to emissions.

9.3.1 The Model

There are three sectors in a small open economy, a formal sector and two informal sectors, where all the sectors operate at close vicinity. Sector 1 is the informal waste recovery and processing sector producing processed waste X_1, using labour and capital. Sector 2 is the informal recycling sector producing a non-traded final manufacturing product, X_2, using labour, capital and processed waste, X_1. Sector 3 is the formal sector producing a manufacturing product, X_3, by using capital and labour. It is assumed that the formal sector is more capital-intensive than the informal sector as a whole. It is also assumed that sector 1 is the tariff-protected import-competing sector while sector 3 is the export sector. This pattern of trade is particularly relevant to the newly industrialising countries that have adopted an export-oriented growth strategy and have emerged to be large manufacturing exporters.[25] Labour in the formal sector earns a contractual wage, $\overline{W}$, while the wage rate in the informal sector, W, is market determined. Due to the assumption of small economy, the product prices of sectors 1 and 3 are internationally given. Production functions exhibit constant returns to scale with diminishing marginal productivity to each factor. Capital and labour are fully employed and are mobile between the three sectors. The endowment of labour in physical units is given. The efficiency of the representative worker, h, is inversely related to the pollution level in the economy. All the workers are assumed to possess identical efficiency functions. Pollution is positively related to X_3 and inversely to X_2.

The general equilibrium is represented by the following set of equations:

$$Wa_{L1} + ra_{K1} = P_1(1 + t) \qquad (9.30)$$

---

[25] See Chaudhuri and Mukhopadhyay (2002).

$$Wa_{L2} + ra_{K2} + P_1(1+t)a_{12} = P_2 \tag{9.31}$$

$$\overline{W}a_{L3} + ra_{K3} = P_3 \tag{9.32}$$

Equations (9.30), (9.31) and (9.32) are the competitive industry equilibrium conditions in the two informal sectors and the formal sector, respectively.

$$a_{12}X_2 = X_1 + M \tag{9.33}$$

Equation (9.33) depicts that the total input requirement of wastes in the recycling sector is satisfied by domestic recovery, X_1, and import of wastes, M. Both are perfect substitutes so that higher the amount of recovered wastes, lower are the imports. Here, a_{12} is assumed to be a constant, to rule out the possibility of substitution between the intermediary waste and other factors of production in sector 2.

Now, it is assumed that the efficiency of a representative worker, h, is inversely related to the level of pollution, Z, in the economy. Environmental pollution leads to health hazards, thus adversely affecting the worker's efficiency (Chaudhuri and Mukhopadhyay, 2006). Since all the three sectors operate at close vicinity it is assumed that pollution affects the efficiency of the entire workforce equally. Thus,

$$h = h(Z); h' < 0 \tag{9.34}$$

where Z is a positive function of net manufacturing production.

$$\text{Thus, } Z = Z(X_3 - X_2); Z' > 0 \tag{9.35}$$

It is assumed that formal sector production is always accompanied by pollution, especially in developing countries with lax in environmental regulations. Even if the formal sector firms abide by whatever regulations that do exist and opt for pollution abatement, some pollution is necessarily generated by them. On the other hand, methods of waste disposal in these countries indirectly affect the environment, through pollution of ground and surface water by leachates from disposal sites, generation of greenhouse gas like methane in landfill sites and air pollution caused by open burning at dumps. Secondary production or recycling, using wastes as raw materials, has obvious advantages in terms of savings in energy and resources and the emission level is also lower than that of primary production (Beukering et al., 1997; USEPA, 1998). Thus, higher the formal sector production and lesser the recycling activities, higher is the level of pollution.

After normalising the labour endowment in physical units to unity, the full-employment of labour in efficiency units implies the following:

$$a_{L1}X_1 + a_{L2}X_2 + a_{L3}X_3 = h(Z(X_3 - X_2)) \tag{9.36}$$

As the labour endowment of the economy in physical units has been normalised to unity, the labour endowment in efficiency units is $h(Z)$.

Complete utilisation of capital in the economy implies that

$$a_{K1}X_1 + a_{K2}X_2 + a_{K3}X_3 = K \tag{9.37}$$

Since the recycled final product, X_2, is internationally non-traded, it is determined by the domestic demand–supply mechanism. The demand for X_2 is represented by D_2 and depends on its price, P_2, and national income, Y. Thus,

$$D_2 = f(P_2, Y);\ f_1 < 0 \text{ and } f_2 > 0$$

Equality in demand and supply for X_2 requires

$$X_2 = f(P_2, Y) \tag{9.38}$$

National income measured at world prices, Y, is expressed as follows:

$$Y = W(a_{L1}X_1 + a_{L2}X_2) + \overline{W}a_{L3}X_3 + rK - tP_1X_1 \tag{9.39}$$

where $W(a_{L1}X_1 + a_{L2}X_2)$gives the total wage income in the two informal sectors of the economy. $\overline{W}\ a_{L3}X_3$ is the amount of the wage income of the labourers employed in the formal sector. rK is the rental income from capital. Finally, $tP_1\ X_1$ measures the cost of tariff protection of the import-competing sector.

There are 10 endogenous variables, W, r, P_2, X_1, X_2, X_3, h, Z, M and Y, which can be solved from the above 10 equations. The system possesses the decomposition property. So the factor prices are determined independently of the output system. As $\overline{W}$ is given, r is found from Equation (9.32). Given r, Equation (9.30) can be solved to get W. Once W is known, the equilibrium value of P_2 is determined from Equation (9.31). If factor prices are known, the factor coefficients, a_{ji} s, are also known. Solving Equations (9.36), (9.37) and (9.38) can yield the product-mix and use of Equation (9.33) gives M. The pollution level Z can be obtained from Equation (9.35). The efficiency of each worker, h, is found from Equation (9.34). Finally, the national income Y can be determined from Equation (9.39).

The model analyses the effects of reduction in tariff on import of non-hazardous wastes and inflow of foreign capital on pollution and solid waste in the presence of informal recovery and recycling sectors, with the latter generating a favourable impact on pollution.

Total differentials of Equations (9.30), (9.31) and (9.32) and use of envelope conditions yield

$$\theta_{L1}\hat{W} + \theta_{K1}\hat{r} = T\hat{t} \tag{9.40}$$

$$\theta_{12}T\hat{t} + \theta_{L2}\hat{W} + \theta_{K2}\hat{r} = \hat{P}_2 \tag{9.41}$$

$$\theta_{K3}\hat{r} = \hat{P}_3 \tag{9.42}$$

where $T = (t/(1+t))$

From Equations (9.40), (9.41) and (9.42), respectively, it follows that

$$\hat{r} = \hat{P}_3/\theta_{K3}; \hat{W} = (\hat{W} - \hat{r}) = (T\hat{t}/\theta_{L1}) \text{ and } \hat{P}_2 = \{(T\hat{t}/\theta_{L1})(\theta_{12}\theta_{L1} + \theta_{L2})\} \quad (9.43)$$

In this model we do not consider the effects of change in the price of X_3 so that $\hat{P}_3 = 0$, implying that $\hat{r} = 0$.

Total differentiation of Equation (9.34) gives

$$Z\hat{Z} = Z'(X_3\hat{X}_3 - X_2\hat{X}_2) \quad (9.44)$$

Total differentiation of Equation (9.33) gives

$$\hat{X}_1 = \lambda_{12}\hat{X}_2 - (M/X_1)\hat{M} \quad (9.45)$$

Differentiating Equation (9.39) one gets

$$\begin{aligned} Y\hat{Y} = {} & (W\lambda_{L1} - tP_1X_1)\hat{X}_1 + W\lambda_{L2}\hat{X}_2 + \overline{W}\lambda_{L3}\hat{X}_3 - W(\lambda_{L1}\theta_{K1} + \lambda_{L2}\theta_{K2})(T\hat{t}/\theta_{L1}) \\ & + (\lambda_{L1} + \lambda_{L2})W(T\hat{t}/\theta_{L1}) - tP_1X_1\hat{t} \end{aligned} \quad (9.46)$$

For simplifying the algebra, the production functions of each sector are assumed to be of the Cobb–Douglas type, implying that the elasticity of substitution between capital and labour in each sector is unity.

Total differentiation of Equations (9.36), (9.37) and (9.38) and use of Equation (9.43), (9.44) and (9.46) yield, respectively,

$$\begin{aligned} & -\lambda_{L1}(M/X_1)\hat{M} + (\lambda_{L2} + h'Z'X_2 + \lambda_{L1}\lambda_{12})\hat{X}_2 + (\lambda_{L3} - h'Z'X_3)\hat{X}_3 = (\lambda_{L1}\theta_{K1} \\ & +\lambda_{L2}\theta_{K2})(T\hat{t}/\theta_{L1}) \end{aligned} \quad (9.47)$$

$$-\lambda_{K1}(M/X_1)\hat{M} + (\lambda_{K2} + \lambda_{K1}\lambda_{12})\hat{X}_2 + \lambda_{K3}\hat{X}_3 = \hat{K} - (\lambda_{K1}\theta_{L1} + \lambda_{K2}\theta_{L2})(T\hat{t}/\theta_{L1}) \quad (9.48)$$

$$\begin{aligned} & -\varepsilon_Y(W\lambda_{L1} - tP_1X_1)(M/X_1)\hat{M} + \{(\varepsilon_Y W\lambda_{L2} - Y) + \varepsilon_Y(W\lambda_{L1} - tP_1X_1)\lambda_{12}\}\hat{X}_2 \\ & \quad +\varepsilon_Y\overline{W}\lambda_{L3}\hat{X}_3 \\ & = \varepsilon_Y W(\lambda_{L1}\theta_{K1} + \lambda_{L2}\theta_{K2})(T\hat{t}/\theta_{L1}) - \varepsilon_Y(\lambda_{L1} + \lambda_{L2})W(T\hat{t}/\theta_{L1}) + \varepsilon_Y tP_1X_1\hat{t} \\ & \quad -\varepsilon_P Y(T\hat{t}/\theta_{L1})(\theta_{L2} + \theta_{12}\theta_{L1}) \end{aligned} \quad (9.49)$$

where ε_P and ε_Y are the elasticities of demand for X_2 with respect to its price P_2 and national income Y, respectively. $\varepsilon_P = (\partial X_2/\partial P_2)(P_2/X_2) < 0$ and $\varepsilon_Y = (\partial X_2/\partial Y)(Y/X_2) > 0$.

Solving Equations (9.47), (9.48) and (9.49) by Cramer's rule and simplifying yield the following expressions:

$$\begin{aligned}\hat{M} = {} & (T\hat{t}/\Delta\theta_{L1})[A\{\lambda_{K3}(\lambda_{L2} + h'Z'X_2 + \lambda_{L1}\lambda_{12}) - (\lambda_{K2} + \lambda_{K1}\lambda_{12})(\lambda_{L3} - h'Z'X_3)\} \\ & +(\lambda_{K1}\theta_{L1} + \lambda_{K2}\theta_{L2})\{(\lambda_{L2} + h'Z'X_2 + \lambda_{L1}\lambda_{12})\varepsilon_Y\overline{W}\lambda_{L3} - (\lambda_{L3} - h'Z'X_3)B\} \\ & +(\lambda_{L1}\theta_{K1} + \lambda_{L2}\theta_{K2})\{(\lambda_{K2} + \lambda_{K1}\lambda_{12})\varepsilon_Y\overline{W}\lambda_{L3} - \lambda_{K3}B\}] + (\hat{K}/\Delta) \\ & [(\lambda_{L3} - h'Z'X_3)B - (\lambda_{L2} + h'Z'X_2 + \lambda_{L1}\lambda_{12})\varepsilon_Y\overline{W}\lambda_{L3}]\end{aligned} \tag{9.50}$$

$$\begin{aligned}\hat{X}_2 = {} & (T\hat{t}/\Delta\theta_{L1})(M/X_1)[A\{\lambda_{L1}\lambda_{K3} - \lambda_{K1}(\lambda_{L3} - h'Z'X_3)\} \\ & +\varepsilon_Y(\lambda_{K1}\theta_{L1} + \lambda_{K2}\theta_{L2})\{\overline{W}\lambda_{L1}\lambda_{L3} - (\lambda_{L3} - h'Z'X_3)(W\lambda_{L1} - tP_1X_1)\} \\ & +\varepsilon_Y(\lambda_{L1}\theta_{K1} + \lambda_{L2}\theta_{K2})\{\overline{W}\lambda_{K1}\lambda_{L3} - \lambda_{K3}(W\lambda_{L1} - tP_1X_1)\}] \\ & +(\hat{K}/\Delta)(M/X_1)\varepsilon_Y[(\lambda_{L3} - h'Z'X_3)(W\lambda_{L1} - tP_1X_1) - \overline{W}\lambda_{L1}\lambda_{L3}]\end{aligned} \tag{9.51}$$

and

$$\begin{aligned}\hat{X}_3 = {} & (T\hat{t}/\Delta\theta_{L1})(M/X_1)[A\{\lambda_{K1}(\lambda_{L2} + h'Z'X_2) - \lambda_{L1}\lambda_{K2}\} \\ & +(\lambda_{K1}\theta_{L1} + \lambda_{K2}\theta_{L2})\{(W\lambda_{L1} - tP_1X_1)\varepsilon_Y(\lambda_{L2} + h'Z'X_2 + \lambda_{L1}\lambda_{12}) - \lambda_{L1}B\} \\ & +(\lambda_{L1}\theta_{K1} + \lambda_{L2}\theta_{K2})\{(\lambda_{K2} + \lambda_{K1}\lambda_{12})\varepsilon_Y(W\lambda_{L1} - tP_1X_1) - \lambda_{K1}B\}] \\ & +(\hat{K}/\Delta)(M/X_1)[\lambda_{L1}B - (W\lambda_{L1} - tP_1X_1)\varepsilon_Y(\lambda_{L2} + h'Z'X_2 + \lambda_{L1}\lambda_{12})]\end{aligned} \tag{9.52}$$

where

$$\begin{aligned}A &= \varepsilon_Y W(\lambda_{L1}\theta_{K1} + \lambda_{L2}\theta_{K2} - \lambda_{L2}) - \varepsilon_P Y(\theta_{L2} + \theta_{12}\theta_{L1}) > 0 \\ B &= (\varepsilon_Y W\lambda_{L2} - Y) + \varepsilon_Y(W\lambda_{L1} - tP_1X_1)\lambda_{12} < 0 \\ \Delta &= (M/X_1)\overline{W}\varepsilon_Y\lambda_{L3}\{\lambda_{K1}(\lambda_{L2} + h'Z'X_2 + \lambda_{L1}\lambda_{12}) - \lambda_{L1}(\lambda_{K2} + \lambda_{K1}\lambda_{12})\} \\ & \quad +B\{\lambda_{L1}\lambda_{K3} - \lambda_{K1}(\lambda_{L3} - h'Z'X_3)\} + \varepsilon_Y(W\lambda_{L1} - tP_1X_1)\{(\lambda_{K2} + \lambda_{K1}\lambda_{12}) \\ & \quad (\lambda_{L3} - h'Z'X_3) - \lambda_{K3}(\lambda_{L2} + h'Z'X_2 + \lambda_{L1}\lambda_{12})\}] < 0 \text{ if } W\lambda_{L1} \geq tP_1X_1\end{aligned}$$

It should be noted that it is assumed here that the formal manufacturing sector (sector 3) is more capital-intensive than the informal sector (as a whole), implying that $(\lambda_{K2}+\lambda_{K1}\lambda_{12})(\lambda_{L3}+h'Z'X_3)-\lambda_{K3}(\lambda_{L2}+h'Z'X_2+\lambda_{L1}\lambda_{12}) < 0$ and the informal recycling sector (sector 2) is more capital-intensive vis-à-vis the informal recovery sector (sector 1) so that $\lambda_{K1}(\lambda_{L2} + h'Z'X_2 + \lambda_{L1}\lambda_{12}) - \lambda_{L1}(\lambda_{K2} + \lambda_{K1}\lambda_{12}) < 0$, even when the indirect input requirements and effects of pollution on the labour endowment (in efficiency units) are taken into account.

9.3.2 Effects of Tariff Reform on the Economy

It is assumed that the capital stock remains unchanged while the tariff rate is reduced. This implies that $\hat{K} = 0$ and $\hat{t} < 0$.

From Equation (9.51) it can be concluded that

$\hat{X}_2 > 0$ when $\hat{t} < 0$ under the following sufficient conditions:

(i) $W\lambda_{L1} \geq tP_1X_1$

(ii) $\overline{W}\lambda_{K1}\lambda_{L3} \geq \lambda_{K3}(W\lambda_{L1} - tP_1X_1)$.

So we can establish the following proposition

Proposition 9.3 *Reduction in tariff rates on import of non-hazardous wastes may lead to increase in recycling of wastes.*

Now by substitution of Equations (9.50) and (9.51) in Equation (9.45) and simplification we get

$$\begin{aligned}\hat{X}_1 = {} & (T\hat{t}/\Delta\theta_{L1})(M/X_1)[A\{\lambda_{K2}(\lambda_{L3} - h'Z'X_3) - \lambda_{K3}(\lambda_{L2} + h'Z'X_2)\} \\ & +(\lambda_{K1}\theta_{L1} + \lambda_{K2}\theta_{L2})\{(\lambda_{L3} - h'Z'X_3)(\varepsilon_Y W\lambda_{L2} - Y) - (\lambda_{L2} + h'Z'X_2)\varepsilon_Y\overline{W}\lambda_{L3}\} \\ & +(\lambda_{L1}\theta_{K1} + \lambda_{L2}\theta_{K2})\{\lambda_{K3}(\varepsilon_Y W\lambda_{L2} - Y) - \varepsilon_Y\overline{W}\lambda_{K2}\lambda_{L3}\}] \\ & +(\hat{K}/\Delta)(M/X_1)[(\lambda_{L2} + h'Z'X_2)\varepsilon_Y\overline{W}\lambda_{L3} - (\lambda_{L3} - h'Z'X_3)(\varepsilon_Y W\lambda_{L2} - Y)]\end{aligned} \tag{9.53}$$

From Equation (9.53) it is evident that $\hat{X}_1 > 0$ when $\hat{t} < 0$ under the following sufficient conditions:

(i) $W\lambda_{L1} \geq tP_1X_1$
(ii) $\lambda_{L2} + h'Z'X_2 < 0$ and
(iii) $[A\{\lambda_{K2}(\lambda_{L3} - h'Z'X_3) - \lambda_{K3}(\lambda_{L2} + h'Z'X_2)\} - (\lambda_{K1}\theta_{L1} + \lambda_{K2}\theta_{L2})(\lambda_{L2} + h'Z'X_2)\varepsilon_Y \overline{W}\lambda_{L3}] > [(\lambda_{K1}\theta_{L1} + \lambda_{K2}\theta_{L2})(\lambda_{L3} - h'Z'X_3)(\varepsilon_Y W\lambda_{L2} - Y) + (\lambda_{L1}\theta_{K1} + \lambda_{L2}\theta_{K2})\{\lambda_{K3}(\varepsilon_Y W\lambda_{L2} - Y) - \varepsilon_Y\overline{W}\lambda_{K2}\lambda_{L3}\}$

So we establish the following proposition.

Proposition 9.4 *Liberalisation of imports of non-hazardous wastes may lead to increase in domestic recovery of wastes, even when imported and domestic wastes are perfect substitutes.*

Propositions 9.3 and 9.4 can be explained as follows. Owing to a reduction in tariff rate the domestic price of the informal recovery sector falls. The informal sector wage rate, W, also falls, which in turn reduces P_2 in order to satisfy the zero-profit condition in sector 2. The informal recycling sector (sector 2) expands in order to satisfy the increased demand for X_2, resulting from a fall in P_2. The fall in W leads to reduction in the wage–rental ratio in the informal sector, inducing the producers to adopt more labour-intensive techniques of production. Given X_1 and X_2 adoption of more labour-intensive techniques means a shortage of labour leading to contraction (expansion) of sectors 1 and 2 (sector 3) as the formal sector is more capital-intensive than the informal sector (as a whole). As a result, the initial increase in X_2 may be partly offset. The effect on national income is somewhat ambiguous. With a fixed wage, $\overline{W}$, and given labour–output ratio, expansion of the formal sector leads to a rise in the formal sector wage income. The contraction of sector 1 plummets the cost of tariff protection and hence raises the national income. The total informal sector labour income is affected due to the following: (i) fall in W, (ii) rise in a_{L1} and a_{L2} and (iii) contraction in X_1 and expansion in X_2. The national income Y increases if the positive effects outweigh the negative ones. This again leads to expansion in X_2 via income effect. The net expansion of sector 2 leads to fall in the pollution level, producing a positive effect on the efficiency of labour so that labour endowment (in efficiency units) rises. This produces a Rybczynski effect so that the informal sectors 1 and 2 expand and the formal sector contracts since the informal sector (as a whole) is more labour-intensive than the formal sector.

There is a net expansion in the recycling sector if the initial expansion due to fall in its price is reinforced by an increase in national income due to labour reallocation and change in output composition, which is possible under the sufficient conditions stated in Proposition 9.3. The recovery sector expands despite the initial contraction if Proposition 9.3 holds, that is, the recycling sector expands and the resulting favourable effect on pollution and efficiency of labour is strong enough to produce a Rybczynski effect that may have sufficient expansionary effect on sector 1 to outweigh the initial contraction. This requires another sufficient condition: $\lambda_{L2} + h'Z'X_2 < 0$. It implies that due to one additional unit of production of X_2, pollution falls by $Z'X_2$, which in turn raises the efficiency of labour by $h'Z'X_2$. Thus instead of λ_{L2} the availability of labour to other sectors decreases by only $\lambda_{L2} + h'Z'X_2$. Now, if $\lambda_{L2} + h'Z'X_2 < 0$ production of an additional unit of X_2 actually raises the availability of labour (in efficiency unit) to the rest of the economy.

Now it would be worthwhile to analyse the effects of tariff reduction on pollution level in the economy.

Substitution of Equations (9.51) and (9.52) in Equation (9.44) yields

$$\begin{aligned}\hat{Z} = {} & (Z'/Z)(T\hat{t}/\Delta\theta_{L1})(M/X_1)[A[X_3\{\lambda_{K1}(\lambda_{L2} + h'Z'X_2) - \lambda_{L1}\lambda_{K2}\} \\ & -X_2\{\lambda_{L1}\lambda_{K3} - \lambda_{K1}(\lambda_{L3} - h'Z'X_3)\}] + (\lambda_{K1}\theta_{L1} + \lambda_{K2}\theta_{L2})[X_3\{(W\lambda_{L1} - tP_1X_1)\varepsilon_Y \\ & (\lambda_{L2} + h'Z'X_2 + \lambda_{L1}\lambda_{12}) - \lambda_{L1}B\} - X_2\{\overline{W}\varepsilon_Y\lambda_{L1}\lambda_{L3} - (\lambda_{L3} - h'Z'X_3)\varepsilon_Y \\ & (W\lambda_{L1} - tP_1X_1)\}] + (\lambda_{L1}\theta_{K1} + \lambda_{L2}\theta_{K2})[X_3\{(\lambda_{K2} + \lambda_{K1}\lambda_{12})\varepsilon_Y(W\lambda_{L1} - tP_1X_1) \\ & -\lambda_{K1}B\} - X_2\{\overline{W}\lambda_{K1}\lambda_{L3} \\ & -\lambda_{K3}(W\lambda_{L1} - tP_1X_1)\}]] + (Z'/Z)(\hat{K}/\Delta)(M/X_1)[X_3\{\lambda_{L1}B - (W\lambda_{L1} - tP_1X_1)\varepsilon_Y \\ & (\lambda_{L2} + h'Z'X_2 + \lambda_{L1}\lambda_{12})\} - X_2\{(\lambda_{L3} - h'Z'X_3)\varepsilon_Y(W\lambda_{L1} - tP_1X_1) - \overline{W}\varepsilon_Y\lambda_{L1}\lambda_{L3}\}]\end{aligned} \tag{9.54}$$

Thus, $\hat{Z} < 0$ when $\hat{t} < 0$ under the following sufficient conditions:

(i) $W\lambda_{L1} \geq tP_1X_1$

(ii) $X_3\{(\lambda_{K2} + \lambda_{K1}\lambda_{12})\varepsilon_Y(W\lambda_{L1} - tP_1X_1) - \lambda_{K1}B\} < X_2\{\lambda_{K1}\overline{W}\lambda_{L3} - \lambda_{K3}(W\lambda_{L1} - tP_1X_1)\}$

(iii) $X_3\{(W\lambda_{L1} - tP_1X_1)\varepsilon_Y(\lambda_{L2} + h'Z'X_2 + \lambda_{L1}\lambda_{12}) - \lambda_{L1}B\} < X_2\{\overline{W}\varepsilon_Y\lambda_{L1}\lambda_{L3} - (\lambda_{L3} - h'Z'X_3)\varepsilon_Y(W\lambda_{L1} - tP_1X_1)\}$

This establishes the following proposition.

Proposition 9.5 *Reduction in tariff rates on import of non-hazardous wastes may lower the pollution level.*

It follows from the explanation for Propositions 9.3 and 9.4 that the expansion of sector 2 produces a favourable effect on the pollution level, raising the efficiency of labour so that labour endowment (in efficiency units) rises. This produces a Rybczynski effect so that the informal sector expands and formal sector contracts, since the informal sector (as a whole) is more labour-intensive than the formal sector. Since pollution is positively related to the magnitude of formal sector production, its contraction lowers the level of pollution. Again, if Proposition 9.3 holds, expansion of the recycling sector has a further lowering effect on pollution.

9.3.3 Effects of Foreign Capital Inflow on the Economy

Now to examine the effects of foreign capital inflow it is assumed that $\hat{t} = 0$ and $\hat{K} > 0$.

From Equation (9.51) it is obtained that $\hat{X}_2 > 0$ when $\hat{K} > 0$ under the following sufficient conditions:

(i) $W\lambda_{L1} \geq tP_1X_1$ and
(ii) $(\lambda_{L3} - h'Z'X_3)(W\lambda_{L1} - tP_1X_1) \leq \overline{W}\lambda_{L1}\lambda_{L3}$

So the following proposition can be established.

Proposition 9.6 *Foreign capital inflow may lead to expansion of the domestic waste recycling sector.*

From Equation (9.53) it is evident that $\hat{X}_1 > 0$ when $\hat{K} > 0$ under the following sufficient conditions:

(i) $W\lambda_{L1} \geq tP_1X_1$
(ii) $(\lambda_{L2} + h'Z'X_2) < 0$
(iii) $(\lambda_{L2} + h'Z'X_2)\varepsilon_Y\overline{W}\lambda_{L3} > (\lambda_{L3} - h'Z'X_3)(\varepsilon_Y W\lambda_{L2} - Y)$

This establishes the following proposition.

Proposition 9.7 *Foreign capital inflow may lead to increase in domestic waste recovery.*

Propositions 9.6 and 9.7 can be explained in the following fashion. An inflow of foreign capital leads to expansion of the formal sector and contraction of the informal sectors 1 and 2 in accordance with the Rybczynski theorem. Since the informal recovery sector is the tariff-protected sector its contraction reduces the cost of tariff protection and hence raises Y. Expansion of the higher wage-paying sector enhances Y as well. On the other hand, the total wage income in the two informal sectors falls, lowering Y. National income augments if the positive effects outweigh the negative effects. This leads to the expansion of X_2. If the rise in X_2 due to income effect is stronger than its initial fall, pollution level reduces so that the labour endowment in efficiency units rises. This produces another Rybczynski effect, leading to fall in the formal sector and expansion of the informal sectors. If the increase in efficiency of labour due to fall in pollution is sufficiently strong, the Rybczynski effect outweighs the initial Rybczynski effect and leads to expansion of the two informal sectors and contraction of the formal sector.

Now the effect of an increase in foreign capital inflow on pollution level in the economy is analysed.

From Equation (9.54) we obtain that $\hat{Z} < 0$ when $\hat{K} > 0$ under the following sufficient conditions:

(i) $W\lambda_{L1} \geq tP_1X_1$
(ii) $\lambda_{L1}B > (W\lambda_{L1} - tP_1X_1)\varepsilon_Y(\lambda_{L2} + h'Z'X_2 + \lambda_{L1}\lambda_{12})$
(iii) $(W\lambda_{L1} - tP_1X_1)\varepsilon_Y(\lambda_{L3} - h'Z'X_3) < \overline{W}\varepsilon_Y\lambda_{L1}\lambda_{L3}$

So we can establish the following proposition.

Proposition 9.8 *An inflow of foreign capital may lower the pollution level in the economy.*

It follows from the explanation for Propositions 9.6 and 9.7 that if national income rises due to inflow of foreign capital and produces strong income effects, sector 2 expands and produces a favourable effect on the pollution level, raising the efficiency of labour so that labour endowment (in efficiency units) rises. This produces a Rybczynski effect so that the informal sector (sectors 1 and 2) expands and the formal sector contracts since the informal sector (as a whole) is more labour-intensive than the formal sector. This leads to lowering of the level of pollution since pollution is positively related to the magnitude of formal sector production and inversely with recycling.

The above model shows that tariff reforms in wastes and foreign capital inflow may produce effects that tend to increase domestic waste recovery as well as recycling and lower the level of pollution in an economy where waste recovery and recycling are carried out in the informal sector.

Appendix 9.1: Derivations of certain expressions

Total differentiation of Equation (9.3) gives

$$
\begin{aligned}
&=-(a_{23}/(X_2)^2)[X_2\{T'(.)(Z'dX_2 - d\overline{Z})\} - T(.)dX_2]\\
&\text{or, } \theta_{K3}\hat{r} + \theta_{23}\hat{P}_2 = (a_{23}/X_2P_3(1+t))T(.)\hat{X}_2 - (a_{23}/P_3(1+t))T'(.)Z'\hat{X}_2\\
&+(a_{23}/X_2P_3(1+t))T'(.)\hat{\overline{Z}}\overline{Z}\\
&\text{or, } \theta_{K3}\theta_{L1}(\hat{P}_2/|\theta|) + \theta_{23}\hat{P}_2 = (\theta_{23}/P_2X_2)T(.)\hat{X}_2 - (\theta_{23}/P_2)T'(.)Z'\hat{X}_2\\
&+(\theta_{23}/P_2X_2)T'(.)\overline{Z}\hat{\overline{Z}}\\
&\text{or, } (\hat{P}_2/|\theta|)[\theta_{K3}\theta_{L1} + \theta_{23}(\theta_{L1} - \theta_{L2})] + (\theta_{23}/P_2X_2)(T'(.)Z'X_2 - T(.))\hat{X}_2\\
&=(\theta_{23}/P_2X_2)(T'(.)\overline{Z}\hat{\overline{Z}})
\end{aligned}
\tag{9.19}
$$

Again differentiation of Equation (9.9) yields

$$
\begin{aligned}
&\lambda_{L1}\hat{X}_1 + (\lambda_{L2} + \lambda_{L3})\hat{X}_2 - (h'(.)Z'X_2/h(.))\hat{X}_2 = -\lambda_{L1}\theta_{K1}\sigma_1(\hat{P}_2/|\theta|)\\
&-\lambda_{L2}\theta_{K2}\sigma_2(\hat{P}_2/|\theta|) - \{\lambda_{L3}\theta_{K3}\theta_{L1}\sigma_3/(1-\theta_{23})\}(\hat{P}_2/|\theta|)
\end{aligned}
$$

Rearranging terms we get

$$
\begin{aligned}
&(\hat{P}_2/|\theta|)[\lambda_{L1}\theta_{K1}\sigma_1 + \lambda_{L2}\theta_{K2}\sigma_2 + (\lambda_{L3}\theta_{K3}\theta_{L1}\sigma_3/(1-\theta_{23})]\\
&+[\lambda_{L2} + \lambda_{L3} - (h'(.)Z'X_2/h(.))]\hat{X}_2 + \lambda_{L1}\hat{X}_1 = 0
\end{aligned}
\tag{9.20}
$$

Finally, differentiation of Equation (9.6) gives

$$
\begin{aligned}
&\lambda_{K1}\hat{X}_1 + (\lambda_{K2} + \lambda_{K3})\hat{X}_2 = \hat{K} + \lambda_{K1}\theta_{L1}\sigma_1(\hat{P}_2/|\theta|) + \lambda_{K2}\theta_{L2}\sigma_2(\hat{P}_2/|\theta|)\\
&+(\lambda_{K3}\theta_{L3}\theta_{L1}\sigma_3/(1-\theta_{23}))(\hat{P}_2/|\theta|)\\
&or,(\hat{P}_2/|\theta|)[-\lambda_{K1}\theta_{L1}\sigma_1 - \lambda_{K2}\theta_{L2}\sigma_2 - \{\lambda_{K3}\theta_{L3}\theta_{L1}\sigma_3/(1-\theta_{23})\}]\\
&+(\lambda_{K2} + \lambda_{K3})\hat{X}_2 + \lambda_{K1}\hat{X}_1 = \hat{K}
\end{aligned}
\tag{9.21}
$$

Appendix 9.2: Derivation of stability condition in the market for the non-traded input

As commodity 2 is internationally non-traded its market must clear domestically through adjustments in its price, P_2.

The stability condition in the market for commodity 2 requires that $\left(\mathrm{d}\left(X_2^D - X_2\right)/\mathrm{d}P_2\right) < 0$. This implies around equilibrium, initially, $X_2^{\mathrm{D}} = X_2$. Thus,

$$\left(\left(\hat{X}_2^D/\hat{P}_2\right) - \left(\hat{X}_2/\hat{P}_2\right)\right) < 0. \tag{A.1}$$

We note that X_1, X_2 and X_3 can be simultaneously solved from Equations (9.3), (9.6) and (9.9) as functions of P_2. Differentiating Equations (9.3), (9.9) and (9.6) and keeping the parameters unchanged, we get the following three expressions, respectively:

$$-G\hat{X}_2 + H\hat{X}_3 = M_1\hat{P}_2; \tag{A.2}$$

$$\lambda_{L1}\hat{X}_1 + \{\lambda_{L2} - (h'(.)Z'X_2/h(.))\}\hat{X}_2 + \lambda_{L3}\hat{X}_3 = -M_2\hat{P}_2; \tag{A.3}$$

and

$$\lambda_{K1}\hat{X}_1 + \lambda_{K2}\hat{X}_2 + \lambda_{K3}\hat{X}_3 = M_3\hat{P}_2 \tag{A.4}$$

where

$$\left.\begin{array}{l} G = (T'(.)Z'X_2/P_3^*X_3) > 0; H = (T(.)/P_3^*X_3) > 0; \\ M_1 = \{(\theta_{K3}\theta_{L1} + \theta_{23}|\theta|)/|\theta|\} = \{\theta_{K3}\theta_{L1} + \theta_{23}(\theta_{L1} - \theta_{L2})\}(1/|\theta|) \\ M_2 = \{\lambda_{L1}\theta_{K1}\sigma_1 + \lambda_{L2}\theta_{K2}\sigma_2 + (\lambda_{L3}\theta_{K3}\theta_{L1}\sigma_3/(1-\theta_{23}))\}(1/|\theta|); \text{ and} \\ M_3 = \{\lambda_{K1}\theta_{L1}\sigma_1 + \lambda_{K2}\theta_{L2}\sigma_2 + (\lambda_{K3}\theta_{L3}\theta_{L1}\sigma_3/(1-\theta_{23}))\}(1/|\theta|) \end{array}\right\} \tag{A.5}$$

Solving Equations (A.2)–(A.4) by Cramer's rule we get

$$\hat{X}_2 = (\hat{P}_2/|\lambda|)[-M_1(\lambda_{L1}\lambda_{K3} - \lambda_{L3}\lambda_{K1}) + H(\lambda_{L1}M_3 + \lambda_{K1}M_2)]; \tag{A.6}$$

and

$$\hat{X}_3 = (\hat{P}_2/|\lambda|)[G(\lambda_{L1}M_3 + \lambda_{K1}M_2) + M_1\lambda_{L1}\lambda_{K2} - M_1\lambda_{K1}\{\lambda_{L2} - (h'(.)Z'X_2/h(.))\}] \tag{A.7}$$

where

$$|\lambda| = [G(\lambda_{L1}\lambda_{K3} - \lambda_{L3}\lambda_{K1}) + H\{\lambda_{L1}\lambda_{K2} - \lambda_{K1}(\lambda_{L2} - h'(.)Z'X_2/h(.))\}] \tag{A.8}$$

From Equation (A.6) we find that

$$(\hat{X}_2/\hat{P}_2) = (1/|\lambda|)[-M_1(\lambda_{L1}\lambda_{K3} - \lambda_{L3}\lambda_{K1}) + H(\lambda_{L1}M_3 + \lambda_{K1}M_2)] \quad \text{(A.9)}$$

Now the demand for the non-traded input is given by
$X_2^{\mathrm{D}} = a_{23}X_3$. Differentiating this equation one gets
$\hat{X}_2^{\mathrm{D}} = \hat{X}_3$. Using Equation (A.7) one can find

$$\left(\hat{X}_2^D/\hat{P}_2\right) = (1/|\lambda|)[G(\lambda_{L1}M_3 + \lambda_{K1}M_2) + M_1\lambda_{L1}\lambda_{K2} - M_1\lambda_{K1}$$
$$\{\lambda_{L2} - (h'(.)Z'X_2/h(.))\}] \quad \text{(A.10)}$$

Using Equations (A.1), (A.9) and (A.10) we find the following stability condition for equilibrium in the market for commodity 2:

$$\left(\left(\hat{X}_2^D/\hat{P}_2\right) - \left(\hat{X}_2/\hat{P}_2\right)\right) = (1/|\lambda|)[G(\lambda_{L1}M_3 + \lambda_{K1}M_2) - H(\lambda_{L1}M_3 + \lambda_{K1}M_2)$$
$$+M_1\{\lambda_{L1}(\lambda_{K2} + \lambda_{K3}) - \lambda_{K1}(\lambda_{L2} + \lambda_{L3} - h'(.)Z'X_2/h(.))\}] < 0$$

Inserting the values of G, H, M_1, M_2 and M_3 from Appendix (A.5) into the above expression and noting that $(1/P_3^* X_3) = (\theta_{23}/P_2X_2)$we get

$$\left(\left(\hat{X}_2^D/\hat{P}_2\right) - \left(\hat{X}_2/\hat{P}_2\right)\right) = (1/|\theta||\lambda|)[\{\theta_{K3}\theta_{L1} + \theta_{23}(\theta_{L1} - \theta_{L2})\}\{\lambda_{L1}(\lambda_{K2} + \lambda_{K3})$$
$$(+)$$
$$-\lambda_{K1}(\lambda_{L2} + \lambda_{L3}) - (h'(.)Z'X_2/h(.))\}$$
$$(+)$$
$$+\{\theta_{23}\{T'(.)Z'X_2 - T(.)\}/P_2X_2\}\{\lambda_{K1}\lambda_{L1}\sigma_1 + \sigma_2(\lambda_{K1}\lambda_{L2}\theta_{K2} + \lambda_{L1}\lambda_{K2}\theta_{L2})$$
$$+(\theta_{L1}\sigma_3/(1 - \theta_{23}))(\lambda_{K1}\lambda_{L3}\theta_{K3} + \lambda_{L1}\lambda_{K3}\theta_{L3})\}] < 0$$
$$(+)$$
$$= (\Delta/|\lambda|) = (\Delta'/|\theta||\lambda|) > 0 \quad \text{(9.25)}$$

where

$$\Delta = (1/|\theta|)[\{\theta_{K3}\theta_{L1} + \theta_{23}(\theta_{L1} - \theta_{L2})\}\{\lambda_{K1}(\lambda_{L2} + \lambda_{L3}) - \lambda_{L1}(\lambda_{K2} + \lambda_{K3})$$
$$(+) \qquad\qquad (-)$$
$$-(\lambda_{K1}h'(.)Z'X_2/h(.))\} - (\theta_{23}/P_2X_2)(T'(.)Z'X_2 - T(.))\{\lambda_{K1}\lambda_{L1}\sigma_1 + \sigma_2(\lambda_{K1}\lambda_{L2}\theta_{K2}$$
$$+\lambda_{L1}\lambda_{K2}\theta_{L2}) + (\theta_{L1}\sigma_3/(1 - \theta_{23}))(\lambda_{K1}\lambda_{L3}\theta_{K3} + \lambda_{L1}\lambda_{K3}\theta_{L3})\}];$$
$$(+) \quad \text{(9.24)}$$

and

$$\Delta\prime = [\{\theta_{K3}\theta_{L1} + \theta_{23}(\theta_{L1} - \theta_{L2})\}\{\lambda_{K1}(\lambda_{L2} + \lambda_{L3} - h'(.)Z'X_2/h(.)) - \lambda_{L1}$$
$$(+)$$
$$(\lambda_{K2} + \lambda_{K3})\}]$$
$$(-)$$
$$-[\theta_{23}\{T'(.)Z'X_2 - T(.)\}/(P_2X_2)][\lambda_{K1}\lambda_{L1}\sigma_1 + \sigma_2(\lambda_{K1}\lambda_{L2}\theta_{K2} + \lambda_{L1}\lambda_{K2}\theta_{L2})$$
$$+(\theta_{L1}\sigma_3/(1 - \theta_{23}))(\lambda_{K1}\lambda_{L3}\theta_{K3} + \lambda_{L1}\lambda_{K3}\theta_{L3})]$$
$$(+) \quad \text{(9.26.1)}$$

Appendix 9.3: Derivation of Equation (9.28)
The effective emission tax rate is given by

$$F = \frac{T(Z(X_2) - \overline{Z})}{X_3}$$

Differentiating F and using Equation (9.18), we get

$$\begin{aligned} F\hat{F}X_3 &= T'(.)Z'X_2\hat{X}_2 - T(.)\hat{X}_2 - T'(.)\overline{Z}\hat{\overline{Z}} \\ &= \hat{X}_2\{T'(.)Z'X_2 - T(.)\} - T'(.)\overline{Z}\hat{\overline{Z}} \end{aligned}$$

Now using Equation (9.22) one gets

$$\begin{aligned} F\hat{F}X_3 = \{T'(.)Z'X_2 - T(.)\}[- (1/\Delta|\theta|)\lambda_{L1}\hat{K}\{\theta_{K3}\theta_{L1} + \theta_{23}(\theta_{L1} - \theta_{L2})\} \\ -\hat{\overline{Z}}\{(\theta_{23}T'(.)\overline{Z})/(\Delta|\theta|P_2X_2)\}C] - T'(.)\overline{Z}\hat{\overline{Z}} \end{aligned}$$

where

$$\begin{aligned} C = [\lambda_{K1}\lambda_{L1}\sigma_1 + \sigma_2(\lambda_{K1}\lambda_{L2}\theta_{K2} + \lambda_{L1}\lambda_{K2}\theta_{L2}) + (\theta_{L1}\sigma_3/(1-\theta_{23})) \\ (\lambda_{K1}\lambda_{L3}\theta_{K3} + \lambda_{L1}\lambda_{K3}\theta_{L3})] > 0. \end{aligned}$$

Use of Equation (9.24) and simplification yield

$$\begin{aligned} F\hat{F}X_3 = -[\{T'(.)Z'X_2 - T(.)\}(\lambda_{L1}/\Delta|\theta|)\{\theta_{K3}\theta_{L1} + \theta_{23}(\theta_{L1} - \theta_{L2})\}]\hat{K} \\ (+) \\ -\{(\theta_{23}T'(.)\overline{Z})/(\Delta|\theta|P_2X_2)\}[\{T'(.)Z'X_2 - T(.)\}C + \{(\Delta|\theta|P_2X_2)/\theta_{23}\}]\hat{\overline{Z}} \end{aligned}$$

Further simplification gives

$$\begin{aligned} F\hat{F}X_3 = \{T'(.)Z'X_2 - T(.)\}[(\lambda_{L1}/\Delta\,|\theta|\,)\{\theta_{K3}\theta_{L1} + \theta_{23}(\theta_{L1} - \theta_{L2})\}]\hat{K} \\ -\{(T'(.)\overline{Z})/(\Delta|\theta|)\}[\{\theta_{K3}\theta_{L1} + \theta_{23}(\theta_{L1} - \theta_{L2})\}\{\lambda_{K1}(\lambda_{L2} + \lambda_{L3} - h'(.)Z'X_2/h(.)) \\ -\lambda_{L1}(\lambda_{K2} + \lambda_{K3})\}]\hat{\overline{Z}} \end{aligned} \quad (9.28)$$

Appendix 9.4: Derivation of Equation (9.29)
Differentiation of Equation (9.12) yields

$$\begin{aligned} \mathrm{d}Y = h(.)\mathrm{d}W + Wh'(.)Z'\mathrm{d}X_2 + (W^* - W)a_{L3}\mathrm{d}X_3 + (W^* - W)X_3\mathrm{d}a_{L3} - a_{L3}X_3\mathrm{d}W \\ +K_D\mathrm{d}r + T'(.)Z'\mathrm{d}X_2 - T(.)\mathrm{d}\overline{Z} - mP_3\mathrm{d}X_3 \end{aligned}$$

or

$$\begin{aligned} Y\hat{Y} = Wh(.)\hat{W} + Wh'(.)Z'X_2\hat{X}_2 + (W^* - W)a_{L3}X_3\hat{X}_3 \\ +(W^* - W)a_{L3}X_3(\theta_{K3}\sigma_3/(1-\theta_{23}))\hat{r} + rK_D\hat{r} \\ -Wa_{L3}X_3\hat{W} + T'(.)Z'X_2\hat{X}_2 - T'(.)\overline{Z}\hat{\overline{Z}} - mP_3X_3\hat{X}_2 \end{aligned}$$

(note that $\hat{a}_{L3} = (\theta_{K3}\sigma_3/(1-\theta_{23}))\hat{r}; (\theta_{L3} + \theta_{K3}) = (1 - \theta_{23})$).

Now substitution of $\hat{X}_2$ in place of $\hat{X}_3$ into the above equation yields

$$Y\hat{Y} = \{h(.)W(1-\lambda_{L3})\}\hat{W} + \{(W^* - W)a_{L3}X_3(\theta_{K3}\sigma_3/(1-\theta_{23})) + rK_D\}\hat{r}$$
$$+[\{Wh'(.)+T'(.)\}Z'X_2 + (W^* - W)h(.)\lambda_{L3} - mP_3X_3]\hat{X}_2 - T'(.)\overline{Z}\hat{\overline{Z}}$$

With the help of Equations (9.15) and (9.16) the above expression becomes

$$Y\hat{Y} = [-Wh(.)\theta_{K1}(1-\lambda_{L3}) + (W^* - W)h(.)\lambda_{L3}(\theta_{K3}\sigma_3\theta_{L1}/(1-\theta_{23}))$$
$$+ rK_D\theta_{L1}](\hat{P}_2/|\theta|) - T'(.)\overline{Z}\hat{\overline{Z}} + [\{T'(.) + Wh'(.)\}Z'X_2$$
$$+ (W^* - W)h(.)\lambda_{L3} - mP_3X_3]\hat{X}_2$$

Using Equations (9.22) and (9.23) we can write

$$Y\hat{Y} = \hat{\overline{Z}}[\{A\theta_{23}T'(.)\overline{Z})/(|\theta|\Delta P_2X_2)\}\{\lambda_{K1}(\lambda_{L2}+\lambda_{L3}-(h'(.)Z'X_2/h(.))$$
$$-\lambda_{L1}(\lambda_{K2}+\lambda_{K3})\}] + \hat{K}[\{A\lambda_{L1}\theta_{23}/|\theta|\Delta P_2X_2\}\{T'(.)Z'X_2 - T(.)\}] - T'(.)\overline{Z}\hat{\overline{Z}}$$
$$-\hat{K}[(B\lambda_{L1}/\Delta|\theta|)\{\theta_{K3}\theta_{L1}+\theta_{23}(\theta_{L1}-\theta_{L2})\}] - \hat{\overline{Z}}[\{(B\theta_{23}T'(.)\overline{Z})/(\Delta|\theta|P_2X_2)\}C]$$

where

$$A = [\{(W^* - W)h(.)\lambda_{L3}\theta_{K3}\theta_{L1}\sigma_3/(1-\theta_{23})\} - Wh(.)\theta_{K1}(1-\lambda_{L3}) + rK_D\theta_{L1}],$$
$$B = [(W^* - W)h(.)\lambda_{L3} - \{T'(.) + h'(.)W\}Z'X_2 - mP_3X_3], \text{ and}$$
$$C = [\lambda_{K1}\lambda_{L1}\sigma_1 + \sigma_2(\lambda_{K1}\lambda_{L2}\theta_{K2} + \lambda_{L1}\lambda_{K2}\theta_{L2}) + (\theta_{L1}\sigma_3/(1-\theta_{23}))(\lambda_{K1}\lambda_{L3}\theta_{K3} + \lambda_{L1}\lambda_{K3}\theta_{L3})] > 0.$$

Further simplification gives

$$Y\hat{Y} = \hat{\overline{Z}}\{(T'(.)\overline{Z})/(\Delta|\theta|P_2X_2)\}[A\theta_{23}\{\lambda_{K1}(\lambda_{L2}+\lambda_{L3}-(h'(.)Z'X_2/h(.))$$
$$\underset{(-)}{-\lambda_{L1}(\lambda_{K2}+\lambda_{K3})\}}$$
$$\underset{(+)}{-B\theta_{23}C - (|\theta|\Delta P_2X_2)]}$$
$$+\hat{K}(\lambda_{L1}/|\theta|\Delta)[(A\theta_{23}/P_2X_2)\{T'(.)Z'X_2 - T(.)\} - \underset{(+)}{B\{\theta_{K3}\theta_{L1}+\theta_{23}(\theta_{L1}-\theta_{L2})\}}] \quad (9.29)$$

Appendix 9.5: Two possible cases

Depending on the different signs and values of $|\theta|$ the following two cases are possible.

Case I: $|\theta| > 0$. From Equations (9.26.2)–(9.26.4) it follows that $|\lambda| > 0$. Then, from the stability condition in the market for commodity 2 (given by (9.25)) one obtains $\Delta > 0$. We have stated in the text that $\Delta > 0$ only if $\{T'(.)Z'X_2 - T(.)\} < 0$, i.e. $E_T < (1 - \overline{Z}/Z)$. Using Equation (9.10.1) it is then easy to check from Equation (9.22) that $\hat{X}_2 < 0$ when $\hat{K} > 0$ and $\hat{X}_2 > 0$when $\hat{\overline{Z}} < 0$.

Again with the help of Equation (9.10.1) from Equation (9.29) we find that $\hat{Y} < 0$ when $\hat{K} > 0$ if (i) $A > 0$ and (ii) $B \geq 0$. On the other hand, $\hat{Y} > 0$ when $\hat{\overline{Z}} < 0$ under the same two sufficient conditions.

Case II: Let us now concentrate on the case where the agricultural sector is more capital (less labour)-intensive than the informal manufacturing sector. In this case, we have $(a_{K1}/a_{L1}) > (a_{K2}/a_{L2})$. This implies that $(\lambda_{L1}\lambda_{K2} - \lambda_{K1}\lambda_{L2}) < 0$ and $|\theta| < 0$. There can be two sub-cases depending on the sign of $|\lambda|$, given by Equation (9.26.2).

Sub-case 1: $|\theta| < 0$ and $|\lambda| > 0$. From Equations (9.25) and (9.26.1) we find that $\Delta > 0$ and $\Delta' < 0$ (as $|\theta| < 0$). A sufficient condition for $\Delta' < 0$ is that $\{T'(.)Z'X_2 - T(.)\} \geq 0$, i.e. $E_T \geq (1 - \overline{Z}/Z)$.

From Equation (9.22) one finds that $\hat{X}_2 > 0$ when $\hat{K} > 0$ and $\hat{X}_2 < 0$ when $\hat{\overline{Z}} < 0$. This from Equation (9.27), in turn, implies that $\hat{Z} > 0$ when $\hat{K} > 0$ and $\hat{Z} < 0$ when $\hat{\overline{Z}} < 0$.

Then from Equation (9.29) it follows that

$\hat{Y} < 0$ when $\hat{K} > 0$ if (i) $B < 0$ and (ii) $A(T'(.)Z'X_2 - T(.)) \geq 0$.

On the contrary, $\hat{Y} > 0$ when $\hat{\overline{Z}} < 0$ if

$$[A\theta_{23}\{\lambda_{K1}(\lambda_{L2} + \lambda_{L3} - h'(.)Z'X_2/h(.)) - \lambda_{L1}(\lambda_{K2} + \lambda_{K3})\} - B\theta_{23}C] \geq 0.$$

or if

$$[A\theta_{23}\{\lambda_{K1}(\lambda_{L2}+\lambda_{L3}-h'(.)Z'X_2/h(.)) - \lambda_{L1}(\lambda_{K2} + \lambda_{K3})\} - (|\theta|\Delta P_2X_2)] \geq (>)0;$$

and $B < (\leq)0$.

Sub-case 2: $|\theta| < 0$ and $|\lambda| < 0$. This implies that for stability of equilibrium in the market for commodity 2 we need $\Delta < 0$, a necessary condition for which is $\{T'(.)Z'X_2 - T(.)\} < 0$, i.e. $E_T < (1 - \overline{Z}/Z)$.

From Equation (9.22) it then follows that $\hat{X}_2 < 0$ when $\hat{K} > 0$ and $\hat{X}_2 > 0$ when $\hat{\overline{Z}} < 0$.

On the other hand, from Equation (9.29), it follows that

$\hat{Y} < 0$ when $\hat{K} > 0$ if (i) $A \geq 0$; (ii) $B \geq 0$; and (iii) either A or B is non-zero.

Also $\hat{Y} > 0$ when $\hat{\overline{Z}} < 0$ if (i) $A \geq 0$ and (ii) $B \geq 0$.

Chapter 10
Conclusion and Comments

Informal sector is essentially an extensive discipline as an element of the production system and labour markets in developing countries. It is not only a segment in a dichotomous economic structure; rather it encompasses an array of multifarious activities, each with its distinct feature. 'Informality' has a multidimensional character. Basically, it is conceived as work characterised by the lack of minimum levels of returns to labour, where the job is performed without legal rights, without opportunities for labour quality enhancement and with no social protection and trade union representation. Apart from such precarious employment in informal units, the recent expansion of informality within the private corporate sector and the public sector with outsourcing, subcontracting, work at home and other typical forms of work that foster unstable and insecure employment relations can safely be construed as unrestrained growth of 'informality'.

The informal sector not only exists but is ubiquitous and has stupendous influence on the workings of the economy, inter-relationships between the economic agents and efficacy of changes in policy parameters. However, most of the enterprises cannot be placed in any of the extreme points of the formal–informal continuum; rather they fall in some place in the intermediate zone. This complexity gets in the way of formulation of appropriate progressive strategies targeted to integrate the informal sector into development.

In this book we endeavour to give an insight into the different dimensions of the informal sector and study its multi-faceted interaction with the other sectors of the economy. Most importantly, we give an outline of the earlier doctrines, elucidate on the newer ones and critically review the contradictions within them to trace the nature and direction of desirable policy parameters that may be relevant in the present scenario. We have stylised the informal sector within different established theoretical frameworks. We have incorporated the informal sector in the traditional Heckscher–Ohlin model and also considered the dualistic approach within the Harris–Todaro framework. We have embraced the theories of dependency and/or underdevelopment where the focus shifts from marginalisation to the structural linkages that exist between the informal and formal sectors. The dependent structural linkages between the informal and formal sectors are shaped by capitalist modes of production that result from the wage and labour strategies of capitalist

S. Chaudhuri, U. Mukhopadhyay, *Revisiting the Informal Sector*,
DOI 10.1007/978-1-4419-1194-0_10,

enterprises, which seek to lower costs by resorting to subcontracting. We have considered situations, albeit in different models, where the informal sector produces internationally traded final commodity, non-traded final commodity, and traded and non-traded intermediaries.

10.1 An Overview

We set off our discussion with the most popular dualistic approach proposed by Harris and Todaro (1970). We explain the Harris–Todaro (HT) migration mechanism and trace out the importance of informal wage in the determination of unionised wage in a segmented urban labour market. In the existing literature on informal sector it is usually assumed that the workers who are unable to find employment in the urban formal sector are automatically absorbed in the informal sector in which the wage rate is perfectly flexible, thereby leaving no room for open unemployment in the migration equilibrium. But empirical evidence strongly suggests that the menace of open unemployment does exist in the urban sector of developing economies despite the existence of an informal sector. An informal sector of a developing economy often is found to consist of small subcontract firms, where workers do not get more than their reservation wages. Besides, there are often strong barriers to entry even into the informal sector, which exclude some workers in finding employment in the informal sector of the economy. We have presented theoretical models that show the simultaneous existence of urban informal sector and open unemployment in a Harris–Todaro model.

A common practice in developing countries is that the governments often implement traditional subsidy policies to ameliorate the problem of rising unemployment in the urban sector. The standard Harris–Todaro result suggests that the key to the solution of the urban unemployment lies in the rural sector of the economy. The HT model advocates that any urban development policy aimed at enhancing employment opportunities in the urban sector is likely to exaggerate unemployment in the urban sector; rather rural development programme is forwarded as a possible solution to the problem.

However, the introduction of dualism in the urban sector, where the informal sector co-exists with the formal sector, may generate results contradicting the standard Harris–Todaro result. It is shown that cases may arise where a rural development policy cannot mitigate urban unemployment resulting from rural–urban migration. On the contrary a surge in the wage or price subsidy to the urban sector may be instrumental in lowering the urban unemployment level. It is assumed that the government procures food from the rural sector and distributes it among the urban consumers so that the government can effectively control the urban labour force by controlling the availability of food in that sector. Subsidy policies to the rural sector increase the availability of food in the urban sector resulting from an increase in total food production, causing the urban labour force to expand. On the other hand, a wage or a price policy in the urban sector raises the level of employment in the urban sector, while keeping the rural sector undisturbed. Thus the urban unemployment level falls. However, here the crucial role of the demand side in determining the level of production in both the manufacturing and rural sectors has been ignored. This lacuna has been dealt with in another model where the importance of demand side in determination of the level of production in all the three sectors is considered. A price or a wage subsidy policy to the rural sector raises the aggregate income of the workers in the economy, which in turn causes an increase in the level of demand in all the three sectors, directly or indirectly. The employment level in each of the three sectors increases, thereby causing reduction in urban unemployment. Also a demand management policy, for example an export promotional scheme in the manufacturing industry, raises the level of employment in each of the three sectors of the economy, directly or indirectly, lowering urban unemployment.

The essence of our discussion is that it can never be assured that urban development programmes will necessarily be effective in solving the urban unemployment problem. Therefore, it seems prudent to avoid these policies. On the other hand, rural development programmes in the form of a wage or price subsidy policy and/or a demand management policy such as an export promotional scheme in the manufacturing sector unambiguously lower the urban unemployment level. However, when the urban unemployment level is demand determined and the government can control it through a demand management policy, then there is little justification of using the indirect policy measures such as price or wage subsidy policy. Thus we provide a theoretical basis for the introduction of export promotional schemes, for example, the formation of duty-free export processing zones (EPZs) to mitigate the unemployment problem in the urban area.

The informal subcontracting is introduced and it is shown that the informal sector firm does not get more than its reservation income in the subcontracting system and that the subcontracting system is the optimal policy to the formal sector firm provided there is imperfection in the credit market. A credit subsidy policy to the informal sector leads to an overall contraction of the formal sector while it expands the informal sector. However, it does not raise the industrial productivity so long as it is engaged in subcontracting arrangement with the formal sector firm.

The common contention now in the perspective of the ongoing process of globalisation is that the problems of all developing countries can be best understood with reference to the international environment, of which they are a part. The problems of underdevelopment must, therefore, first and foremost be perceived in a global context. We try to explore different aspects of the informal sector in the backdrop of globalisation.

We analyse the effects of liberalised trade and investment policies on welfare and open unemployment in a developing economy. A conventional result in the literature on trade and development is that growth with foreign capital is immiserising in a tariff-distorted economy. Having discussed this result that had been obtained in a number of studies in both HOS and Harris–Todaro (1970) frameworks, we show in a three-sector Harris–Todaro (1970) type general equilibrium model, with the assumption of wage rigidity in the two urban sectors, leading to the simultaneous existence of open unemployment and an urban informal sector in the migration equilibrium, that an inflow of foreign capital in either of the two broad sectors of the economy may be welfare improving mainly through the fall in urban unemployment. On the other hand, a reduction in import tariff may lower national welfare. This is in contradiction to the traditional result that envisages removal of distortions to facilitate more efficient allocation of resources. Besides, an inflow of foreign capital into the urban sector (a reduction in import tariff) leads to an expansion (a contraction) of the urban sector of the economy. This policy is likely to ameliorate (aggravate) the problem of urban unemployment. These results are completely opposite to those generated by the standard Harris–Todaro model.

We also show that even in a 2×2 decomposable production structure there may be welfare gains from foreign capital. This happens if the labour reallocation effect of foreign capital inflow outweighs the output effect (of the import-competing sector). However, the existence of labour market distortion is a necessity to obtain the counterintuitive result and any attempt to lower the magnitude of labour market distortion lowers the possibility of welfare gain from foreign capital. A liberalising developing economy, yearning for foreign capital, therefore, ought to be vigilant while undertaking labour market reform policy. This is because there is a trade-off between the growth with foreign capital and labour market reform policy. However, it is also true that in obtaining welfare-improving result of foreign capital, the presence of labour market distortion is necessary only in the absence of technology transfer. In case foreign capital inflow is accompanied by technology transfer, welfare of the economy may increase even if there is no labour market distortion. Foreign capital leads to an increase in the efficiency of domestic labour, effectively raising the labour supply. As a consequence, the tariff-protected sector does not necessarily expand. With additional labour supply it is quite likely that domestic income rises and foreign capital is welfare-improving if the labour endowment effect is sufficiently large. Thus, investment liberalisation policy and labour market reform may be undertaken concomitantly in the presence of technology transfer.

Empirical evidence points out that trade and investment liberalisation have so far failed to provide any substantial welfare gains to the liberalising countries, which seems quite puzzling. One possible explanation may be that the liberalising countries have tried to free their economy in every possible way and at a very brisk pace, without pre-calculating their possible outcomes. Whether a country should follow every aspect of the WTO-prescribed policy package is a vital question. We have shown that an inflow of foreign capital is desirable only if there exists a certain degree of labour market distortion. So, again this calls for a very cautious tread towards labour market reform. If labour market distortion is removed beyond a certain limit, gainful effects of investment and trade liberalisation policies cannot be achieved and in the extreme cases these may even be counterproductive. On the other hand, a tariff reform measure has been found to be relatively safe in the existing set-up. In the Harris–Todaro setting an inflow of foreign capital has been found to be immiserising. The welfare consequences of tariff and labour market reforms have been found to depend crucially on the presence and magnitude of foreign capital in the economy. If the magnitude of foreign capital is relatively small, deregulation of the labour market is likely to produce a favourable effect on national welfare while a tariff reform will be counterproductive. But these results are likely to get reversed in the presence of substantial amount of foreign capital in the economy.

With substantial evidences of 'informalisation' in the developing countries, generally attributed to liberalised policies, it becomes imperative to examine the effects of such policies on the welfare of informal sector workers, which can fairly be assessed by the informal wage rate. We have shown that trade liberalisation, except in a very special case, produces depressing effect on the informal wage while inflows of foreign capital and/or structural reforms like deregulating the labour market are likely to produce favourable effects on the wage earnings of the poor workers. The latter result is extremely crucial as it explains why labour market reform should form an integral constituent of the liberalised economic package in the liberalising countries. Furthermore, these results do not hinge on the nature of the capital mobility between the formal and informal sectors and, therefore, are robust. So, removal of the protectionist policy, which aims at reduction of commodity market distortion, must be undertaken very cautiously as it is likely to hurt the interest of the poorer group of the workforce. On the other hand, investment and labour market reforms may be encouraged.

In accordance with the Stolper–Samuelson theorem it is predicted that liberalised policies are likely to lower the prevailing wage inequality between skilled and unskilled labour. But empirical evidences in a number of developing countries are in sharp contradiction to this conjecture. We have shown that the wage inequality rises unambiguously due to policies like an increase in the relative price of the high-skill commodity and a reduction of import tariff from the low-skill manufacturing sector. On the other hand, an increase in capital endowment due to, for example, an inflow of foreign capital improves the wage inequality if the skill-intensive sector is not more capital-intensive (in a special sense) vis-à-vis the low-skill manufacturing sector. Interestingly, contrary to the common wisdom a decline in the trade union power of the unskilled labour that results from a policy of labour market reform does not necessarily lead to deterioration in the skilled–unskilled wage inequality. In fact, such a policy may improve the wage inequality under reasonable condition. This result is important, especially when many of the developing countries are hesitant to undertake labour market reforms seriously in the fear that such a move would be vehemently resisted by the political parties and trade unions on the plea that it would lead to general wage reductions of the poorer groups of the working population engaged in different sectors of the economy and accentuate the wage inequality. But we have shown that there is very little substance in such a common and populist belief. The vast section of the poor working population engaged in the different unorganised sectors of the economy will ultimately be benefited from such a policy and the wage inequality is also very much likely to get better.

A vital point that emerges is that the reform policy/ies to be undertaken essentially depends on the nature of the target group, whose welfare the government envisages to safeguard. Liberalisation policies that improve overall national welfare may be detrimental for the poorer section of the society or may intensify inequality in terms of wages. This can be indicative of the fact that the benefits accruing to the relatively well-off section greatly outweigh the harm inflicted on the poor.

Thus it rests with the respective governments to choose from the alternative reform strategies and implement them in accordance with their objectives of egalitarianism, uplifting the downtrodden or mitigating social inequality.

The social menace of child labour is inextricably linked to the informal sector of developing countries. Almost the entire child labour force is employed in the informal sector in these countries. Poverty and lack of educational facilities are often referred to in the literature as the primary factors responsible for the incidence of child labour. Liberalised trade and investment policies and provision of better and free education are largely recommended as remedial measures. It is advocated that policies like tariff reforms and/or inflow of foreign capital in substantial amounts are likely to take the developing countries into higher growth orbits, the benefits of which would eventually percolate down to the bottom rungs of the society and reduce poverty. A reduction in poverty, in turn, would exert a downward pressure on the incidence of child labour and urban unemployment of adult labour. On the other hand, betterment of educational facilities coupled with allied incentive schemes would also be able to deliver the goods by keeping the children from poor families into schools and refraining them from entering the job market. However, empirical evidences from developing economies embarking on economic liberalisation are not quite encouraging. The incidence of child labour has plummeted over the last few decades but not at the expected rate. Even in some high growth-prone areas, the incidence has been on the rise. Why globalisation and betterment of educational opportunities have not so far been able to produce the desired results is quite puzzling.

We have shown that if different trade and investment liberalisation programmes and a free education policy are undertaken simultaneously in a transition economy, their overall effect on the supply of child labour may not be quite satisfactory as different policies produce mutually opposite effects on the incidence of child labour, thereby nullifying each other's effects, at least partially.

Even in an H–T model inflow of foreign capital in the economy and/or a free education policy may raise the supply of child labour in the urban sector by forcing rural workers to migrate to the urban sector with their children and accentuate the problem of urban unemployment of adult labour. Besides, trade reforms like tariff reductions on the urban final manufacturing product or rise in the price of the export commodity resulting from worldwide liberalised trade policies in agriculture and the education subsidy policy lower the welfare of the run of the meal people of the urban sector while foreign capital inflow unambiguously improves their welfare. The analysis made in this book can serve to question the effectiveness of these policies as a general proposition. The policymakers should decide which policies to be given priority and carried out in order to mitigate the incidence of poverty-induced child labour in the system only after taking into account all parameter values to get the desired results.

Quite interestingly, the informal sector has its share of contribution in the environment too by way of perpetuating as well as mitigating environmental pollution. In developing countries reduction of the permissible level of pollution by pollution-regulating authorities is a conventional policy to arrest further environmental degradation. Although both the formal and informal manufacturing units cause industrial pollution, the extent of pollution generated by the informal sector firms is significantly greater than that generated by their formal sector counterparts. With limited access to Environmentally Sound Technology (EST) the informal sector firms, largely using backward technology, are responsible for a major share of pollutants. The formal sector firms in developing countries often subcontract the informal sector units to undertake a number of tasks and processes that are 'dirty' from the environmental point of view. The informal sector firms being unregistered are difficult to control and so they face fewer incentives to prevent pollution. In the circumstances, an indirect way to control environmental pollution is to impose pollution emission tax on the formal sector firms if the level of industrial pollution created exceeds a certain permissible level. This is expected to persuade them to minimise harmful discharges by cutting down the use of intermediaries produced by the informal sector and thus improve the environmental quality. A pertinent question is whether this indirect way of controlling pollution can actually deliver the goods.

We have analysed the efficacy of such a policy in a three-sector general equilibrium model with a polluting informal sector, which produces a non-traded intermediate input for the formal sector. It is shown that even if the permissible pollution level is reduced, the polluting sector may expand and lead to a deterioration in the environmental standard. Quite unexpectedly, this policy may improve welfare of the economy. This has a very important policy implication due to the counterintuitive results of direct environmental policies. On the contrary, an inflow of foreign capital may be effective in lowering the level of pollution although it may affect welfare of the economy adversely. Therefore, there might exist a trade-off between the economy's objectives of lowering the level of pollution and improving national welfare. This calls for designing appropriate policies since reduction of pollution level and improvement of national welfare feature as priorities for a developing economy.

It is believed that pollution and solid waste generation are unavoidable accomplices of industrial production. To tackle the solid wastes, the well-known 'waste management hierarchy' proposes waste minimisation, reuse, recycle, recovery and disposal, and it is believed that waste minimisation is the best approach. But in developing countries with less-stringent pollution norms and environmental standards, waste minimisation is often not prioritised; rather rampant industrial activities with heavily polluting and waste-generating effects are indulged in. Waste dumping and open burnings can cause severe harmful effects; landfill has its own problems as well since it encroaches into the already scarce land in these countries with massive rates of urbanisation. Hence, recycling, although not the best, may be the only viable solution for managing solid wastes in these countries.

The informal sector plays a crucial role in recovery, processing and recycling of solid wastes in developing countries, which are some of the largest importers of recyclable wastes that are mainly used in the informal recycling industries as intermediate goods. International agreements like the Basel Convention prohibit trade in hazardous wastes, but there exists controversies regarding effects of free trade in non-hazardous recyclable wastes.

We show that foreign capital inflow and tariff reforms in wastes may produce effects that tend to increase domestic waste recovery as well as recycling and lower the level of pollution in an economy where waste recovery and recycling are carried out in the informal sector.

10.2 Concluding Remarks

Although having dealt with a number of issues, we perhaps have been unable to do justice to an extensive topic like informal sector within our limitations. There still remain pertinent issues that demand theoretical exposition. A few of them have been discussed below with a view to provide an outline for further research.

Self-employment has assumed remarkable significance, more in the recent years, accounting, in average, for more than 30% of the labour force. The importance of self-employment had long been sketched by Hart (1971) who emphasised, 'The distinction between formal and informal income opportunities is based essentially on that between wage earning and self-employment.' Although it was an overtly simplified categorisation, it indicated self-employment as an important part of the informal sector. It offers a choice between underemployment as informal wage earners or to be self-employed, and involves a micro-level decision of individuals whether to work for themselves or commoditise their labour. Self-employment may again be dichotomous in nature. On the one hand it consists of artisans, shoe shine boys, street vendors, repairmen, depicting lower income than formal sector wage-earning activities, while, on the other, it comprises small business enterprises that operate on an informal basis to circumvent regulations that often earn higher than informal wage earners. The recent surge in informal self-employment can be broadly ascribed to the effects of flexible deregulation of labour markets in most of the developing world embracing economic reform, which encourage temporary contract modalities or the lack of it.

The informal self-employed serve the community by providing cheaper goods, ready access to goods, employment for the unskilled and an employment 'cushion' for bad times. Despite globalisation and the resulting competition, informal self-employment has recently played a major role in poverty alleviation through employment and income generation. However, theoretical literature on informal self-employment is scarce. While substantial research has been focused towards the workings of informal wage employment and the implications that liberalisation has on informal workers, the repercussions on those self-employed in the informal sector are rarely studied.

Secondly, empirical evidences indicate an overwhelming representation of women in informal sector employment. In some countries in sub-Saharan Africa, virtually all of the female non-agricultural labour force is in the informal sector: for example, the informal sector accounts for over 95% of women workers outside agriculture in Benin, Chad and Mali. In India and Indonesia, the informal sector accounts for nine out of every ten women working outside agriculture. In ten Latin American and four East Asian countries, for which data are available, half or more of the female non-agricultural workforce is in the informal sector. Thus, the informal sector is a larger source of employment for women than for men (Charmes, 1998; UN, 2000; Chen, 2001).

Although it is very difficult to accurately count the women workers in the informal sector, street hawkers and vendors probably account for a large proportion of the women working in commerce as family or 'own account' workers. Other forms of women's informal employment include domestic service, contracting or subcontracting and prostitution. Women's problems in informal sector employment include low earnings, lack of skills, lack of knowledge of commerce and local bureaucracies, no access to wholesale suppliers and credit, and illiteracy.

Globalisation and the resulting restructuring of production foster outsourcing of production to home workers who remain outside the formal workforce. There is a predominance of women in the export processing zones, for example in the garment industry of Bangladesh. Notwithstanding the fact that women's informal work contributes substantially to GDP and global trade, women informal workers are overtly synonymous with poverty and vulnerability.

Although average incomes of both men and women are lower in the informal sector than in the formal sector, the gender gap in income and wages appears higher in the informal sector than in the formal sector and exists even when women are not wage workers. This is largely due to the fact that women are under-represented in high-income activities (like informal entrepreneur, self-employed) and over-represented in low-income activities (like casual worker and subcontract worker).

They are constrained to work in the neighbourhood of their residence and can access jobs only through informal contacts, both of which reduce their bargaining power considerably. The tendency for specialised activities to be concentrated in different geographic locations of a city further restricts the possibility of women workers being engaged in diverse jobs and thus aggravates the situation of an excess supply of labour in a particular activity. Constrained choice, limited contacts of women and physical segmentation of the labour market perpetuate forces that entrap women workers in a low-income situation with worse outcomes than those of their male counterparts (Mitra, 2005).

Regulations regarding minimum wage, literacy campaign with the onus on women education along with vocational and on-the-job training are some of the recommendations found in the literature to improve the conditions of women within the informal sector. Unfortunately, theoretical literature to capture the gender dimension in the informal sector is scarce. It is necessary to trace out the labour market conditions and intriguing discrepancies in the wages of women workers and evaluate different policies with respect to trade and reforms in the light of women informal workers since they are likely to affect the latter in a different manner.

Third, illegal immigration has been a source of predicament for not only many developed but developing countries as well. For example, in spite of efforts by the respective governments to restrict immigrants, the number of illegal immigrants from Mexico to United States and from Bangladesh and Nepal to India has been on the rise. The illegal immigrants in the developing countries are mostly the unskilled workers of the neighbouring countries that permeate through the borders, largely motivated by the economic benefits in terms of higher wages or employability in the host country and end up in the informal sector, with virtually no barriers to entry.

The welfare effects of illegal immigration in the host country have been subject to substantial debate. However, the unfavourable effects seem to be quite overwhelming. The influx of unskilled labour tends to exert a downward pressure on the competitive informal wage. With unemployment already existing in these developing host countries, unskilled immigrants are likely to displace native workers and also become a source of burden for the government since they tend not to pay taxes by the virtue of their illegality.

There exist a number of instruments for the government to control illegal immigration. The stringency in border enforcement and penalties for immigrants that are nabbed along with internal enforcement whereby illegal immigrants are apprehended and expelled from the country may be palpable methods to resist them. Some countries provide foreign aid to the country of origin in order to reduce income differentials and thus the incentive to immigrate.

There exists a considerable theoretical literature on illegal immigration (Ethier, 1986; Bond and Chen, 1987; Bandyopadhyay, 2006 to name only a few). However, the interaction of illegal immigrants with the informal sector has not received adequate attention, but needs in-depth study before formulating policies to deal with illegal immigration.

Fourth, the recent financial and economic crisis that initiated in 2008 mainly in the advanced countries has started to permeate into the developing countries with crisis impending in their wage and employment levels. The global slump has critically affected poverty and income distribution and triggered rising joblessness in the developing countries. According to a study by the Labour Bureau of Ministry of Labour and Employment in India, about half a million people were rendered jobless between October and December 2008 due to the recession. According to official Chinese figures, by January, 2009, 15.3% of China's 130 million migrant workers had lost their jobs and returned home. This aggregate figure of migrant job loss does not include those who stayed back in cities in search of new jobs and fell back upon the informal sector, at least temporarily.

These conditions of increasing unemployment are anticipated to have large repercussions on the informal sector. Over 55% of non-agricultural employment in the developing world is informal and these already high figures of informality are likely to increase even further. According to the annual Global Employment Trends report (2009) by the ILO the number of people joining the ranks of the unemployed, working poor and those in vulnerable employment are expected to increase dramatically. The Asian Development Bank predicts that the number of self-employed people and unpaid family workers will increase by 21 million, if current conditions hold, or by 60 million if the situation worsens. Empirical evidences from Argentina and many

Asian countries support the predicted shift towards more informal employment in times of economic downturn.

There are mainly three mechanisms through which the global recession has affected the informal sector: first, the fall in the imports of developed countries from developing ones and the consequent decline in commodity prices have severely hit the export-oriented informal sector that either produces final export goods or supplies intermediaries for the export industries. Developing countries that depend on primary and processed products have impinged the rural agricultural informal sector. Second, during economic crises, informal employment acts as a cushion when people are laid off in the formal sector and need to find new job opportunities. Furthermore, an economy going into recession might experience a shift from the tradable to the non-tradable sectors, which again would strengthen informality. Third, the advanced countries may be expected to outsource more production aspects to the developing ones to curtail their costs, with the potential of generating new jobs and business.

Since informal employment can offer only temporary job prospects that are more vulnerable in times of recession, the increasing informality can be construed as jobs of inferior quality, high risks and insufficient social protection that are likely to increase poverty levels in the developing countries. To counter this situation and strive towards the Millennium Development Goals, governmental intervention to improve social protection and empowerment for those in the informal sector seems crucial. The ILO suggests that people will be more willing to work under flexible terms if they have a better social safety network to fall back on. This would also reduce pressure on employers to provide welfare measures. Also, better social security is likely to minimise possibilities of social unrest.

Better social security may be ensured by extending existing formal mechanisms to the informal sector or scaling up support mechanisms for the informal sector so that it could act as a shock absorber to prevent people from falling into the poverty trap. Examples include the strengthening of conditional cash transfer programmes, enhancing public works and giving a boost to (micro)-insurance schemes that protect against basic risks like health shocks. Steps must also be taken to increase the productivity of informal businesses by providing better infrastructure and access to resources.

The above discussion constitutes the general and perceptible insights into the impact of economic recession on the growth of informal sector. With only few studies delving into the nuances of the linkages between economic downturn and informal sector, such as Rogerson (1988) and Meagher (2008), the present global recession calls for extensive study on the issue.

Selected Bibliography

Addison, T., Bhalotra, S. and Heady, C. (1997). *Child Labour in Pakistan and Ghana*. University of Warwick, *Mimeo*, Coventry.

Agenor, P.R. (1996). 'The Labour Market and Economic Adjustment', *IMF Staff Papers*, 32, pp. 261–355.

Agenor, P.R. and Montiel, P. (1995). *Development Macroeconomics*. Princeton University Press, New Jersey.

Aghion, P., Burgess, R., Redding, S. and Zilibotti, F. (2003). 'The Unequal Effects of Liberalisation: Theory and Evidence from India', *Mimeo*. Harvard, LSE, and IIES.

Ali, S.M., Cotton, A. and Coad, A., (1993). 'Informal Sector Waste Recycling', *Paper presented at the 19th WEDC Conference on Water, Sanitation, Environment and Development*, 153–155 Accra, Ghana.

Arias, O. and Sosa, E.W. (2004) *Subjective and Objective Poverty in Bolivia*, Background paper for the 2005 World Bank Bolivia Poverty Assessment.

Baland, J. and Robinson, J.A. (2000). 'Is Child Labour Inefficient?', *Journal of Political Economy*, 108(4), pp. 663–679.

Bandyopadhyay, S. (2006). 'Illegal Immigration and Second Best Import Tariffs', *Review of International Economics*, 14(1), pp. 93–103.

Banerjee, B. (1983). 'The Role of the Informal Sector in the Migration Process: A Test of Probabilistic Migration Models and Labour Market Segmentation for India', *Oxford Economic Papers*, 35(3), pp. 399–422.

Banerjee, B. (1986). *Rural to Urban Migration and the Urban Labour Market: A Case Study of Delhi*. Himalaya Publishing House, Mumbai.

Bartone, C., Leith, L., Triche, T. and Schertenleid, R. (1991). 'Private Sector Participation in Municipal Solid Waste Service: Experiences in Latin America', *Waste Management and Research*, 9, pp. 495–509.

Basu, K. (1984). *The Less Developed Economy*. Oxford University Press, New Delhi.

Basu, K. (1998). *Analytical Development Economics: The Less Developed Economy Revisited*. Oxford University Press, Delhi, Calcutta, Chennai, Mumbai, Chapter13.

Basu, K. (1999). 'Child Labour: Cause, Consequence, and Cure, with Remarks on International Labour Standards', *Journal of Economic Literature*, 37 (September), pp. 1083–1119.

Basu, K. and Bell, C. (1991). 'Fragmented Duopoly: Theory and Applications to Backward Agriculture', *Journal of Development Economics*, 36, pp. 259–81.

Basu, K. and Van, P.H. (1998). 'The Economics of Child Labour', *American Economic Review*, 88(3), pp. 412–427.

Batra, R.N. (1973). *Studies in the Pure Theory of International Trade*. Macmillan, London.

Baud, I., Huysman, M. and Schenk, H. (1994). *New Approaches to Urban Solid Waste Management: Linkages Between Formal and Informal Systems of Source Separation, Collection and Recycling in Indian Cities*. University of Amsterdam, The Netherlands.

Baud, I. and Schenk H. (eds.) (1994). *Solid Waste Management: Modes, Assessments, Appraisals and Linkages in Bangalore*. Manohar, New Delhi.

S. Chaudhuri, U. Mukhopadhyay, *Revisiting the Informal Sector*,
DOI 10.1007/978-1-4419-1194-0,

Bedi, A.S. and Garg, A. (2000). 'The Effectiveness of Private Versus Public Schools: The Case of Indonesia', *Journal of Development Economics*, 61, pp. 463–494.

Beker, V.A. (2000). *Globalisation and Unemployment: The Case of Argentina*. Universidad de Belgrano, Buenos Aires.

Beladi, H. and Marjit, S. (1992a). 'Foreign Capital and Protectionism', *Canadian Journal of Economics*, 25, pp. 233–238.

Beladi, H. and Marjit, S. (1992b). 'Foreign Capital, Unemployment and National Welfare', *Japan and the World Economy*, 4, pp. 311–317.

Beladi, H. and Yabuuchi, S. (2001). 'Tariff-induced Capital Inflow and Welfare in the Presence of Unemployment and Informal Sector', *Japan and the World Economy*, 13, pp. 51–60.

Beneria, L. (1989). 'Subcontracting and Employment Dynamics in Mexico City', in Portes, A., Castells, M. and Benton, L.A. (eds), *The Informal Economy*. Johns Hopkins University Press, Baltimore, Maryland.

Bentley, E. (1988). *Struggle for Survival; Organizing the Paper Pickers of Ahmedabad*. Mahila SEWA Trust, Ahmedabad, India.

Beukering, P. and Sharma V. (ed.) (1996). 'International Trade and Recycling in Developing Countries: the Case of Wastepaper in India', *CREED Report*. International Institute or Environment and Development (IIED), London.

Beukering, P. et al. (1997). 'Trends and Issues in the Plastics Cycle in China with Special Emphasis on Trade and Recycling', *CREED Working Paper No. 16*, International Institute or Environment and Development (IIED), London.

Beyer, H., Rojas, P. and Vergara, R. (1999). 'Trade Liberalisation and Wage Inequality', *Journal of Development Economics*, 59(1), pp. 103–123.

Bhaduri, A. (1977). 'On the Formation of Usurious Interest Rates in Backward Agriculture', *Cambridge Journal of Economics*, 1, pp. 341–352.

Bhalotra, S. (1999). *Child Labour in Rural Pakistan: Myths and Data*, Draft, Department of Applied Economics, University of Cambridge, Cambridge.

Bhalotra, S. (2000). 'Is Child Work Necessary?', *Discussion Paper* no. 26, STICERD, London School of Economics, August.

Bhalotra, S. (2002). *The Impact of Economic Liberalisation on Employment and Wages in India*. ILO, Geneva.

Biller, D. and Quintero, J.D. (1995). *Policy Options to Address Informal Sector Contamination in Urban Latin America: The Case of Leather Tanneries in Bogota, Colombia*. The World Bank, Latin America Technical Department, Environment Division, Washington.

Blackman, A. and Bannister, G.J. (1996). 'Community Pressure and Clean Technologies in the Informal Sector: An Econometric Analysis of the Adoption of Propane by Traditional Brickmakers in Cd. Juárez, Mexico', *Discussion Paper* 97–16.

Boeri, T. and Garibaldi, P. (2002). 'Shadow Activity and Unemployment in a Depressed Labour Market', *CEPR Discussion Paper* No. 3433.

Bond, E.W. and Chen, T.J. (1987). 'The Welfare Effects of Illegal Immigration', *Journal of International Economics*, 23, pp. 315–328.

Bose, A.N. (1978). *Calcutta and Rural Bengal: Small Sector Symbiosis*. Minerva Publications, New Delhi.

Botero, J., Djankov, S., La Porta, R., Lopez-de-Silanes, F. and Schleifer, A. (2003). 'The Regulation of Labour', *NBER Working Paper* 9756, National Bureau of Economic Research, Cambridge, MA.

Bottomley, A. (1975). 'Interest Determination in Underdeveloped Rural Areas', *American Journal of Agricultural Economics*, 57, pp. 279–291.

Brecher, R.A. and Alejandro, C.F.D. (1977). 'Tariffs, Foreign Capital and Immiserizing Growth', *Journal of International Economics*, 7, pp. 317–322.

Brown, D.K., Deardorff, A.V. and Stern, R.M. (2001). 'Child Labour: Theory, Evidence and Policy', *Discussion Paper* No. 474, Research Seminar in International economics, School of Public Policy, The University of Michigan.

Burra, N. (1997). *Born to Work: Child Labour in India*. Oxford University Press, Delhi.

Capalleja, D.E. (1994). 'Regulaciones labourales y mercado de trabajo en México', in Marquez, G. (eds.), *Regulacion del Mercado de Trabajo en America Latina*. Centro Internacional para el Desarrollo Economico, San Francisco.

CAPS. (1992). *A Case Study of a Privately-Initiated Solid Waste Collection Management in San Juan, Metro Manila*. World Bank Metropolitan Environmental Improvement Programme, Manila, The Philippines.

Carruth, A.A. and Oswald, A.J. (1981). 'The Determination of Union and Non-union Wage Rates', *European Economic Review*, 16, pp. 285–302.

Castells, M. and Portes, A. (1989). 'World Underneath: The Origins, Dynamics and Effects of the Informal Economy', in Portes, A., Castells, M. and Benton, L.A. (eds), *The Informal Economy: Studies in Advanced and Less Developed Countries*, John Hopkins University Press, Baltimore, Maryland.

Caves, R.E., Frankel, J.A. and Jones, R.W. (1990). *World Trade and Payments* (5th edition). Brown Higher Education, Scott, Foresman and Little, London.

Chandra, V. and Khan, M.A. (1993). 'Foreign Investment in the Presence of an Informal Sector', *Economica*, 60, pp. 79–103.

Chandra, V., Nganou, J. and Noel, C. (2002). 'Constraints to Growth in Johannesburg's Black Informal Sector: Evidence from the 1999 Informal Sector Survey', *World Bank Report No. 24449-ZA*, June.

Charmes, J. (1998). *Street Vendors in Africa: Data and Methods*. United Nations Statistics Division, New York.

Charmes, J. (2000). 'Progress in Measurement of the Informal Sector: Employment and Share of GDP', in *Handbook of National Accounting. Household accounting: Experiences in the Use of Concepts and their Compilation*, Vol. 1. Household Sector Accounts, New York, United Nations, pp. 153–168.

Chaudhuri, S. (2000). 'Rural–Urban Migration, Informal Sector, Urban Unemployment and Development Policies – A Theoretical Analysis', *Review of Development Economics*, 4, pp. 353–364.

Chaudhuri, S. (2001). 'Foreign Capital Inflow, Non-traded Intermediary, Urban Unemployment and Welfare in a Small Open Economy: A Theoretical Analysis', *Pakistan Development Review*, 40(3), pp. 225–235.

Chaudhuri, S. (2003). 'How and How far to Liberalize a Developing Country with Informal Sector and Factor Market Distortions', *Journal of International Trade and Economic Development*, 12(4), pp. 403–428.

Chaudhuri, S. (2005). 'Labour Market Distortion, Technology Transfer and Gainful Effects of Foreign Capital', *The Manchester School*, 73(2), pp. 214–227.

Chaudhuri, S. (2007). 'Foreign Capital, Welfare and Unemployment in the Presence of Agricultural Dualism', *Japan and the World Economy*, 19(2), pp. 149–165.

Chaudhuri, S. and Banerjee, D. (2007). 'Economic Liberalisation, Capital Mobility and Informal Wage in a Small Open Economy: A theoretical Analysis', *Economic Modelling*, 24(6), 924–940.

Chaudhuri, S. and Dwibedi, J.K. (2006). 'Trade Liberalisation in Agriculture in Developed Nations and Incidence of Child Labour in a Developing Economy', *Bulletin of Economic Research*, 58(2), pp. 129–150.

Chaudhuri, S. and Dwibedi, J.K. (2007). 'Foreign Capital Inflow, Fiscal Policies and Incidence of Child Labour in A Developing Economy', *Manchester School*, 75(1), pp. 17–46.

Chaudhuri, S. and Gupta, M.R. (2004). 'Child Labour and Trade Liberalisation in a Developing Economy', *Japanese Economic Review*, 55(2), pp. 201–211.

Chaudhuri, S. and Mukherjee, U. (2002). 'Removal of Protectionism, Foreign Investment and Welfare in a Model of Informal Sector', *Japan and the World Economy*, 14, pp. 101–116.

Chaudhuri, S. and Mukhopadhyay, U. (2002). 'Economic Liberalisation and Welfare in a Model with an Informal Sector', *The Economics of Transition*, 10, pp. 143–172.

Chaudhuri, S. and Mukhopadhyay, U. (2006). 'Pollution and Informal Sector: A Theoretical Analysis', *Journal of Economic Integration*, 21(2), pp. 363–378.

Chaudhuri, S. and Yabuuchi, S. (2007). 'Economic Liberalisation and Wage Inequality in the Presence of Labour Market Imperfection', *International Review of Economics and Finance*, 16(4), pp. 592–603.

Chaudhuri, S., Yabuuchi, S. and Mukhopadhyay, U. (2006). 'Inflow of Foreign Capital and Trade Liberalisation in a Model with an Informal Sector and Urban Unemployment', *Pacific Economic Review*, 11(1), pp. 87–103.

Chen, M., Jhabvala, R. and Lund, F. (2002). 'Supporting Workers in the Informal Economy: A Policy Framework', Geneva, *Working Paper on the Informal Economy 2*. International Labour Office, Geneva.

Chen, M.A. (2001). 'Women in the Informal Sector: A Global Picture, the Global Movement', *SAIS Review*, Winter–Spring 2001.

Choi, J.P. and Thum, M.P. (2005). 'Corruption and the Shadow Economy', *International Economic Review*, 46(3), pp. 817–836.

Cichello, P. (2005). 'Hindrances to Self employment: Evidence from the 2000 Khayelitsha Mitchell's Plain Survey', CSSR Working Paper.

Cichello, P., Almeleh, C., Ncube, L. and Oosthuizen, M. (2005). 'Perceived Barriers to Entry Into Self Employment in Khayelitsha, South Africa: Crime, Risk and Start-up Capital Dominate Profit Concerns', Prepared for the Northeast University Development Consortium (NEUDC) Conference, September.

Cointreau-Levine, S. (1994). Private Sector Participation in Municipal Solid Waste Services in Developing Countries, Vol. 1. The Formal Sector, *Urban Management Programme Discussion Paper* No. 13. World Bank. Washington, United States.

Cole, W.E. and Sanders, R.D. (1983). 'Interstate Migration in Mexico: Variations on the Todaro Theme', *Journal of Development Economics*, 12, pp. 341–354.

Cole, W.E. and Sanders, R.D. (1985). 'Internal Migration and Urban Employment in the Third World', *American Economic Review*, 75(3), pp. 481–494.

Consultora Nordeste. (1998). Investigacion del Mercado de Creditos para Microempresas en las Ciudades de San Salvador de Jujuy y Palpala, Resistencia, Chaco, Argentina.

Corden, W.M. and Findlay, R. (1975). 'Urban Unemployment, Intersectoral Capital Mobility and Development Policy in a Dual Economy', *Economica*, 42, pp. 59–78.

Cunningham, W. and Maloney, W.F. (2001). 'Heterogeneity in the Mexican Micro-enterprise Sector: An Application of Factor and Cluster Analysis', *Economic Development and Cultural Change*, 5, pp.131–156.

Currie, J. and Harrison, A. (1997). 'Trade Reform and Labour Market Adjustment in Morocco', *Journal of Labour Economics*, 15(s3), pp. S44–S71.

Dasgupta, P. and Ray, D. (1990). Adapting to Undernourishment: The Biological Evidence and Its Implications, in Dreze, J. and Sen, A., (eds.), *The Political Economy of Hunger,*. Clarendon Press, Oxford.

Datta Chaudhuri, T. (1989). 'A Theoretical Analysis of the Informal Sector', *World Development*, 17(3), pp. 351–355.

De Soto, H. (1989). *The Other Path: The Invisible Revolution in the Third World*. Harper and Row, New York.

Dessy, S. and Pallage, S. (2003). 'Taxes, Inequality and the Size of the Informal Sector', *Journal of Development Economics*, 70, pp. 225–233.

Dessy, S.E. (2000). 'A Defense of Compulsive Measures against Child Labour', *Journal of Development Economics*, 62, pp. 261–275.

Dev, M. (2000). 'Economic Liberalisation and Employment in South Asia', *Economic and Political Weekly*, (January), pp. 40–51.

Djankov, S. (2003). 'The Informal Economy: Large and Growing in Most Developing Countries', *The World Bank Archived Discussion*, June.

Duraiappah, A. et al. (1999). 'The Plastics Sector in China: Issues in Production, Recycling and International Trade', *CREED Working Paper No. 27*, International Institute or Environment and Development (IIED), London. http://www.iied.org/docs/eep/creed27e.pdf

Edmonds, E. and Pavcnik, N. (2005). 'The Effect of Trade Liberalisation on Child Labour', *Journal of International Economics*, 65, pp. 401–419.

Edmonds, E., Pavcnik, N. and Topalova, P. (2007). 'Trade Adjustment and Human Capital Investments: Evidence from Indian Tariff Reform', *Working paper no. 12884*. National Bureau of Economic Research, Inc, USA.

EQI (1991). *The Recycling of Solid Waste in Cairo, Egypt,* WAREN project, WASTE Consultants. Gouda, The Netherlands.

Eswaran, M. (1996). 'Fertility, Literacy, and the Institution of Child Labour', *CRESP Discussion Paper: DP No. 36*, The University of British Columbia.

Ethier, W.J. (1986). 'Illegal Immigration: The Host-Country Problem', *American Economic Review*, 76(1), pp. 56–71.

Feenstra, R.C. and Hanson, G.H. (1996). 'Foreign Investment, Outsourcing and Relative Wages', in Feenstra, R., Grossman, G. and Irwin, D. (eds.), *Political Economy of Trade Policies: Essays in Honor of J. N. Bhagwati*. MIT Press, Cambridge, MA.

Feenstra, R.C. and Hanson, G.H. (1997). 'Foreign Direct Investment and Relative Wages: Evidence from Mexico's Maquiladoras', *Journal of International Economics*, 42, pp. 371–394.

Fei, J.C.H. and Ranis, G. (1964). *Development of the Labour Surplus Economy: Theory and Policy*. Richard A. Irwin, Inc., Homewood, IL.

Feige, E.L. (1989). *The Underground Economies: Tax Evasion and Information Distortion* (ed). Cambridge University Press, Cambridge.

Fields, G.S. (1975). 'Rural–Urban Migration, Urban Unemployment and Underemployment, and Job Search Activity in LDC's', *Journal of Development Economics*, 2, pp. 165–188.

Fields, G.S. (1990). 'Labour Market Modeling and the Urban Informal Sector: Theory and Evidence', in Turnham, D., Salomé, B. and Schwarz, A. (eds.), *The Informal Sector Revisited*. Development Centre of the Organisation for Economic Co-Operation and Development, Paris.

Findlay, R. (1978). 'Relative Backwardness, Direct Foreign Investment and the Transfer of Technology: A Simple Dynamic Model', *Quarterly Journal of Economics*, 92, pp. 1–16.

Flórez, C.E. (2002). 'The Function of the Urban Informal Sector in Employment: Evidence from Colombia 1984–2000', *Documento CEDE* No. 2002–04, Abril. Universidad de Los Andes.

Flórez, C.E. (2003). 'Migration and the Urban Informal Sector in Colombia', *Paper prepared for Conference on African Migration in Comparative Perspective*, Johannesburg, South Africa, 4–7 June.

Fortin, B., Marceau, N. and Savard, L. (1997). 'Taxation, Wage Controls and the Informal Sector', *Journal of Public Economics*, 66(2), pp. 239–312.

Gandhi-Kingdon, G. and Knight, J. (2001). 'Unemployment in South Africa: The Nature of the Beast,' Centre for the Study of African Economies, University of Oxford, WPS/2001–15.

Geertz, C. (1963). *Peddlers and Princes: Social Change and Economic Modernization in Two Indonesian Towns*. University of Chicago, Chicago.

Gindling, T.H. and Terrell, K. (2005). 'The Effect of Minimum Wages on Actual Wages in Formal and Informal Sectors in Costa Rica', *World Development*, 33, pp. 1905–1921.

Goldberg, P.K. and Pavcnik, N. (2003). 'The Response of the Informal Sector to Trade Liberalisation', *Journal of Development Economics*, 72, pp. 463–496.

Grace, R. et al. (1978). 'Secondary Materials and International Trade', *Journal of Environmental Economics and Management*, 5, pp.172–186.

Gramlich, E. (1976). 'The Impact of Minimum Wages on Other Wages, Employment, and Family Incomes', *Brookings Papers on Economic Activity*, 2(76), pp. 409–451.

Grinols, E. (1991). 'Unemployment and Foreign Capital: The Relative Opportunity Costs of Domestic Labour and Welfare', *Economica*, 58, pp. 107–121.

Grootaert, C. and Kanbur, R. (1995). 'Child labour: A Review', *Background Paper for the 1995 World Developent Report on Labour*, World Bank.

Grote, U., Basu, A.K. and Weinhold, D. (1998). *Child Labour and the International Policy Debate – The Education/Child Labour Trade Off and the Consequences of Trade Sanctions.* ZEF (publ.), ZEF-Discussion Papers on Development Policy No.1, Bonn.

Gupta, M.R. (1993). 'Rural–Urban Migration, Informal Sector and Development Policies: A Theoretical Analysis', *Journal of Development Economics*, 41, pp. 137–151.

Gupta, M.R. (1994). 'Duty-Free Zone, Unemployment and Welfare: A Note', *Journal of Economics*, 59(2), 217–236.

Gupta, M.R. (1995). 'Foreign Capital, Income Inequality and Welfare in a Harris-Todaro Model', *Journal of Development Economics*, 45(2), pp. 407–414.

Gupta, M.R. (1997). 'Foreign Capital and Informal Sector: Comments on Chandra and Khan', *Economica*, 64, pp. 353–363.

Gupta, M.R. (2000). 'Wage Determination of a Child Worker: A Theoretical Analysis', *Review of Development Economics*, 4(2), pp. 219–228.

Gupta, M.R. (2002). 'Trade Sanctions, Adult Unemployment and the Supply of Child Labour: A Theoretical Analysis', *Development Policy Review*, 20(3), pp. 317–332.

Hamid, S. (1994). 'A Micro Analysis of Urban Child Labour: Some Determinants of Labour and Its Conditions', *Pakistan Development Review*, 33(3), pp. 1249–1271.

Hanson, G.H. and Harrison, A. (1999). 'Trade Liberalisation and Wage Inequality in Mexico', *Industrial and Labour Relations Review*, 52(2), pp. 271–288.

Harberger, A.C. (1971). 'On Measuring the Social Opportunity Cost of Labour', *International Labour Review*, 103, pp. 559–579.

Harding, P. and Jenkins, R. (1989). *The Myth of the Hidden Economy: Towards a New Understanding of Informal Economic Activity.* Open University Press, Milton Keynes, Philadelphia.

Harris, J.R. and Todaro, M.P. (1970). 'Migration, Unemployment and Development: A Theoretical Analysis', *American Economic Review*, 60, pp.126–142.

Harrison, A. and Hanson, G. (1999). 'Who Gains from Trade Reform? Some Remaining Puzzles', *Journal of Development Economics*, 59(1), pp. 125–154.

Hart, K. (1971). 'Informal Income Opportunities and Urban Employment in Ghana', in Jolly, R. et al. (eds.), *Third World Employment: Problems and Strategy*. Penguin, Harmondsworth.

Hasan, A. (2002). 'The Changing Nature of the Informal Sector in Karachi as a Result of Global Restructuring and Liberalisation', *Environment & Urbanization*, 14(1), pp. 69–78.

Hausmann, R. and Gavin, M. (1996). 'Security Stability and Growth in a Shock-prone Region: the Policy Challenge for Latin America,' *IADB Working Paper Series*, 315, Washington, DC.

House, W.J. (1984). 'Nairobi's Informal Sector: Dynamic Entrepreneurs or Surplus Labour?', *Economic Development and Cultural Change*, 32, pp. 277–302.

Ihrig, J. and Moe, K. (2004). 'Lurking in the Shadows: The Informal Sector and Government Policy', *Journal of Development Economics*, 73(2), pp. 541–557.

International Labour Organization (2006). *Global Employment Trends Brief.* ILO, Geneva.

International Labour Organization (1972). *Employment, Incomes and Equality: A Strategy for Increasing Productive Employment in Kenya.* ILO, Geneva.

International Labour Organization (2000). *Every Child Counts*, see www.ilo.org/public/english/standards/ipec/simpoc/others/globalest.pdf

International Labour Organization (2002a). *Decent Work in the Informal Economy*. ILO, Geneva.

International Labour Organization (2002b). 'A Future Without Child Labour?', *International Labour Conference, 90th Session June 2002*. International Labour Office, Geneva.

International Labour Organization (2003). *Guidelines concerning a statistical definition of informal employment, endorsed by the Seventeenth International Conference of Labour Statisticians (November–December 2003)*; in: *Seventeenth International Conference of Labour Statisticians (Geneva, 24 November–3 December 2003), Report of the Conference*; Doc. ICLS/17/2003/R; International Labour Office, Geneva.

International Labour Organization (2005). *Facts on Child Labour*, see www.ilo.org/communication.

International Monetary Fund (1998). *World Economic Outlook*, May, Washington, DC.

Jafarey, S. and Lahiri, S. (2002). 'Will Trade Sanctions Reduce Child Labour? The Role of Credit Markets', *Journal of Development Economics*, 68(1), pp. 137–156.

Jenkins, C. and Knight, J. (2002). *The Economic Decline of Zimbabwe: Neither Growth nor Equity*. Palgrave, London.

Jhabvala, R., Sudarshan, R.M. and Unni, J. (2003). *Informal Economy Centrestage: New Structures of Employment*. Sage Publications, New Delhi.

Jimenez, E. and Lockheed, M. (1995). 'Public and Private Secondary Education in Developing Countries: A Comparative Study', *World Bank Discussion Paper*, no. 309. The World Bank, Washington, DC.

Johnson, S., Kauffman, D. and Shleifer, A. (1997). 'The Unofficial Economy in Transition', *Brookings Papers on Economic Activity*, 2, pp. 159–239.

Jones, P. (1997). 'The Impact of Minimum Wage Legislation in Developing Countries where Coverage is Incomplete', *WPS/98-2*, Centre for the Study of African Economies, Institute of Economics and Statistics, University of Oxford.

Jones, R.W. (1965). 'The Structure of Simple General Equilibrium Models', *Journal of Political Economy*, 73, pp. 551–572.

Jones, R.W. (1971). 'A Three-factor Model in Theory, Trade and History', in Bhagwati, J., et al. (eds.), *Trade, Balance of Payments and Growth*, North-Holland, Amsterdam.

Jones, R.W. and Marjit, S. (1992). 'International Trade and Endogenous Production Structures', in Neuefeind, W. and Riezman, R. (eds.), *Economic Theory and International Trade: Essays in Memoriam J. Trout Rader*. Springer, Verlag, pp. 173–196.

Jones, R.W. and Marjit, S. (2003). 'Economic Development, Trade and Wages', *German Economic Review*, 4(1), pp. 1–17.

Jones, R.W. and Neary, P. (1984). 'Positive Theory of International Trade', Jones, R.W. and Kenen, P.B. (eds.), *Handbook of Development Economics* Vol. 1. North-Holland, Amsterdam, pp. 1–62.

Joshi, H. and Joshi, V. (1976). *Surplus Labour and the City: A Study of Bombay*. Oxford University Press, New Delhi.

Kaplinsky, R. (2001). 'Globalisation and Economic Insecurity', *IDS Bulletin*, 32(2), pp. 13–24.

Kar, S. and Marjit, S. (2001). 'Informal Sector in General Equilibrium: Welfare Effects of Trade Policy Reforms', *International Review of Economics and Finance*, 10, pp. 289–300.

Katz, E. and Stark, O. (1986). 'Labour Migration and Risk Aversion in Less-developed Countries', *Journal of Labour Economics*, 4(1), pp. 134–149.

Khan, A.R. (1998). 'The Impact of Globalisation in South Asia', in A.S. Bhalla (ed.), *Globalisation, Growth and Marginalization*. Macmillan India Ltd, New Delhi.

Khan, M.A. (1982). 'Tariffs, Foreign Capital and Immiserizing Growth with Urban Unemployment and Specific Factors of Production', *Journal of Development Economics*, 10, pp. 245–256.

Kingdon, G. and Knight, J. (2005). 'How Flexible are Wages in Response to Local Unemployment in South Africa?', Centre for the Study of African Economies, University of Oxford, *Working Paper* GPRG-WPS–015.

Kingdon, G. and Knight, J. (2007). 'Unemployment in South Africa, 1995–2003: Causes, Problems and Policies', *Journal of African Economies*, 16(5), pp. 813–848.

Knight, J. (2007). 'China, South Africa and the Lewis Model', Paper for the WIDER workshop, *Southern Engines of Growth*, Beijing, January 12–13.

Knight, J. and Song, L. (2005). *Towards a Labour Market in China*, Oxford: Oxford University Press.

Koizumi, T. and Kopecky, K.J. (1977). 'Economic Growth, Capital Movements and the International Transfer of Technical Knowledge', *Journal of International Economics*, 7, pp. 45–65.

Kolstad, C.D. (2000). *Environmental Economics*, Oxford University Press, Oxford.

Kruger, D. (2007). 'Coffee Production Effects on Child Labour and Schooling in Rural Brazil', *Journal of Development Economics*, 82, pp. 448–463.

Kugler, A. (1999). 'The Impact of Firing Costs on Turnover and Unemployment: Evidence from The Colombian Labour Market Reform', *International Tax and Public Finance Journal*, 6(3), pp. 389–410.

Kumar, N. (2001). 'Informal Sector in India: Case of Micro-enterprises in Services Sector', in Oberai, A.S. and Chadha, G.K. (eds.), *Job Creation in Urban Informal Sector in India: Issues and Policy Options* (New Delhi, ILO/SAAT).

Lee, E. (1998). *The Asian Financial Crisis: The Challenge for Social Policy*, International Labour Organization, Geneva.

Leite, P.G., McKinley, T. and Osorio, R.G. (2006). 'The Post-apartheid Evolution of Earnings Inequality in South Africa, 1995-2004', *Working Paper No. 32*, International Poverty Centre, UNDP, Brazil.

Leonard, M. (2001). *Invisible work,* op. cit.; and idem: "Coping strategies in developed and developing societies", op. cit. See also K. Gërxhani: *Politico-economic institutions and the informal sector: A spontaneous free market in Albania,* discussion paper (Amsterdam, Tinbergen Institute and University of Amsterdam, 2000); ILO: *Report of the Technical Workshop on Old and New Facets of Informality, in* Geneva, 2 Mar.

Lewis, A. (1954). 'Economic Development with Unlimited Supply of Labour', *Manchester School*, 22, pp. 139–191. Reprinted in A.N. Agarwal and S.P. Singh (eds.) *Economics of Underdevelopment* (1958), Oxford University Press.

Loayza, N.V. (1996). 'The Economics of the Informal Sector: A Simple Model and Some Empirical Evidence from Latin America', *Carneige-Rochester Conference Series on Public Policy*, 45, pp. 129–162.

Majumdar, D. (1993). 'Labour Markets and Adjustments in Open Asian Economies: The Republic of Korea and Malaysia', *World Bank Economic Review*, 7, pp. 349–380.

Maldonado, C. (1995). 'The Informal Sector Legislation or Laissez-faire?', in *ILO Trade Unions and The Informal Sector: Towards a Comprehensive Strategy*, Geneva.

Maloney, W.F. (2004). 'Informality Revisited', *World Development*, 32(7), pp. 1159–1178.

Mansfield, E.M. (1961). 'Technical Change and the Rate of Imitation', *Econometrica*, 29, pp. 741–766.

Mansfield, E.M. (1968). *Industrial Research and Technological Innovation*, New York, Norton.

Marcouiller, D., Castilla, V.R. and Woodruff, C. (1997). 'Formal Measures of the Informal Sector Wage Gap in Mexico, El Salvador, and Peru', *Economic Development and Cultural Change*, 45, pp. 367–392.

Marjit, S. (1991). 'Agro-based Industry and Rural–Urban Migration: A Case for an Urban Employment Subsidy', *Journal of Development Economics*, 35(2), pp. 393–398.

Marjit, S. (2003). 'Economic Reform and Informal Wage – A General Equilibrium Analysis', *Journal of Development Economics*, 72(1), pp. 371–378.

Marjit, S. and Acharyya, R. (2003). *International Trade, Wage Inequality and the Developing Economy – A General Equilibrium Approach*, Germany: Springer-Verlag.

Marjit, S. and Beladi, H. (1996). 'Protection and Gainful Effects of Foreign Capital', *Economics Letters*, 53 (3), pp. 311–316.

Marjit, S. and Beladi, H. (2002). 'The Stolper-Samuelson Theorem in a Wage Differential Framework', *Japanese Economic Review*, 53(2), pp. 177–181.

Marjit, S., Beladi, H. and Chakrabarti, A. (2004). 'Trade and Wage Inequality in Developing Countries', *Economic Inquiry*, 42(2), pp. 295–303.

Marjit, S., Broll, U. and Sengupta, S. (2000). 'Trade and Wage-gap in Poor Countries: The Role of the Informal Sector', in A. Bose et al. (eds.), *Macroeconomics, Trade and Institutions: Essays in Honour of M.K. Rakshit*, Oxford University Press, Kolkata.

Marjit, S. and Kar, S. (2005). 'Emigration and Wage Inequality', *Economics Letters*, 88, pp. 141–145.

Markusen, J.R. (1995). 'The Boundaries of Multinational Enterprises and the Theory of International Trade', *Journal of Economic Perspectives*, 9, pp. 169–189.

Markusen, J.R. (2002). *Multinational Firms and the Theory of International Trade*, Cambridge: MIT Press.

Mazumdar, D. (1976). 'The Urban Informal Sector', *World Development*, 4 (8), pp. 655–679.
Mazumdar, D. (1983). 'Segmented Labour Markets in LDCs', *American Economic Review*, 73, pp. 254–259.
McGee, T.G. (1971). *The Urbanized Process in the Third World*, London, G. Bell and Sons.
McGee, T.G. (1973). 'Peasants in the Cities: A Paradox, A Paradox, A Most Ingenious Paradox', *Human Organization*, 32(2), pp. 135–142.
Meagher, K. (2008). 'Crisis, Informalization and the Urban Informal Sector in Sub-Saharan Africa', *Development and Change*, 26 (2), pp. 259–284.
Medina, M. and Dows, M. (2000). 'A Short History of Scavenging', *Comparative Civilizations Review*, 42, 7–17.
Mincer, J. (1976). 'Unemployment Effects of Minimum Wage', *Journal of Political Economy*, 84(4), Part Two, pp. S87–S104.
Mingione, E. (1984). 'The Informal Sector and the Development of Third World Cities', *Regional Development Dialogue*, 5(2), pp. 63–76.
Mishra, A. (1994). 'Clientelization and Fragmentation in Backward Agriculture: Forward Induction and Entry Deterrence', *Journal of Development Economics*, 45, pp. 271–285.
Mitra, A. (2005). 'Women in the Urban Informal Sector: Perpetuation of Meagre Earnings', *Development and Change*, 36 (2), pp. 291–316.
Mohsin, N. (1996). 'Counting and Accounting of Child Labour in Unorganized Sectors', *Labour and Development*, 1(2) Jan–June.
Moser, C.O.N. (1978). 'Informal Sector or Petty Commodity Production: Dualism or Dependence in Urban Development?', *World Development*, 6, (9/10), pp. 1041–1064.
Motta, M. (1992). 'Multinational Firm and the Tariff-jumping Argument: A Game Theoretic Analysis with Some Unconventional Conclusions', *European Economic Review*, 36(8), pp. 1557–1571.
Mukhopadhyay, U. (2007). 'International Trade in Wastes, Recycling and the Informal Sector - A Theoretical Analysis', *The Journal of Solid Waste Technology and Management*, 33 (4), pp. 210–218.
Neary, J.P. (2002). 'Foreign Direct Investment and the Single Market', *The Manchester School*, 70 (3), pp. 291–314.
Neary, J.P. (2003). 'Cross-Border Mergers as Instruments of Comparative Advantage', *Working Paper*, University College Dublin.
Norback, P.J. and Persson, L. (2002). 'Investment Liberalisation: Who Benefits from Cross-Border Mergers and Acquisitions?', CEPR Discussion paper 3166.
Ogilvie, S.M. (1996). '*Opportunities and Barriers to Plastics Recycling*', AEAT- 0114, Prepared by the Recycling Advisory Unit of the National Environmental Technology Centre for the Department of Trade and Industry, NETC, Oxfordshire.
Osmani, S.R. (1990). 'Nutrition and the Economics of Food: Implications of Some Recent Controversies', in Dreze, J. and Sen, A. (eds.), *The Political Economy of Hunger*, Clarendon Press, Oxford.
Osmani, S.R. (1991). 'Wage Determination in Rural Labour Markets: The Theory of Implicit Cooperation', *Journal of Development Economics*, 34, pp. 3–23.
Papola, T.S. (1981). *Urban Informal Sector in a Developing Economy*, New Delhi, Vikas Publishing House.
Portes, A. and Schauffler, R. (1993). 'Competing Perspectives on the Latin American Informal Sector', *Population and Development Review*, 19(1), pp. 33–60.
Quijano, A. (1974). 'The Marginal Pole of the Economy and the Marginalized Labour Force', *Economy and Society*, 3(4), pp. 393–428.
Ranis, G. and Stewart, F. (1999). 'V-Goods and the Role of the Urban Informal Sector in Development', *Economic Development and Cultural Change*, 47(2), pp. 259–288.
Ranjan, P. (1999). 'An Economic Analysis of Child Labour', *Economic Letters*, 64, pp. 99–105.

Ranjan, P. (2001). 'Credit Constraints and the Phenomenon of Child Labour', *Journal of Development Economics*, 64, pp. 81–102.
Rauch, J. (1991). 'Modelling the Informal Sector Formally', *Journal of Development Economics*, 35, pp. 33–47.
Ravallion, M. and Wodon, Q. (1999). 'Does Child Labour Displace Schooling? Evidence on Behavioural Responses to an Enrollment Subsidy', Paper presented at the Annual Conference of the Royal Economic Society 1999, at the University of Nottingham, England.
Ravallion, M. and Wodon, Q. (2000). 'Does Cheaper Schooling Mean Less Child Labour? Evidence from Behavioural Responses to an Enrollment Subsidy', *Economic Journal*, 110, pp. C158–C175.
Ray, D. (1998). *Development Economics*, Princeton University Press, New Jersey.
Ray, R. (1999). 'Poverty, Household Size and Child Welfare in India', University of Tasmania, *Mimeo*.
Ray, R. (2000). 'Analysis of Child Labour in Peru and Pakistan: A Comparative Study', *Journal of Population Economics*, 13, pp. 3–19.
Ray, R. (2002). 'Simultaneous Analysis of Child Labour and Child Schooling: Comparative Evidence from Nepal and Pakistan', *Economic and Political Weekly*, Dec. 28, pp. 5215–5224.
Revenga, A. (1997). 'Employment and Wage Effects of Trade Liberalisation: The Case of Mexican Manufacturing', *Journal of Labour Economics*, 15(3) pp. S20–S43.
Robbins, D. (1994a). 'Malaysian Wage Structure and Its Causes', Harvard Institute for International Development (HIID).
Robbins, D. (1994b). 'Philippine Wage and Employment Structure 1978–1983', HIID.
Robbins, D. (1995a). 'Earnings Dispersion in Chile after Trade Liberalisation', HIID.
Robbins, D. (1995b). 'Trade, Trade Liberalisation and Inequality in Latin America and East Asia: Synthesis of Seven Country Studies', HIID.
Robbins, D. (1996a). 'Stolper-Samuelson Lost in the Tropics – Trade liberalisation and Wages in Columbia', HIID.
Robbins, D. (1996b). 'HOS Hits Facts: Facts Win: Evidence on Trade and Wages in Developing World', HIID.
Roberts, B.D. (1989). 'Employment Structure, Life Cycle and Life Chances: Formal and Informal Sectors in Guadalajara', in Portes, A., Castells, M. and Benton, L.A. (eds), *The Informal Economy*, Johns Hopkins University Press, Baltimore, Maryland.
Rogerson, C.M. (1988). 'Recession and the Informal Sector in South Africa', *Development Southern Africa*, 5(1), pp. 88–96.
Romatet, E. (1983). 'Calcutta's Informal Sector: Theory and Reality', *Economic and Political Weekly*, 18(50), pp. 2115–2128.
Rudra, A. (1982). *Indian Agricultural Economics: Myths and Realities*, Allied Publishers Private Limited, New Delhi.
Ruffer, T. and Knight, J. (2007). *Informal Sector Labour Markets in Developing Countries*, Oxford Policy Management, Oxford.
Rybczynski, T.M. (1955). 'Factor Endowment and Relative Commodity Prices', *Economica*, XXII, (Nov), pp. 336–341.
Santos, M. (1979). *The Shared Space: The Two Circuits of the Urban Economy in Underdeveloped Countries*, London, Metheuen.
Sarte, P.G. (2000). 'Informality and Rent-Seeking Bureaucracies in a Model of Long Run Growth', *Journal of Monetary Economics*, 46, pp. 173–197.
Schneider, F. and Enste, D.H. (2000). 'Shadow Economies: Size, Causes, and Consequences', *Journal of Economic Literature*, 38, pp. 77–114.
Sethuraman, S.V. (1981). *The Urban Informal Sector in Developing Countries: Employment, Poverty and Environment*, ILO, Geneva.
Sethuraman, S.V. (1984). *The Urban Informal Sector in Developing Countries: Employment, Poverty and Environment* (2nd Ed.), ILO, Geneva.
Sethuraman, S.V. and Maldonado, C. (eds.) (1992). *Technological Capability in the Informal Sector*, International Labour Office Staff, Geneva.

Sistema de Informacion, Monitoreo y Evaluacion de Programas Sociales (SIEMPRO). (1998). Perfiles del Microempresario en Argentina, Secretaria de Desarrollo Social, Presidencia de la Nación, Buenos Aires.

Skinner, C. (2005). 'Constraints to Growth and Employment: Evidence from the Informal Economy', *School of Development Studies Research Report No.65*. University of KwaZulu Natal, Durban.

Stiglitz, J.E. (1982). 'The Structure of Labour Markets and Shadow Prices in LDCs', in R.H. Sabot (ed.), *Migration and the Labour Market in Developing Countries*. Westview Press, Boulder.

Stiglitz, J.E. (2002). *Globalisation and Its Discontents*, Allen Lane, The Penguin Press.

Stolper, W.F. and Samuelson, P.A. (1941). 'Protection and Real Wages', *Review of Economic Studies*, IX, Nov, pp. 58–73.

Suryahadi, A., Widyanti, W., Perwira, D. and Sumarto, S. (2003). 'Minimum Wage Policy and Its Impact on Employment in the Urban Formal Sector', *Bulletin of Indonesian Economic Studies*, 39 (1), pp. 29–50.

Swaminathan, M. (1991). 'Understanding the Informal Sector: A Survey', *Working Paper 95*. WIDER, Finland.

Swaminathan, M. (1998). 'Economic Growth and the Persistence of Child Labour: Evidence from an Indian City', *World Development*, 26 (8), pp. 1513–1528.

Te Velde, D.W. and Morrissey, O. (2002). 'Foreign Direct Investment, Skills and Wage in the Informal Economy', *SoDS Research Report 65*, University of KwaZulu-Natal.

Tendulkar, S., Sundaram, D.K. and Jain, L.R. (1996). Macroeconomic Policies and Poverty in India 1966–67 to 1993–94, *Manuscript*. ILO, New Delhi.

Todaro, M.P. (1969). 'A Model of Labour Migration and Urban Unemployment in Less Developed Countries', *American Economic Review*, 39, pp. 138–148.

Tokman, V. (1987). 'El Sector Informal en America Latina, 15 años después', *EL Trimestre Económico*, 54 (215), Julio-Septiembre, pp. 513–536.

Tokman, V.E. (1992). 'The Informal Sector in Latin America: From Underground to Legality', in V.E. Tokman (ed.), *Beyond Regulation: The Informal Economy in Latin America*. Colorado, Lynne Rienner Publishers, Boulder.

Turnham, D. (1993). *Employment and Development: A New Review of Evidence*, Paris: OECD.

UN (2000). *The World's Women 2000: Trends and Statistics*. New York, UN Statistical Division.

UNCTAD (1996). *Statistical Review of International Trade in Paper and Plastic Waste*, UNCTAD Commodities Division, Geneva.

UNCTAD (2000). *The Least Developed Countries 2000 Report: Overview by the Secretary-General of UNCTAD*, Geneva.

UNICEF (1997). *The State of the World's Children*. Oxford: Oxford University Press.

United States Environment Protection Agency (1998). '*Solid Waste and Emergency Response*', EPA530-K-97-008, http://www.epa.gov/osw.

Weeks, J. (1975). 'Policies for Expanding Employment in the Informal Urban Sector of Developing Economies', *International Labour Review*, 3 (1), pp. 1–13.

Weiner, M. (1991). *The Child and the State in India: Child Labor and Education Policy in Comparative Perspective*, Oxford University Press, Delhi.

Wilson, A., (1994). 'GATT, Trade Liberalisation and the Environment: An Economic Analysis', A Report by the Congressional Research Service, USA.

Wilson, D.C., Velis, C. and Cheeseman, C. (2006). 'Role of Informal Sector Recycling in Waste Management in Developing Countries', *Habitat International*, 30, pp. 797–808.

Wood, A. (1997). 'Openness and Wage Inequality in Developing Countries: The Latin American Challenge to East Asian Conventional Wisdom', *World Bank Research Observer*, January.

World Development Report (2006). 'Equity and Development', Published by Oxford University Press for the World Bank.

Yabuuchi, S. and Chaudhuri, S. (2007). 'International Migration of Labour and Skilled-Unskilled Wage Inequality in a Developing Economy', *Economic Modelling*, 24(1), pp. 128–137.

Yanagawa, N. (1990) 'Tariff Jumping Foreign Direct Investment', *The Economic Studies Quarterly*, 41(4), p. 353–366.

Index

Kolibri 360 GmbH
Ferdinand-Jühlke-Straße 7
99095 Erfurt, Deutschland
produktsicherheit@kolibri360.de